1 H 51

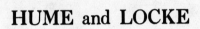

HUME and LOCKE

HUME and LOCKE

THOMAS HILL GREEN

THOMAS Y. CROWELL COMPANY
NEW YORK   ESTABLISHED 1834

INTRODUCTION.

1. *Green's Life, Work, and Influence.* Thomas Hill Green
was born April 7, 1836, at Birkin, a village in Yorkshire, and
died from blood poisoning March 26, 1882, in Oxford. He
was the youngest in a family of four children, two sons and
two daughters. His mother died when he was only a year
old, and the children were brought up by their father, who
was rector at Birkin. In 1850 Green went to school at Rugby,
and in 1855 entered Balliol College in Oxford, where his un-
dergraduate tutor was Benjamin Jowett. The remainder of
his life was spent at Oxford, with the exception of a period of
about a year in 1865–66, which he spent travelling about in-
specting schools as a member of a schools' inquiry commission.
In 1860 he began lecturing at Balliol, in the same year was
elected a fellow of the college, and in 1878 was appointed
Whyte's Professor of Moral Philosophy. He married in 1871,
but never had any children.

The impression Green made upon his contemporaries at Oxford is analogous in some respects, but only in some respects,
to that made by Ludwig Wittgenstein upon his contemporaries
at Cambridge during the thirties and forties. As Wittgenstein was perhaps the dominant philosophical figure at Cambridge during this latter period, so Green was the dominant
philosophical figure at Oxford from the early 1870's until his
death. His presence and activity excited an enthusiasm
among certain of his Oxford contemporaries somewhat similar
to that excited among certain of his contemporaries by Wittgenstein.

Green was convinced that the true result of Hume's philosophy was the demonstration of the bankruptcy implicit in the
empiricistic principles of Locke and Berkeley, that Kant and

Hegel had pointed the way to an acceptable alternative account of experience and knowledge, and that nineteenth-century British philosophy, and especially that of the two leading British philosophers of that century, John Stuart Mill and Herbert Spencer, was consequently anachronistic, since it sought to continue along the bankrupt lines laid down by Hume, ignoring the work of Kant and Hegel.

Much of his philosophical labor was devoted to exhibiting in detail the untenability of empiricism, the anachronistic character of British philosophy of the nineteenth century, and the need for a return to Kant and Hegel. This labor led to a change in the climate of British philosophy that persisted for almost fifty years, for Green is as responsible as any other thinker for the shift away from traditional British empiricism and toward Kantian and Hegelian idealism that dominated British philosophy in the last quarter of the nineteenth century and the first quarter of the twentieth. Green is the first in the line of British idealists that includes R. L. Nettleship (1846–92), F. H. Bradley (1846–1924), Bernard Bosanquet (1848–1923), and H. H. Joachim (1868–1938) at Oxford, and J. M. E. McTaggart (1866–1925) at Cambridge.

But whereas Wittgenstein excited only philosophers, Green exercised considerable influence among nonphilosophers. He was, for example, the original of the Mr. Grey of *Robert Elsmere*. And whereas Wittgenstein's influence was exclusively philosophical, Green's was religious, social, and political as well as philosophical. Though he regarded himself as a "questionable churchman," he was sufficiently orthodox in religion to remain within the Church of England, and though he regarded the moral and social teaching of the Christian religion as immeasurably more important than an allegiance to creeds, dogmas, and institutions, the eternal consciousness for which he argues in many of his writings, particularly in the *Prolegomena to Ethics,* is quite akin to a kind of god; and on his deathbed he expressed a belief in God and immortality, and requested that the eighth chapter of St. Paul's Epistle to the Romans be read to him. Yet study of his religious writings in the third volume of his *Works* reveals his essential liberalism in religion and his belief that what is of fundamental importance in the Christian message is its moral and social teaching.

His interest in social and political questions was practical as well as theoretical—it was manifested in practical, even prosaic, activity as well as in his philosophical conversation, lecturing, and writing. Prior to Green's active participation in local politics, Oxford dons had lived in something of an ivory tower, isolated from any practical involvement in the day-to-day social and political problems and activities of the Oxford townspeople. Green did not consider it condescension but his simple duty to mix with and work with these ordinary folk in an attempt to do what he could to assist in the solution of their problems.

One of his primary concerns was the improvement of the English educational system so that no English child would be deprived of the opportunity to develop his capacities to the fullest because of the absence of educational opportunity. This interest is evidenced not only by his lectures on education, such as those included in the third volume of his *Works,* but also by his work on the schools inquiry commission and by his being elected to the Oxford school board in 1874. He was also involved in the temperance movement of his day, believing that excessive drinking was sapping the energies of many among the working classes. This belief he expressed not merely by speaking publicly for temperance, but also by holding office in temperance societies and by setting up a coffee tavern in 1875.

He participated also in political activities of a more general nature, and made speeches both in Oxford and in other cities in support of liberal policies and legislation. His lecture on "Liberal Legislation and Freedom of Contract," delivered at Leicester in 1881 in support of two liberal measures of the preceding year, applies to these two acts the principles of the liberalism elaborated at considerably greater length in his *Lectures on the Principles of Political Obligation.*

This work constitutes a turning point in the history of the philosophy of liberalism, and remains even today the classic statement of the philosophical foundations of contemporary liberalism, as distinguished from the liberalism of the nineteenth century prior to its publication. Until its publication nineteenth-century liberalism, as exemplified philosophically in the writings of John Stuart Mill (at least in those written before he began to change his views toward the end of his life) and Herbert Spencer, had been more or less laissez-faire, contending that the function of the state is limited primarily to the protection of individual liberty.

What Green does is to argue that the state has a more positive function to perform as well as this rather negative function—that it has the task not only of protecting the negative freedom of individuals, i.e., of protecting them from unjustifiable coercive restrictions upon their freedom of speech and action, but also the task of promoting the positive freedom of every person within the state, i.e., of establishing and maintaining those conditions the presence of which is necessary if each person is to have the opportunity, and therefore the freedom, to develop fully his highest potentialities. Green was convinced that if the activities of the state were limited merely to the protection of negative freedom, the positive freedom of many persons within the state would be nonexistent and their negative freedom insignificant, if not in many cases also nonexistent.

2. *Green's Writings.* Green's Introductions to Hume's *Treatise of Human Nature* were first published in 1874, in the four-volume edition of Hume's philosophical works edited by Green and T. H. Grose. The first volume contained Book I of the *Treatise,* "Of the Understanding," along with Green's long Introduction to Book I. The second contained Books II and III of the *Treatise,* entitled respectively "Of the Passions" and "Of Morals," along with Green's Introduction to Books II and III. The third contained Hume's *Essays Moral, Political, and Literary,* along with a history of the editions of Hume's works, about the same length as Green's Introduction to Books II and III of the *Treatise,* written by Grose. The fourth volume contained Hume's *Enquiry Concerning Human Understanding,* his *Dissertation on the Passions,* his *Enquiry Concerning the Principles of Morals,* his *Natural History of Religion,* a dialogue, and a dozen withdrawn and unpublished essays. The only significant philosophical work of Hume's not included in the Green and Grose edition is his *Dialogues Concerning Natural Religion.*

Green's Introductions to Hume's *Treatise* were later included, in 1885, as part of Volume I of his *Works,* edited by R. L. Nettleship. Green's *Works,* as edited by Nettleship, comprise three volumes. Volume I contains, along with the

"Introductions" to Hume, a series of five essays entitled "Mr. Herbert Spencer and Mr. G. H. Lewes: Their Application of the Doctrine of Evolution to Thought." The first three and the fifth of these were initially published in the *Contemporary Review,* in 1877–78 and January 1881 respectively; the fourth would have also been published in the *Contemporary Review* but was withheld from publication because of Lewes' death in 1878. The second volume of Green's *Works,* first published in 1886, consists of various series of lectures Green gave in his capacity as a lecturer at Oxford. Altogether there are three series of lectures—"Lectures on the Philosophy of Kant," "Lectures on Logic," and "Lectures on the Principles of Political Obligation." They were composed and delivered between 1874 and 1880. The third volume, published in 1888, contains a long memoir of Green by the editor, Nettleship; various philosophical essays and reviews; extracts from lectures on St. Paul's Epistles to the Galatians and to the Romans and on the Fourth Gospel; addresses or lay sermons on texts from St. Paul's Epistles to the Romans and to the Corinthians; four lectures on the English Revolution; four lectures on elementary and secondary schools; and the important lecture on "Liberal Legislation and Freedom of Contract."

The only important philosophical work of Green's not included in Nettleship's edition of his *Works* is his *Prolegomena to Ethics.* Green, according to a letter written shortly before his death, still had some twenty or thirty pages to add to this work when he died. What he had written was edited by A. C. Bradley and published in 1883. There are various unpublished essays, lectures, and letters among Green's papers in the Balliol College Library, but an examination of them has convinced me that all his important philosophical writing is included in Nettleship's edition of his *Works* and in his *Prolegomena to Ethics.*

The Green and Grose edition of Hume's philosophical works, Green's *Works,* and his *Prolegomena to Ethics* were reprinted several times. His *Lectures on the Principles of Political Obligation* was reprinted as a separate volume in 1941, and has also been reprinted as late as 1966. This, however, is the only one of his works to be reprinted in over fifty years.

The continued reprinting of this work has been due, at least in part, to the fact that political philosophers and scientists

have continued to hold it in higher esteem than philosophers
have continued to hold Green's *Prolegomena to Ethics* and his
epistemological and metaphysical writings. On the other
hand, the continued reprinting of his work in political philosophy has in turn contributed to the persistence of the high
regard for this work that political philosophers and scientists
continue to have.

Had his *Prolegomena to Ethics* and his epistemological and
metaphysical writings received the same continued reprinting,
it is possible that Green would be remembered not only as a
political philosopher of some distinction, but also as an episte-
mologist, metaphysician, and moral philosopher of some merit.
It is at least probable that his epistemological, metaphysical,
and moral writings would be more widely read today. The
only one of his works still widely read is his work in political
philosophy, which has become recognized as a classic and therefore as required reading for the serious student of political
philosophy.

The fact that Green's Introductions to Hume have not been
reprinted in over fifty years has meant that they have become
almost inaccessible to the serious student of either Green or
Hume who is interested in owning his own copy of them. The
study of them is essential for an adequate understanding of
Green's own epistemological and metaphysical position. It
is true that in them he is primarily concerned with showing the
impossibility of accounting for experience and knowledge in
terms of the principles accepted by Locke, Berkeley, and
Hume. But in the course of doing so, he presents arguments
that he later develops in his criticism of Mill's logic in his
Lectures on Logic and in his criticism of the attempts of
Spencer and Lewes to substitute a natural history of the development of experience and knowledge for a philosophical
analysis along Kantian lines of the a priori conditions of experience and knowledge.

Green also presents, in the course of his criticism, hints of
the positive epistemological and metaphysical position that he
later develops systematically in Book I of the *Prolegomena to
Ethics,* on the "Metaphysics of Knowledge." But the study
of his Introductions is essential not only for these reasons, but
also, and perhaps even more so, for any one interested in a

detailed, meticulous, and systematic examination of the attempts of Locke, Berkeley, and Hume to account for experience and knowledge along empiricistic lines.

Leibniz in his *New Essays Concerning Human Understanding* had subjected Locke's essay to such an examination, and Reid and Kant, each in his own way, had attempted to reply to Hume, not by means of the detailed criticism to which Leibniz had subjected Locke's essay, but by presenting alternative positive accounts of knowledge intended as replies to Hume. But whereas Leibniz subjects only Locke to detailed criticism, Green subjects both Locke and Hume to a criticism as sustained and unsparing as that to which any philosopher has ever subjected them.

3. *Green's Introductions to Hume.* In two respects Green's Introductions to Hume are somewhat unusual. Green and Grose had been commissioned to edit a four-volume edition of Hume's philosophical works, and one would ordinarily expect a philosopher who thinks the work of some previous philosopher of sufficient importance to assist in the publication of a new edition of it to expand at length in a philosophical introduction upon the merits of the work he is editing. Yet this is precisely what Green does not do. The only real merit Green finds in Hume's *Treatise* is that in it Hume is so faithful to the presuppositions of Locke's *Essay Concerning Human Understanding* and so persistent and consistent in elaborating the consequences of these presuppositions that an assiduous study of the *Treatise* reveals the impossibility of accounting for human experience and knowledge in terms of these presuppositions.

To the reader it will doubtlessly seem, as he winds his way through the involved, unremitting, and at times tedious criticism in Green's pages, that Green never gives Hume the benefit of the doubt—that he invariably places the more damaging of two interpretations upon Hume's words when alternative interpretations are possible. Yet the attentive reader will also find, I believe, that the interpretation Green places upon Hume's words is usually, if not indeed invariably, required by Hume's initial contentions that all perceptions are either impressions or ideas, and all ideas are copies of impressions. It is clear, then, that in his Introduc-

tions Green did not come to praise Hume, but to bury him.
He does, however, deliver the following eulogy before the
burial:

> . . . those who understand the difference between philosophical
> failures, which are so because they are anachronisms, and those
> which in their failure have brought out a new truth and compelled
> a step forward in the progress of thought, will understand that a
> process, which looks like pulling a great philosopher to pieces, may
> be the true way of showing reverence for his greatness. . . . The
> genius of Locke and Hume was their readiness to follow the lead
> of Ideas: their spirit was the Spirit of Rationalism—the spirit
> which, however baffled and forced into inconsistent admissions, is still
> governed by the faith that all things may ultimately be understood.
> We best do reverence to their genius, we most truly appropriate
> their spirit, in so exploring the difficulties to which their enquiry
> led, as to find in them the suggestion of a theory which may help
> us to walk firmly where they stumbled and fell.

The positions of Mill, Spencer, and other empiricists of the
nineteenth century were simply anachronistic; the ideas of
Locke and Hume were theses the statement of which was
necessary if they were to be transcended by the work of
Kant. Kant would have continued to slumber had Hume not
awakened him.

The second peculiarity of Green's Introductions is that they
are as much an introduction to Locke as to Hume, for Green
devotes almost as much space to a critical examination of
Locke's *Essay* as he does to Hume's *Treatise*. There are 126
pages of meticulous and unsparing criticism of Locke in the
Introduction to Book I of the *Treatise,* and 138 pages of such
criticism of Hume. Berkeley gets off more lightly with only
thirty pages of criticism, but only because, according to Green,
Alexander Campbell Fraser, in his edition of Berkeley's
works, had already supplied a sufficient explanation of
Berkeley's system.

The reason Green devotes so much space to Locke in an introduction to Hume is twofold. First, Hume began by accepting the empiricistic premises of Locke and sought to
elucidate consistently their implications; secondly, Hume
sought to remove the inconsistencies that erupted in Locke's
Essay as a consequence of Locke's failing to see clearly and to
adhere completely to the implications of his premises. What
Green seeks to do in his treatment of Locke is to show in detail
what these inconsistencies are. What he seeks to do in his

treatment of Hume is to show that Hume succeeds in removing these inconsistencies and in drawing out and adhering to the implications of Locke's presuppositions only at the cost of ending with an account of experience and knowledge that in fact fails to account for them.

Green's critique of Locke and Hume is essentially Kantian. Like Kant, he does not begin with the question, "Is knowledge of nature possible?" Instead he assumes that it is possible. G. E. Moore was only following in his footsteps when he insisted in his "Defence of Common Sense" that at least one of the ultimate tests of the adequacy of any philosophical position is its compatibility with common sense. Green, no less than Moore, would insist that if a philosopher's development of the consequences of his presuppositions led him to assert positions incompatible with common sense and science and the ordinary language and language of science which express the beliefs of common sense and science, then we may rest assured either that the presuppositions of the philosopher are faulty or else that he has made some mistake in deriving his conclusions.

Common sense and science both assume that nature is real and that knowledge of it is possible—that an objective order of objects and persons standing in various relations to one another exists independently of any particular person's experience or knowledge of it, and that knowledge of this order is possible. Thus for Green, as for Kant, the important question is not, "*Is* knowledge of nature possible?" Instead it is, "*How* is knowledge of nature possible?" The traditional rationalistic answer from Plato's time down to that of Descartes and Leibniz had been that it is possible only through the organization and interpretation of sense experience in terms of innate ideas or principles. Kant's answer was basically the same as that of the rationalists, though he couched it in a different terminology—it is possible only through the organization and interpretation of sense experience by means of a priori concepts and judgments of the understanding. Thus the rationalistic answer from Plato through Descartes and Leibniz to Kant is that knowledge of nature is possible only through a union of two elements neither of which can be reduced to the other—a material or empirical element on the one hand and a formal, rational, innate, or a priori element on the other.

What Locke and Hume attempt to do, according to Green, is to account for knowledge of nature in terms of only one of these elements—the material or empirical element. Thus Locke maintains (1) that there are no innate ideas, (2) that all objects of the human understanding are ideas, (3) that knowledge is the perception of the agreement or disagreement of these ideas, (4) that all ideas are either simple or complex, (5) that simple ideas fall into two classes—simple ideas of sensation and simple ideas of reflection, (6) that simple ideas cannot be made by the understanding, but are given either in sensation or in reflection, (7) that all complex ideas are constructed by the understanding, through compounding, abstracting from, and placing simple ideas in various relations to one another, (8) that simple ideas are therefore revelatory of a reality external to them which produces them and to which they thus stand as effects to cause, simple ideas of sensation being the effects of the causal agency of material substances and simple ideas of reflection being the effects of the causal agency of spiritual substances, and (9) that complex ideas, being the immediate effects of the activity of the understanding, may or may not also reflect the nature of a reality external to the understanding.

Hume substantially accepts theses (1) through (7), but expresses them differently and modifies them somewhat. Thus he (a) uses the terminology of perceptions, impressions, and ideas, maintaining that all perceptions of the human mind are impressions and ideas, that the former are more lively and forceful than the latter, and that the latter are copies of the former; (b) introduces a distinction between "natural" and "philosophical" relations; (c) maintains, though not always consistently, that causal relations obtain only among perceptions, and not among perceptions and objects that are not perceptions; and (d) contends that the identity and continued existence of objects and the self is a "fiction" of the mind, and thus that the notion of substance is neither an impression nor an idea but a fiction.

Green agrees with Hume that if Locke's first seven theses are accepted, then Hume's conclusions (c) and (d) must also be accepted. But (c) and (d) are incompatible with the possibility of a knowledge of nature—i.e., with the possibility of a knowledge of a system of objects and persons standing in various relations to one another independently of any human being's knowledge of this system—and therefore are to be rejected. More specifically, if all perceptions are either impressions or ideas, and if all ideas are copies of impressions, then there cannot even be an *idea* of such a system, much less any knowledge of it, since there can be no impression of it. But since there is an idea of it and even, Green insists, some knowledge of it, it is impossible that all ideas should be copies of impressions. Moreover, Green argues, if reality consisted entirely of successions and coexistences of impressions and ideas and nothing more, then we could never know it, for there can be no impression of such a complex system of successions and coexistences as reality would be, and therefore no idea either, and hence no knowledge. For where there are no impressions there are no ideas, and where there are no ideas there is no knowledge.

Indeed, if all ideas were merely copies of impressions, the question of whether reality is or is not identical with such a system of successions and coexistences could not even arise. But the question does arise, since it can be asked; therefore, again, it is impossible that all ideas should be copies of impressions. These consequences of Hume's doctrine of ideas are hidden from the unwary reader, Green contends, by Hume's use of ordinary language to expound his position, for everyday language presupposes the possibility of a knowledge of an order of objects and persons that would be impossible if Hume's theory of ideas were true. Thus Hume uses language to present his ideas that could not exist if his theory of ideas were true; reading this language, the unsuspecting reader reads into Hume's words conceptions that he could not possibly have if Hume's theory were true.

Both Locke and Hume then, according to Green, can only state their position by employing the very a priori concepts and by making the very a priori judgments the existence of which they deny. Green's assault upon Locke and Hume is therefore an argument for rationalism and Kantianism by way of an attempt to reduce empiricism to absurdity. But the kind of rationalism for which he argues, both in his Introductions to Hume and in his later work, is Kantian, and the kind of Kantianism for which he argues is rationalistic. His rationalism is Kantian because he regards Kant's theory of a priori concepts and judgments and of the synthetic a priori as constituting an advance over previous rationalistic theories of innate ideas. And his Kantianism is rationalistic because he regards the work of the understanding, in organizing the materials of sense by means of a system of a priori concepts and judgments, as constitutive of a world of reality, and not merely of a world of phenomena or appearances.

For Green, as for Hegel, the rational is the real. Thus to say that his rationalism is Kantian and his Kantianism rationalistic is to say that his position is Hegelian, or at least, idealistic. Intimations of his idealism are clearly present in his Introductions to Hume. His argument for idealism, however—both in his Introductions to Hume and as stated in a more developed form in his later writings—is at best questionable. It rests ultimately upon a certain ambiguity in his contention that nature, as a system of objects and persons existing independently of anyone's conception of it, can exist only for thought. If by this Green meant only that it can be *known,* even in part, only by means of thinking that employs ideas some of which at least cannot be mere copies of impressions, then it amounts only to a rejection of empiricism and an acceptance of rationalism. But Green does not mean only this. He means not merely that the system of nature can be *known* only by thought, but also that it can *exist* only as the object of thought, and this not merely the thought of a perishing human being who can at best know this system only in part, but the thought of an eternal and omniscient consciousness. But though one may question that Green succeeds in showing the necessity of concluding the existence of such an eternal consciousness, one can by no means reply so easily to the barrage of criticism he has levelled against the empiricism of Locke and Hume. If empiricism is to be defended, Green's criticisms must be answered. Such an answer, so far as I know, has not been presented in the more than ninety years since Green first published them.

RAMON M. LEMOS

Department of Philosophy
University of Miami
Coral Gables, Florida

CONTENTS

II. Introduction to the Moral Part of Hume's 'Treatise.'

INTRODUCTIONS

TO

HUME'S TREATISE OF HUMAN NATURE.

INTRODUCTION.

—◦◦◦—

THERE is a view of the history of mankind, by this time familiarised to Englishmen, which detaches from the chaos of events a connected series of ruling actions and beliefs— the achievement of great men and great epochs, and assigns to these in a special sense the term 'historical.' According to this theory—which indeed, if there is to be a theory of History at all, alone gives the needful simplification—the mass of nations must be regarded as left in swamps and shallows outside the main stream of human development. They have either never come within the reach of the hopes and institutions which make history a progress instead of a cycle, or they have stiffened these into a dead body of ceremony and caste, or at some great epoch they have failed to discern the sign of the times and rejected the counsel of God against themselves. Thus permanently or for generations, with no principle of motion but unsatisfied want, without the assimilative ideas which from the strife of passions elicit moral results, they have trodden the old round of war, trade, and faction, adding nothing to the spiritual heritage of man. It would seem that the historian need not trouble himself with them, except so far as relation to them determines the activity of the progressive nations.

2. A corresponding theory may with some confidence be applied to simplify the history of philosophical opinion. The common plan of seeking this history in compendia of the systems of philosophical writers, taken in the gross or with no discrimination except in regard to time and popularity, is mainly to blame for the common notion that metaphysical enquiry is an endless process of threshing old straw. Such enquiry is really progressive, and has a real history, but it is a history represented by a few great names. At rare epochs there appear men, or sets of men, with the true speculative

impulse to begin at the beginning and go to the end, and
with the faculty of discerning the true point of departure
which previous speculation has fixed for them.   The intervals
are occupied by commentators and exponents of the last true
philosopher, if it has been his mission to construct; if it has
been sceptical, by writers who cannot understand the fatal
question that he has asked, and thus still dig in the old vein
which he had exhausted, and of which his final dilemma had
shown the bottom.   Such an interval was that which in the
growth of continental philosophy followed on the epoch of
Leibnitz; an interval of academic exposition or formulation,
in which the system, that had been to the master an incomplete enquiry, became in the hands of his disciples a one-
sided dogmatism.   In the line of speculation more dis-
tinctively English, a like *régime* of 'strenua inertia' has
prevailed since the time of Hume.   In the manner of its un-
profitableness, indeed, it has differed from the Wolfian period
in Germany, just as the disinterested scepticism of Hume
differed from the system-making for purposes of edification
to which Leibnitz applied himself.   It has been unprofitable,
because its representatives have persisted in philosophising
upon principles which Hume had pursued to their legitimate
issue and had shown, not as their enemy but as their advo-
cate, to render all philosophy futile.   Adopting the premises
and method of Locke, he cleared them of all illogical adaptations to popular belief, and experimented with them on the
body of professed knowledge, as one only could do who had
neither any twist of vice nor any bias for doing good, but
was a philosopher because he could not help it.

3. As the result of the experiment, the method, which
began with professing to explain knowledge, showed knowledge to be impossible. Hume himself was perfectly cognisant
of this result, but his successors in England and Scotland
would seem so far to have been unable to look it in the face.
They have either thrust their heads again into the bush of
uncriticised belief, or they have gone on elaborating Hume's
doctrine of association, in apparent forgetfulness of Hume's
own proof of its insufficiency to account for an intelligent, as
opposed to a merely instinctive or habitual, experience.   An
enquiry, however, so thorough and passionless as the 'Treatise
of Human Nature,' could not be in vain ; and if no English
athlete had strength to carry on the torch, it was transferred

to a more vigorous line in Germany. It awoke Kant, as he used to say, from his 'dogmatic slumber,' to put him into that state of mind by some called wonder, by others doubt, in which all true philosophy begins. This state, with less ambiguity of terms, may be described as that of freedom from presuppositions. It was because Kant, reading Hume with the eyes of Leibnitz and Leibnitz with the eyes of Hume, was able to a great extent to rid himself of the presuppositions of both, that he started that new method of philosophy which, as elaborated by Hegel, claims to set man free from the artificial impotence of his own false logic, and thus qualify him for a complete interpretation of his own achievement in knowledge and morality. Thus the 'Treatise of Human Nature' and the 'Critic of Pure Reason,' taken together, form the real bridge between the old world of philosophy and the new. They are the essential 'Propædeutik,' without which no one is a qualified student of modern philosophy. The close correspondence between the two works becomes more apparent the more each is studied. It is such as to give a strong presumption that Kant had studied Hume's doctrine in its original and complete expression, and not merely as it was made easy in the 'Essays.' The one with full and reasoned articulation asks the question, which the other with equal fulness seeks to answer. It is probably because the question in its complete statement has been so little studied among us, that the intellectual necessity of the Kantian answer has been so little appreciated. To trace the origin and bring out the points of the question, in order to the exhibition of that necessity, will be the object of the following treatise. To do this thoroughly, indeed, would carry us back through Hobbes to Bacon. But as present limits do not allow of so long a journey, we must be content with showing Hume's direct filiation to Locke, who, indeed, sufficiently gathered up the results of the 'empirical' philosophy of his predecessors.

4. Such a task is very different from an ordinary undertaking in literary history, and requires different treatment. To the historian of literature a philosopher is interesting, if at all, on account of the personal qualities which make a great writer, and have a permanent effect on letters and general culture. Locke and Hume undoubtedly had these qualities and produced such an effect—an effect in Locke's case more

intense upon the immediately following generations, but in
Hume's more remarkable as having reappeared after near a
century of apparent forgetfulness. Each, indeed, like every
true philosopher, was the mouth-piece of a certain system of
thought determined for him by the stage at which he found
the dialectic movement that constitutes the progress of philosophy, but each gave to this system the stamp of that
personal power which persuades men. Their mode of expression had none of that academic or 'ex cathedra' character,
which has made German philosophy almost a foreign literature in the country of its birth. They wrote as citizens and
men of the world, anxious (in no bad sense) for effect; and
even when their conclusions were remote from popular belief,
still presented them in the flesh and blood of current terms
used in the current senses. It is not, however, in their
human individuality and its effects upon literature, but as
the vehicles of a system of thought, that it is proposed here
to treat them; and this purpose will best be fulfilled if we
follow the line of their speculation without divergence into
literary criticism or history, without remarks either on the
peculiarities of their genius or on any of the secondary
influences which affected their writings or arose out of them.
For a method of this sort, it would seem, there is some need
among us. We have been learning of late to know much
more about philosophers, but it is possible for knowledge
about philosophers to flourish inversely as the knowledge of
philosophy. The revived interest which is noticeable in the
history of philosophy may be an indication either of philosophical vigour or of philosophical decay. In those whom
intellectual indolence, or a misunderstood and disavowed
metaphysic, has landed in scepticism there often survives a
curiosity about the literary history of philosophy, and the
writings which this curiosity produces tend further to spread
the notion that philosophy is a matter about which there
has been much guessing by great intellects, but no definite
truth is to be attained. It is otherwise with those who see in
philosophy a progressive effort towards a fully-articulated
conception of the world as rational. To them its past history
is of interest as representing steps in this progress which
have already been taken for us, and which, if we will make
them our own, carry us so far on our way towards the freedom
of perfect understanding; while to ignore them is not to

return to the simplicity of a pre-philosophic age, but to condemn ourselves to grope in the maze of 'cultivated opinion,' itself the confused result of those past systems of thought which we will not trouble ourselves to think out.

5. The value of that system of thought, which found its clearest expression in Hume, lies in its being an effort to think to their logical issue certain notions which since then have become commonplaces with educated Englishmen, but which, for that reason, we must detach ourselves from popular controversy to appreciate rightly. We are familiar enough with these in the form to which adaptation to the needs of plausibility has gradually reduced them, but because we do not think them out with the consistency of their original exponents, we miss their true value. They do not carry us, as they will do if we restore their original significance, by an intellectual necessity to those truer notions which, in fact, have been their sequel in the development of philosophy, but have not yet found their way into the ' culture' of our time. An attempt to restore their value, however, if this be the right view of its nature, cannot but seem at first sight invidious. It will seem as if, while we talk of their value, we were impertinently trying to ' pull them to pieces.' But those who understand the difference between philosophical failures, which are so because they are anachronisms, and those which in their failure have brought out a new truth and compelled a step forward in the progress of thought, will understand that a process, which looks like pulling a great philosopher to pieces, may be the true way of showing reverence for his greatness. It is a Pharisaical way of building the sepulchres of philosophers to profess their doctrine or extol their genius without making their spirit our own. The genius of Locke and Hume was their readiness to follow the lead of Ideas: their spirit was the spirit of Rationalism—the spirit which, however baffled and forced into inconsistent admissions, is still governed by the faith that all things may ultimately be understood. We best do reverence to their genius, we most truly appropriate their spirit, in so exploring the difficulties to which their enquiry led, as to find in them the suggestion of a theory which may help us to walk firmly where they stumbled and fell.

6. About Locke, as about every other philosopher, the essential questions are, What was his problem, and what was

his method? Locke, as a man of business, gives us the answers at starting. His problem was the origin of 'ideas' in the individual man, and their connection as constituting knowledge: his method that of simply 'looking into his own understanding and seeing how it wrought.' These answers commend themselves to common sense, and still form the text of popular psychology. If its confidence in their value, as explained by Locke, is at all beginning to be shaken, this is not because, according to a strict logical development, they issued in Hume's unanswered scepticism, which was too subtle for popular effect, but because they are now open to a rougher battery from the physiologists. Our concern at present is merely to show their precise meaning, and the difficulties which according to this meaning they involve.

7. There are two propositions on which Locke is constantly insisting: one, that the object of his investigation is *his own* mind; the other, that his attitude towards this object is that of mere observation. He speaks of his own mind, it is to be noticed, just as he might of his own body. It meant something born with, and dependent on, the particular animal organism that first saw the light at Wrington on a particular day in 1632. It was as exclusive of other minds as his body of other bodies, and he could only infer a resemblance between them and it. With all his animosity to the coarse spiritualism of the doctrine of innate ideas, he was the victim of the same notion which gave that doctrine its falsehood and grotesqueness. He, just as much as the untutored Cartesian, regarded the 'minds' of different men as so many different things; and his refutation of the objectionable hypothesis proceeds wholly from this view. Whether the mind is put complete into the body, or is born and grows with it; whether it has certain characters stamped upon it to begin with, or receives all its ideas through the senses; whether it is simple and therefore indiscerptible, or compound and therefore perishable—all these questions to Locke, as to his opponents, concern a multitude of 'thinking things' in him and them, merely individual, but happening to be pretty much alike.

8. This 'thinking thing,' then, as he finds it in himself, the philosopher, according to Locke, has merely and passively to observe, in order to understand the nature of knowledge. 'I could look into nobody's understanding but my own to see how it wrought,' he says, but 'I think the intellectual

faculties are made and operate alike in most men. But if it should happen not to be so, I can only make it my humble request, in my own name and in the name of those that are of my size, who find their minds work, reason, and know in the same low way that mine does, that the men of a more happy genius will show us the way of their nobler flights.'—(Second Letter to Bishop of Worcester.) As will appear in the sequel, it is from this imaginary method of ascertaining the origin and nature of knowledge by passive observation of what goes on in one's own mind that the embarrassments of Locke's system flow. It was the function of Hume to exhibit the radical flaw in his master's method by following it with more than his master's rigour.

9. As an observation of the 'thinking thing,' the 'philosophy of mind' seems to assume the character of a natural science, and thus at once acquires definiteness, and if not certainty, at least plausibility. To deny the possibility of such observation, in any proper sense of the word, is for most men to tamper with the unquestioned heritage of all educated intelligence. Hence the unpalatability of a consistent Positivism; hence, too, on the other side, the general conviction that the Hegelian reduction of Psychology to Metaphysics is either an intellectual juggle, or a wilful return of the philosophy, which psychologists had washed, to the mire of scholasticism. It is the more important to ascertain what the observation in question precisely means. What observes, and what is observed? According to Locke (and empirical psychology has never substantially varied the answer) the matter to be observed consists for each man firstly in certain impressions of his own individual mind, by which this mind from being a mere blank has become furnished—by which, in other words, his mind has become actually a mind; and, secondly, in certain operations, which the mind, thus constituted, performs upon the materials which constitute it. The observer, all the while, is the constituted mind itself. The question at once arises, how the developed man can observe in himself (and it is only to himself, according to Locke, that he can look) that primitive state in which his mind was a 'tabula rasa.' In the first place, that only can be observed which is present; and the state in question to the supposed observer is past. If it be replied that it is recalled by memory, there is the farther objection that memory only recalls

what has been previously known, and how is a man's own primitive consciousness, as yet void of the content which is supposed to come to it through impressions, originally known to him ?   How can the 'tabula rasa' be cognisant of itself?

10. The cover under which this difficulty was hidden from Locke, as from popular psychologists ever since, consists in the implicit assumption of certain ideas, either as possessed by or acting upon the mind in the supposed primitive state, which are yet held to be arrived at by a gradual process of comparison, abstraction, and generalisation.   This assumption, which renders the whole system resting upon the interrogation of consciousness a paralogism, is yet the condition of its apparent possibility.   It is only as already charged with a content which is yet (and for the individual, truly) maintained to be the gradual acquisition of experience, that the primitive consciousness has any answer to give to its interrogator.

11. Let us consider the passage where Locke sums up his theory of the 'original of our ideas.' (Book II. chap. i. sec. 23, 24.)   ' Since there appear not to be any ideas in the mind, before the senses have conveyed any in, I conceive that ideas in the understanding are coeval with sensation; which is such an impression, made in some part of the body, as produces some perception in the understanding.   It is about these impressions made on our senses by outward objects, that the mind seems first to employ itself in such operations as we call perception, remembering, consideration, reasoning, &c.   In time the mind comes to reflect on its own operations about the ideas got by sensation, and thereby stores itself with a new set of ideas, which I call ideas of reflection.   These impressions that are made on our senses by outward objects, that are extrinsical to the mind; and its own operations, proceeding from powers intrinsical and proper to itself, which, when reflected on by itself, become also objects of its contemplation, are, as I have said, the original of all knowledge.'

12. Can we from this passage elicit a distinct account of the beginning of intelligence ?   In the first place it consists in an 'idea,' and an idea is elsewhere (Introduction, sec. 8) stated to be 'whatsoever is the object of the understanding, when a man thinks.'   But the primary idea is an 'idea of sensation.'   Does this mean that the primary idea *is* a sen-

sation, or is a distinction to be made between the sensation and the idea thereof? The passage before us would seem to imply such a distinction. Looking merely to it, we should probably say that by *sensation* Locke meant ' an impression or motion in some part of the body;' by the *idea of sensation* ' a perception in the understanding,' which this impression produces. The account of perception itself gives a different result. (Book II. chap. ix. sec. 3.) ' Whatever impressions are made on the outward parts, if they are not taken notice of within, there is no perception. Fire may burn our bodies with no other effect than it does a billet, unless the motion be continued to the brain, and there the *sense* of heat or *idea* of pain be produced in the mind, wherein consists actual *perception.*' Here sensation is identified at once with the idea and with perception, as opposed to the impression on the bodily organs.[1] To confound the confusion still farther, in a passage immediately preceding the above, ' Perception,' here identified with the idea of sensation, has been distinguished from it, as ' exercised about it.' ' Perception, as it is the first faculty of the mind exercised about our ideas, so it is the first and simplest idea we have from reflection.' Taking Locke at his word, then, we find the beginning of intelligence to consist in having an idea of sensation. This idea, however, we perceive, and to perceive is to have an idea ; i.e. to have an idea of an idea of sensation. But of perception again we have a simple or primitive idea. Therefore the beginning of intelligence consists in having an idea of an idea of an idea of sensation.

13. By insisting on Locke's account of the relation between the ideas of sensation and those of reflection we might be brought to a different but not more luminous conclusion. In the passages quoted above, where this relation is most fully spoken of, it appears that the latter are essentially sequent to those of sensation. ' *In time* the mind comes to reflect on its own operations, about the ideas got by sensation, and thereby stores itself with a new set of ideas, which I call ideas of reflection.' Of these only two are primary and ori-

---

[1] Cf. Book II. chap. xix. sec. 1. ' The *perception*, which actually accompanies and is annexed to any impression on the body, made by an external object, being distinct from all other modifications of thinking, furnishes the mind with a distinct idea which we call *sensation ;* which is, as it were, the actual entrance of any idea into the understanding by the senses.'

ginal (Book II. c. xxi. sec. 73), viz. motivity or power of moving, with which we are not at present concerned, and perceptivity or power of perception. But according to Locke, as we have seen, there cannot be any, the simplest, idea of sensation without perception.   If, then, the *idea* of perception is only given later and upon reflection, we must suppose perception to take place without any idea of it.   But with Locke to have an idea and to perceive are equivalent terms.   We must thus conclude that the beginning of knowledge is an unperceived perception, which is against his express statement elsewhere (Book II. c. xxvii. sec. 9), that it is 'impossible for any one to perceive without perceiving that he does perceive.'

14. Meanwhile a perpetual equivocation is kept up between a supposed impression on the 'outward parts,' and a supposed impression on the 'tablet of the mind.' It is not the impression upon, or a motion in, the outward parts, as Locke admits, that constitutes the idea of sensation.   It is not an agitation in the tympanum of the ear, or a picture on the retina of the eye, that we are conscious of when we see a sight or hear a sound.[1] The motion or impression, however, has only, as he seems to suppose, to be 'continued to the brain,' and it becomes an idea of sensation. Notwithstanding the rough line of distinction between soul and body, which he draws elsewhere, his theory was practically governed by the supposition of a cerebral something, in which, as in a third equivocal tablet, the imaginary mental and bodily tablets are blended.   If, however, the idea of sensation, as an object of the understanding when a man thinks, differs absolutely from 'a motion of the outward parts,' it does so no less absolutely, however language and metaphor may disguise the difference, from such motion as 'continued to the brain.'   An instructed man, doubtless, may come to think about a motion in his brain, as about a motion of the earth round the sun, but to speak of such motion as an idea of sensation or an immediate object of intelligent sense, is to confuse between the object of consciousness and a possible physical theory of the conditions of that consciousness.   It is

[1] Cf. Locke's own statement (Book III. iv. sec. 10). 'The cause of any sensation, and the sensation itself, in all the simple ideas of one sense, are two ideas; and two ideas so different and distant one from another, that no two can be more so.'

only, however, by such an equivocation that any idea, according to Locke's account of the idea, can be described as an 'impression' at all, or that the representation of the mind as a tablet, whether born blank or with characters stamped on it, has even an apparent meaning. A metaphor, interpreted as a fact, becomes the basis of his philosophical system.

15. As applied to the ideas of reflection, indeed, the metaphor loses even its plausibility. In its application to the ideas of sensation it gains popular acceptance from the ready confusion of thought and matter in the imaginary cerebral tablet, and the supposition of actual impact upon this by 'outward things.' But in the case of ideas of reflection, it is the mind that at once gives and takes the impression. It must be supposed, that is, to make impressions on itself. There is the further difficulty that as perception is necessary in order to give *an idea* of sensation, the impress of perception must be taken by the mind in its earliest receptivity; or, in other words, it must impress itself while still a blank, still void of any 'furniture' wherewith to make the impression. There is no escape from this result unless we suppose perception to precede the idea of it by some interval of time, which lands us, as we have seen, in the counter difficulty of supposing an unperceived perception. Locke disguises the difficulty from himself and his reader by constantly shifting both the receptive subject and the impressive matter. We find the 'tablet' perpetually receding. First it is the 'outward part' or bodily organ. Then it is the brain, to which the impression received by the outward part must somehow be continued, in order to produce sensation. Then it is the perceptive mind, which takes an impression of the sensation or has an idea of it. Finally, it is the reflective mind, upon which in turn the perceptive mind makes impressions. But the hasty reader, when he is told that the mind is passively impressed with ideas of reflection, is apt to forget that the matter which thus impresses it is, according to Locke's showing, simply its perceptive, i.e. its passive, self.

16. The real source of these embarrassments in Locke's theory, it must be noted, lies in the attempt to make the individual consciousness give an answer to its interrogator as to the beginning of knowledge. The individual looking back on an imaginary earliest experience pronounces himself in that experience to have been simply sensitive and passive.

But by this he means consciously sensitive *of something* and consciously passive *in relation to something*. That is, he supposes the primitive experience to have involved consciousness of a self on the one hand and of a thing on the other, as well as of a relation between the two. In the ' idea of sensation' as Locke conceived it, such a consciousness is clearly implied, notwithstanding his confusion of terms. The idea is a perception, or consciousness *of a thing*, as opposed to a sensation proper or affection of the bodily organs. Of the perception, again, there is an idea, i.e. a consciousness by the man, in the perception, of himself in negative relation to the thing that is his object, and this consciousness (if we would make Locke consistent in excluding an unperceived perception) must be taken to go along with the perceptive act itself. No less than this indeed can be involved in any act that is to be the beginning of knowledge at all. It is the minimum of possible thought or intelligence, and the thinking man, looking for this beginning in the earliest experience of the individual human animal, must needs find it there. But this means no less than that he is finding there already the conceptions of substance and relation. Hence a double contradiction : firstly, a contradiction between the primariness of self-conscious cognisance of a thing, as the beginning of possible knowledge, on the one hand, and the primariness of animal sensation in the history of the individual man on the other ; secondly, a contradiction between the primariness in knowledge of the ideas of substance and relation, and the seemingly gradual attainment of these ' abstractions' by the individual intellect. The former of these contradictions is blurred by Locke in the two main confusions which we have so far noticed : (*a*) the confusion between sensation proper and perception, which is covered under the phrase ' idea of sensation ; ' a phrase which, if sensation means the first act of intelligence, is pleonastic, and if it means the ' motion of the outward parts continued to the brain,' is unmeaning ; and (*b*) the confusion between the physical affection of the brain and the act of the self-conscious subject, covered under the equivocal metaphor of impression. The latter contradiction, that concerning the ideas of substance and relation, has to be further considered.

17. It is not difficult to show that to have a simple idea, according to Locke's account of it, means to have already the

conception of substance and relation, which are yet according to him 'complex and derived ideas,' 'the workmanship of the mind' in opposition to its original material, the result of its action in opposition to what is given it as passive. The equivocation in terms under which this contradiction is generally covered is that between 'idea' and 'quality.' 'Whatever the mind perceives in itself, or is the immediate object of perception, thought, or understanding, that I call *idea*; and the power to produce that idea I call quality of the subject wherein that power is. Thus a snowball having power to produce in us the ideas of white, cold, and round, the powers to produce these ideas in us, as they are in the snowball, I call qualities; and as they are sensations or perceptions in our understandings, I call them ideas; which ideas, if I speak of sometimes as in the things themselves, I would be understood to mean those qualities in the object which produce them in us.' (Book II. chap. viii. sec. 8.)

18. An equivocation is not the less so because it is announced. It is just because Locke allows himself at his convenience to interchange the terms 'idea' and 'quality' that his doctrine is at once so plausible and so hollow. The essential question is whether the 'simple idea,' as the original of knowledge, is on the one hand a mere feeling, or on the other a thing or quality of a thing. This question is the crux of empirical psychology. Adopting the one alternative, we have to face the difficulty of the genesis of knowledge, as an apprehension of the real, out of mere feeling; adopting the other, we virtually endow the nascent intelligence with the conception of substance. By playing fast and loose with 'idea' and 'quality,' Locke disguised the dilemma from himself. Here again the metaphor of Impression did him yeoman's service. The idea, or 'immediate object of thought,' being confused with the affection of the sensitive organs, and this again being accounted for as the result of actual impact, it was easy to represent the idea itself as caused by the action of an outward body on the 'mental tablet.' Thus Locke speaks of the 'objects of our senses obtruding their particular ideas on our minds, whether we will or no.' (Book II. chap. i. sec. 25.) This sentence holds in solution an assumption and two fallacies. The assumption (with which we have no further concern here) is the physical theory that matter affects the sensitive organs in the way of actual

impact. Of the fallacies, one is the confusion between this affection and the idea of which it is the occasion to the individual; the other is the implication that this idea, as such, in its prime simplicity, recognises itself as the result of, and refers itself as a quality to, the matter supposed to cause it. This recognition and reference, it is clearly implied, are involved in the idea itself, not merely made by the philosopher theorising it. Otherwise the 'obtrusion' would be described as of a property or effect, not of an idea, which means, it must be remembered, the object of consciousness just as the object of consciousness. Of the same purport is the statement that 'the mind is furnished with simple ideas as they are found in exterior things.' (Book II. chap. xxiii. sec. 1.) It only requires a moment's consideration, indeed, to see that the beginning of consciousness cannot be a physical theory, which, however true it may be and however natural it may have become to us, involves not only the complex conception of material impact, but the application of this to a case having no palpable likeness to it. But the 'interrogator of consciousness' finds in its primitive state just what he puts there, and thus Locke, with all his pains ' to set his mind at a distance from itself,' involuntarily supposes it, in the first element of intelligence, to 'report' that action of matter upon itself, which, as the result of a familiar theory—involving not merely the conceptions of substance, power, and relation, but special qualifications of these—it reports to the educated man.

19. This will appear more clearly upon an examination of his doctrine of 'the ideas of primary and secondary qualities of bodies.' The distinction between them he states as follows. The primary qualities of bodies are ' the bulk, figure, number, situation, motion, and rest of their solid parts; these are in them, whether ws perceive them or no; and when they are of that size that we can discover them, we have by these an idea of the thing as it is in itself.' . . . Thus 'the ideas of primary qualities are resemblances of them, and their patterns do really exist in the bodies themselves. But the ideas produced in us by the secondary qualities have no resemblance of them at all. There is nothing like them existing in the bodies themselves. They are in the bodies, we denominate from them, only a power to produce these sensations in us; and what is sweet, blue, or warm in idea is but

the certain bulk, figure, and motion of the insensible parts
in the bodies themselves which we call so.' This power is
then explained to be of two sorts : (a) ' The power that is in
any body, by reason of its insensible primary qualities, to
operate after a peculiar manner on any of our senses, and
thereby produce in us the different ideas of several colours,
sounds, smells, tastes, &c. These are usually called sensible
qualities. (b) The power that is in any body, by reason of the
particular constitution of its primary qualities, to make such
a change in the bulk, figure, texture, and motion of another
body, as to make it operate differently on our senses from
what it did before. Thus the sun has a power to make wax
white, and fire to make lead fluid. These are usually called
powers.' (Book ii. chap. viii. sec. 15, 23.)

20. What we have here is a theory of the causes of simple
ideas; but we shall find Locke constantly representing this
theory as a simple idea itself, or the simple idea as involving
this theory. By this unconscious device he is enabled readily
to exhibit the genesis of knowledge out of ' simple ideas,'
but it is at the cost of converting these into ' creations of the
mind,' which with him are the antitheses of ' facts ' or
' reality.' The process of conversion takes a different form
as applied respectively to the ideas of primary and to those
of secondary qualities. We propose to follow it in the latter
application first.

21. The simple idea caused by a quality he calls the idea
of that quality. Under cover of this phrase, he not only
identifies the idea of a primary quality with the quality itself
of which he supposes it to be a copy, but he also habitually
regards the idea of a secondary quality as the consciousness
of a quality of a thing, though under warning that the quality
as it is to consciousness is not as it is in the thing. This re-
servation rather adds to the confusion. There are in fact, according to Locke, as appears from his distinction between
the ' nominal' and 'real essence,' two different things denoted
by every common noun; the thing as it is in itself or in
nature, and the thing as it is for consciousness. The former
is the thing as constituted by a certain configuration of par-
ticles, which is only an object for the physical philosopher,
and never fully cognisable even by him ; [1] the latter is the

---

[1] This distinction is more fully treated below, paragraphs 88, &c.

thing as we see and hear and smell it. Now to a thing in
this latter sense, according to Locke, such a simple idea as
to the philosopher is one of a secondary quality (i.e. not a copy,
but an effect, of something in a body), is already in the
origin of knowledge referred as a quality, though without
distinction of primary and secondary. He does not indeed
state this in so many words. To have done so might have
forced him to reconsider his doctrine of the mere passivity
of the mind in respect of simple ideas. But it is implied in
his constant use of such phrases as 'reports of the senses,'
'inlet through the senses'—which have no meaning unless
something is reported, something let in—and in the familiar
comparison of the understanding to a 'closet, wholly shut
from light, with only some little opening left, to let in
external visible resemblances, or ideas, of things without.'
(Book II. chap. xi. sec. 17.)

22. Phraseology of this kind, the standing heritage of the
philosophy which seeks the origin of knowledge in sensation,
assumes that the individual sensation is from the first consciously representative; that it is more than what it is simply
in itself—fleeting, momentary, unnameable (because, while we
name it, it has become another), and for the same reason unknowable, the very negation of knowability; that it shows the
presence of something, whether this be a 'body' to which it is
referred as a quality, or a mind of which it is a modification,
or be ultimately reduced to the permanent conditions of its
own possibility. This assumption for the present has merely
to be pointed out; its legitimacy need not be discussed. Nor
need we now discuss the attempts that have been made since
Locke to show that mere sensations, dumb to begin with, may
yet become articulate upon repetition and combination; which
in fact endow them with a faculty of inference, and suppose
that though primarily they report nothing beyond themselves,
they yet somehow come to do so as an explanation of their
own recurrence. The sensational theory in Locke is still, so
to speak, unsophisticated. It is true that, in concert with
that 'thinking gentleman,' Mr. Molyneux, he had satisfied
himself that what we reckon simple ideas are often really
inferences from such ideas which by habit have become instinctive; but his account of this habitual process presupposes
the reference of sensation to a thing. 'When we set before
our eyes a round globe of any uniform colour, it is certain

that the idea thereby imprinted in our mind is of a flat circle, variously shadowed with several degrees of light and brightness coming to our eyes. But we having by use been accustomed to perceive what kind of appearance convex bodies are wont to make in us, what alterations are made in the reflections of light by the difference of the sensible figures of bodies; the judgment presently, by an habitual custom, alters the appearances into their causes. So that from that which truly is variety of colour or shadow, collecting the figure, it makes it pass for a mark of figure, and frames to itself the perception of a convex figure, and an uniform colour.' (Book II. chap. ix. sec. 8.) The theory here stated involves two assumptions, each inconsistent with the simplicity of the simple idea. (a) The actual impression of the 'plane variously coloured' is supposed to pronounce itself to be of something outward. Once call the sensation an 'impression,' indeed, or call it anything, and this or an analogous substantiation of it is implied. It is only as thus reporting something 'objective' that the simple idea of the plane variously coloured gives anything to be corrected by the 'perception of the kind of appearance convex bodies are wont to make in us,' i.e. 'of the alterations made in the reflections of light by the difference of the sensible figure of bodies.' This perception, indeed, as described, is already itself just the instinctive judgment which has to be accounted for, and though this objection might be met by a better statement, yet no statement could serve Locke's purpose which did not make assumption (b) that sensations of light and colour—' simple ideas of secondary qualities '—are in the very beginning of knowledge *appearances*, if not of *convex* bodies, yet of bodies; if not of bodies, yet of something which they reveal, which remains there while they pass away.

23. The same assumption is patent in Locke's account of the distinction between 'real and fantastic,' 'adequate and inadequate,' ideas. This distinction rests upon that between the thing as archetype, and the idea as the corresponding ectype. Simple ideas he holds to be necessarily ' real ' and ' adequate,' because necessarily answering to their archetypes. ' Not that they are all of them images or representations of what does exist : . . . whiteness and coldness are no more in snow than pain is : . . . yet are they real ideas in us, whereby we distinguish the qualities that are really in

things themselves.   For these several appearances being designed to be the marks whereby we are to know and
distinguish things which we have to do with, our ideas do as
well serve us to that purpose, and are as real distinguishing
characters, whether they be only constant effects, or else
exact resemblances of something in the things themselves.'
(Book II. chap. xxx. sec. 2.)   The simple idea, then, is a
'mark' or 'distinguishing character,' either as a copy or as
an effect, of something other than itself.   Only as thus
regarded, does the distinction between real and fantastic
possibly apply to it.   So too with the distinction between
true and false ideas.   As Locke himself points out, the simple
idea in itself is neither true nor false. It can become so only
as 'referred to something extraneous to it.'   (Book II. chap.
xxxii. sec. 4.)   For all that, he speaks of simple ideas as
true and necessarily true, because 'being barely such perceptions as God has fitted us to receive, and given power to
external objects to produce in us by established laws and
ways . . .   their truth consists in nothing else but in
such appearances as are produced in us, and must be suitable
to those powers He has placed in external objects, or else
they could not be produced in us.'   (Book II. chap. xxxii.
sec. 14.)   Here again we are brought to the same point.
The idea is an 'appearance' of something, necessarily true
when it cannot seem to be the appearance of anything else
than that of which it is the appearance.   We thus come to
the following dilemma.   Either the simple idea is referred to
a thing, as its pattern or its cause, or it cannot be regarded
as either real or true.   If it is still objected that it need not
be so referred in the beginning of knowledge, though it comes
to be so in the developed intelligence, the answer is the
further question, how can that be knowledge even in its most
elementary phase—the phase of the reception of simple ideas
—which is not a capacity of distinction between real and
apparent, between true and false ?   If its beginning is a mode
of consciousness, such as mere sensation would be—which,
because excluding all reference, excludes that reference of
itself to something else without which there could be no consciousness of a distinction between an 'is' and an 'is not,'
and therefore no true judgment at all—how can any repetition of such modes give such a judgment ?[1]

[1] Cf. the ground of distinction
between clearness and obscurity of
ideas: (Book II. chap. xxix. sec. 2)
'Our simple ideas are clear when they

24. The fact is that the 'simple idea' with Locke, as the beginning of knowledge, is already, at its minimum, the judgment, 'I have an idea different from other ideas, which I did not make for myself.' His confusion of this judgment with sensation is merely the fundamental confusion, on which all empirical psychology rests, between two essentially distinct questions—one metaphysical, What is the simplest element of knowledge? the other physiological, What are the conditions in the individual human organism in virtue of which it becomes a vehicle of knowledge? Though he failed, however, to distinguish these questions, their difference made itself appear in a certain divergence between the second and fourth books of his Essay. So far we have limited our consideration to passages in the second book, in which he treats *eo nomine* of ideas; of simple ideas as the original of knowledge, of complex ones as formed in its process. Here the physical theory is predominant. The beginning of knowledge is that without which the animal is incapable of it, viz. sensation regarded as an impression through 'animal spirits' on the brain. But it can only be so represented because sensation is identified with that which later psychology distinguished from it as Perception, and for which no physical theory can account. As we have seen, the whole theory of this (the second) book turns upon the supposition that the simple idea of sensation is in every case an idea of a sensible quality, and that it is so, not merely for us, considering it *ex parte post*, but consciously for the individual subject, which can mean nothing else than that it distinguishes itself from, and refers itself to, a thing. Locke himself, indeed, according to his plan of bringing in a 'faculty of the mind' whenever it is convenient, would perhaps rather have said that it is so distinguished and referred 'by the mind.' He considers the simple idea not, as it truly is, the mind itself in a certain relation, but a datum or material of the mind, upon which it performs certain operations as upon something other than itself, though all the while it is constituted, at least in its actuality, by this material. Between the reference of the simple idea to the thing, however, by itself and 'by the mind,'

are such as the objects themselves, whence they are taken, did or might in a well-ordered sensation or perception, present them.' As Locke always assumes that immediate consciousness can tell whether an idea is clear or not, it follows that immediate consciousness must tell of 'the object itself, whence the idea is taken.'

there is no essential difference. In either case the reference
is inconsistent with the simplicity of the simple idea; and if
the latter expression avoids the seeming awkwardness of
ascribing activity to the idea, it yet ascribes it to the mind
in that elementary stage in which, according to Locke, it is
merely receptive.

25. So much for the theory ' of ideas.' As if, however, in
treating of ideas he had been treating of anything else than
knowledge, he afterwards considers ' knowledge' in a book
by itself (the fourth) under that title, and here the question
as to the relation between idea and thing comes before him
in a somewhat different shape. According to his well-known
definition, knowledge is the perception of the agreement or
disagreement of any of our ideas. The agreement or disagreement may be of four sorts. It may be in the way (1)
of identity, (2) of relation, (3) of co-existence, (4) of real existence. In his account of the last sort of agreement, it may
be remarked by the way, he departs at once and openly from
his definition, making it an agreement, not of idea with idea,
but of an idea with ' actual real existence.' The fatal but
connatural wound in his system, which this inconsistency
marks, will appear more fully below. For the present, our
concern is for the adjustment of the definition of knowledge
to the doctrine of the simple idea as the beginning of knowledge. According to the definition, it cannot be the simple
idea, as such, that constitutes this beginning, but only the
perception of agreement or disagreement between simple
ideas. 'There could be no room,' says Locke distinctly, 'for
any positive knowledge at all, if we could not distinguish
any relation beween our ideas.' (Book IV. chap. i. sec. 5.)
Yet in the very context where he makes this statement, the
perception of relation is put as a distinct kind of knowledge apart from others. In his account of the other kinds,
however, he is faithful to his definition, and treats each as a
perception (i.e. a judgment) of a relation in the way of agreement or disagreement. The primary knowledge is that of
identity—the knowledge of an idea as identical with itself.
' A man infallibly knows, as soon as ever he has them in his
mind, that the ideas he calls *white* and *round*, are the very
ideas they are, and not other ideas which he calls *red* and
square .' (Book IV. chap. i. sec. 4.) Now, as Hume afterwards pointed out, identity is not simple unity. It cannot

be predicated of the 'idea' as merely single, but only as a manifold in singleness. To speak of an idea as the 'same with itself' is unmeaning unless it mean 'same with itself *in its manifold appearances,*' i.e. unless the idea is distinguished, as an object existing continuously, from its present appearance. Thus 'the infallible knowledge,' which Locke describes in the above passage, consists in this, that on the occurrence of a certain 'idea' the man *recognises* it as one, which at other times of its occurrence he has called '*white.*' Such a 'synthesis of recognition,' however, expressed by the application of a common term, implies the reference of a present sensation to a permanent object of thought, in this case the object thought under the term 'white,' so that the sensation becomes an idea of that object. Were there no such objects, there would be no significant names, but only noises; and were the present sensation not so referred, it would not be named. It may be said indeed that the 'permanent object of thought' is merely the instinctive result of a series of past resembling sensations, and that the common name is merely the register of this result. But the question is thus merely thrown further back. Unless the single fleeting sensation was, to begin with, fixed and defined by relation to and distinction from something permanent—in other words, unless it ceased to be a mere sensation—how did it happen that other sensations were referred to it, as different cases of an identical phenomenon, to which the noise suggested by it might be applied as a sign?

26. This primary distinction and relation of the simple idea Locke implicitly acknowledges when he substitutes for the simple idea, as in the passage last quoted, the man's knowledge that he has the idea; for such knowledge implies the distinction of the idea from its permanent conscious subject, and its determination by that negative relation.[1] Thus determined, it becomes itself a permanent object, or (which comes to the same) an idea *of an object;* a phrase which Locke at his convenience substitutes for the mere idea, whenever it is wanted for making his theory of knowledge square with knowledge itself. Once become such an object, it is a

---

[1] Cf. the passage in Book II. chap. vii. sec. 7. 'When ideas are in our minds, we consider them as being actually there.' The mere 'idea' is in fact essentially different from the 'considera- tion of it as actually there,' as sensation is different from thought. The 'con- sideration, &c.,' really means the *thought* of the 'idea' (sensation) as determined by relation to the conscious subject.

basis to which other sensations, like and unlike, may be
referred as differentiating attributes. Its identity becomes a
definite identity.

27. Upon analysis, then, of Locke's account of the most
elementary knowledge, the perception of identity or agreement of an idea with itself, we find that like the 'simple
idea,' which he elsewhere makes the beginning of knowledge,
it really means the reference of a sensation to a conception
of a permanent object or subject,[1] either in such a judgment
as 'this is white' (sc. a white thing), or in the more elementary one, 'this is an object to me.' In the latter form
the judgment represents what Locke puts as the consciousness, 'I have an idea,' or as the 'consideration that the idea
is actually there;' in the former it represents what he calls
'the knowledge that the idea which I have in my mind and
which I call white is the very idea it is, and not the idea
which I call red.' It is only because *referred*, as above, that
the sensation is in Locke's phraseology 'a testimony' or
'report' of something. As we said above, his notion of the
beginning of knowledge is expressed not merely in the formula
'I have an idea different from other ideas,' but with the
addition, 'which I did not make for myself.'[2] The simple
idea is supposed to testify to something without that caused
it, and it is this interpretation of it which makes it with him
the ultimate criterion of reality. But unless it were at once
distinguished from and referred to both a thing of which it
is an effect and a subject of which it is an experience, it could
not in the first place testify to anything, nor secondly to a
thing as made for, not by, the subject. This brings us, however, upon Locke's whole theory of 'real existence,' which
requires fuller consideration.

28. It is a theory, we must premise, which is nowhere
explicitly stated. It has to be gathered chiefly from those
passages of the second book in which he treats of 'complex'
or 'artificial' ideas in distinction from simple ones, which
are necessarily real, and from the discussion in the fourth
book of the 'extent' and 'reality' of knowledge. We have,
however, to begin with, in the enumeration of simple ideas, a

---

[1] For a recognition by Locke of the
correlativity of these (of which more
will have to be said below) cf. Book II.
chap. xxiii. sec. 15. 'Whilst I know
by seeing or hearing, &c., that there is

some corporeal being without me, the
object of that sensation, I do more certainly know that there is some spiritual
being within me that sees and hears.'
[2] Cf. Book II. chap. xii. sec. 1.

mention of 'existence,' as one of those 'received alike through all the ways of sensation and reflection.' It is an idea 'suggested to the understanding by every object without and every idea within. When ideas are in our minds, we consider them as being actually there, as well as we consider things to be actually without us; which is, that they exist, or have existence.' (Book II. chap. vii. sec. 7.)

29. The two considerations here mentioned, of 'ideas as actually in our minds,' of 'things as actually without us,' are meant severally to represent the two ways of reflection and sensation, by which the idea of existence is supposed to be suggested. But sensation, according to Locke, is an organ of 'ideas,' just as much as reflection. Taking his doctrine strictly, there are no 'objects' but 'ideas' to suggest the idea of existence, whether by the way of sensation or by that of reflection, and no ideas that are not 'in the mind.' (Book II. chap. ix. sec. 3, &c.)

30. The designation of the idea of existence, then, as 'suggested by every idea within,' covers every possible suggestion. It can mean nothing else than that it is given in every act and mode of consciousness; that it is inseparable from feeling as such, being itself at the same time a distinct simple idea. This, we may remark by the way, involves the conclusion that every idea is composite, made up of whatever distinguishes it from other ideas together with the idea of existence. Of this idea of existence itself, however, it will be impossible to say anything distinctive; for, as it accompanies all possible objects of consciousness, there will be no cases where it is absent to be distinguished from those where it is present. Not merely will it be undefinable, as every simple idea is; it will be impossible 'to send a man to his senses' (according to Locke's favourite subterfuge) in order to know what it is, since it is neither given in one sense as distinct from another, nor in all senses as distinct from any other modification of consciousness. Thus regarded, to treat it as a simple idea alongside of other simple ideas is a palpable contradiction. It is the mere 'It is felt,' the abstraction of consciousness, no more to be reckoned as one among other ideas than colour in general is to be co-ordinated with red, white, and blue. Whether I smell a rose in the summer or recall the smell in winter; whether I see a horse or a ghost, or imagine a centaur or think of gravitation or the

philosopher's stone—in every case alike the idea or 'immediate object of the mind' *exists*. Yet we find Locke distinguishing between real ideas, as those that 'have a conformity
with the existence of things,' and fantastic ideas, as those
which have no such conformity (Book II. chap. xxx. sec. 1);
and again in the fourth book (chap. i. sec. 7, chap. iii.
sec. 21, &c.) he makes the perception of the agreement of an
idea with existence a special kind of knowledge, different
from that of agreement of idea with idea; and having done
so, raises the question whether we have such a knowledge of
existence at all, and decides that our knowledge of it is very
narrow.

31. How are such a distinction and such a question to be
reconciled with the attribution of existence to every idea?
The answer of course will be, that when he speaks of ideas as
not conforming to existence, and makes knowledge or the
agreement of ideas with each other something different from
their agreement with existence, he means and generally says
'real actual existence,' or the 'existence of *things*,' i.e. an
existence, whatever it be, which is opposed to mere existence
in consciousness. Doubtless he so means, but this implies
that upon mere consciousness, or the simple presence of
ideas, there has supervened a distinction, which has to be
accounted for, of ideas from things which they represent on
the one hand, and from a mind of which they are affections
on the other. Even in the passage first quoted (Book II.
chap. vii. sec. 7), where existence is ascribed to every idea,
on looking closely we find this distinction obtruding itself,
though without explicit acknowledgment. In the very same
breath, so to speak, in which the idea of existence is said to
be suggested by every idea, it is further described as being
either of two considerations—either the consideration of an
idea as actually in our mind, or of a thing as actually without
us. Such considerations at once imply the supervention of
that distinction between 'mind' and 'thing,' which gives a
wholly new meaning to 'existence.' They are not, in truth,
as Locke supposed, two separate considerations, one or other
of which, as the case may be, is interchangeable with the
'idea of existence.' One is correlative with the other, and
neither is the same as simple feeling. Considered as actually
in the mind, the feeling is distinguished from the mind as an
affection from the subject thereof, and just in virtue of this

distinction is referred to a thing as the cause of the affection, or becomes representative of a thing. But for such consideration there would for us, if the doctrine of ideas means anything, be no 'thing without us' at all. To 'consider things as actually without us' is to consider them as causes of the ideas in our mind, and this is to have an idea of existence quite different from mere consciousness. It is to have an idea of it which at once suggests the question whether the existence is real or apparent; in other words, whether the thing, to which an affection of the mind is referred as its cause, is really its cause or no.

32. Between these two meanings of existence—its meaning as interchangeable with simple consciousness, and its meaning as reality—Locke failed to distinguish. Just as, having announced 'ideas' to be the sole 'materials of knowledge,' he allows himself at his convenience to put 'things' in the place of ideas; so having identified existence with momentary consciouness or the simple idea, he substitutes for existence in this sense *reality*, and in consequence finds reality given solely in the simple idea. Thus when the conceptions of cause or substance, or relations of any kind, come under view, since these cannot be represented as given in momentary consciousness, they have to be pronounced not to exist, and since existence is reality, to be unreal or 'fictions of the mind.' But without these unreal relations there could be no knowledge, and if they are not given in the elements of knowledge, it is difficult to see how they are introduced, or to avoid the appearance of constructing knowledge out of the unknown. Given in the elements of knowledge, however, they cannot be, if these are simple ideas or momentary recurrences of the 'it is felt.' But by help of Locke's equivocation between the two meanings of existence, they can be covertly introduced as the real. Existence is given in the simple idea, existence equals the real, therefore the real is given in the simple idea. But think or speak of the real as we will, we find that it exhibits itself as substance, as cause, and as related; i.e. according to Locke as a 'complex' or 'invented' or 'superinduced' idea.

33. In the second book of his Essay, which treats of ideas, he makes the grand distinction between 'the simple ideas which are all from things themselves, and of which the mind can have no more or other than what are suggested to it,' and

the 'complex ideas which are the workmanship of the mind.'
(Book II. chap. xii.) In his account of the latter there are
some curious cross-divisions, but he finally enumerates them
as ideas either of *modes, substances,* or *relations.* The character of these ideas he then proceeds to explain in the order
given, one after the other, and as if each were independent
of the rest ; though according to his own statement the idea
of mode presupposes that of substance, and the idea of
substance involves that of relation.   'Modes I call such
complex ideas, which, however compounded, contain not in
them the supposition of subsisting by themselves, but are
considered as dependencies on, or affections of, substances ;
such are the ideas signified by the words 'triangle,' 'grati-
tude,' 'murder,' &c. Of these there are two sorts. First,
there are some which are only variations or different combinations of the same simple idea without the mixture of any
other—as a dozen, or score—which are nothing but the ideas
of so many distinct units added together; and these I call
simple modes, as being contained within the bounds of one
simple idea.   Secondly, there are others compounded of
simple ideas of several kinds, put together to make one
complex one ; e. g. beauty, ... and these I call *mixed
modes.'* (Book II. chap. xii. secs. 4, 5.) So soon as he comes
to speak more in detail of simple modes, he falls into apparent
contradiction with his doctrine that, as complex ideas, they
are the mere workmanship of the mind.   All particular
sounds and colours are simple modes of the simple ideas of
sound and colour.   (Book II. chap. xviii. secs. 3, 4.) Again,
the ideas of figure, place, distance, as of all particular figures,
places, and distances, are simple modes of the simple idea of
space.   (Book II. chap. xiii.) To maintain, however, that
the ideas of space, sound, or colour *in general* (as simple
ideas) were taken from things themselves, while those of
particular spaces, sounds, and colours (as complex ideas)
were 'made by the mind,' was for Locke impossible.   Thus
in the very next chapter after that in which he has opposed
all complex ideas, those of simple modes included, as made
by the mind to all simple ones as taken from things themselves, he speaks of simple modes 'either *as found in things
existing,* or as made by the mind within itself.' (Book II.
chap. xiii. sec. 1.) It was not for Locke to get over this confusion by denying the entithesis between that which the

mind 'makes' and that which it 'takes from existing things,' and for the present we must leave it as it stands. We must further note that a mode being considered ' as an affection of a substance,' space must be to the particular spaces which are its simple modes, as a substance to its modifications. So too colour to particular colours, &c., &c. But the idea of a substance is a complex idea ' framed by the mind.' Therefore the idea of space—at any rate such an idea as we have of it when we think of distances, places, or figures, and when else do we think of it at all?—must be a complex and artificial idea. But according to Locke the idea of space is emphatically a simple idea, given immediately *both* by sight and touch, concerning which if a man enquire, he 'sends him to his senses.' (Book II. chap. v.)

34. These contradictions are not avoidable blunders, due to carelessness or want of a clear head in the individual writer. 'The complex idea of substance' will not be exorcised ; the mind will show its workmanship in the very elements of knowledge towards which its relation seems most passive—in the ' existing things' which are the conditions of its experience no less than in the individual's conscious reaction upon them. The interrogator of the individual consciousness seeks to know that consciousness, and just for that reason must find in it at every stage those formal conceptions, such as substance and cause, without which there can be no object of knowledge at all. He thus substantiates sensation, while he thinks that he merely observes it, and calls it a sensible thing. Sensations, thus unconsciously transformed, are for him the real, the actually existent. Whatever is not given by immediate sense, outer or inner, he reckons a mere 'thing of the mind.' The ideas of substance and relation, then, not being given by sense, must in his eyes be things of the mind, in distinction from really existent things. But speech bewrayeth him. He cannot state anything that he knows save in terms which imply that substance and relation are in the things known ; and hence an inevitable obtrusion of 'things of the mind' in the place of real existence, just where the opposition between them is being insisted on. Again, as a man seems to observe consciousness in himself and others, it has nothing that it has not received. It is a blank to begin with, but passive of that which is without, and through its passivity it becomes

informed. If the 'mind,' then, means this or that individual
consciousness, the things of the mind must be gradually developed from an original passivity. On the other hand, let
anyone try to know this original passive consciousness, and
in it, as in every other known object-matter, he must find
these things of the mind, substance and relations. If nature
is the object. he must find them in nature; if his own self-
consciousness, he must find them in that consciousness.
But while nature knows not what is in herself, self-consciousness, it would seem, *ex vi termini*, does know. Therefore not
merely substance and relation must be found in the original
consciousness, but the knowledge, the ideas, of them.

35. As we follow Locke's treatment of these ideas more in
detail, we shall find the logical see-saw, here accounted for,
appearing with scarcely a disguise. His account of the
origin of the 'complex ideas of substances' is as follows.
'The mind being furnished with a great number of the
simple ideas, conveyed in by the senses, as they are found in
exterior things, or by reflection on its own operations, takes
notice also that a certain number of these simple ideas go
constantly together; which being presumed to belong to one
thing, and words being suited to common apprehensions and
made use of for quick despatch, are called, so united in one
subject, by one name; which by inadvertency we are apt
afterwards to talk of and consider as one simple idea, which
indeed is a complication of many ideas together; because,
as I have said, not imagining how these simple ideas can
subsist by themselves, we accustom ourselves to suppose
some *substratum*, wherein they do subsist, and from which
they do result; which therefore we call *substance*.' (Book
II. chap. xxiii. sec. 1.) In the controversy with Stillingfleet,
which arose out of this chapter, Locke was constrained
further to distinguish (as he certainly did not do in the
original text) between the 'ideas of distinct substances, such
as man, horse,' and the 'general idea of substance.' It is to
ideas of the former sort that he must be taken to refer in the
above passage, when he speaks of them as formed by 'complication of many ideas together,' and these alone are *complex*
in the strict sense. The *general* idea of substance on the
other hand, which like all general ideas (according to Locke)
is made by abstraction, means the idea of a 'substratum
which we accustom ourselves to suppose' as that wherein

the complicated ideas 'do subsist, and from which they do result.' This, however, he regards as itself one, 'the first and chief,' among the ideas which make up any of the ' distinct substances.' (Book II. chap. xii. sec. 6.) Nor is he faithful to the distinction between the general and the complex. In one passage of the first letter to Stillingfleet, he distinctly speaks of the *general* idea of substance as a ' *complex* idea made up of the idea of something plus that of relation to qualities.'[1] Notwithstanding this confusion of terms, however, he no doubt had before him what seemed a clear distinction between the ' abstract general idea ' of substance, as such, i.e. of ' something related as a support to accidents,' but which does not include ideas of any particular accidents, and the composite idea of a substance, made up of a multitude of simple ideas plus that of the something related to them as a support. We shall find each of these ideas, according to Locke's statement, presupposing the other.

36. In the passage above quoted, our aptness to consider a complication of simple ideas, which we notice to go constantly together, as one simple idea, is accounted for as the result of a presumption that they belong to one thing. This presumption is again described in the words that ' we accustom ourselves to suppose some substratum, wherein they do subsist, and from which they do result; which therefore we call substance.' Here it is implied that the idea of substance, i. e. ' the general idea of something related as a support to accidents,' is one gradually formed upon observation of the regular coincidence of certain simple ideas. In the sequel (sec. 3 of the same chapter[2]) we are told that such an idea—' an obscure and relative idea of substance in general —being thus made, we come to have the ideas of particular sorts of substances by collecting such combinations of simple ideas as are, by experience and observation of men's senses, taken notice of to exist together.' Thus a *general* idea of

---

[1] Upon a reference to the chapter on 'complex ideas' (Book II. chap. xii.), it will appear that the term is used in a stricter and a looser sense. In the looser sense it is not confined to *compound* ideas, but in opposition to simple ones includes those of relation and even ' abstract general ideas.' When Locke thinks of the *general* idea of substance apart from the complication of accidents referred to it, he opposes it to the complex idea, according to the stricter sense of that term. On the other hand, when he thinks of it as ' made up ' of the idea of *something* plus that of relation to qualities (as if there could be an idea of something apart from such relation), it seems to him to have two elements, and therefore to be complex.

[2] I. xxiii.

substance having been formed by one gradual process, ideas
of particular sorts of substances are formed by another and
later one.　But then the very same 'collection of such combinations of simple ideas as are taken notice of to exist
together,' which (according to sec. 3) constitutes the later
process and follows upon the formation of the *general* idea of
substance, has been previously described as preceding and
conditioning that formation.　It is the complication of
simple ideas, noticed to go constantly together, that (according to sec. 1) leads to the 'idea of substance in general.'
To this see-saw between the process preceding and that following the formation of the idea in question must be added
the difficulty, that Locke's account makes the general idea
precede the particular, which is against the whole tenor of
his doctrine of abstraction as an operation whereby 'the
mind makes the particular ideas, received from particular
objects, to become general.'　(Book II. chap. xi. sec. 9.)

37. It may be said perhaps that Locke's self-contradiction
in this regard is more apparent than real; that the two processes of combining simple ideas are essentially different,
just because in the later process they are combined by a conscious act of the mind as accidents of a 'something,' of
which the *general* idea has been previously formed, whereas
in the earlier one they are merely presented together 'by
nature,' and, *ex hypothesi*, though they gradually suggest, do
not carry with them any reference to a 'substratum.'　But
upon this we must remark that the presentation of ideas 'by
nature' or 'by God,' though a mode of speech of which
Locke in his account of the origin of knowledge freely avails
himself, means nothing else than their relation to a 'substratum,' if not 'wherein they do subsist,' yet 'from which
they do result.'　If then it is for consciousness that ideas
are presented together by nature, they already carry with
them that reference to a substratum which is supposed gradually to result from their concurrence.　If it is not for consciousness that they are so presented, if they do not *severally*
carry with them a reference to 'something,' how is it they
come to do so in the gross?　If a single sensation of heat is
not referred to a hot thing, why should it be so referred on
the thousandth recurrence?　Because perhaps, recurring
constantly in the same relations, it compels the inference of
permanent antecedents?　But the 'same relations' mean

relations to the same things, and the observation of these relations presupposes just that conception of *the thing* which it is sought to account for.

38. We are estopped, however, from any such explanation of Locke as would suggest these ulterior questions by his explicit statement that ' all simple ideas, all sensible qualities, carry with them a supposition of a substratum to exist in, and of a substance wherein they inhere.' The vindication of himself against the pathetic complaint of Stillingfleet, that he had ' almost discarded substance out of the reasonable part of the world,' in which this statement occurs, was certainly not needed. Already in the original text the simple ideas, of which the association suggests the idea of substance, are such as ' the mind finds in exterior things or by reflection on its own operations.' But to find them in an exterior thing is to find them in a substance, a ' something it knows not what,' regarded as outward, just as to find them by reflection on its own operations, as its own, is to find them in such a substance regarded as inward. The process then by which, according to Locke, the general idea of substance is arrived at, presupposes this idea just as much as the process, by which ideas of particular sorts of substances are got, presupposes it, and the distinction between the two processes, as he puts it, disappears.

39. The same paralogism appears under a slightly altered form when it is stated (in the first letter to Stillingfleet) that the idea of substance as the ' general indetermined idea of *something* is by the abstraction of the mind derived from the simple ideas of sensation and reflection.' Now ' abstraction ' with Locke means the ' separation of an idea from all other ideas that accompany it in its real existence.' (Book II. chap. xii. sec. 1.) It is clear then that it is impossible to abstract an idea which is not *there*, in real existence, to be abstracted. Accordingly, if the ' general idea of something' is derived by abstraction from simple ideas of sensation and reflection, it must be originally given with these ideas, or it would not afterwards be separated from them. Conversely they must carry this idea with them, and cannot be simple ideas at all, but compound ones, each made up of ' the general idea of something or being,' and of an accident which this something supports. How then does the general idea of substance or ' something,' *as derived*, differ from the

idea of ' something,' as given in the original ideas of sensation and reflection from which the supposed process of abstraction starts? What can be said of the one that cannot
be said of the other? If the derived general idea is of
something related to qualities, what, according to Locke, are
the original ideas but those of qualities related to something?
It is true that the general idea is of something, of which
nothing further is known, related to qualities in general, not
to any particular qualities. But the ' simple idea ' in like
manner can only be of an indeterminate quality, for in order
to any determination of it, the idea must be put together
with another idea, and so cease to be simple; and the ' something,' to which it is referred, must for the same reason be a
purely indeterminate something. If, in order to avoid concluding that Locke thus unwittingly identified the abstract
general idea of substance with any simple idea, we say that
the simple idea, because not abstract, is not indeterminate
but of a real quality, defined by manifold relations, we
fall upon the new difficulty that, if so, not only does the
simple idea become manifoldly complex, but just such
an ' idea of a particular sort of substance ' as, according
to Locke, is derived from the derived idea of substance in
general. As an idea of a quality, it is also necessarily an
idea of a correlative ' something;' and if it is an idea of a
quality in its reality, i. e. as determined by various relations,
it must be an idea of a variously qualified something, i. e. of
a particular substance. Then not merely the middle of the
twofold process by which we are supposed to get at ' complex
ideas of substances '— i. e. the *abstract* something; but its
end—i. e. the *particular* something—turns out to be the
same as its beginning.

40. The fact is, that in making the general idea of substance precede particular ideas of sorts of substances (as he
certainly however confusedly does, in the 23rd chapter of
the Second Book,[1] as well as by implication in his doctrine
of modes, Book II. chap. xii. sec. 4), Locke stumbled upon a
truth which he was not aware of, and which will not fit into
his ordinary doctrine of general ideas : the truth that knowledge is a process from the more abstract to the more concrete, not the reverse, as is commonly supposed, and as

---

[1] See above, paragraph 35.

Locke's definition of abstraction implies. Throughout his prolix discussion of ' substance ' and ' essence ' we find two opposite notions perpetually cross each other : one that knowledge begins with the simple idea, the other that it begins with the real thing as particularized by manifold relations. According to the former notion, simple ideas being given, void of relation, as the real, the mind of its own act proceeds to bring them into relation and compound them : according to the latter, a thing of various properties (i. e. relations[1]) being given as the real, the mind proceeds to separate these from each other. According to the one notion the intellectual process, as one of complication, ends just where, according to the other notion, as one of abstraction, it began.

41. The chief verbal equivocation, under which Locke disguises the confusion of these two notions, is to be found in the use of the word ' particular,' which is sometimes used for the mere individual having no community with anything else, sometimes for the thing qualified by relation to a multitude of other things. The simple idea or sensation; the ' something ' which the simple idea is supposed to ' report,' and which Locke at his pleasure identifies with it; the complex idea; and the thing as the collection of the properties which the simple idea ' reports,' all are merged by Locke under the one term ' particulars.' As the only consistency in his use of the term seems to lie in its opposition to ' generals,' we naturally turn to the passage where this opposition is spoken of most at large.

42. ' General and universal belong not to the real existence of things, but are the inventions and creatures of the understanding, made by it for its own use, and concern only signs, whether words or ideas. Words are general when used for signs of general ideas, and so are applicable indifferently to many particular things ; and ideas are general, when they are set up as the representatives of many particular things ; but universality belongs not to things themselves, which are all of them particular in their existence, even those words and ideas which in their signification are general. When

---

[1] Cf. BOOK ii. chap. xxiii. sec. 37. ' Most of the simple ideas that make up our complex ideas of substances are only powers . . . e. g. the greater part of the ideas which make up our complex idea of gold . . . are nothing else *but so many relations* to other substances.'

therefore we quit particulars, the generals that rest are only creatures of our own making, their general nature being nothing but the capacity they are put into by the understanding, of signifying or representing many particulars. For the signification they have is nothing but a relation that by the mind of man is added to them. . . . The sorting of things under names is the workmanship of the understanding, taking occasion from the similitude it observes among them to make abstract general ideas, and set them up in the mind, with names annexed to them, as patterns or forms (for in that sense the word form has a very proper signification), to which as particular things are found to agree, so they come to be of that species, have that denomination, or are put into that classis. For when we say this is a man, that a horse; this justice, that cruelty, what do we else but rank things under different specific names, as agreeing to those abstract ideas, of which we have made those names the signs ? And what are the essences of those species, set out and marked by names, but those abstract ideas in the mind ; which are, as it were, the bonds between particular things that exist, and the names they are to be ranked under ? ' (Book III. chap. iii. secs. 11 and 13.)

43. In the first of these remarkable passages we begin with the familiar opposition between ideas as ' the creatures of the mind ' and real things. Ideas, and the words which express them, may be general, but things cannot. ' They are all of them particular in their existence.' Then the ideas and words themselves appear as things, and as such ' in their existence ' can only be particular. It is only in its signification, i.e. in its relation to other ideas which it represents, that an idea, particular itself, becomes general, and this relation does not belong to the ' existence ' of the idea or to the idea in itself, but ' by the mind of man is added to it.' The relation being thus a fictitious addition to reality, ' general and universal are mere inventions and creatures of the understanding.' The next passage, in spite of the warning that all ideas are particular in their existence, still speaks of general ideas, but only as ' set up in the mind.' To these ' particular things existing are found to agree,' and the agreement is expressed in such judgments as ' this is a man, that a horse ; this is justice, that cruelty ; ' the ' this ' and ' that ' representing ' particular existing

things,' 'horse' and 'cruelty' abstract general ideas to which these are found to agree.

44. One antithesis is certainly maintained throughout these passages—that between 'real existence which is always particular, and the workmanship of the mind,' which 'invents' generality. Real existence, however, is ascribed (a) to things themselves, (b) to words and ideas, even those which become of general signification, (c) to mixed modes, for in the proposition 'this is justice,' the 'this' must represent a mixed mode. (Cf. II. xii. 5.) The characteristic of the 'really existent,' which distinguishes it from the workmanship of the mind, would seem to be mere individuality, exclusive of all relation. The simple 'this' and 'that,' apart from the relation expressed in the judgment, being mere individuals, are really existent; and conversely, ideas, which in themselves have real existence, when a relation, in virtue of which they become significant, has been 'added to them by the mind,' become 'inventions of the understanding.' This consists with the express statement in the chapter on 'relation' (II. xxv. 8), that it is 'not contained in the existence of things, but is something extraneous and superinduced.' Thus generality, as a relation between any one of a multitude of *single* (not necessarily *simple*) ideas, e.g. single ideas of horses, and all the rest—a relation which belongs not to any one of them singly—is superinduced by the understanding upon their *real*, i.e. their *single* existence. Apart from this relation, it would seem, or in their mere singleness, even ideas of mixed modes, e.g. *this act* of justice, may have real existence.

45. The result of Locke's statement, thus examined, clearly is that real existence belongs to the present momentary act of consciousness, and to that alone. Ascribed as it is to the 'thing itself,' to the idea which, *as general*, has it not, and to the mixed mode, it is in each case the momentary presence to consciousness that constitutes it. To a thing itself, as distinct from the presentation to consciousness, it cannot belong, for such a 'thing' means that which remains identical with itself under manifold appearances, and both identity and appearance imply relation, i.e. 'an invention of the mind.' As little can it belong to the *content* of any idea, since this is in all cases constituted by relation to other ideas. Thus if I judge 'this is sweet,' the real existence lies

in the simple ' this,' in the mere form of presentation at an
individual *now*, not in the relation of this to other flavours
which constitutes the determinate sweetness, or to a sweetness at other times tasted. If I judge ' this is a horse,' a
present vision really exists, but not so its relation to other
sensations of sight or touch, closely precedent or sequent,
which make up the ' total impression ;' much less its relation
to other like impressions thought of, in consideration of
which a common name is applied to it. If, again, I judge
' this is an act of justice,' the present thought of the act,
as present, really exists; not so those relations of the act
which either make it just, or make me apply the name to it.
It is true that according to this doctrine the ' really existent '
is the unmeaning, and that any statement about it is impossible. We cannot judge of it without bringing it into
relation, in which it ceases to be what in its mere singleness
it is, and thus loses its reality, overlaid by the ' invention of
the understanding.' Nay, if we say that it is the mere
' this ' or ' that,' as such—the simple ' here ' and ' now '—
the very ' this,' in being mentioned or judged of, becomes
related to other things which we have called ' this,' and the
' now' to other ' nows.' Thus each acquires a generality,
and with it becomes fictitious. As Plato long ago taught—
though the lesson seems to require to be taught anew to
each generation of philosophers—a consistent sensationalism
must be speechless. Locke, himself, in one of the passages
quoted, implicitly admits this by indicating that only through
relations or in their generality are ideas ' significant.'

46. He was not the man, however, to become speechless
out of sheer consistency. He has a redundancy of terms
and tropes for disguising from himself and his reader the
real import of his doctrine. In the latter part of the
passage quoted we find that the relation or community
between ideas, which the understanding invents, is occasioned by a ' similitude which it observes among things.'
The general idea having been thus invented, ' things are
found to agree with it '—as is natural since they suggested it.
Hereupon we are forced to ask how, if all relation is superinduced upon real existence by the understanding, an *observed*
relation of similitude among things can occasion the superinduction ; and again how it happens, if all generality of ideas
is a fiction of the mind, that ' things are found to agree with

general ideas.' How can the real existence called 'this' or 'that,' which only really exists so far as nothing can be said of it but that it is 'this' or 'that,' agree with anything whatever? Agreement implies some content, some determination by properties, i.e. by relations, in the things agreeing, whereas the really existent excludes relation. How then can it agree with the abstract general idea, the import of which, according to Locke's own showing, depends solely on relation?

47. Such questions did not occur to Locke, because while asserting the mere individuality of things existent, and the simplicity of all ideas as *given*, i.e. as real, he never fully recognised the meaning of his own assertion. Under the shelter of the ambiguous 'particular' he could at any time substitute for the *mere* individual the *determinate* individual, or individual qualified by community with other things ; just as, again, under covering of the 'simple idea' he could substitute for the mere momentary consciousness the perception of a definite thing. Thus when he speaks of the judgment 'this is gold' as expressing the agreement of a real (i.e. individual) thing with a general idea, he thinks of 'this' as already having, apart from the judgment, the determination which it first receives in the judgment. He thinks of it, in other words, not as the mere 'perishing' sensation[1] or individual void of relation, but as a sensation symbolical of other possibilities of sensation which, as so many relations of a *thing* to us or to other things, are connoted by the common noun 'gold.' It thus 'agrees' with the abstract idea or conception of qualities, i.e. because it is already the 'creature of the understanding,' determined by relations which constitute a generality and community between it and other things. Such a notion of the really existent thing— wholly inconsistent with his doctrine of relation and of the general—Locke has before him when he speaks of general ideas as formed by abstraction of certain qualities from real things, or of certain ideas from other ideas that accompany them in real existence. 'When some one first lit on a parcel of that sort of substance we denote by the word *gold*, . . . its peculiar colour, perhaps, and weight were the first he abstracted from it, to make the complex idea of that species . . . another perhaps added to these the ideas of fusibility

---

[1] 'All impressions are perishing existences.'—HUME. See below, paragraph 208.

and fixedness . . . another its ductility and solubility in aqua regia. These, or part of these, put together, usually make the complex idea in men's minds of that sort of body we call *gold*.' (Book II. chap. xxxi. sec. 9.) Here the supposition is that a thing, multitudinously qualified, is given apart from any action of the understanding, which then proceeds to act in the way of successively detaching ('abstracting') these qualities and recombining them as the idea of a species. Such a recombination, indeed, would seem but wasted labour. The qualities are assumed to be already found by the understanding and found as in a thing ; otherwise the understanding could not abstract them from it.   Why should it then painfully put together in imperfect combination what has been previously given to it complete ?   Of the complex idea which results from the work of abstraction, nothing can be said but a small part of what is predicable of the known thing which the possibility of such abstraction presupposes.

48. 'The complex idea of a species,' spoken of in the passage last quoted, corresponds to what, in Locke's theory of substance, is called the 'idea of a particular sort of substance.'   In considering that theory we saw that, according to his account, the beginning of the process by which the 'abstract idea of substance' was formed, was either that abstract idea itself, the mere 'something,' or by a double contradiction the 'complex idea of a particular sort of substance' which yet we only come to have *after* the abstract idea has been formed.   In the passage now before us there is no direct mention of the abstraction of the 'substratum,' as such, but only of the quality, and hence there is no ambiguity about the paralogism.   It is not a mere 'something' that the man 'lights upon,' and thus it is not this that holds the place at once of the given and the derived, but a something having manifold qualities to be abstracted. In other words, it is the 'idea of a particular sort of substance' that he starts from, and it is just this again to which, as a 'complex idea of a species,' his understanding is supposed gradually to lead him.   The understanding, indeed, according to Locke, is never adequate to nature, and accordingly the qualities abstracted and recombined in the complex idea always fall vastly short of the fulness of those

given in the real thing; or as he states it in terms of the multiplication table (Book II. chap. xxxi. sec. 10), ' some who have examined this species more accurately could, I believe, enumerate ten times as many properties in gold, all of them as inseparable from its internal constitution, as its colour or weight; and it is probable if any one knew all the properties that are by divers men known of this metal, there would an hundred times as many ideas go to the complex idea of gold, as any one man has yet in his; and yet perhaps that would not be the thousandth part of what is to be discovered in it.' These two million properties, and upwards, which await abstraction in gold, are all, it must be noted, according to Locke's statement elsewhere (Book II. chap xxiii. sec. 37), ' nothing but so many relations to other substances.' It is just on account of these multitudinous relations of the real thing that the understanding is inadequate to its comprehension. Yet according to Locke's doctrine of relation these must all be themselves 'superinductions of the mind,' and the greater the fulness which they constitute, the further is the distance from the *mere* individuality which elsewhere, in contrast with the fictitiousness of ' generals,' appears as the equivalent of real existence.

49. The real thing and the creation of the understanding thus change places. That which is given to the understanding as the real, which it finds and does not make, is not now the bare atom upon which relations have to be artificially superinduced. Nor is it the mere present feeling, which has ' by the mind of man ' to be made ' significant,' or representative of past experience. It is itself an inexhaustible complex of relations, whether they are considered as subsisting between it and other things, or between the sensations which it is ' fitted to produce in us.' These are the real, which is thus a system, a community; and if the ' general,' as Locke says, is that which ' has the capacity of representing many particulars,' the real thing itself is general, for it represents —nay, is constituted by—the manifold particular feelings which, mediately or immediately, it excites in us. On the other hand, the invention of the understanding, instead of giving ' significance ' or content to the mere individuality of the real, as it does according to Locke's theory of ' generals,' now appears as detaching fragments from the fulness of the

real to recombine them in an 'abstract essence' of its own.
Instead of adding complexity to the simple, it subtracts from
the complex.

50. To gather up, then, the lines of contradiction which
traverse Locke's doctrine of real existence as it appears
in his account of general and complex ideas :—The idea
of substance is an abstract general idea, not given directly in sensation or reflection, but 'invented by the understanding,' as by consequence must be ideas of particular
sorts of substances which presuppose the abstract idea.   On
the other hand, the ideas of sensation and reflection, from
which the idea of substance is abstracted, and to which as
real it as an *invention* is opposed, are ideas of 'something,'
and are only real as representative of something.   But this
idea of something = the idea of substance.   Therefore the
idea of substance is the presupposition, and the condition
of the reality, of the very ideas from which it is said to be
derived.   Again, if the general idea of substance is got by
abstraction, it must be originally given in conjunction with
the ideas of sensation or reflection from which it is afterwards
abstracted, i.e. separated.   But in such conjunction it constitutes the ideas of particular sorts of substances.   Therefore these latter ideas, which yet we 'come to have ' after
the general idea of substance, form the prior experience from
which this general idea is abstracted.   Further, this original
experience, from which abstraction starts, being of 'sorts of
substances,' and these sorts being constituted by relations, it
follows that relation is given in the original experience.
But that which is so given is 'real existence' in opposition
to the invention of the understanding.   Therefore these
relations, and the community which they constitute, really
exist.   On the other hand, mere individuals alone really
exist, while relations between them are superinduced by the
mind.   Once more, the simple idea given in sensation or
reflection, as it is made *for* not *by* us, has or results from real
existence, whereas general and complex ideas are the workmanship of the mind.   But this workmanship consists in the
abstraction of ideas from each other, and from that to which
they are related as qualities.   It thus presupposes at once
the general idea of 'something' or substance, and the complex idea of qualities of the something.   Therefore it must
be general and complex ideas that are real, as made for and

not by us, and that afford the inventive understanding its material. Yet if so—if they are *given*—why make them over again by abstraction and recomplication?

51. We may get over the last difficulty, indeed, by distinguishing between the complex and confused, between abstraction and analysis. We may say that what is originally given in experience is the confused, which to us is simple, or in other words has no definite content, because, till it has been analysed, nothing can be said of it, though in itself it is infinetely complex; that thus the process, which Locke roughly calls abstraction, and which, as he describes it, consists merely in taking grains from the big heap that is given in order to make a little heap of one's own, is yet, rightly understood, the true process of knowledge—a process which may be said at once to begin with the complex and to end with it, to take from the concrete and to constitute it, because it begins with that which is in itself the fulness of reality, but which only becomes so for us as it is gradually spelt out by our analysis. To put the case thus, however, is not to correct Locke's statement, but wholly to change his doctrine. It renders futile his easy method of ' sending a man to his senses ' for the discovery of reality, and destroys the supposition that the elements of knowledge can be ascertained by the interrogation of the individual consciousness. Such consciousness can tell nothing of its own beginning, if of this beginning, as of the purely indefinite, nothing can be said; if it only becomes defined through relations, which in its state of primitive potentiality are not actually in it. The senses again, so far from being, in that mere passivity which Locke ascribes to them, organs of ready-made reality, can have nothing to tell, if it is only through the active processes of ' discerning, comparing, and compounding,' that they acquire a definite content. But to admit this is nothing else than, in order to avoid a contradiction of which Locke was not aware, to efface just that characteristic of his doctrine which commends it to ' common sense '—the supposition, namely, that the simple datum of sense, as it is for sense or in its mere individuality, is the real, in opposition to the ' invention of the mind.' That this supposition is to make the real the unmeaning, the empty, of which nothing can be said, he did not see because, under an unconscious delusion of words, even while asserting

that the names of simple ideas are undefinable (Book III.
chap. iv. sec. 4), which means that nothing can be said of
such ideas, and while admitting that the processes of discerning, comparing, and compounding ideas, which mean
nothing else than the bringing them into relation[1] or the
superinduction upon them of fictions of the mind, are
necessary to constitute even the beginnings of knowledge, he
yet allows himself to invest the simple idea, as the real, with
those definite qualities which can only accrue to it, according
to his showing, from the 'inventive' action of the understanding.

52. Thus invested, it is already substance or symbolical of
substance, not a mere feeling but a felt thing, recognised
either under that minimum of qualification which enables us
merely to say that it is 'something,' or (in Locke's language)
abstract substance, or under the greater complication of
qualities which constitutes a 'particular sort of substance'—
gold, horse, water, &c. Real existence thus means substance.
It is not the simple idea or sensation by itself that is real,
but this idea as caused by a thing. It is the thing that is
primarily the real; the idea only secondarily so, because it
results from a power in the thing. As we have seen, Locke's
doctrine of the necessary adequacy, reality, and truth of the
simple idea turns upon the supposition that it is, and announces itself as, an 'ectype' of an 'archetype.' But there
is not a different archetype to each sensation; if there were,
in 'reporting' it the sensation would do no more than report
itself. It is the supposed single cause of manifold different
sensations or simple ideas, to which a single name is applied.
'If sugar produce in us the ideas which we call whiteness
and sweetness, we are sure there is a power in sugar to
produce those ideas in our minds. . . . . And so each sensation answering the power that operates on any of our senses,
the idea so produced is a real idea (and not a fiction of the
mind, which has no power to produce any single idea), and

---

[1] Locke only states this explicitly of
comparison, 'an operation of the mind
about its ideas, upon which depends all
that large tribe of ideas, comprehended
under relation.' (Book II. chap. xi. sec.
4.) It is clear, however, that the same
remark must apply to the 'discernment
of ideas,' which is strictly correlative
to comparison, and to their composition,

which means that they are brought into
relation as constituents of a whole.

That these three processes are necessary to constitute the beginnings of
knowledge, according to Locke, appears
from Book II. chap. xi. sec. 15, taken in
connection with what precedes in that
chapter.

cannot but be adequate . . . . and so all simple ideas are
adequate.' (Book II. chap. xxxi. sec. 2.) The sugar, which
is here the 'archetype' and the source of reality in the idea,
is just what Locke elsewhere calls 'a particular sort of
substance,' as the 'something' from which a certain set of
sensations result, and in which, as sensible qualities, they
inhere. Strictly speaking, however, according to Locke, that
which inheres in the thing is not the quality, as it is to us,
but a power to produce it. (Book II. chap. viii. sec. 23, and
c. xxiii. 37.)

53. In calling a sensation or idea the product of a power,
substance is presupposed just as much as in calling it a
sensible quality; only that with Locke 'quality' conveyed
the notion of inherence in the substance, power that of
relation to an effect not *in* the substance itself. 'Secondary
qualities are nothing but the powers which *substances* have to
produce several ideas in us by our senses, which ideas are
not in the things themselves, otherwise than as anything is
in its cause.' (Book II. chap. xxiii. sec. 9.) 'Most of the
simple ideas, that make up our complex ideas of substances,
are only powers . . . . or relations to other substances (or,
as he explains elsewhere, 'relations to our perceptions,'[1]), and
are not really in the substance considered barely in itself.'
(Book II. chap. xxiii. sec. 37, and xxxi. 8.) That this implies
the inclusion of the idea of cause in that of substance, appears
from Locke's statement that 'whatever is considered by us
to operate to the producing any particular simple idea which
did not before exist, hath thereby in our minds the relation
of a cause.' (Book II. chap. xxvi. sec. 1.) Thus to be conscious of the reality of a simple idea, as that which is not
made by the subject of the idea, but results from a power in
a thing, is to have the idea of substance as cause. This
latter idea must be the condition of the consciousness of
reality. If the consciousness of reality is implied in the beginning of knowledge, so must the correlative ideas be of
cause and substance.

54. On examining Locke's second rehearsal of his theory
in the fourth book of the Essay—that 'On Knowledge'—
we are led to this result quite as inevitably as in the book
'On Ideas.' He has a special chapter on the 'reality of
human knowledge,' where he puts the problem thus :—' It is

[1] Book II. chap. xxi. sec. 3.

evident the mind knows not things immediately, but only by
the intervention of the ideas it has of them.   Our knowledge
therefore is real only so far as there is a conformity between
our ideas and the reality of things.   But what shall be here
the criterion?   How shall the mind, when it perceives nothing but its own ideas, know that they agree with things
themselves ? '   (Book IV. chap. iv. sec. 3.)   It knows this, he
proceeds to show, in the case of simple ideas, because ' since
the mind can by no means make them to itself, they must be
the product of things operating on the mind in a natural
way. . . . . Simple ideas are not fictions of our fancies, but
the natural and regular productions of things without us,
really operating upon us ; and so carry with them all the
conformity which is intended, or which our state requires,
for they represent to us things under those appearances
which they are fitted to produce in us ; whereby we are enabled to distinguish the sorts of particular substances,' &c.
&c. (Book IV. chap. iv. sec. 4.)   The whole force of this
passage depends on the notion that simple ideas are already
to the subject of them not his own making, but the product
of a thing, which in its relation to these ideas is a ' particular
sort of substance.'   It is the reception of such ideas, so
related, that Locke calls ' sensitive knowledge of particular
existence,' or a ' perception of the mind, employed about the
particular existence of finite beings without us.'   (Book iv.
chap. ii. sec. 14.)   This, however, he distinguishes from two
other ' degrees of knowledge or certainty,' ' intuition ' and
' demonstration,' of which the former is attained when the
agreement or disagreement of two ideas is perceived immediately, the latter when it is perceived mediately through the
intervention of certain other agreements or disagreements
(less or more), each of which must in turn be perceived
immediately. ·Demonstration, being thus really but a series
of intuitions, carries the same certainty as intuition, only it
is a certainty which it requires more or less pains and attention to apprehend.   (Book IV. chap. ii. sec. 4.)   Of the
' other perception of the mind, employed about the particular
existence of finite beings without us,' which ' passes under
the name of knowledge,' he explains that although ' going
beyond bare probability, it reaches not perfectly to either of
the foregoing degrees of certainty.'   ' There can be nothing
more certain,' he proceeds, ' than that the idea we receive

from an external object is in our minds; this is intuitive knowledge. But whether there be anything more than barely that idea in our minds, whether we can thence certainly infer the existence of anything without us which corresponds to that idea, is that whereof some men think there may be a question made; because men may have such ideas in their minds, when no such thing exists, no such object affects their senses.' (Book IV. chap. ii. sec. 14.)

55. It is clear that here in his very statement of the question Locke begs the answer. If the intuitive certainty is that ' the idea we *receive from an external object* is in our minds,'[1] how is it possible to doubt whether such an object exists and affects our senses? This impossibility of speaking of the simple idea, except as received from an object, may account for Locke's apparent inconsistency in finding the assurance of the reality of knowledge (under the phrase ' evidence of the senses ') just in that ' perception ' which reaches not to intuitive or demonstrative certainty, and only ' passes under the name of knowledge.' In the passage just quoted he shows that he is cognizant of the distinction between the simple idea and the perception of an existence corresponding to it, and in consequence distinguishes this perception from proper intuition, but in the very statement of the distinction it eludes him. The simple idea, as he speaks of it, becomes itself, as consciously ' received from an external object,' the perception of existence; just as we have previously seen it become the judgment of identity or perception of the ' agreement of an idea with itself,' which is his first kind of knowledge.

56. In short, with Locke the simple idea, the perception of existence corresponding to the idea, and the judgment of identity, are absolutely merged, and in mutual involution, sometimes under one designation, sometimes under another, are alike presented as the beginning of knowledge. As occasion requires, each does duty for the other. Thus, if the ' reality of knowledge ' be in question, the simple idea, which is given, is treated as involving the perception of existence, and the reality is established. If in turn this perception is distinguished from the simple idea, and it is asked whether

---

[1] I do not now raise the question, What are here the ideas, which must be immediately perceived to agree or disagree in order to make it a case of ' intuitive certainty ' or knowledge according to Locke's definition. See below, paragraphs 59, 101, and 147.

the correspondence between idea and existence is properly
matter of knowledge, the simple idea has only to be treated
as involving the judgment of identity, which again involves
that of existence, and the question is answered.   So in the
context under consideration (Book IV. chap. ii. sec. 14), after
raising the question as to the existence of a thing corresponding to the idea, he answers it by the counter question,
' whether anyone is not invincibly conscious to himself of a
different perception, when he looks on the sun by day, and
thinks on it by night; when he actually tastes wormwood,
or smells a rose, or only thinks on that savour or odour ?
We as plainly find the difference there is between any idea
revived in our minds by our own memory, and actually coming into our minds by our senses, as we do between any two
distinct ideas.'   The force of the above lies in its appeal to
the perception of identity, or—to apply the language in
which Locke describes this perception—the knowledge that
the idea which a man calls the smell of a rose is the very
idea it is.[1]   The mere difference in liveliness between the
present and the recalled idea, which, as Berkeley and Hume
rightly maintained, is the only difference between them as
mere ideas, cannot by itself constitute the difference between
the knowledge of the presence of a thing answering to the
idea and the knowledge of its absence.   It can only do this
if the more lively idea is *identified* with past lively ideas as
a representation of one and the same thing which ' agrees
with itself' in contrast to the multiplicity of the sensations,
its signs.   Only in virtue of this identification can either the
liveliness of the idea show that the thing—the sun or the
rose—is there, or the want of liveliness that it is not, for
without it there would be no thing to be there or not to be
there.   It is because this identification is what Locke understands by the first sort of perception of agreement between
ideas, and because he virtually finds this perception again in
the simple idea, that the simple idea is to him the index of
reality.   But if so, the idea in its primitive simplicity is the
sign of a thing that is ever the same in the same relations,
and we find the ' workmanship of the mind,' its inventions
of substance, cause, and relation, in the very rudiments of
knowledge.

57. With that curious tendency to reduplication, which is

[1] See above, paragraph 25.

one of his characteristics, Locke, after devoting a chapter to the 'reality of human knowledge,' of which the salient passage as to simple ideas has been already quoted, has another upon our 'knowledge of existence.' Here again it is the sensitive knowledge of things actually present to our senses, which with him is merely a synonym for the simple idea, that is the prime criterion. (Book IV. chap. iii. secs. 5 and 2, and chap. ii. sec. 2.) After speaking of the knowledge of our own being and of the existence of a God (about which more will be said below), he proceeds, 'No particular man can know the existence of any other being, but only when, by actually operating upon him, it makes itself perceived by him. For the having the idea of anything in our mind no more proves the existence of that thing, than the picture of a man evidences his being in the world, or the visions of a dream make thereby a true history. It is therefore the actual receiving of ideas from without, that gives us notice of the existence of other things, and makes us know that something doth exist at that time without us, which causes that idea in us, though perhaps we neither know nor consider how it does it; for it takes not from the certainty of our senses and the ideas we receive by them, that we know not the manner wherein they are produced; e. g. whilst I write this, I have, by the paper affecting my eyes, that idea produced in my mind, which, whatever object causes, I call *white*; by which I know that the quality or accident (i. e. whose appearance before my eyes always causes that idea) doth really exist, and hath a being without me. And of this the greatest assurance I can possibly have, and to which my faculties can attain, is the testimony of my eyes, which are the proper and sole judges of this thing, whose testimony I have reason to rely on, as so certain, that I can no more doubt whilst I write this, that I see white and black, and that something really exists that causes that sensation in me, than that I write and move my hand.' (Book IV. chap. xi. secs. 1, 2.)

58. Reasons are afterwards given for the assurance that the 'perceptions' in question are produced in us by 'exterior causes affecting our senses.' The first (*a*) is, that 'those that want the organs of any sense never can have the ideas belonging to that sense produced in their mind.' The next (*b*), that whereas 'if I turn my eyes at noon toward the sun,

I cannot avoid the ideas which the light or the sun then produces in me;' on the other hand, ' when my eyes are shut or
windows fast, as I can at pleasure recall to my mind the ideas
of light or the sun, which former sensations had lodged in
my memory, so I can at pleasure lay them by.' Again (c),
' many of those ideas are produced in us with pain which
afterwards we remember without the least offence. Thus
the pain of heat or cold, when the idea of it is revived in
our minds, gives us no disturbance; which, when felt, was
very troublesome, and is again, when actually repeated;
which is occasioned by the disorder the external object
causes in our body, when applied to it.' Finally (d), ' our
senses in many cases bear witness to the truth of each other's
report, concerning the existence of sensible things without
us. He that sees a fire may, if he doubt whether it be anything more than a bare fancy, feel it too.' Then comes the
conclusion, dangerously qualified : ' When our senses do
actually convey into our understandings any idea, we cannot but be satisfied that there doth something at that time
really exist without us, which doth affect our senses, and by
them give notice of itself to our apprehensive faculties, and
actually produce that idea which we then perceive ; and we
cannot so far distrust their testimony as to doubt that such
collections of simple ideas, as we have observed by our senses
to be united together, actually exist together. But this
knowledge extends as far as the present testimony of our
senses, employed about particular objects, that do then affect
them, and no further. For if I saw such a collection of
simple ideas as is wont to be called man, existing together
one minute since, and am now alone; I cannot be certain
that the same man exists now, since there is no necessary
connexion of his existence a minute since with his existence
now. By a thousand ways he may cease to be, since I had
the testimony of my senses for his existence.' (Book iv.
chap. xi. sec. 9.)

59. Upon the ' knowledge of the existence of things,' thus
established, it has to be remarked in the first place that,
after all, according to Locke's explicit statement, it is not
properly knowledge. It is ' an assurance that deserves the
name of knowledge ' (Book iv. chap. ii. sec. 14, and xi. sec. 3),
yet being neither itself an intuition of agreement between
ideas, nor resoluble into a series of such intuitions, the de-

finition of knowledge excludes it. Only if existence were itself an 'idea,' would the consciousness of the agreement of the idea with it be a case of knowledge; but to make existence an idea is to make the whole question about the agreement of ideas, as such, with existence, as such, unmeaning. To seek escape from this dilemma by calling the consciousness of the agreement in question an 'assurance' instead of knowledge is a mere verbal subterfuge. There can be no assurance of agreement between an idea and that which is no object of consciousness at all. If, however, existence is an object of consciousness, it can, according to Locke, be nothing but an idea, and the question as to the *assurance* of agreement is no less unmeaning than the question as to the *knowledge* of it. The raising of the question in fact, as Locke puts it, implies the impossibility of answering it. It cannot be raised with any significance, unless existence is external to and other than an idea. It cannot be answered unless existence is, or is given in, an object of consciousness, i. e. an idea.

60. As usual, Locke disguises this difficulty from himself, because in answering the question he alters it. The question, *as he asks it*, is whether, given the idea, we can have posterior assurance of something else corresponding to it. The question, *as he answers it*, is whether the idea includes the consciousness of a real thing as a constituent; and the answer consists in the simple assertion, variously repeated, that it does. It is clear, however, that this answer to the latter question does not answer, but renders unmeaning, the question as it is originally asked. If, according to Locke's own showing, there is nowhere for anything to be found by us but in our 'ideas' or our consciousness—if the *thing* is given in and with the idea, so that the idea is merely the thing *ex parte nostrâ*—then to ask if the idea agrees with the thing is as futile as to ask whether hearing agrees with sound, or the voice with the words it utters. That the thing is so given is implied throughout Locke's statement of the 'assurance we have of the existence of material beings,' as well as of the confirmations of this assurance. If the 'idea which I call white' means the knowledge that 'the property or accident (i. e. whose appearance before my eyes always causes that idea) doth really exist and hath a being without me,' then consciousness of existence—outward, permanent, substantive.

and causative existence—is involved in the idea, and no ulterior question of agreement between idea and existence can
properly arise. But unless the simple idea is so interpreted,
the senses have no testimony to give. If it is so interpreted,
no extraneous 'reason to rely upon the testimony' can be
discovered, for such reason can only be a repetition of the
testimony itself.

61. This becomes clearer upon a view of the confirmations
of the testimony, as Locke gives them. They all, we may
remark by the way, presuppose a distinction between the
simple idea as originally represented and the same as recalled
or revived.   This distinction, fixed by the verbal one between
'impression' and 'idea,' we shall find constantly maintained
and all-important in Hume's system; but in Locke, though
upon it (as we shall see) rests his distinction between real
and nominal essence and his confinement of general knowledge to the latter, it seems only to turn up as an afterthought.
In the account of the reality and adequacy of ideas it does
not appear at all.   There the distinction is merely between
the simple idea, as such, and the complex, as such, without
any further discrimination of the simple idea as originally
produced from the same as recalled. So, too, in the opening
account of the reception of simple ideas (Book II. chap. xii.
sec. 1), 'Perception,' 'Retention,' and 'Discerning' are all
reckoned together as alike forms of the *passivity* of the mind,
in contrast with its activity in combination and abstraction,
though retention and discerning have been previously described in terms which imply activity. In the ' confirmations'
before us, however, the distinction between the originally
produced and the revived is essential.

62. The first turns upon the impossibility of producing an
idea *de novo* without the action of sensitive organs; the two
next upon the difference between the idea as produced through
these organs and the like idea as revived at the will of the
individual.   It is hence inferred that the idea as originally
produced is the work of a thing, which must exist *in rerum
natura*, and by way of a fourth 'confirmation' the man who
doubts this in the case of one sensation is invited to try it in
another.   If, on seeing a fire, he thinks it ' bare fancy,' i. e.
doubts whether his idea is caused by a thing, let him put his
hand into it.   This last ' confirmation ' need not be further
noticed here, since the operation of a producing thing is as

certain or as doubtful for one sensation as for another.[1] Two
certainties are not more sure than one, nor can two doubts
make a certainty. The other ' confirmations ' alike lie in the
words ' product ' and ' organ.' A man has a certain ' idea :'
afterwards he has another like it, but differing in liveliness
and in the accompanying pleasure or pain. If he already
has, or if the ideas severally bring with them, the idea of a
producing outward thing to which parts of his body are
organs, on the one hand, and of a self ' having power ' on the
other, then the liveliness, and the accompanying pleasure or
pain, may become indications of the action of the thing, as
their absence may be so of the action of the man's self; but
not otherwise. Locke throughout, in speaking of the simple
ideas as produced or recalled, implies that they carry with
them the consciousness of a cause, either an outward thing
or the self, and only by so doing can he find in them the
needful ' confirmations ' of the ' testimony of the senses.'
This testimony is confirmed just because it distinguishes
of itself between the work of ' nature,' which is real, and
the work of the man, which is a fiction. In other words,
the confirmation is nothing else than the testimony itself
—a testimony which, as we have seen, since it supposes
consciousness, as such, to be consciousness *of a thing*,
eliminates by anticipation the question as to the agreement
of consciousness with things, as with the extraneous.

63. The distinction between the real and the fantastic,
according to the passages under consideration, thus depends
upon that between the work of nature and the work of man.
It is the confusion between the two works that renders the
fantastic possible, while it is the consciousness of the distinction that sets us upon correcting it. Where all is the work
of man and professes to be no more, as in the case of ' mixed
modes,' there is no room for the fantastic (Book II. chap. xxx.
sec. 4, and Book IV. chap. iv. sec. 7); and where there is
ever so much of the fantastic, it would not be so for us, unless we were conscious of a ' work of nature,' to which to
oppose it. But on looking a little closer we find that to be
conscious of an idea as the work of nature, in opposition to

---

[1] To feel the object, in the sense of
touching it, had a special significance
for Locke, since touch with him was the
primary ' revelation ' of body, as the
solid. More will be said of this when
we come to consider his doctrine of
' real essence,' as constituted by primary
qualities of body. See below, paragraph 101.

the work of man, is to be conscious of it under relations which, according to Locke, are the inventions of man. It is nothing else than to be conscious of it as the result of ' something having power to produce it ' (Book ii. chap. xxxi. sec. 2), i. e. of a substance, to which it is related as a quality. ' Nature ' is just the ' something we know not what,' which is substance according to the ' *abstract* idea ' thereof. Producing ideas, it exercises powers, as it essentially belongs to substance to do, according to our *complex* idea of it. (Book ii. chap. xxiii. secs. 9, 10.) But substance, according to Locke, whether as abstract or complex idea, is the ' workmanship of the mind,' and power, as a relation (Book ii. chap. xxi. sec. 3, and chap. xxv. sec. 8), ' is not contained in the real existence of things.' Again, the idea of substance, as a source of power, is the same as the idea of cause. ' Whatever is considered by us to operate to the producing any particular simple idea, which did not before exist, hath thereby in our minds the relation of a cause.' (Book ii. chap. xxvi. sec. 1.) But the idea of cause is not one ' that the mind has of things as they are in themselves,' but one that it gets by its own act in ' bringing things to, and setting them by, one another.' (Book ii. chap. xxv. sec. 1.) Thus it is with the very ideas, which are the workmanship of man, that the simple idea has to be clothed upon, in order to ' testify ' to its being real, i. e. (in Locke's sense) not the work of man.

64. Thus invested, the simple idea has clearly lost its simplicity. It is not the momentary, isolated consciousness, but the representation of a thing determined by relations to other things in an order of nature, and causing an infinite series of resembling sensations to which a common name is applied. Thus in all the instances of sensuous testimony mentioned in the chapter before us, it is not really a simple sensation that is spoken of, but a sensation referred to a thing—not a mere smell, or taste, or sight, or feeling, but the smell of a rose, the taste of a pine-apple, the sight of the sun, the feeling of fire. (Book iv. chap. xi. secs. 4–7.) Immediately afterwards, however, reverting or attempting to revert to his strict doctrine of the mere individuality of the simple idea, he says that the testimony of the senses is a ' present testimony employed about particular objects, that do then affect them,' and that sensitive knowledge extends

no farther than such testimony. This statement, taken by itself, is ambiguous. Does it mean that sensation testifies to the momentary presence to the individual of a continuous existence, or is the existence itself as momentary as its presence to sense? The instance that follows does not remove the doubt. 'If I saw such a collection of simple ideas as is wont to be called *man*, existing together one minute since, and am now alone; I cannot be certain that the same man exists now, since there is no necessary connection of his existence a minute since with his existence now.' (Book iv. chap. xi. sec. 9.) At first sight, these words might seem to decide that the existence is merely coincident with the presence of the sensation—a decision fatal to the distinction between the real and fantastic, since, if the thing is only present with the sensation, there can be no combination of qualities in reality other than the momentary coincidence of sensations in us. Memory or imagination, indeed, might recall these in a different order from that in which they originally occurred; but, if this original order had no being after the occurrence, there could be no ground for contrasting it with the order of reproduction as the real with the merely apparent.

65. In the very sentence, however, where Locke restricts the testimony of sensation to existence present along with it, he uses language inconsistent with this restriction. The particular existence which he instances as 'testified to' is that of 'such a collection of simple ideas as is wont to be called man.' But these ideas can only be present in succession. (See Book ii. chap. vii. sec. 9, and chap. xiv. sec. 3.) Even the surface of the man's body can only be taken in by successive acts of vision; and, more obviously, the states of consciousness in which his qualities of motion and action are presented occupy separate times. If then sensation only testifies to an existence present along with it, how can it testify to the co-existence (say) of an erect attitude, of which I have a present sight, with the risibility which I saw a minute ago? How can the 'collection of ideas wont to be called man,' *as co-existing*, be formed at all? and, if it cannot, how can the present existence of an object so-called be testified to by sense any more than the past? The same doctrine, which is fatal to the supposition of 'a necessary connexion between the man's existence a minute since and his

existence now,' is in fact fatal to the supposition of his
existence as a complex of qualities at all. It does not merely
mean that, for anything we know, the man may have died.
Of course he may, and yet there may be continuity of existence
according to natural laws, though not one for which we
have the testimony of present sense, between the living body
and the dead. What Locke had in his mind was the notion
that, as existence is testified to only by present sensation,
and each sensation is merely individual and momentary,
there could be no testimony to the continued existence of
anything. He could not, however, do such violence to the
actual fabric of knowledge as would have been implied in the
logical development of this doctrine, and thus he allowed
himself to speak of sense as testifying to the co-existence of
sensible qualities in a thing, though the individual sensation
could only testify to the presence of one at a time, and could
never testify to their *nexus* in a common cause at all. This
testimony to co-existence in a present thing once admitted,
he naturally allowed himself in the further assumption that
the testimony, on its recurrence, is a testimony to the same
co-existence and the same thing. The existence of the same
man (he evidently supposes), to which sensation testified an
hour ago, may be testified to by a like sensation now. This
means that resemblance of sensation becomes identity of a
thing—that like sensations occurring at different times are
interpreted as representing the same thing, which continuously exists, though not testified to by sense, between the
times.

66. In short, as we have seen the simple idea of sensation
emerge from Locke's inquiry as to the beginning of knowledge transformed into the judgment, ' I have an idea different
from other ideas which I did not make for myself,' so now
from the inquiry as to the correspondence between knowledge
and reality it emerges as the consciousness of a thing now
acting upon me, which has continued to exist since it acted
on me before, and in which, as in a common cause, have
existed together powers to affect me which have never affected
me together. If in the one form the operation of thought
in sense, the ' creation of the understanding ' within the simple idea, is only latent or potential, in the other it is actual
and explicit. The relations of substance and quality, of
cause and effect, and of identity—all ' inventions of the

mind '—are necessarily involved in the immediate, spontaneous testimony of passive sense.

67. It will be noticed that it is upon the first of these, the relation of substance and quality, that our examination of Locke's Essay has so far chiefly gathered. In this it follows the course taken by Locke himself. Of the idea of substance, *eo nomine*, he treats at large: of cause and identity (apart from the special question of personal identity) he says little. So, too, the 'report of the senses' is commonly exhibited as announcing the sensible qualities of a thing rather than the agency of a cause or continuity of existence. The difference, of course, is mainly verbal. Sensible qualities being, as Locke constantly insists, nothing but 'powers to operate on our senses' directly or indirectly, the substance or thing, as the source of these, takes the character of a cause. Again, as the sensible quality is supposed to be one and the same in manifold separate cases of being felt, it has identity in contrast with the variety of these cases, even as the thing has, on its part, in contrast with the variety of its qualities. Something, however, remains to be said of Locke's treatment of the ideas of cause and identity in the short passages where he treats of them expressly. Here, too, we shall find the same contrast between the given and the invented, tacitly contradicted by an account of the given in terms of the invented.

68. The relation of cause and effect, according to Locke's general statement as to relation, must be something 'not contained in the real existence of things, but extraneous and superinduced.' (Book II. chap. xxv. sec. 8.) It is a 'complex idea,' not belonging to things as they are in themselves, which the mind makes by its own act. (Book II. chap xii. secs. 1, 7, and chap. xxv. sec. 1.) Its origin, however, is thus described :—' In the notice that our senses take of the constant vicissitude of things, we cannot but observe that several particular, both qualities and substances, begin to exist; and that they receive this their existence from the due application and operation of some other being. From this observation we get our ideas of cause and effect. That which produces any simple or complex idea we denote by the general name cause; and that which is produced, effect. Thus, finding that in that substance which we call wax, fluidity, which is a simple idea that was not in it before, is constantly pro-

duced by the application of a certain degree of heat, we call the simple idea of heat, in relation to fluidity in wax, the cause of it, and fluidity the effect. So, also, finding that the substance, wood, which is a certain collection of simple ideas so-called, by the application of fire is turned into another substance called ashes, i.e. another complex idea, consisting of a collection of simple ideas, quite different from that complex idea which we call wood; we consider fire, in relation to ashes, as cause, and the ashes as effect.' Here we find that the 'given,' upon which the relation of cause and effect is 'superinduced' or from which the 'idea of it is got' (to give Locke the benefit of both expressions), professedly, according to the first sentence of the passage quoted, involves the complex or derived idea of substance. The sentence, indeed, is a remarkable instance of the double refraction which arises from redundant phraseology. Our senses are supposed to 'take notice of a constant vicissitude of things,' or substances. Thereupon we observe, what is necessarily implied in this vicissitude, a beginning of existence in substances or their qualities, 'received from the due application or operation of some other being.' Thereupon we infer, what is simply another name for existence thus given and received, a relation of cause and effect. Thus not only does the *datum* of the process of 'invention' in question, i.e. the observation of change in a thing, involve a *derived* idea, but a derived idea which presupposes just this process of invention.

69. Here again it is necessary to guard against the notion that Locke's obvious *petitio principii* might be avoided by a better statement without essential change in his doctrine of ideas. It is true that 'a notice of the vicissitude of things' includes that 'invention of the understanding' which it is supposed to suggest, but state the primary knowledge otherwise—reduce the vicissitude of things, as it ought to be reduced, in order to make Locke consistent, to the mere multiplicity of sensations—and the appearance of suggestion ceases. Change or 'vicissitude' is quite other than mere diversity. It is diversity relative to something which maintains an identity. This identity, which ulterior analysis may find in a 'law of nature,' Locke found in 'things' or 'substances.' By the same unconscious subreption, by which with him a sensible thing takes the place of sensation, 'vicissitude of things' takes the place of multiplicity of sensa-

tions, carrying with it the observation that the changed state of the thing is due to something else. The mere multiplicity of sensations could convey no such 'observation,' any more than the sight of counters in a row would convey the notion that one 'received its existence' from the other. Only so far as the manifold appearances are referred, as its vicissitudes, to something which remains one, does any need of accounting for their diverse existence, or in consequence any observation of its derivation 'from some other being,' arise. Locke, it is true, after stating that it is upon a notice of the vicissitude of things that the observation in question rests, goes on to speak as if an *origination* of substances, which is just the opposite of their vicissitude, might be observed; and the second instance of production which he gives—that of ashes upon the burning of wood—seems intended for an instance of the production of a substance, as distinct from the production of a quality. He is here, however, as he often does, using the term 'substance' loosely, for 'a certain collection of simple ideas,' without reference to the 'substratum wherein they do subsist,' which he would have admitted to be ultimately the same for the wood and for the ashes. The conception, indeed, of such a substratum, whether vaguely as 'nature,' or more precisely as a 'real constitution of insensible parts' (Book III. chap. iii. secs. 18, &c.), governed all his speculation, and rendered to him what he here calls *substance* virtually a *mode*, and its production properly a 'vicissitude.'

70. We thus find that it is only so far as simple ideas are referred to things—only so far as each in turn, to use Locke's instance, is regarded as an appearance 'in a substance which was not in it before'—that our sensitive experience, the supposed *datum* of knowledge, is an experience of the vicissitudes of things; and again, that only as an experience of such vicissitude does it furnish the 'observation from which we get our ideas of cause and effect.' But the reference of a sensation to a sensible thing means its reference to a cause. In other words, the invented relation of cause and effect must be found in the primary experience in order that it may be got from it. [1]

---

[1] Locke's contradiction of himself in regard to this relation might be exhibited in a still more striking light by putting side by side with his account of it his account of the idea of power. The two are precisely similar, the idea of power being represented as got by a notice of the alteration of simple ideas

71. The same holds of that other 'product of the mind,' the relation of identity. This 'idea' according to Locke, is formed when, 'considering anything as existing at any determined time and place, we compare it with itself existing at another time.' 'In this consists identity,' he adds, 'when the ideas it is attributed to, vary not at all from what they were that moment wherein we consider their former existence, and to which we compare the present; for we never finding nor conceiving it possible that two things of the same kind should exist in the same place at the same time, we rightly conclude that whatever exists anywhere, at any time, excludes all of the same kind, and is there itself alone. When, therefore, we demand whether anything be the same or no? it refers always to something that existed such a time in such a place, which it was certain at that instant was the same with itself, and no other; from whence it follows that one thing cannot have two beginnings of existence, nor two things one beginning; it being impossible for two things of the same kind to be or exist in the same instant in the very same place, or one and the same thing in different places. That, therefore, that had one beginning, is the same thing; and that which had a different beginning in time and place from that is not the same, but diverse.' He goes on to inquire about the *principium individuationis*, which he decides is 'existence itself, which determines a being of any sort to a particular time and place, incommunicable to two beings of the same kind . . . for being at that instant what it is and nothing else, it is the same, and so must continue as long as its existence is continued; for so long it will be the same, and no other.' (Book II. chap. xxvii. secs. 1—3).

72. It is essential to bear in mind with regard to identity, as with regard to cause and effect, that no distinction according to Locke can legitimately be made between the relation and the idea of the relation. As to substance, it is true, he was driven in his controversy with Stillingfleet to distinguish between 'the being and the idea thereof,' but in dealing with relation he does not attempt any such violence to his proper system. Between the 'idea' as such and

---

in things without (Book II. chap. xxi. sec. 1), just as the idea of cause and effect is. Power, too, he expressly says, is a relation. Yet, although the idea of it, both as derived and as of a relation, ought to be complex, he reckons it a simple and original one, and by using it interchangeably with 'sensible quality' makes it a primary *datum* of sense.

'being' as such, his 'new way of ideas,' as Stillingfleet
plaintively called it, left no fair room for distinction. In
this indeed lay its permanent value for speculative thought.
The distinction by which alone it could consistently seek to
replace the old one, so as to meet the exigencies of language
and knowledge, was that between simple ideas, as given and
necessarily real, and the reproductions or combinations in
which the mind may alter them. But since every relation
implies a putting together of ideas, and is thus always, as Locke
avows, a complex idea or the work of the mind, a distinction
between its being and the idea thereof, in that sense of the
distinction in which alone it can ever be consistently admitted
by Locke, was clearly inadmissible. Thus in the passages
before us the relation of identity is not explicitly treated as
an original 'being' or 'existence.' It is an idea formed by
the mind upon a certain 'consideration of things' being or
existent. But on looking closely at Locke's account, we find
that it is only so far as it already belongs to, nay constitutes,
the things, that it is formed upon consideration of them.

73. When it is said that the idea of identity, or of any other
relation, is formed upon consideration of things as existing
in a certain way, this is naturally understood to mean—indeed,
otherwise it is unmeaning—that the things are first *known* as
existing, and that afterwards the idea of the relation in question is formed. But according to Locke, as we have seen,[1]
the first and simplest act of knowledge possible is the perception of identity between ideas. Either then the 'things,'
upon consideration of which the idea of identity is formed,
are not known at all, or the knowledge of them involves the
very idea afterwards formed on consideration of them. Locke,
having at whatever cost of self-contradiction to make his
theory fit the exigencies of language, virtually adopts the
latter alternative, though with an ambiguity of expression
which makes a definite meaning difficult to elicit. We have,
however, the positive statement to begin with, that the
comparison in which the relation originates, is of a thing
with itself as existing at another time. Again, the 'ideas'
(used interchangeably with 'things'), to which identity is
attributed, 'vary not at all from what they were at that
moment wherein we consider their former existence.' It is
here clearly implied that 'things' or 'ideas' *exist*, i.e. are

[1] See above, paragraph 25.

given to us in the spontaneous consciousness which we do
not make, as each one and the same throughout a multiplicity
of times. This, again, means that the relation of identity or
sameness, i.e. unity of thing under multiplicity of appearance,
belongs to or consists in the 'very being' of those given
objects of consciousness, which are in Locke's sense the real,
and upon which according to him all relation is superinduced
by an after-act of thought. So long as each such object
'continues to exist,' so long its 'sameness with itself must
continue,' and this sameness is the complex idea, the relation,
of identity. Just as before, following Locke's lead, we found
the simple idea, as the element of knowledge, become complex—a perceived identity of ideas; so now mere existence,
the 'very being of things' (which with Locke is only another
name for the simple idea), resolves itself into a relation,
which it requires 'consideration by the mind' to constitute.

74. The process of self-contradiction, by which a 'creation
of the mind' finds its way into the real or given, must also
appear in a contradictory conception of the real itself. Kept
pure of all that Locke reckons intellectual fiction, it can be
nothing but a simple chaos of individual units : only by the
superinduction of relation can there be sameness, or continuity of existence, in the minutest of these for successive
moments. Locke presents it arbitrarily under the conception
of mere individuality or of continuity, according as its distinction from the work of the mind, or its intelligible content,
happens to be before him. A like see-saw in his account of
the individuality and generality of ideas has already been
noticed.[1] In his discussion of identity the contradiction is
partly disguised by a confusion between mere unity on the
one hand, and sameness or unity in difference, on the other.
Thus, after starting with an account of identity as belonging
to ideas which are the same *at different times*, he goes on to
speak of a thing as the same with itself, *at a single instant*.
So, too, by the *principium individuationis*, he understands
'existence itself, which determines a being of any sort to a
particular time and place.' As it is clear from the context
that by the *principium individuationis* he meant the source
of identity or sameness, it will follow that by 'sameness' he
understood singleness of a thing in a single time and place.
Whence then the plurality, without which 'sameness' is

[1] See above, paragraphs 43, and the following.

unmeaning ? In fact, Locke, having excluded it in his definition, covertly brings it back again in his instance, which is
that of ' an atom, i.e. a continued body under one immutable
superficies, existing in a determined time and place.' This,
' considered in any instant of its existence, is in that instant
the same with itself.' But it is so because—and, if we suppose
the consideration of plurality of *times* excluded, *only* because
—it is a ' *continued* ' body, which implies, though its place be
determined, that it exists in a *plurality of parts of space.*
Either this plurality, or that of instants of its existence, must
be recognised in contrast with the unity of body, if this unity
is to become ' sameness with itself.' In adding that not only
at the supposed instant is the atom the same, but ' so must
continue as long as its existence continues,' Locke shows that
he really thought of the identical body under a plurality of
times *ex parte post,* if not *ex parte ante.*

75. But how is this continuity, or sameness of existence in
plurality of times or spaces, compatible with the constitution
of ' real existence ' by mere *individua ?* The difficulty is the
same, according to Locke's premisses, whether the simple
ideas by themselves are taken for the real *individua,* or
whether each is taken to represent a single separate thing.
In his chapter on identity he expressly says that 'things whose
existence is in succession ' do not admit of identity. Such,
he adds, are motion and thought; ' because, each perishing
the moment it begins, they cannot exist in different times or
in different places as permanent beings can at different times
exist in distant places.' (Book I. chap. xxvii. sec. 2.) What
he here calls ' thought ' clearly includes the passive consciousness in which alone, according to his strict doctrine, reality
is given. So elsewhere (Book II. chap. vii. sec. 9), in accounting for the ' simple idea of succession,' he says generally that
' if we look immediately into ourselves we shall find our ideas
always, whilst we have any thought, passing in train, one
going and another coming, without intermission.'[1] No statement of the 'perpetual flux' of ideas, as each having a separate beginning and end, and ending in the very moment

[1] It is true that in this place Locke
distinguishes between the ' suggestion
by our senses' of the idea of succession,
and that which passes in our ' minds,'
by which it is ' more constantly offered
us.' But since, according to him, the
idea of sensation must be ' produced in
the mind' if there is to be any either
sensation or idea at all (Book II. chap.
ix. secs. 3 and 4), the distinction between the 'suggestion by our senses'
and what ' passes in our minds' cannot
be maintained.

when it begins, can be stronger than the above. If 'ideas' of any sort, according to this account of them, are to consti‧ tute real existence, no sameness can be found in reality. It must indeed be a relation 'invented by the mind.'

76. This, it may be said, is just the conclusion that was wanted in order to make Locke's doctrine of the particular relation of identity correspond with his general doctrine of the fictitiousness of relations. To complete the consistency, however, his whole account of the origin of the relation (or of the idea in which it consists) must be changed, since it supposes it to be derived from an observation of things or existence, which again is to suppose sameness to be in the things or to be real. This change made, philosophy would have to start anew with the problem of accounting for the origin of the fictitious idea. It would have to explain how it comes to pass that the mind, if its function consists solely in reproducing and combining given ideas, or again in 'abstracting' combined ideas from each other, should be able to invent a relation which is neither a given idea, nor a reproduction, combination, or abstract residuum of given ideas. This is the great problem which we shall find Hume attempting. Locke really never saw its necessity, because the dominion of language—a dominion which, as he did not recognise it, he had no need to account for—always, in spite of his assertion that simple ideas are the sole *data* of consciousness, held him to the belief in another *datum* of which ideas are the appearances, viz., a thing having identity, because the same with itself in the manifold times of its appearance. This *datum*, under various guises, but in each demonstrably, according to Locke's showing, a 'creation of thought,' has met us in all the modes of his theory, as the condition of knowledge. As the 'abstract idea' of substance it renders 'perishing' ideas into qualities by which objects may be discerned. (Book II. chap. xi. sec. 1.) As the relative idea of cause, it makes them 'affections' to be accounted for. As the fiction of a universal, it is the condition of their mutual qualification as constituents of a whole. Finally, as the 'superinduced' relation of sameness, the direct negative of the perpetual beginning and ending of 'ideas,' it constitutes the 'very being of things.'

77. 'The very being of things,' let it be noticed, according to what Locke reckoned their 'real,' as distinct from their

'nominal,' essence. The consideration of this distinction
has been hitherto postponed; but the discussion of the relation of identity, as subsisting between the parts of a 'continued body,' brings us upon the doctrine of matter and its
'primary qualities,' which cannot be properly treated except
in connection with the other doctrine (which Locke unhap-
pily kept apart) of the two sorts of 'essence.' So far, it will
be remembered, the 'facts' or *given* ideas, which we have
found him unawares converting into theories or 'invented'
ideas, have been those of the 'secondary qualities of body.'[1]
It is these which are united into things or substances,
having been already 'found in them:' it is from these that
we 'infer' the relation of cause and effect, because as
'vicissitudes of things' or 'affections of sense' they presuppose it: it is these again which, as 'received from without,' testify the present existence of something, because in
being so received they are already interpreted as 'appearances of something.' That the 'thing,' by reference to which
these ideas are judged to be 'real,' 'adequate,' and 'true'—
or, in other words, become elements of a knowledge—is yet
itself according to Locke's doctrine of substance and relation a 'fiction of thought,' has been sufficiently shown.
That it is so no less according to his doctrine of essence will
also appear. The question will then be, whether by the
same showing the ideas of body, of the self, and of God, can
be other than fictions, and the way will be cleared for Hume's
philosophic adventure of accounting for them as such.

78. In Locke's doctrine of 'ideas of substances,' the
'thing' appeared in two inconsistent positions: on the one
hand, as that in which they 'are found;' on the other, as
that which results from their concretion, or which, such
concretion having been made, we accustom ourselves to
suppose as its basis. This inconsistency, latent to Locke
himself in the theory of substance, comes to the surface in
the theory of essence, where it is (as he thought) overcome,
but in truth only made more definite, by a distinction of
terms.

79. This latter theory has so far become part and parcel
of the 'common sense' of educated men, that it might seem
scarcely to need restatement. It is generally regarded as
completing the work, which Bacon had begun, of transferring

[1] See above, paragraph 20.

philosophy from the scholastic bondage of words to the fruitful discipline of facts. In the process of transmission and popular adaptation, however, its true significance has been lost sight of, and it has been forgotten that to its original exponent implicitly—explicitly to his more logical disciple—· though it did indeed distinguish effectively between things and the meaning of words, it was the analysis of the latter only, and not the understanding of things, that it left as the possible function of knowledge. It will be well, then, in what follows, first briefly to restate the theory in its general form; then to show how it conflicts with the actual knowledge which mankind supposes itself to have attained; and finally to exhibit at once the necessity of this conflict as a result of Locke's governing ideas, and the ambiguities by which he disguised it from himself.

80. The essence of a thing with Locke, in the only sense in which we can know or intelligibly speak of it, is the meaning of its name. This, again, is an 'abstract or general idea,' which means that it is an idea 'separated from the circumstances of time and place, and any other ideas that may determine it to this or that particular existence. By this way of abstraction it is made capable of representing more individuals than one; each of which, having in it a conformity to that abstract idea, is (as we call it) of that sort.' (Book III. chap. iii. sec. 6.) That which is given in immediate experience, as he proceeds to explain, is this or that 'particular existence,' Peter or James, Mary or Jane, such particular existence being already a complex idea.[1] That it should be so is indeed in direct contradiction to his doctrine of the primariness of the simple idea, but is necessary to his doctrine of abstraction. Some part of the complex idea (it is supposed)—less or more—we proceed to leave out. The minimum of subtraction would seem to be that of the 'circumstances of time and place,' in which the particular existence is given. This is the 'separation of ideas,' first made, and alone suffices to constitute an 'abstract idea,' even though, as is the case with the idea of the sun, there is only one 'particular substance' to agree with it. (Book III. chap. vi. sec. 1.) In proportion as the particular substances compared are more various, the subtraction of ideas is larger, but, be it less or more, the remainder is the abstract

[1] Book III. chap. iii. sec. 7, at the end.

idea, to which a name—e.g. man—is annexed, and to which as a 'species' or 'standard' other particular existences, on being 'found to agree with it,' may be referred, so as to be called by the same name. These ideas then, 'tied together by a name,' form the essence of each particular existence, to which the same name is applied (Book III. chap. iii. secs. 12 and the following.) Such essence, however, according to Locke, is 'nominal,' not 'real.' It is a complex—fuller or emptier—of ideas in us, which, though it is a 'uniting medium between a general name and particular beings,'[1] in no way represents the qualities of the latter. These, consisting in an 'internal constitution of insensible parts,' form the 'real essence' of the particular beings; an essence, however, of which we can know nothing. (Book III. chap. vi. sec. 21, and ix. sec. 12.)

81. It is the formation of 'nominal essences' that renders general propositions possible. 'General certainty,' says Locke, 'is never to be found but in our ideas. Whenever we go to seek it elsewhere in experiment or observation without us, our knowledge goes not beyond particulars. It is the contemplation of our own abstract ideas, that alone is able to afford us general knowledge.' (Book IV. chap. vi. sec. 16.) 'General knowledge,' he says again, 'lies only in our own thoughts.'[2] (Book IV. chap. vi. sec. 13.) This use of 'our ideas' and 'our own thoughts' as equivalent phrases, each antithetical to 'real existence,' tells the old tale of a deviation from 'the new way of ideas' into easier paths. According to this new way in its strictness, as we have sufficiently seen, there is nowhere for anything to be found but 'in our ideas.' It therefore in no way distinguishes general knowledge or certainty that it cannot be found elsewhere. Locke, however, having allowed himself in the supposition that simple ideas report a real existence, other than themselves, but to which they are related as ectype to archetype, tacitly proceeds to convert them into real existences, to which ideas in general, as mere thoughts of our own, may be opposed. Along with this conversion, there supervenes upon the original distinction between simple and complex ideas, which alone does duty in the Second Book of the Essay, another distinction, essential to Locke's doctrine of the 'reality' of knowledge—that between the idea, whether

[1] Book III. chap. iii. sec. 13.   [2] Cf. Book IV. chap. iii. sec. 31.

simple or complex, as originally given in sensation, and the
same as retained or reproduced in the mind.   It is only in
the former form that the idea, however simple, reports, and
thus (with Locke) itself is, a real existence.   Such real existence is a 'particular' existence, and our knowledge of it
a 'particular' knowledge.   In other words, according to the
only consistent doctrine that we have been able to elicit from
Locke, [1] it is a knowledge which consists in a consciousness,
upon occasion of a present sensation—say, a sensation of
redness—that some object is present here and now causing
the sensation; an object which, accordingly, must be 'particular' or transitory as the sensation.   The 'here and now,'
as in such a case they constitute the particularity of the
object of consciousness, so also render it a real existence.
Separate these ('the circumstances of time and place' [2])
from it, and it at once loses its real existence and becomes an
'abstract idea,' one of 'our own thoughts,' of which as 'in
the mind' agreement or disagreement with some other abstract idea can be asserted in a general proposition; e.g. 'red
is not blue.'   (Book IV. chap. vii. sec. 4.) [3]

82. It is between simple ideas, it will be noticed, that a
relation is here asserted, and in this respect the proposition
differs from such an one as may be formed when simple ideas
have been compounded into the nominal essence of a thing,
and in which some one of these may be asserted of the
thing, being already included within the meaning of its
name; e.g. 'a rose has leaves.'   But as expressing a relation
between ideas 'abstract' or 'in the mind,' in distinction
from present sensations received from without, the two sorts
of proposition, according to the doctrine of Locke's Fourth
Book, stand on the same footing. [4]   It is a nominal essence
with which both alike are concerned, and on this depends
the general certainty or self-evidence, by which they are
distinguished from 'experiment or observation without us.'
These can never 'reach with certainty farther than the bare

[1] See above, paragraph 56.
[2] Book III. chap. iii. sec. 6.
[3] In case there should be any doubt
as to Locke's meaning in this passage,
it may be well to compare Book IV.
chap. ix. sec. 1.   There he distinctly
opposes the consideration of ideas in the
understanding to the knowledge of real
existence.   Here (Book IV. chap. vii.

sec. 4) he distinctly speaks of the proposition 'red is not blue' as expressing
a consideration of ideas in the understanding.   It follows that it is not a
proposition as to real existence.
[4] Already in Book II. (chap. xxxi. sec.
12), the simple idea, as abstract, is
spoken of as a nominal essence.

instance' (Book iv. chap. vi. sec. 7) : i.e., though the only channels by which we can reach real existence, they can never tell more than the presence of this or that sensation as caused by an unknown thing without, or the present disagreement of such present sensations with each other. As to the recurrence of such sensations, or any permanently real relation between them, they can tell us nothing. Nothing as to their recurrence, because, though in each case they show the presence of something causing the sensations, they show nothing of the real essence upon which their recurrence depends.[1] Nothing as to any permanently real relation between them, because, although the disagreement between ideas of blue and red, and the agreement between one idea of red and another, *as in the mind*, is self-evident, yet as thus in the mind they are not ' actual sensations ' at all (Book iv. chap. xi. sec. 6), nor do they convey that 'sensitive knowledge of particular existence,' which is the only possible knowledge of it. (Book iv. chap. iii. sec. 21.) As actual sensations and indices of reality, they do indeed differ in this or that ' bare instance,' but can convey no certainty that the real thing or ' parcel of matter ' (Book iii. chap. iii. sec. 18), which now causes the sensation of (and thus *is*) red, may not at another time cause the sensation of (and thus *be*) blue.[2]

83. We thus come upon the crucial antithesis between relations of ideas and matters of fact, with the exclusion of general certainty as to the latter, which was to prove such a potent weapon of scepticism in the hands of Hume. Of

---

[1] Cf. Book iv. chap. vi. sec. 5. ' If we could certainly know (which is impossible) where a real essence, which we know not, is—e.g. in what parcels of matter the real essence of gold is; yet could we not be sure, that this or that quality could with truth be affirmed of gold; since it is impossible for us to know that this or that quality or idea has a necessary connexion with a real essence, of which we have no idea at all.'

Several passages, of course, can be adduced from Locke which are inconsistent with the statement in the text: e.g. Book iv. chap. iv. sec. 12. 'To make knowledge real concerning substances, the ideas must be taken from the real existence of things. Whatever simple ideas have been found to coexist in any substance, these we may with confidence join together again, and so make abstract ideas of substances. For whatever have once had an union in nature, may be united again.' In all such passages, however, as will appear below, the strict opposition between the real and the mental is lost sight of, the 'nature' or 'substance,' in which ideas ' have a union,' or are ' found to coexist,' being a system of relations which, according to Locke, it requires a mind to constitute, and thus itself a 'nominal essence.'

[2] Cf. Book iv. chap. iii. sec. 29; Book iv. chap. vi. sec. 14; Book iv. chap. xi. sec. 11.

its incompatibility with recognized science we can have no
stronger sign than the fact that, after more than a century
has elapsed since Locke's premisses were pushed to their
legitimate conclusion, the received system of logic among
us is one which, while professing to accept Locke's doctrine
of essence, and with it the antithesis in question, throughout
assumes the possibility of general propositions as to matters
of fact, and seeks in their methodical discovery and proof
that science of nature which Locke already 'suspected' to
be impossible. (Book IV. chap. xii. sec. 10.)

84. That, so far as any inference from past to future
uniformities is necessary to the science of nature, his doctrine
does more than justify such 'suspicion,' is plain enough.
Does it, however, leave room for so much as a knowledge of
past uniformities of fact, in which the natural philosopher,
accepting the doctrine, might probably seek refuge? At
first sight, it might seem to do so. 'As, when our senses
are actually employed about any object, we do know that it
does exist; so by our memory we may be assured that here-
tofore things that affected our senses have existed—and
thus we have knowledge of the past existence of several
things, whereof our senses having informed us, our memories
still retain the ideas.' (Book IV. chap. xi. sec. 11.) Let us
see, however, how this knowledge is restricted. 'Seeing
water at this instant, it is an unquestionable truth to me
that water doth exist; and remembering that I saw it
yesterday, it will also be always true, and as long as my
memory retains it, always an undoubted proposition to me,
that water did exist the 18th of July, 1688; as it will also
be equally true that a certain number of very fine colours
did exist, which at the same time I saw on a bubble of that
water; but being now quite out of sight both of the water
and bubbles too, it is no more certainly known to me that
the water doth now exist, than that the bubbles and colours
therein do so; it being no more necessary that water should
exist to-day because it existed yesterday, than that the
colours or bubbles exist to-day because they existed yesterday.'—(*Ibid.*)

85. The result is that though I may enumerate a multitude of past matters-of-fact about water, I cannot gather
them up in any general statement about it as a real existence. So soon as I do so, I pass from water as a real

existence to its 'nominal essence,' i.e., to the ideas retained in my mind and put together in a fictitious substance, to which I have annexed the name 'water.' If we proceed to apply this doctrine to the supposed past matters-of-fact themselves, we shall find these too attenuating themselves to nonentity. Subtract in every case from the 'particular existence' of which we have 'sensitive knowledge' the qualification by ideas which, as retained in the mind, do not testify to a present real existence, and what remains? There is a certainty, according to Locke (Book IV. chap. xi. sec. 11), not, indeed, that water exists to-day because it existed yesterday—this is only 'probable'—but that it has, as a past matter-of-fact, at this time and that 'continued long in existence,' because this has been 'observed;' which must mean (Book IV. chap. ii. secs. 1, 5, and 9), because there has been a continued 'actual sensation' of it. 'Water,' however, is a complex idea of a substance, and of the elements of this complex idea those only which at any moment are given in 'actual sensation' may be accounted to 'really exist.' First, then, must disappear from reality the 'something,' that unknown substratum of ideas, of which the idea is emphatically 'abstract.' This gone, we naturally fall back upon a fact of co-existence between ideas, as being a reality, though the 'thing' be a fiction. But if this co-existence is to be real or to represent a reality, the ideas between which it obtains must be 'actual sensations.' These, whatever they may be, are at least opposed by Locke to ideas retained in the mind, which only form a nominal essence. But it is the association of such nominal essence, in the supposed observation of water, with the actual sensation that alone gives the latter a meaning. Set this aside as unreal, and the reality, which the sensation reveals, is at any rate one of which nothing can be said. It cannot be a relation between sensations, for such relation implies a consideration of them by the mind, whereby, according to Locke, they must cease to be 'real existences.' (Book II. chap. xxv. sec. 1.) It cannot even be a single sensation *as continuously observed*, for every present moment of such observation has at the next become a past, and thus the sensation observed in it has lost its 'actuality,' and cannot, *as a 'real existence,'* qualify the sensation observed in the next. Restrict the 'real existence,' in short, as Locke does, to an 'actual present sensation,' which can only be defined by opposition to an idea retained in the mind, and at every instant of its existence it has passed into the mind and thus ceased really to exist. Reality is in perpetual process of disappearing into the unreality of thought. No point can be fixed either in the flux of time or in the imaginary process from ' without ' to ' within ' the mind, on the one side of which can be placed ' real existence,' on the other the ' mere idea.' It is only because Locke unawares defines to himself the ' actual sensation ' as representative of a real essence, of which, however, according to him, as itself unknown, the presence is merely inferred from the sensation, that the ' actual sensation ' itself is saved from the limbo of nominal essence, to which ideas, as abstract or in the mind, are consigned. Only, again, so far as it is thus illogically saved, are we entitled to that distinction between ' facts ' and ' things of the mind,' which Locke once for all fixed for English philosophy.

86. By this time we are familiar with the difficulties which this antithesis has in store for a philosophy which yet admits that it is only in the mind or in relation to consciousness —in one word, as ' ideas '—that facts are to be found at all, while by the ' mind ' it understands an abstract generalization from the many minds which severally are born and grow, sleep and wake, with each of us. The antithesis itself, like every other form in which the impulse after true knowledge finds expression, implies a distinction between the seeming and the real; or between that which exists for the consciousness of the individual and that which really exists. But outside itself consciousness cannot get. It is there that the real must, at any rate, manifest itself, if it is to be found at all. Yet the original antithesis between the mind and its unknown opposite still prevails, and in consequence that alone which, though indeed in the mind, is yet given to it by no act of its own, is held to represent the real. This is the notion which dominates Locke. He strips from the formed content of consciousness all that the mind seems to have done for itself, and the abstract residuum, that of which the individual cannot help being conscious at each moment of his existence, is or ' reports ' the real, in opposition to the mind's creation. This is Feeling; or more strictly—since it exists, and whatever does so must exist as one in a number (Book II. chap. vii. sec. 7)—it is the multitude

of single feelings, 'each perishing the moment it begins' (Book II. chap. xxvii. sec. 2), from which all the definiteness that comes of composition and relation must be supposed absent. Thus, in trying to get at what shall be the mere fact in detachment from mental accretions, Locke comes to what is still consciousness, but the merely indefinite in consciousness. He seeks the real and finds the void. Of the real as outside consciousness nothing can be said; and of that again within consciousness, which is supposed to represent it, nothing can be said.

87. We have already seen how Locke, in his doctrine of secondary qualities of substances, practically gets over this difficulty; how he first projects out of the simple ideas, under relations which it requires a mind to constitute, a cognisable system of things, and then gives content and definiteness to the simple ideas in us by treating them as manifestations of this system of things. In the doctrine of propositions, the proper correlative to the reduction of the real to the present simple idea, as that of which we cannot get rid, would be the reduction of the 'real proposition' to the mere 'it is now felt.' If the matter-of-fact is to be that in consciousness which is independent of the 'work of the mind' in comparing and compounding, this is the only possible expression for it. It states the only possible 'real essence,' which yet is an essence of nothing, for any reference of it to a thing, if the thing is outside consciousness, is an impossibility; and if it is within consciousness, implies an 'invention of the mind' both in the creation of a thing, 'always the same with itself,' out of perishing feelings, and in the reference of the feelings to such a thing. Thus carried out, the antithesis between 'fact' and 'creation of the mind' becomes self-destructive, for, one feeling being as real as another, it leaves no room for that distinction between the real and fantastic, to the uncritical sense of which it owes its birth. To avoid this fusion of dream-land and the waking world, Locke avails himself of the distinction between the idea (i.e. feeling) as in the mind, which is not convertible with reality, and the idea as somewhere else, no one can say where—'the actual sensation'—which is so convertible. The distinction, however, must either consist in degrees of liveliness, in which case there must be a corresponding infinity of degrees of reality or unreality, or else must presuppose a

real existence from which the feeling, if 'actual sensation,' *is*—if merely 'in the mind' *is not*—derived. Such a real existence either is an object of consciousness, or is not. If it is not, no distinction between one kind of feeling and another can for consciousness be derived from it. If it is, then, granted the distinction between given feelings and creations of the mind, it must fall to the latter, and a 'thing of the mind' turns out to be the ground upon which 'fact' is opposed to 'things of the mind.'

88. It remains to exhibit briefly the disguises under which these inherent difficulties of his theory of essence appear in Locke. Throughout, instead of treating 'essence' altogether as a fiction of the mind—as it must be if feelings in simplicity and singleness are alone the real—he treats indeed as a merely 'nominal essence' every possible combination of ideas of which we can speak, but still supposes another essence which is 'real.' But a real essence of what? Clearly, according to his statements, of the same 'thing' of which the combination of ideas in the mind is the nominal essence. Indeed, there is no meaning in the antithesis unless the 'something,' of which the latter essence is so nominally, is that of which it is not so really. So says Locke, 'the nominal essence of gold is that complex idea the word gold stands for; let it be, for instance, a body yellow, of a certain weight, malleable, fusible, and fixed. But the real essence is the constitution of the insensible parts *of that body*, on which those qualities and all the other properties of gold depend.' (Book III. chap. vi. sec. 2.) Here the notion clearly is that of one and the same thing, of which we can only say that it is a 'body,' a certain complex of ideas— yellowness, fusibility, &c.—is the nominal, a certain constitution of insensible parts the real, essence. It is on the real essence, moreover, that the ideas which constitute the nominal depend. Yet while they are known, the real essence (as appears from the context) is wholly unknown. In this case, it would seem, the cause is not known from its effects.

89. There are lurking here two opposite views of the relation between the nominal essence and the real thing. According to one view, which prevails in the later chapters of the Second Book and in certain passages of the third, the relation between them is that with which we have already become familiar in the doctrine of substance—that, namely,

between ideas as in us and the same as in the thing. (Book II.
chap. xxiii. secs. 9 and 10.)　No distinction is made between
the 'idea in the mind' and the 'actual sensation.'　The
ideas in the mind are also in the thing, and thus are called
its qualities, though for the most part they are so only
secondarily, i.e. as effects of other qualities, which, as copied
directly in our ideas, are called primary, and relatively to
these effects are called powers.　These powers have yet in-
numerable effects to produce in us which they have not yet
produced. (Book II. chap. xxxi. sec. 10.)　Those which
have been so far produced, being gathered up in a complex
idea to which a name is annexed, form the 'nominal essence'
of the thing.　Some of them are of primary qualities, more
are of secondary.　The originals of the former, the powers to
produce the latter, together with powers to produce an indefinite multitude more, will constitute the 'real essence,'
which is thus 'a standard made by nature,' to which the
nominal essence is opposed merely as the inadequate to the
adequate.　The ideas, that is to say, which are indicated by
the name of a thing, have been really 'found in it' or 'produced by it,' but are only a part of those that remain to be
found in it or produced by it.　It is in this sense that Locke
opposes the adequacy between nominal and real essence in
the case of mixed modes to their perpetual inadequacy in
the case of ideas of substances.　The combination in the
one case is artificially made, in the other is found and being
perpetually enlarged.　This he illustrates by imagining the
processes which led Adam severally to the idea of the mixed
mode 'jealousy' and that of the substance 'gold.'　In the
former process Adam 'put ideas together only by his own
imagination, not taken from the existence of anything
. . . . . . the standard there was of his own making.'　In
the latter, 'he has a standard made by nature; and therefore being to represent that to himself by the idea he has of
it, even when it is absent, he puts no simple idea into his
complex one, but what he has the perception of from the
thing itself.　He takes care that his idea be conformable to
this archetype.' (Book III. chap. vi. secs. 46, 47.)　'It is
plain,' however, 'that the idea made after this fashion by
this archetype will be always inadequate.'

90. The nominal essence of a thing, then, according to
this view, being no other than the 'complex idea of a sub-

stance,' is a copy of reality, just as the simple idea is. It is
' a picture or representation in the mind of a thing that does
exist by ideas of those qualities that are discoverable in it.'
(Book II. chap. xxxi. secs. 6, 8.) It only differs from the
simple idea (which is itself, as abstract, a nominal essence)[1] in
respect of reality, because the latter is a copy or effect produced singly and involuntarily, whereas we may put ideas
together, as if in a thing, which have never been so presented
together, and, on the other hand, never can put together all
that exist together. (Book II. chap. xxx. sec. 5, and xxxi. 10.)
So far as Locke maintains this view, the difficulty about
general propositions concerning real existence need not arise.
A statement which affirmed of gold one of the qualities included
in the complex idea of that substance, would not express
merely an analysis of an idea in the mind, but would represent a relation of qualities in the existing thing from which
the idea 'has been taken.' These qualities, as in the thing,
doubtless would not be, as in us, feelings (or, as Locke should
rather have said in more recent phraseology, possibilities of
feeling), but powers to produce feeling, nor could any relation between these, as in the thing, be affirmed but such as
had produced its copy or effect in actual experience. No
coexistence of qualities could be truly affirmed, which had
not been found; but, once found—being a coexistence of
qualities and not simply a momentary coincidence of feelings—it could be affirmed as permanent in a general proposition. That a relation can be stated universally between
ideas collected in the mind, no one denies, and if such
collection 'is taken from a combination of simple ideas
existing together constantly in things' (Book II. chap. xxxii.
sec. 18), the statement will hold equally of such existence.
Thus Locke contrasts mixed modes, which, for the most
part, 'being actions which perish in the birth, are not
capable of a lasting duration,' with 'substances, which are
the actors; and wherein the simple ideas that make up
the complex ideas designed by the name have a lasting
union.' (Book III. chap. vi. sec. 42.)

91. In such a doctrine Locke, starting whence he did,
could not remain at rest. We need not here repeat what has
been said of it above in the consideration of his doctrine of
substance. Taken strictly, it implies that 'real existence'

---

[1] Book II. chap. xxxi. sec. 12.

consists in a permanent relation of ideas, said to be of secondary qualities, to each other in dependence on other ideas, said to be of primary qualities. In other words, in order to constitute reality, it takes ideas out of that particularity in time and place, which is yet pronounced the condition of reality, to give them an 'abstract generality' which is fictitious, and then treats them as constituents of a system of which the 'invented' relations of cause and effect and of identity are the framework. In short, it brings reality wholly within the region of thought, distinguishing it from the system of complex ideas or nominal essences which constitute our knowledge, not as the unknown opposite of all possible thought, but only as the complete from the incomplete. To one who logically carried out this view, the ground of distinction between fact and fancy would have to be found in the relation between thought as 'objective,' or in the world, and thought as so far communicated to us. Here, however, it could scarcely be found by Locke, with whom 'thought' meant simply a faculty of the 'thinking thing,' called a 'soul,' which might ride in a coach with him from Oxford to London. (Book II. chap. xxiii. sec. 20.) Was the distinction then to disappear altogether?

92. It is saved, though at the cost of abandoning the 'new way of ideas,' as it had been followed in the Second Book, by the transfer of real existence from the thing in which ideas are found, and whose qualities the complex of ideas in us, though inadequate, represents, to something called 'body,' necessarily unknown, because no ideas in us are in any way representative of it. To such an unknown body unknown qualities are supposed to belong under the designation 'real essence.' The subject of the nominal essence, just because its qualities, being matter of knowledge, are ideas in our minds, is a wholly different and a fictitious thing.

93. This change of ground is of course not recognized by Locke himself. It is the perpetual crossing of the inconsistent doctrines that renders his 'immortal Third Book' a web of contradictions. As was said above, he constantly speaks as if the subject of the real essence were the same with that of the nominal, and never explicitly allows it to be different. The equivocation under which the difference is disguised lies in the use of the term 'body.' A 'particular body' is the subject both of the nominal and real essence

' gold ' But ' body,' as that in which ' ideas are found,' and in which they permanently coexist according to a natural law, is one thing ; ' body,' as the abstraction of the unknown, is quite another. It is body in the former sense that is the real thing when nominal essence (the complex of ideas in us) is treated as representative, though inadequately so, of the real thing ; it is body in the latter sense that is the real thing when this is treated as wholly outside possible consciousness, and its essence as wholly unrepresented by possible ideas. By a jumble of the two meanings Locke obtains an amphibious entity which is at once independent of relation to ideas, as is body in the latter sense, and a source of ideas representative of it, as is body in the former sense—which thus carries with it that opposition to the mental which is supposed necessary to the real, while yet it seems to manifest itself in ideas. Meanwhile a third conception of the real keeps thrusting itself upon the other two —the view, namely, that body in both senses is a fiction of thought, and that the mere present feeling is alone the real.

94. Where Locke is insisting on the opposition between the real essence and any essence that can be known, the former is generally ascribed either to a ' particular being ' or to a ' parcel of matter.' The passage which brings the opposition into the strongest relief is perhaps the following :—' I would ask any one, what is sufficient to make an essential difference in nature between any two particular beings, without any regard had to some abstract idea, which is looked upon as the essence and standard of a species ? All such patterns and standards being quite laid aside, particular beings, considered barely in themselves, will be found to have all their qualities equally essential ; and everything, in each individual, will be essential to it, or, which is more, nothing at all. For though it may be reasonable to ask whether obeying the magnet be essential to iron ; yet I think it is very improper and insignificant to ask whether it be essential to the particular parcel of matter I cut my pen with, without considering it under the name *iron*, or as being of a certain species.' (Book III. chap. vi. sec. 5.)[1] Here, it will be seen, the exclusion of the abstract idea from reality carries with it the exclusion of that ' standard made

---

[1] To the same purpose is a passage in Book III. chap. x. sec. 19, towards the end.

by nature,' which according to the passages already quoted, is the 'thing itself' from which the abstract idea is taken, and from which, if correctly taken, it derives reality. This exclusion, again, means nothing else than the disappearance from 'nature' (which with Locke is interchangeable with 'reality') of all essential difference. There remain, however, as the 'real,' 'particular beings,' or 'individuals,' or 'parcels of matter.' In each of these, 'considered barely in itself, everything will be essential to it, or, which is more, nothing at all.'

95. We have already seen,[1] that if by a 'particular being' is meant the mere *individuum*, as it would be upon abstraction of all relations which according to Locke are fictitious, and constitute a community or generality, it certainly can have no essential qualities, since it has no qualities at all. It is a something which equals nothing. The notion of this bare *individuum* being the real is the 'protoplasm' of Locke's philosophy, to which, though he never quite recognized it himself, after the removal of a certain number of accretions we may always penetrate. It is so because his unacknowledged method of finding the real consisted in abstracting from the formed content of consciousness till he came to that which could not be got rid of. This is the momentarily present relation of subject and object, which, considered on the side of the object, gives the mere atom, and on the side of the subject, the mere 'it is felt.' Even in this ultimate abstraction the 'fiction of thought' still survives, for the atom is determined to its mere individuality by relation to other individuals, and the feeling is determined to the present moment or 'the now' by relation to other 'nows.'

96. To this ultimate abstraction, however, Locke, though constantly on the road to it, never quite penetrates. He is farthest from it—indeed, as far from it as possible—where he is most acceptable to common sense, as in his ordinary doctrine of abstraction, where the real, from which the process of abstraction is supposed to begin, is already the individual in the fullness of its qualities, James and John, this man or this gold. He is nearest to it when the only qualification of the 'particular being,' which has to be removed by thought in order to its losing its reality and

---

[1] See above, paragraph 45.

becoming an abstract idea, is supposed to consist in 'circumstances of time and place.'

97. It is of these circumstances, as the constituents of
the real, that he is thinking in the passage last quoted. As
qualified by 'circumstances of place' the real is a parcel of
matter, and under this designation Locke thought of it as a
subject of 'primary qualities of body.'[1] These, indeed, as he
enumerates them, may be shown to imply relations going far
beyond that of simple distinctness between atoms, and thus
to involve much more of the creative action of thought; but
we need be the less concerned for this usurpation on the part
of the particular being, since that which he illegitimately
conveys to it as derived from 'circumstances of place,' he
virtually takes away from it again by limitation in time.
The 'particular being' has indeed on the one hand a real
essence, consisting of certain primary qualities, but on the
other it has no continued identity. It is only real as present
to feeling at this or that time. The particular being of one
moment is not the particular being of the next. Thus the
primary qualities which are a real essence, i.e. an essence of
a particular being, at one moment, are not its real essence at
the next, because, while they as represented in the mind
remain the same, the 'it,' the particular being is different.
An *immutable* essence for that very reason cannot be real.
The immutability can only lie in a relation between a certain
abstract (i.e. unreal) idea and a certain sound. (Book III.
chap. iii. sec. 19.) 'The real constitution of things,' on the
other hand, 'begin and perish with them. All things that
exist are liable to change.' (*Ibid.*) Locke, it is true (as is
implied in the term *change*[2]) never quite drops the notion of
there being a real identity in some unknown background, but
this makes no difference in the bearing of his doctrine upon
the possibility of 'real' knowledge. It only means that for
an indefinite particularity of 'beings' there is substituted one
'being' under an indefinite peculiarity of forms. Though the
reality of the thing *in itself* be immutable, yet its reality *for*

---

[1] According to Locke's ordinary usage
of the terms, no distinction appears between 'matter' and 'body.' In Book
III. chap. x. sec. 15, however, he distinguishes matter from body as the less
determinate conception from the more.
The one implies solidity merely, the
other extension and figure also, so that
we may talk of the 'matter of bodies,'
but not of the 'body of matters.' But
since solidity, according to Locke's
definition, involves the other 'primary
qualities,' this distinction does not avail
him much.

[2] See above, paragraph 69.

us is in perpetual flux. 'In itself' it is a substance without an essence, a 'something we know not what' without any ideas to 'support;' a 'parcel of matter,' indeed, but one in which no quality is really essential, because its real essence, consisting in its momentary presentation to sense, changes with the moments.[1]

98. We have previously noticed[2] Locke's pregnant remark, that 'things whose existence is in succession' do not admit of identity. (Book II. chap. xxvii. sec. 2.) So far, then, as the 'real,' in distinction from the 'abstract,' is constituted by particularity in time, or has its existence in succession, it excludes the relation of identity. 'It perishes in every moment that it begins.' Had Locke been master of this notion, instead of being irregularly mastered by it, he might have anticipated all that Hume had to say. As it is, even in passages such as those to which reference has just been made, where he follows its lead the farthest, he is still pulled up by inconsistent conceptions with which common sense, acting through common language, restrains the most adventurous philosophy. Thus, even from his illustration of the liability of all existence to change—'that which was grass to-day is to-morrow the flesh of a sheep, and within a few days after will become part of a man'[3]—we find that, just as he does not pursue the individualization of the real in space so far but that it still remains 'a constitution of parts,' so he does not pursue it in time so far but that a coexistence of real elements over a certain duration is possible. To a more thorough analysis, indeed, there is no alternative between finding reality in relations of thought, which, because relations of thought, are not in time and therefore are immutable, and submitting it to such subdivision of time as excludes all real coexistence because what is real, as present, at one moment is unreal, as past, at the next. This alternative could not present itself in its clearness to Locke, because, according to his method of interrogating consciousness, he inevitably found in its supposed beginning, which he identified with the real, those products of thought which he opposed to the real, and thus read into the simple feeling of the moment that which, if it were the simple feeling of the moment, it

---

[1] Cf. Book III. chap. vi. sec. 4: 'Take but away the abstract ideas by which we sort individuals and rank them under common names, and then the thought of anything essential to any of them instantly vanishes,' &c.

[2] See above, paragraph 75.

[3] Book III. chap. iii. sec. 10.

could not contain. Thus throughout the Second Book of the Essay the simple idea is supposed to represent either as copy or as effect a permanent reality, whether body or mind : and in the later books, even where the *representation* of such reality in knowledge comes in question, its existence as constituted by 'primary qualities of body' is throughout assumed, though general propositions with regard to it are declared impossible. It is a feeling referred to body, or, in the language of subsequent psychology, a feeling of the *outward* sense,[1] that Locke means by an 'actual present sensation,' and it is properly in virtue of this reference that such sensation is supposed to be, or to report, the real.

99. According to the doctrine of primary qualities, as originally stated, the antithesis lies between body as it is in itself and body as it is for us, not between body as it is for us in 'actual sensation,' and body as it is for us according to 'ideas in the mind.' The primary qualities 'are in bodies whether we perceive them or no.' (Book ii. chap. viii. sec. 23.) As he puts it elsewhere (Book ii. chap. xxxi. sec. 2), it is just because 'solidity and extension and the termination of it, figure, with motion and rest, whereof we have the ideas, would be really in the world as they are whether there were any sensible being to perceive them or no,' that they are to be looked on as the *real* modifications of matter. A change in them, unlike one in the secondary qualities, or such as is relative to sense, is a *real* alteration *in body*. 'Pound an almond, and the clear white colour will be altered into a dirty one, and the sweet taste into an oily one. What alteration can the beating of the pestle make in any body, but an alteration of the texture of it?' (Book ii. chap. viii. sec. 20.) It is implied then in the notion of the real as body that it should be outside consciousness. It is that which seems to remain when everything belonging to consciousness has been thought

---

[1] For the germs of the distinction between outer and inner sense, see Locke's Essay, Book ii. chap. i. sec. 14: 'This source of ideas (the perception of the operations of the mind) every man has wholly in himself; and though it be not sense, as having nothing to do with external objects, yet it is very like it, and might properly enough be called internal sense.' For the notion of outer sense Cf. Book ii. chap. ix. sec. 6, where he is distinguishing the ideas of hunger and warmth, which he supposes children to receive in the womb from the 'innate principles which some contend for.' 'These (the ideas of hunger and warmth) being the effects of sensation, are only from some affections of the body which happen to them there, and so depend on something exterior to the mind, not otherwise differing in their manner of production from other ideas derived from sense, but only in the precedency of time.'

away. Yet it is brought within consciousness again by the supposition that it has qualities which copy themselves in our ideas and are 'the exciting causes of all our various sensations from bodies.' (Book II. chap. xxxi. sec. 3.) Again, however, the antithesis between the real and consciousness prevails, and the qualities of matter or body having been brought within the latter, are opposed to a 'substance of body'—otherwise spoken of as 'the nature, cause, or manner of producing the ideas of primary qualities'—which remains outside it, unknown and unknowable. (Book II. chap. xxiii. sec. 30, &c.)

100. The doctrine of primary qualities was naturally the one upon which the criticism of Berkeley and Hume first fastened, as the most obvious aberration from the 'new way of ideas.' That the very notion of the senses as 'reporting' anything, under secondary no less than under primary qualities, implies the presence of 'fictions of thought' in the primitive consciousness, may become clear upon analysis; but it lies on the surface and is avowed by Locke himself (Book II. chap. viii. secs. 2, 7), that the conception of primary qualities is only possible upon distinction being made between ideas as in our minds, and the 'nature of things existing without us,' which cannot be given in the simple feeling itself. This admitted, the distinction might either be traced to the presence within intelligent consciousness of another factor than simple ideas, or be accounted for as a gradual 'invention of the mind.' In neither way, however, could Locke regard it and yet retain his distinction between fact and fancy, as resting upon that between the nature of things and the mind of man. The way of escape lay in a figure of speech, the figure of the wax or the mirror. 'The ideas of primary qualities are resemblances of them.' (Book II. chap. viii. sec. 15.) These qualities then may be treated, according to occasion, either as primitive data of consciousness, or as the essence of that which is the unknown opposite of consciousness—in the latter way when the antithesis between nature and mind is in view, in the former when nature has yet to be represented as knowable.

101. How, asked Berkeley, can an idea be like anything that is not an idea? Put the question in its proper strength —How can an idea be like that of which the sole and simple determination is just that it is not an idea (and such with

Locke is body 'in itself' or as the real)—and it is clearly
unanswerable. The process by which Locke was prevented
from putting it to himself is not difficult to trace. 'Body'
and 'the solid' are with him virtually convertible terms.
Each indifferently holds the place of the substance, of which
the primary qualities are so many determinations.[1] It is
true that where solidity has to be defined, it is defined as an
attribute of body, but conversely body itself is treated as a
'texture of solid parts,' i.e. as a mode of the solid. Body, in
short, so soon as thought of, resolves itself into a relation of
bodies, and the solid into a relation of solids, but Locke, by
a shuffle of the two terms—representing body as a relation
between solids and the solid as a relation between bodies—
gains the appearance of explaining each in turn by relation
to a simpler idea. Body, as the unknown, is revealed to us
by the idea of solidity, which sense conveys to us; while
solidity is explained by reference to the idea of body. The
idea of solidity, we are told, is a simple idea which comes into
the mind solely by the sense of touch. (Book II. chap. iii.
sec. 1.) But no sooner has he thus identified it with an immediate feeling than, in disregard of his own doctrine, that
'an idea which has no composition' is undefinable,[2] he converts it into a theory of the cause of that feeling. 'It arises
from the resistance which we find in body to the entrance of
any other body into the place it possesses till it has left it;'
and he at once proceeds to treat it as the consciousness of
such resistance. 'Whether we move or rest, in what posture
soever we are, we always feel something under us that supports us, and hinders our farther sinking downwards: and
the bodies which we daily handle make us perceive that
whilst they remain between them, they do by an insurmount-
able force hinder the approach of the parts of our hands that
press them. That which then hinders the approach of two
bodies, when they are moving one towards another, I call
solidity.' (Book II. chap. iv. sec 1.)

102. Now 'body' in this theory is by no means outside
consciousness. It is emphatically 'in the mind,' a 'nominal
essence,' determined by the relation which the theory assigns

[1] See Book II. chap. viii. sec. 23: The
primary 'qualities that are in bodies,
are the bulk, figure, number, situation,
and motion or rest, *of their solid parts.*'
Cf. Book II. chap. xiii. sec. 11: 'Solidity
is so inseparable an idea from body, that
upon that depends its filling of space,
its contact, impulse, and communication of motion upon impulse.'

[2] See Book III. chap. iv. sec. 7.

to it, and which, like every relation according to Locke, is a 'thing of the mind.' This relation is that of outwardness to other bodies, and among these to the sensitive body through which we receive ' ideas of sensation '—a body which, on its side, as determined by the relation, has its essence from the mind. It is, then, not as the unknown opposite of the mind, but as determined by an intelligible relation which the mind constitutes, and of which the members are each ' nominal essences,' that body is outward to the sensitive subject. But to Locke, substituting for body as a nominal essence body as the unknown thing in itself, and identifying the sensitive subject with the mind, outwardness in the above sense—an outwardness constituted by the mind—becomes outwardness *to* the mind of an unknown opposite of the mind. Solidity, then, and the properties which its definition involves (and it involves all the ' primary qualities '), become something wholly alien to the mind, which ' would exist without any sensible being to perceive them.' As such, they do duty as a real essence, when the opposition of this to everything in the mind has to be asserted. Yet must they be in some sort ideas, for of these alone (as Locke fully admits) can we think and speak; and if ideas, in the mind. How is this contradiction to be overcome? By the notion that though not in or of the mind, they yet copy themselves upon it in virtue of an impulse in body, correlative to that resistance of which touch conveys the idea. (Book II. chap. viii. sec. 11).[1] This explanation, however, is derived from the equivocation between the two meanings of mind and body respectively. The problem to be explained is the relation between the mind and that which is only qualified as the negation of mind ; and the explanation is found in a relation, only existing for the mind, between a sensitive and a non-sensitive body.

103. The case then stands as follows. All that Locke says of body as the real thing-in-itself, and of its qualities as the essence of such thing, comes according to his own showing of an action of the mind which he reckons the source of fictions. ' Body in itself' is a substratum of ideas which the mind ' accustoms itself to suppose.' It perpetually recedes, as what was at first a substance becomes in turn a complex of qualities for which a more remote substratum has to be

[1] Cf. also the passage from Book II. chap. xiii. sec. 11, quoted above, p. 82, note 1.

supposed—a 'substance of body,' a productive cause of matter. But the substance, however remote, is determined by the qualities to which it is correlative, as the cause by its effects ; and every one of these—whether the most primary, solidity, or those which 'the mind finds inseparable from every particle of matter,' i.e. from the 'solid parts of a body,'[1] —as defined by Locke, is a relation such as the mind, 'bringing one thing to and setting it by another' (Book II. chap. xxv. sec. 1), can alone constitute. To Locke, however, overcome by the necessity of intelligence, as gradually developing itself in each of us, to regard the intelligible world as there before it is known, the real must be something which would be what it is if thought were not. Strictly taken, this must mean that it is that of which nothing can be said, and some expression must be found by means of which it may do double duty as at once apart from consciousness and in it. This is done by converting the primary qualities of body, though obviously complex ideas of relation, into simple feelings of touch,[2] and supposing the subject of this sensation to be related to its object as wax to the seal. If we suppose this relation, again, which is really within the mind and constituted by it, to be one between the mind itself, as passive, and the real, we obtain a 'real' which exists apart from the mind, yet copies itself upon it. The mind, then, so far as it takes such a copy, becomes an 'outer sense,' as to which it may be conveniently forgotten that it is a mode of mind at all. Thus every modification of it, as an 'actual present sensation,' comes to be opposed to every idea of memory or imagination, as that which is not of the mind to that which is ; though there is no assignable difference between one and the other, except an indefinite one in degree of vivacity, that is not derived from the action of the mind in referring the one to an object, constituted by itself, to which it does not refer the other.

104. Let us now consider whether by this reference to body, feeling becomes any the more a source of general knowledge concerning matters of fact. As we have seen, if we

[1] Cf. Book II. chap. viii. sec. 9. The primary qualities of body are 'such as sense constantly finds in every particle of matter, which has bulk enough to be perceived, and the mind finds inseparable from every particle of matter, though less than to make itself singly be perceived by our senses.'

[2] I write advisedly 'touch' only, not 'sight and touch,' because, though Locke (Book II. chap. v.) speaks of the ideas of extension, figure, motion, and rest of bodies, as received both by sight and touch, these are all involved in the previous definition of solidity, of which the idea is ascribed to touch only.

identify the real with feeling simply, its distinction from 'bare vision' disappears. This difficulty it is sought to overcome by distinguishing feeling as merely in the mind from actually present sensation. But on reflection we find that sensation after all is feeling, and that one feeling is as much present as another, though present only to become at the next moment past, and thus, if it is the presence that is the condition of reality, unreal. The distinction then must lie in the *actuality* of the sensation. But does not this actuality mean simply derivation from the real, i.e. derivation from the idea which has to be derived from it? If, in the spirit of Locke, we answer, 'No, it means that the feeling belongs to the outer sense'; the rejoinder will be that this means either that it is a feeling of touch—and what should give the feeling of touch this singular privilege over other feelings of not being in the mind while they are in it?—or that it is a feeling referred to body, which still implies the presupposition of the real, only under the special relations of resistance and impulse. The latter alternative is the one which Locke virtually adopts, and in adopting it he makes the actuality, by which sensation is distinguished from 'feelings in the mind,' itself a creation of the mind. But though it is by an intellectual interpretation of the feeling of touch, not by the feeling itself, that there is given that idea of body, by reference to which actual sensation is distinguished from the mere idea, still with Locke the feeling of touch is necessary to the interpretation. Thus, supposing his notion to be carried out consistently, the actual present sensation, as reporting the real, must either be a feeling of touch, or, if of another sort, e.g., sight or hearing, must be referable to an object of touch. In other words, the real will exist for us so long only as it is touched, and ideas in us will constitute a real essence so long only as they may be referred to an object now touched. Let the object cease to be touched, and the ideas become a nominal essence in the mind, the knowledge which they constitute ceases to be real, and the proposition which expresses it ceases to concern matter of fact. Truth as to matters of fact or bodies, then, must be confined to singular propositions such as 'this is touched now,' ' that was touched then;' 'what is touched now is bitter,' ' what was then touched was red.'[1]

<hr />

[1] Thus the conviction that an object seen is not 'bare fancy,' which is gained by 'putting the hand to it' (Book IV. chap. xi. sec. 17), as it conveys the idea

105. All that is gained, then, by the conversion of the feeling of touch, pure and simple, into the idea of a body touched, is the supposition that *there is* a real existence which does not come and go with the sensations. As to *what* this existence is, as to its real essence, we can have no knowledge but such as is given in a present sensation.[1] Any essence of it, otherwise known, could only be a nominal essence, a relation of ideas in our minds : it would lack the condition in virtue of which alone a datum of consciousness can claim to be representative of reality, that of being an impression made by a body now operating upon us. (Book III. chap. v. sec. 2, and Book IV. chap. xi. sec. 1.) The memory of such impression, however faithful, will still only report a *past* reality. It will itself be merely ' an idea in the mind.' Neither it nor its relation to any present sensation result from the immediate impact of body, and in consequence neither ' really exists.' All that can be known, then, of the real, in other words, the whole real essence of body, as it is for us, reduces itself to that which can at any moment be ' revealed ' in a single sensation apart from all relation to past sensations ; and this, as we have seen, is nothing at all.

106. Thus that reduction of reality to that of which nothing can be said, which follows from its identification with particularity in time, follows equally from its identification with the resistance of body, or (which comes to the same) from the notion of an ' outer sense ' being its organ ; since it is only that which *now* resists, not a general possibility of resistance nor a relation between the resistances of different times, that can be regarded as outside the mind. In Locke's language, it is only a particular parcel of matter that can be so regarded. Of such a parcel, as he rightly says, it is absurd to ask what is its essence, for it can have none at all. (See above, paragraph 94.) As real, it has no quality save that of being a body or of being now touched—a quality, which as all things real have it and have none other, cannot be a *differentia* of it. When we consider that this quality may be

of solidity, is properly, according to Locke's doctrine, not one among other ' confirmations of the testimony of the senses,' but the source of all such testimony, as a testimony to the real, i.e. to body. See above, paragraph 62.

[1] Cf. Book III. chap. vi. sec. 6: ' As to the real essences of substances, we only suppose their being, without precisely knowing what they are.' The appearance of the qualification ' precisely,' as we shall see below, marks an oscillation from the view, according to which ' real essence ' is the negation of the knowable to the view according to which our knowledge of it is merely inadequate.

regarded equally as immutable and as changing from moment to moment, we shall see the ground of Locke's contradiction of himself in speaking of the real thing sometimes as indestructible, sometimes as in continual dissolution. 'The real constitutions of things begin and perish with them.' (Book III. chap. iii. sec. 19.) That is, the thing at one moment makes an impact on the sensitive tablet—in the fact that it does so lie at once its existence and its essence—but the next moment the impact is over, and with it thing and essence, *as real*, have disappeared. Another impact, and thus another thing, has taken its place. But of this the real essence is just the same as that of the previous thing, namely, that it may be touched, or is solid, or a body, or a parcel of matter; nor can this essence be really lost, since than it there is no other reality, all difference of essence, as Locke expressly says,[1] being constituted by abstract ideas and the work of the mind. It follows that *real* change is impossible. A parcel of matter at one time is a parcel of matter at all times. Thus we have only to forget that the relation of continuity between the parcels, not being an idea caused by impact, should properly fall to the unreal—though only on the same principle as should that of distinctness between the times—and we find the real in a continuity of matter, unchangeable because it has no qualities to change. It may seem strange that when this notion of the formless continuity of the real being gets the better of Locke, a man should be the real being which he takes as his instance. 'Nothing I have is essential to me. An accident or disease may very much alter my colour or shape; a fever or fall may take away my reason or memory, or both; and an apoplexy leave neither sense nor understanding, no, nor life.' (Book III. chap. vi. sec. 4.) But as the sequel shows, the man or the 'I' is here considered simply as 'a particular corporeal being,' i.e. as the 'parcel of matter' which alone (according to the doctrine of reality now in view) can be the real in man, and upon which all qualities are 'superinductions of the mind.'[2]

107. We may now discern the precise point where the

---

[1] Book III. chap. vi. sec. 4: 'Take but away the abstract ideas by which we sort individuals, and then the thought of anything essential to any of them instantly vanishes.'

[2] See a few lines below the passage quoted: 'So that if it be asked, whether it be essential to me, or any other particular corporeal being, to have reason? I say, no; no more than it is essential to this white thing I write on to have words in it.'

qualm as to clothing reality with such superinductions commonly returns upon Locke. The conversion of feeling into
body felt and of the particular time of the feeling into an
individuality of the body, and, further, the fusion of the individual bodies, manifold as the times of sensation, into one
continued body, he passes without scruple. So long as these
are all the traces of mental fiction which 'matter,' or 'body,'
or 'nature' bears upon it, he regards it undoubtingly as the
pure 'privation' of whatever belongs to the mind. But so
soon as cognisable qualities, forming an essence, come to be
ascribed to body, the reflection arises that these qualities are
on our side ideas, and that so far as they are permanent or
continuous they are not ideas of the sort which can alone represent body as the 'real' opposite of mind; they are not the
result of momentary impact; they are not 'actually present
sensations.' Suppose them, however, to have no permanence
—suppose their reality to be confined to the fleeting 'now'
—and they are no qualities, no essence, at all. There is then
for us no *real* essence of body or nature; what we call so is
a creation of the mind.

108. This implies the degradation of the 'primary qualities of body' from the position which they hold in the Second
Book of the Essay, as the real, *par excellence*, to that of a
nominal essence. In the Second Book, just as the complex
of ideas, received and to be received from a substance, is taken
for the real thing without disturbance from the antithesis
between reality and 'ideas in the mind,' so the primary qualities of body are taken not only as real, but as the sources of
all other reality. Body, the real thing, copying itself upon
the mind in an idea of sensation (that of solidity), carries
with it from reality into the mind those qualities which 'the
mind finds inseparable from it,' with all their modes. 'A
piece of manna of a sensible bulk is able to produce in us the
idea of a round or square figure, and, by being removed
from one place to another, the idea of motion. This idea of
motion represents it, as it really is in the manna, moving; a
circle or square are the same, whether in idea or existence,
in the mind or in the manna; and this both motion and figure
are really in the manna, whether we take notice of them or
no.' (Book II. chap. viii. sec. 18.) To the unsophisticated
man, taking for granted that the 'sensible bulk' of the
manna is a 'real essence,' this statement will raise no diffi-

culties.   But when he has learnt from Locke himself that the
' sensible bulk,' so far as we can think and speak of it, must
consist in the ideas which it is said to produce, the question
as to the real existence of these must arise.   It turns out
that they ' really exist,' so far as they represent the impact
of a body copying itself in actually present sensation, and
that from their reality, accordingly, must be excluded all
qualities that accrue to the present sensation from its relation to the past.   Can the ' primary qualities' escape this
exclusion ?

109. To obtain a direct and compendious answer to this
question from Locke's own mouth is not easy, owing to the
want of adjustment between the several passages where he
treats of the primary qualities.   They are originally enumerated as the ' bulk, figure, number, situation, and motion or
rest of the solid parts of bodies' (Book ii. chap. viii. sec. 23),
and, as we have seen, are treated as all involved in that idea
of solidity which is given in the sensation of touch.   We
have no further account of them till we come to the chapters on ' simple modes of space and duration' (Book ii.
chaps. xiii. &c.), which are introduced by the remark, that in
the previous part of the book simple ideas have been treated
' rather in the way that they come into the mind than as
distinguished from others more compounded.'   As the simple
idea, according to Locke, is that which comes first into the
mind, the two ways of treatment ought to coincide; but
there follows an explanation of the simple modes in question,
of which to a critical reader the plain result is that the idea
of body, which, according to the imaginary theory of ' the
way that it came into the mind' is simple and equivalent to
the sensation of touch, turns out to be a complex of relations
of which the simplest is called space.

110. To know what space itself is, ' we are sent to our
senses' of sight and touch.   It is ' as needless to go to prove
that men perceive by their sight a distance between bodies
of different colours, or between the parts of the same body,
as that they see colours themselves; nor is it less obvious
that they can do so in the dark by feeling and touch.'
(Book ii. chap. xiii. sec. 2.)   Space being thus explained
by reference to distance, and distance *between bodies*, it might
be supposed that distance and body were simpler ideas.   In
the next paragraph, however, distance is itself explained to

be a mode of space. It is 'space considered barely in length between any two beings,' and is distinguished (*a*) from 'capacity' or 'space considered in length, breadth, and thickness;' (*b*) from 'figure, which is nothing but the relation which the parts of the termination of extension, or circumscribed space, have among themselves;' (*c*) from 'place, which is the relation of distance between anything and any two or more points which are considered as keeping the same distance one with another, and so as at rest.' It is then shown at large (Book II. chap. xiii. sec. 11), as against the Cartesians, that extension, which is 'space in whatsoever manner considered,' is a 'distinct idea from body.' The ground of the distinction plainly lies in the greater complexity of the idea of body. Throughout the definition just given 'space' is presupposed as the simpler idea of which capacity, figure, and place are severally modifications; and these again, as 'primary qualities,' though with a slight difference of designation,[1] are not only all declared inseparable from body, but are involved in it under a further modification **as** '*qualities of its solid parts*,' i.e., of parts so related to each other that each will change its place sooner than admit another into it. (Book II. chap. iv. sec. 2, and chap. viii. sec. 23.) Yet, though body is thus a complex of relations—all, according to Locke's doctrine of relation, inventions of the mind—and though it must be proportionately remote from the simple idea which 'comes first into the mind,' yet, on the other hand, it is in body, as an object previously given, that these relations are said to be found, and found by the senses. (Book II. chap. xiii. secs. 2, 27.)[2]

111. It will readily be seen that 'body' here is a mode of the idea of substance, and, like it,[3] appears in two inconsistent positions as at once the beginning and the end of the process of knowledge—as on the one hand that in which ideas are found and from which they are abstracted, and on the other hand that which results from their complication. As the attempt either to treat particular qualities as given and substance as an abstraction gradually made, or conversely to treat the 'thing' as given, and relations as gradually superinduced, necessarily fails for the simple reason

---

[1] In the enumeration of primary qualities, 'capacity' is represented by 'bulk,' 'place' by 'situation.'

[2] In the second of the passages referred to, it will be seen that 'matter' is used interchangeably with 'body.'

[3] See above, paragraph 39.

that substance and relations each presuppose the other, so body presupposes the primary qualities as so many relations which form its essence or make it what it is, while these again presuppose body as the matter which they determine. It is because Locke substitutes for this intellectual order of mutual presupposition a succession of sensations in time, that he finds himself in the confusion we have noticed—now giving the priority to sensations in which the idea of body is supposed to be conveyed, and from it deriving the ideas of the primary qualities, now giving it to these ideas themselves, and deriving the idea of body from their complication. This is just such a contradiction as it would be to put to-day before yesterday. *We* may escape it by the consideration that in the case before us it is not a succession of sensations in time that we have to do with at all ; that ' the real ' is an intellectual order, or mind, in which every element, being correlative to every other, at once presupposes and is presupposed by every other ; but that this order communicates itself to us piecemeal, in a process of which the first condition on our part is the conception that there *is* an order, or something related to something else ; and that thus the conception of qualified substance, which in its definite articulation is the end of all our knowledge, is yet in another form, that may be called indifferently either abstract or confused,[1] its beginning. This way of escape, however, was not open to Locke, because with him it was the condition of reality in the idea of the body and its qualities that they should be ' actually present sensations.' The priority then of body to the relations of extension, distance, &c., as of that in which these relations are found, must, if body and extension are to be more than nominal essences, be a priority of sensations in time. But, on the other hand, the priority of the idea of space to the ideas of its several modes, and of these again to the idea of body, as of the simpler to the more complex, must no less than the other, if the ideas in question are to be real, be one in time. Locke's contradiction, then, is that of supposing that of two sensations each is actually present, of two impacts on the sensitive tablet each is actually made, before the other.

112. From such a contradiction, even though he was not

___

[1] ' Indifferently either abstract or confused,' because of the conception that is most confused the least can be said ; and it is thus most abstract.

distinctly aware of it, he could not but seek a way of escape.
From his point of view two ways might at first sight seem
to be open—the priority in sensitive experience, and with it
reality, might be assigned exclusively either to the idea of
body or to that of space. To whichever of the two it is
assigned, the other must become a nominal essence. If it
is the idea of body that is conveyed to the mind directly
from without through sensation, then it must be by a process in the mind that the spatial relations are abstracted
from it; and conversely, if it is the latter that are given in
sensation, it must be by a mental operation of compounding
that the idea of body is obtained from them. Now, according to Locke's fundamental notion, that the reality of an
idea depends upon its being in consciousness a copy *through
impact* of that which is not in consciousness, any attempt to
retain it in the idea of space while sacrificing it in that of
body would be obviously self-destructive. Nor, however we
might re-write his account of the relations of space as 'found
in bodies,' could we avoid speaking of them as relations of
some sort; and if relations, then derived from the 'mind's
carrying its view from one thing to another,' and not
'actually present sensations.' We shall not, then, be surprised to find Locke tending to the other alternative, and
gradually forgetting his assertion that 'a circle or a square
are the same whether in idea or in existence,' and his
elaborate maintenance of the 'real existence' of a vacuum,
i.e., extension without body. (Book II. chap. xiii. secs. 21
and the following, and xvii. 4.) In the Fourth Book it is
body alone that has real existence, an existence revealed
by actually present sensation, while all mathematical ideas,
the ideas of the circle and the square, have 'barely an ideal
existence' (Book IV. chap. iv. sec. 6); and this means nothing
else than the reduction of the primary qualities of body to a
nominal essence. Our ideas of them are general (Book IV.
chap. iii. sec. 24), or merely in the mind. 'There is no individual parcel of matter, to which any of these qualities
are so annexed as to be essential to it or inseparable from it.'
(Book III. chap. vi. sec. 6.) How should there be, when the
'individual parcel' means that which copies itself by impact
in the present sensation, while the qualities in question are
relations which cannot be so copied? Yet, except as attaching to such a parcel, they have no 'real existence;' and,

conversely, the 'body,' from which they *are* inseparable, not
being an individual parcel of matter in the above sense,
must itself be unreal and belong merely to the mind. The
'body' which is real has for us no qualities, and that reference
to it of the 'actually present sensation' by which such sensation is distinguished from other feeling, is a reference to
something of which nothing can be said. It is a reference
which cannot be stated in any proposition *really* true; and
the difference which it constitutes between 'bare vision' and
the feeling to which reality corresponds, must be either
itself unreal or unintelligible.

113. We have now pursued the antithesis between reality
and the work of the mind along all the lines which Locke
indicates, and find that it everywhere eludes us. The distinction, which only appeared incidentally in the doctrine of
substance, between 'the being and the idea thereof'—between substance as 'found' and substance as that which
'we accustom ourselves to suppose'—becomes definite and
explicit as that between real and nominal essence, but it
does so only that the essence, which is merely real, may disappear. Whether we suppose it the quality of a mere
sensation, as such, or of mere body, as such, we find that
we are unawares defining it by relations which are themselves the work of the mind, and that after abstraction of
these nothing remains to give the antithesis to the work of
the mind any meaning. Meanwhile the attitude of thought,
when it has cleared the antithesis of disguise, but has not
yet found that each of the opposites derives itself from
thought as much as the other, is so awkward and painful
that an instinctive reluctance to make the clearance is not
to be wondered at. Over against the world of knowledge,
which is the work of the mind, stands a real world of which
we can say nothing but that it is there, that it makes us
aware of its presence in every sensation, while our interpretation of what it is, the system of relations which we
read into it, is our own invention. The interpretation is not
even to be called a shadow, for a shadow, however dim, still
reflects the reality; it is an arbitrary fiction, and a fiction
of which the possibility is as unaccountable as the induce-
ment to make it. It is commonly presented as consisting in
abstraction from the concrete. But the concrete, just so far
as concrete, i.e., a complex world of relations, cannot be the

real if the separation of the real from the work of the mind
is to be maintained. It must itself be the work of the compounding mind, which must be supposed again in 'abstraction' to decompose what it has previously compounded.
Now, it is of the essence of the doctrine in question that it
denies all power of origination to the mind except in the way
of compounding and abstracting given impressions. Its
supposition is, that whatever precedes the work of composition and abstraction must be real[1] because the mind
passively receives it : a supposition which, if the mind could
originate, would not hold. How, then, does it come to pass
that a 'nominal essence,' consisting of definite qualities, is
constructed by a mind, which originates nothing, out of a
'real' matter, which, apart from such construction, has no
qualities at all ? And why, granted the construction, should
the mind in 'abstraction' go through the Penelopean exercise of perpetually unweaving the web which it has just
woven ?

114. It is Hume's more logical version of Locke's doctrine
that first forces these questions to the front. In Locke himself they are kept back by inconsistencies, which we have
already dwelt upon. For the real, absolutely void of intelligible qualities, because these are relative to the mind,
he is perpetually substituting a real constituted by such
qualities, only with a complexity which we cannot exhaust.
By so doing, though at the cost of sacrificing the opposition
between the real and the mental, he avoids the necessity of
admitting that the system of the sciences is a mere language,
well—or ill—constructed, but unaccountably and without
reference to things. Finally, he so far forgets the opposition
altogether as to find the reality of 'moral and mathematical'
knowledge in their 'bare ideality' itself. (Book IV. chap. iv.
sec. 6, &c.) Thus with him the divorce between knowledge
and reality is never complete, and sometimes they appear in
perfect fusion. A consideration of his doctrine of propositions will show finally how the case between them stands,
as he left it.

115. In the Fourth Book of the Essay the same ground
has to be thrice traversed under the several titles of 'knowledge,' 'truth,' and 'propositions.' Knowledge being the

---

[1] 'Simple ideas, since the mind can
by no means make them to itself, must
necessarily be the product of things
operating on the mind.' (Book IV.
chap. v. sec. 4.)

perception of agreement or disagreement between ideas, the
proposition is the putting together or separation of words,
as the signs of ideas, in affirmative or negative sentences
(Book IV. chap. v. sec. 5), and truth—the expression of
certainty [1]—consists in the correspondence between the conjunction or separation of the signs and the agreement or
disagreement of the ideas. (Book IV. chap. v. sec. 2.) Thus,
the question between the real and the mental affects all
these. Does this or that perception of agreement between
ideas represent an agreement in real existence ? Is its certainty a real certainty ? Does such or such a proposition,
being a correct expression of an agreement between ideas,
also through this express an agreement between things ? Is
its truth real, or merely verbal ?

116. To answer these questions, according to Locke, we
must consider whether the knowledge, or the proposition
which expresses it, concerns substances, i.e., 'the co-existence
of ideas in nature,' on the one hand ; or, on the other, either
the properties of a mathematical figure or 'moral ideas.' If
it is of the latter sort, the agreement of the ideas in the
mind is itself their agreement in reality, since the ideas
themselves are archetypes. (Book IV. chap. iv. secs. 6, 7.)
It is only when the ideas are ectypes, as is the case when the
proposition concerns substances, that the doubt arises
whether the agreement between them represents an agreement in reality. The distinction made here virtually corresponds to that which appears in the chapters on the reality
and adequacy of ideas in the Second Book, and again in
those on 'names' in the Third. There the 'complex ideas
of modes and relation' are pronounced necessarily real
adequate and true, because, 'being themselves archetypes,
they cannot differ from their archetypes.' (Book II. chap.
xxx. sec. 4.) [2] With them are contrasted simple ideas and
complex ideas of substances, which are alike ectypes, but

All knowledge is certain according
to Locke (Cf. IV. chap. vi. sec. 13,
'certainty is requisite to knowledge'),
though the knowledge must be expressed before the term 'certainty' is
naturally applied to it. (Book IV.
chap. vi. sec. 3.) 'Certainty of knowledge' is thus a pleonastic phrase, which
only seems not to be so because we conceive knowledge to have a relation to
things which Locke's definition denies

it, and by 'certainty,' in distinction
from this, understand its relation to the
subject.

'Certainty of truth' is, in like manner, a pleonastic phrase, there being no
difference between the definition of it
(Book IV. chap. vi. sec. 3) and that of
'truth' simply, given in Book IV.
chap. v. sec. 2.

[2] Cf. Book II. chap. xxxi. sec. 3, and
xxxii. sec. 17.

with this difference from each other, that the simple ideas cannot but be faithful copies of their archetypes, while the ideas of substances cannot but be otherwise. (Book II. chap. xxxi. secs. 2, 11, &c.) Thus, 'the names of simple ideas and substances, with the abstract ideas in the mind which they immediately signify, intimate also some real existence, from which was derived their original pattern. But the names of mixed modes terminate in the idea that is in the mind.' (Book III. chap. iv. sec. 2.)   'The names of simple ideas and modes,' it is added, 'signify always the real as well as nominal essence of their species'—a statement which, if it is to express Locke's doctrine strictly, must be confined to names of simple ideas, while in respect of modes it should run, that 'the nominal essence which the names of these signify is itself the real.'

117. But though the distinction between different kinds of knowledge in regard to reality cannot but rest on the same principle as that drawn between different kinds of ideas in the same regard, it is to be noticed that in the doctrine of the Fourth Book 'knowledge concerning substances,' in contrast with that in which ' our thoughts terminate in the abstract ideas,' has by itself to cover the ground which, in the Second and Third Book, simple ideas and complex ideas of substances cover together. This is to be explained by the observation, already set forth at large,[1] that the simple idea has in Locke's Fourth Book become explicitly what in the previous books it was implicitly, not a feeling proper, but the conscious reference of a feeling to a thing or substance. Only because it is thus converted, as we have seen, can it constitute the beginning of a knowledge which is not a simple idea but a conscious relation between ideas, or have (what yet it must have if it can be expressed in a proposition) that capacity of being true or false, which implies 'the reference by the mind of an idea to something extraneous to it.' (Book II. chap. xxxii. sec. 4.) Thus, what is said of the 'simple idea' in the Second and Third Books, is in the Fourth transferred to one form of knowledge concerning substances, to that, namely, which consists in 'particular experiment and observation,' and is expressed in singular propositions, such as ' this is yellow,' ' this gold is now solved in aqua regia.' Such knowledge cannot but be real, the

[1] See above, paragraph 25.

proposition which expresses it cannot but have *real* certainty, because it is the effect of a 'body actually operating upon us' (Book IV. chap. xi. sec. 1), just as the simple idea is an ectype directly made by an archetype. It is otherwise with complex ideas of substances and with general knowledge or propositions about them. A group of ideas, each of which, when first produced by a 'body,' has been real, when retained in the mind as representing the body, becomes unreal. The complex idea of gold is only a nominal essence or the signification of a name ; the qualities which compose it are merely ideas in the mind, and that general truth which consists in a correct statement of the relation between one of them and another or the whole—e.g., ' gold is soluble in aqua regia '— holds merely for the mind ;[1] but it is not therefore to be classed with those other mental truths, which constitute mathematical and moral knowledge, and which, just because ' merely ideal,' are therefore real. Its merely mental character renders it in Locke's language a ' trifling proposition,' but does not therefore save it from being *really* untrue. It is a ' trifling proposition,' for, unless solubility in aqua regia is included in the complex idea which the sound ' gold' stands for, the proposition which asserts it of gold is not certain, not a truth at all. If it is so included, then the proposition is but ' playing with sounds.' It may serve to remind an opponent of a definition which he has made but is forgetting, but ' carries no knowledge with it but of the signification of a word, however certain it be.' (Book IV. chap. viii. secs. 5 & 9.) Yet there is a real gold, outside the mind, of which the complex idea of gold in the mind must needs try to be a copy, though the conditions of real existence are such that no ' complex idea in the mind ' can possibly be a copy of it. Thus the verbal truth, which general propositions concerning substances express, is under a perpetual doom of being really untrue. The exemption of mathematical and moral knowledge from this doom remains an unexplained mercy. Because merely mental, such knowledge is real—there being no reality for it to *mis*represent— and yet not trifling. The proposition that ' the external angle of all triangles is bigger than either of the opposite internal angles,' has that general certainty which is never to be found but in our ideas, yet ' conveys instructive real

---

[1] Book IV. chap. xi. sec. 13, xii, 9, &c.

knowledge,' the predicate being 'a necessary consequence of
the precise complex idea' which forms the subject, yet 'not
contained in it.' (Book IV. chap. viii. sec. 8.) [1] The same
might be said apparently, according to Locke's judgment
(though he is not so explicit about this), of a proposition in
morals, such as ' God is to be feared and obeyed by man.'
(Book IV. chap. xi. sec. 13.) [2] But how are such propositions,
at once abstract and real, general and instructive, to be
accounted for? There is no ' workmanship of the mind' recognised by Locke but that which consists in compounding
and abstracting (i.e., separating) ideas of which 'it cannot
originate one.' The ' abstract ideas' of mathematics, the
' mixed modes' of morals, just as much as the ideas of substances, must be derived by such mental artifice from a
material given in simple feeling, and ' real' because so given.
Yet, while this derivation renders ideas of substances unreal
in contrast with their real ' originals,' and general propositions about them ' trifling,' because, while 'intimating an
existence,' they tell nothing about it, on the other hand it
actually constitutes the reality of moral and mathematical
ideas. Their relation to an original disappears ; they are
themselves archetypes, from which the mind, by its own act,
can elicit other ideas not already involved in the meaning of
their names. But this can only mean that the mind has
some other function than that of uniting what it has 'found'
in separation, and separating again what it has thus united
—that it can itself originate.

118. A genius of such native force as Locke's could not
be applied to philosophy without determining the lines of
future speculation, even though to itself they remained obscure. He stumbles upon truths when he is not looking for
them, and the inconsistencies or accidents of his system are
its most valuable part. Thus, in a certain sense, he may
claim the authorship at once of the popular empiricism of
the modern world, and of its refutation. He fixed the prime
article of its creed, that thought has nothing to do with the
constitution of facts, but only with the representation of
them by signs and the rehearsal to itself of what its signs
have signified—in brief, that its function is merely the
analytical judgment ; yet his admissions about mathematical

[1] Just as according to Kant such a
proposition expresses a judgment ' synthetical,' yet ' à-priori.'

[2] Cf. Book IV. chap. iii. sec. 18, and
Book III. chap. xi. sec. 16.

knowledge rendered inevitable the Kantian question, 'How are synthetic judgments à-priori possible?'—which was to lead to the recognition of thought as constituting the objective world, and thus to get rid of the antithesis between thought and reality. In his separation of the datum of experience from the work of thought he was merely following the Syllogistic Logic, which really assigns no work to the thought, whose office it professes to magnify, but the analysis of given ideas. Taking the work as that Logic conceived it (and as it must be conceived if the separation is to be maintained) he showed—conclusively as against Scholasticism—the 'trifling' character of the necessary and universal truths with which it dealt. Experience, the manifestation of the real, regarded as a series of events which to us are sensations, can only yield propositions singular as the events, and having a truth like them contingent. By consequence, necessity and universality of connection can only be found in what the mind does for itself, without reference to reality, when it analyses the complex idea which it retains as the memorandum of its past single experiences; i.e., in a relation between ideas or propositions of which one explicitly includes the other. Upon this relation syllogistic reasoning rests, and, except so far as it may be of use for convicting an opponent (or oneself) of inconsistency, it has nothing to say against such nominalism as the above. Hence, with those followers of Locke who have been most faithful to their master, it has remained the standing rule to make the generality of a truth consist in its being analytical of the meaning of a name, and its necessity in its being included in one previously conceded. Yet if such were the true account of the generality and necessity of mathematical propositions, their truth according to Locke's explicit statement would be 'verbal and trifling,' not, as it is, 'real and instructive.'

119. The point of this, the most obvious, contradiction inherent in Locke's empiricism, is more or less striking according to the fidelity with which the notion of matter-of-fact, or of the reality that is not of the mind, proper to that system, is adhered to. When the popular Logic derived from Locke has so far forgotten the pit whence it was digged as to hold that propositions of a certainty at once real and general can be derived from experience, and to speak without question of 'general matters-of-fact' in a sense which to Locke

almost, to Hume altogether, would have been a contradiction
in terms, it naturally finds no disturbance in regarding
mathematical certainty as different not in kind, but only in
degree, from that of any other 'generalisation from experience.' Not aware that the distinction of mathematical from
empirical generality is the condition upon which, according to
Locke, the former escapes condemnation as 'trifling,' it does
not see any need for distinguishing the sources from which
the two are derived, and hence goes on asserting against
imaginary or insignificant opponents that mathematical
truth is derived from 'experience;' which, if 'experience'
be so changed from what Locke understood by it as to yield
general propositions concerning matters-of-fact of other than
analytical purport, no one need care to deny. That it can
yield such propositions is, doubtless, the supposition of the
physical sciences; nor, we must repeat, is it the *correctness*
of this supposition that is in question, but the validity, upon
its admission, of that antithesis between experience and the
work of thought, which is the 'be-all and end-all' of the
popular Logic.

120. Locke, as we have seen, after all the encroachments
made unawares by thought within the limits of that experience which he opposes to it—or, to put it conversely,
after all that he allows 'nature' to take without acknowledgment from 'mind'—is still so far faithful to the opposition as to 'suspect a science of nature to be impossible.'
This suspicion, which is but a hesitating expression of the
doctrine that general propositions concerning substances are
merely verbal, is the exact counterpart of the doctrine pronounced without hesitation that mathematical truths, being
at once real and general, do not concern nature at all. Real
knowledge concerning nature being given by single impressions of bodies at single times operating upon us, and by
consequence being expressible only in singular propositions,
any reality which general propositions state must belong
merely to the mind, and a mind which can originate a reality
other than nature's cannot be a passive receptacle of natural
impressions. Locke admits the real generality of mathematical truths, but does not face its consequences. Hume,
seeing the difficulty, will not admit the real generality. The
modern Logic, founded on Locke, believing in the possibility
of propositions at once real and general concerning nature,

does not see the difficulty at all. It reckons mathematical to be the same in kind with natural knowledge, each alike being real notwithstanding its generality; not aware that by so doing, instead of getting rid, as it fancies, of the originative function of thought in respect of mathematical knowledge, it only necessitates the supposition of its being originative in respect of the knowledge of nature as well.

121. It may find some excuse for itself in the hesitation with which Locke pronounces the impossibility of real generality in the knowledge of nature—an hesitation which necessarily results from the ambiguities, already noticed, in his doctrine of real and nominal essence. So far as the opposition between the nominal and real essences of substances is maintained in its absoluteness, as that between every possible collection of ideas on the one side, and something wholly apart from thought on the other, this impossibility follows of necessity. But so far as the notion is admitted of the nominal essence being in some way, however inadequately, representative of the real, there is an opening, however indefinite, for general propositions concerning the latter. On the one hand we have the express statement that ' universal propositions, of whose truth and falsehood we can have certain knowledge, concern not existence' (Book IV. chap. ix. sec. 1). They are founded only on the 'relations and habitudes of abstract ideas' (Book IV. chap xii. sec. 7); and since it is the proper operation of the mind in abstraction to consider an idea under no other existence but what it has in the understanding, they represent no knowledge of *real* existence at all (Book IV. chap. ix. sec. 1). Here Locke is consistently following his doctrine that the ' particularity in time,' of which abstraction is made when we consider ideas as in the understanding, is what specially distinguishes the real; which thus can only be represented by ' actually present sensation.' It properly results from this doctrine that the proposition representing particular experiment and observation is only true of real existence so long as the sensation, in which the experiment consists, continues present. Not only is the possibility excluded of such experiment yielding a certainty which shall be general as well as real, but the particular proposition itself can only be *really* true so far as the qualities, whose co-existence it asserts, are present sensations. The for-

mer of these limitations to real truth we find Locke generally
recognising, and consequently suspecting a science of nature
to be impossible; but the latter, which would be fatal to the
supposition of there being a real nature at all, even when he
carries furthest the reduction of reality to present feeling, he
virtually ignores. On the other hand, there keeps appearing
the notion that, inasmuch as the combination of ideas which
make up the nominal essence of a substance is taken from a
combination in nature or reality, whenever the connexion
between any of these is necessary, it warrants a proposition
universally true in virtue of the necessary connexion between
the ideas, and *really* true in virtue of the ideas being taken
from reality. According to this notion, though 'the certainty
of universal propositions concerning substances is very narrow
and scanty,' it is yet possible (Book IV. chap. vi. sec. 13). It
is not recognised as involving that contradiction which it must
involve if the antithesis between reality and ideas in the mind
is absolutely adhered to. Nay, inasmuch as certain ideas of
primary qualities, *e.g.* those of solidity and of the receiving or
communicating motion upon impulse, are necessarily connected,
it is supposed actually to exist (Book IV. chap iii. sec. 14). It is
only because, as a matter of fact, our knowledge of the relation
between secondary qualities and primary is so limited that it
cannot be carried further. That they are related as effects and
causes, it would seem, we know; and that the 'causes work
steadily, and effects constantly flow from them,' we know also;
but 'their connexions and dependencies are not discoverable
in our ideas' (Book IV. chap. iii. sec. 29). That, if discoverable
in our ideas, just because there discovered, the connexion
would not be a real co-existence, Locke never expressly says.
He does not so clearly articulate the antithesis between relations of ideas and matters of fact. If he had done so, he must
also have excluded from real existence those abstract ideas of
body which constitute the scanty knowledge of it that according to him we do possess (Book IV. chap. iii. sec. 24). He is
more disposed to sigh for discoveries that would make physics
capable of the same general certainty as mathematics, than
to purge the former of those mathematical propositions—
really true only because having no reference to reality—which
to him formed the only scientific element in them.

122. The ambiguity of his position will become clearer if
we resort to his favourite 'instances in gold.' The proposi-

tion, 'all gold is soluble in aqua regia,' is certainly true, if such solubility is included in the complex idea which the word 'gold' stands for, and if such inclusion is all that the proposition purports to state.   It is equally certain and equally trifling with the proposition, 'a centaur is four-footed.' But, in fact, as a proposition concerning substance, it purports to state more than this, viz. that a 'body whose complex idea is made up of yellow, very weighty, ductile, fusible, and fixed,' is always soluble in aqua regia.   In other words, it states the invariable co-existence in a body of the complex idea, 'solubility in aqua regia,' with the group of ideas indicated by 'gold.'   Thus understood—as instructive or synthetical—it has not the certainty which would belong to it if it were 'trifling,' or analytical, 'since we can never, from the consideration of the ideas themselves, with certainty affirm' their co-existence (Book IV. chap. vi. sec 9).   If we see the solution actually going on, or can recall the sight of it by memory, we can affirm its co-existence with the ideas in question in that 'bare instance;' and thus, on the principle that 'whatever ideas have once been united in nature may be so united again' (Book IV. chap. iv. sec. 12), infer a capacity of co-existence between the ideas, but that is all.   'Constant observation may assist our judgments in guessing' an invariable actual co-existence (Book IV. chap. viii. sec. 9); but beyond guessing we cannot get.   If our instructive proposition concerning co-existence is to be general it must remain problematical.   It is otherwise with mathematical propositions.   'If the three angles of a triangle were once equal to two right angles, it is certain that they always will be so;' but only because such a proposition concerns merely 'the habitudes and relations of ideas.'   'If the perception that the same ideas will eternally have the same habitudes and relations be not a sufficient ground of knowledge, there could be no knowledge of general propositions in mathematics; for no mathematical demonstration could be other than particular: and when a man had demonstrated any proposition concerning one triangle and circle, his knowledge would not reach beyond that particular diagram' (Book IV. chap. i. sec. 9).

123. To a reader, fresh from our popular treatises on Logic, such language would probably at first present no difficulty. He would merely lament that Locke, as a successor of Bacon,

was not better acquainted with the 'Inductive methods,' and
thus did not understand how an observation of co-existence
in the bare instance, if the instance be of the right sort, may
warrant a universal affirmation. Or he may take the other
side, and regard Locke's restriction upon general certainty as
conveying, not any doubt as to the validity of the inference
from an observed case to all cases where the conditions are
ascertainably the same, but a true sense of the difficulty of
ascertaining in any other case that the conditions are the
same. On looking closer, however, he will see that, so far
from Locke's doctrine legitimately allowing of such an adaptation to the exigencies of science, it is inconsistent with
itself in admitting the reality of most of the conditions in the
case supposed to be observed, and thus in allowing the real
truth even of the singular proposition. This purports to
state, according to Locke's terminology, that certain 'ideas'
do now or did once co-exist in a body. But the ideas, thus
stated to co-exist, according to Locke's doctrine that real
existence is only testified to by actual present sensation, differ
from each other as that which *really* exists from that which
does not. In the particular experiment of gold being solved
in aqua regia, from the complex idea of solubility an indefinite deduction would have to be made for qualification by
ideas retained in the understanding before we could reach
the present sensation ; and not only so, but the group of
ideas indicated by 'gold,' to whose co-existence with solubility the experiment is said to testify, as Locke himself says,
form merely a nominal essence, while the body to which we
ascribe this essence is something which we 'accustom ourselves to suppose,' not any 'parcel of matter' having a real
existence in nature.[1] In asserting the co-existence of the
ideas forming such a nominal essence with the actual sensation supposed to be given in the experiment, we change the
meaning of 'existence,' between the beginning and end of
the assertion, from that according to which all ideas exist to
that according to which existence has no 'connexion with any
other of our ideas but those of ourselves and God,' but is testified to by present sensation.[2] This paralogism escapes Locke
just as his equivocal use of the term 'idea' escapes him. The
distinction, fixed in Hume's terminology as that between im-

[1] See above, paragraphs 35, 94, &c.
[2] See above, paragraph 30 and the following.

pression and idea, forces itself upon him, as we have seen, in the Fourth book of the Essay, where the whole doctrine of real existence turns upon it, but alongside of it survives the notion that ideas, though 'in the mind' and forming a nominal essence, are yet, if rightly taken from things, ectypes of reality. Thus he does not see that the co-existence of ideas, to which the particular experiment, as he describes it, testifies, is nothing else than the co-existence of an event with a conception—of that which is in a particular time, and (according to him) only for that reason real, with that which is not in time at all but is an unreal abstraction of the mind's making.[1] The reality given in the actual sensation cannot, as a matter of fact, be discovered to have a necessary connexion with the ideas that form the nominal essence, and therefore cannot be asserted universally to co-exist with them; but with better faculties, he thinks, the discovery might be made (BOOK IV. chap. iii. sec. 16). It does not to him imply such a contradiction as it must have done if he had steadily kept in view his doctrine that of particular (*i.e.* real) existence our 'knowledge' is not properly knowledge at all, but simply sensation—such a contradiction as was to Hume involved in the notion of deducing a matter of fact.

124. It results that those followers of Locke, who hold the distinction between propositions of mathematical certainty and those concerning real existence to be one rather of degree than of kind, though they have the express words of their master against them, can find much in his way of thinking on their side. This, however, does not mean that he in any case drops the antithesis between matters of fact and relations of ideas in favour of matters of fact, so as to admit that mathematical propositions concern matters of fact, but that he sometimes drops it in favour of relations of ideas, so as to represent real existence as consisting in such relations. If the matter of fact, or real existence, is to be found only in the event constituted or reported by present feeling, such a relation of ideas, by no manner of means reducible to an event, as the mathematical proposition states, can have no sort of connection with it. But if real existence is such that the relations of ideas, called primary qualities of matter, constitute it, and the qualities included in our nominal essences are

---

[1] See above, paragraphs 45, 80, 85, 97.

its copies or effects, then, as on the one side our complex
ideas of substances only fail of reality through want of fulness, or through mistakes in the process by which they are
'taken from things,' so, on the other side, the mental truth
of mathematical propositions need only fail to be real because
the ideas, whose relations they state, are considered in abstraction from conditions which qualify them in real existence.   'If it is true of the idea of a triangle that its three
angles equal two right ones, it is true also of a triangle,
wherever it really exists " (BOOK IV. chap. iv. sec. 6). There
is, then, no incompatibility between the idea and real existence.   Mathematical ideas might fairly be reckoned, like
those of substances, to be taken from real existence; but
though, like these, inadequate to its complexity, to be saved
from the necessary infirmities which attach to ideas of substances because not considered as so taken, but merely as in
the mind.   There is language about mathematics in Locke
that may be interpreted in this direction, though his most
explicit statements are on the other side.   It is not our
business to adjust them, but merely to point out the opposite tendencies between which a clear-sighted operator
on the material given by Locke would find that he had to
choose.

125. On the one hand there is the identification of real
existence with the momentary sensible event. This view, of
which the proper result is the exclusion of predication concerning real existence altogether, appears in Locke's restriction of such predication to the singular proposition, and in
his converse assertion that propositions of mathematical certainty ' concern not existence' (BOOK IV. chap.iv.sec. 8). The
embarrassment resulting from such a doctrine is that it leads
round to the admission of the originativeness of thought and
of the reality of its originations, with the denial of which it
starts.[1] It leads Locke himself along a track, which his later
followers scarcely seem to have noticed, when he treats the
'never enough to be admired discoveries of Mr. Newton' as
having to do merely with the relations of ideas in distinction
from things, and looks for a true extension of knowledge—
neither in syllogism which can yield no instructive, nor in
experiment which can yield no general, certainty—but only
in a further process of ' singling out and laying in order in-

---

[1] See above, paragraph 117, sub. fin.

termediate ideas,' which are 'real as well as nominal essences of their species,' because they have no reference to archetypes elsewhere than in the mind (BOOK IV. chap. vii. sec. 11, and BOOK IV. chap. xii. sec. 7). On the other hand there is the notion that ideas, without distinction between 'actual sensation' and 'idea in the mind,' are taken from permanent things, and are real if correctly so taken. From this it results that propositions, universally true as representing a necessary relation between ideas of primary qualities, are true also of real existence; and that an extension of such real certainty through the discovery of a necessary connexion between ideas of primary and those of secondary qualities, though scarcely to be hoped for, has no inherent impossibility. It is this notion, again, that unwittingly gives even that limited significance to the particular experiment which Locke assigns to it, as indicating a co-existence between ideas present as sensations and those which can only be regarded as in the mind. Nor is it the intrinsic import so much as the expression of this notion that is altered when Locke substitutes an order of nature for substance as that in which the ideas co-exist. In his Fourth Book he so far departs from the doctrine implied in his chapters on the reality and adequacy of ideas and on the names of substances, as to treat the notion of several single subjects in which ideas co-exist (which he still holds to be the proper notion of substances), as a fiction of thought. There are no such single subjects. What we deem so are really 'retainers to other parts of nature.' 'Their observable qualities, actions, and powers are owing to something without them; and there is not so complete and perfect a part that we know of nature, which does not owe the being it has, and the excellencies of it, to its neighbours' (BOOK IV. chap. vi. sec. 11). As thus conceived of, the 'objective order' which our experience represents is doubtless other than that collection of fixed separate 'things,' implied in the language about substances which Locke found in vogue, but it remains an objective order still—an order of 'qualities, actions, and powers' which no multitude of sensible events could constitute, but apart from which no sensible event could have such significance as to render even a singular proposition of real truth possible.

126. It remains to inquire how, with Locke, the ideas of self and God escape subjection to those solvents of reality

which, with more or less of consistency and consciousness, he applied to the conceptions on which the science of nature rests. Such an enquiry forms the natural transition to the next stage in the history of his philosophy. It was Berkeley's practical interest in these ideas that held him back from a development of his master's principles, in which he would have anticipated Hume, and finally brought him to attach that other meaning to the 'new way of ideas' faintly adumbrated in the later sections of his 'Siris,' which gives to Reason the functions that Locke had assigned to Sense.

127. The dominant notion of the self in Locke is that of the inward substance, or 'substratum of ideas,' co-ordinate with the outward, 'wherein they do subsist, and from which they do result.' 'Sensation convinces that there are solid extended substances, and reflection that there are thinking ones' (BOOK II. chap. xxiii. sec. 29). We have already seen how, without disturbance from his doctrine of the fictitiousness of universals, he treats the simple idea as carrying with it the distinction of outward and inward, or relations severally to a 'thing' and to a 'mind.' It reports itself ambiguously as a quality of each of these separate substances. It is now, or was to begin with, the result of an outward thing 'actually operating upon us;' for 'of simple ideas the mind cannot make one to itself:' on the other hand, it is a 'perception,' and perception is an 'operation of the mind.' In other words it is at once a modification of the mind by something of which it is consciously not conscious, and a modification of the mind by itself—the two sources of one and the same modification being each determined only as the contradictory of the other. Thus, when we come to probe the familiar metaphors under which Locke describes Reflection, as a 'fountain of ideas' other than sensation, we find that the confusions which we have already explored in dealing with the ideas of sensation recur under added circumstances of embarrassment. Not only does the simple idea of reflection, like that of sensation, turn out to be already complicated in its simplicity with the superinduced ideas of cause and relation, but the causal substance in question turns out to be one which, from being actually nothing, becomes something by acting upon itself; while all the time the result of this action is indistinguishable from that ascribed to the opposite, the external, cause.

128. To a reader to whom Locke's language has always seemed to be—as indeed it is—simply that of common sense and life, in writing the above we shall seem to be creating a difficulty where none is to be found. Let us turn, then, to one of the less prolix passages, in which the distinction between the two sources of ideas is expressed: ' External objects furnish the mind with the ideas of sensible qualities, which are all those different perceptions they produce in us; and the mind furnishes the understanding with ideas of its own operations' (BOOK II. chap. i. sec. 5). We have seen already that with Locke perception and idea are equivalent terms. It only needs further to be pointed out that no distinction can be maintained between his usage of ' mind ' and of ' understanding,'[1] and that the simple ideas of the mind's own operations are those of perception and power, which must be given in and with every idea of a sensible quality.[2] Avoiding synonyms, then, and recalling the results of our examination of the terms involved in the first clause of the passage before us, we may re-write the whole thus: " Creations of the mind, which yet are external to it, produce in it those perceptions of their qualities which they do produce; and the mind produces in itself the perception of these, its own, perceptions.'

129. This attempt to present Locke's doctrine of the relation between the mind and the world, as it would be without phraseological disguises, must not be ascribed to any polemical interest in making a great writer seem to talk nonsense. The greatest writer must fall into confusions when he brings under the conceptions of cause and substance the self-conscious thought which is their source; and nothing else than this is involved in Locke's avowed enterprise of knowing that which renders knowledge possible as he might know any other object. The enterprise naturally falls into two parts, corresponding to that distinction of subject and object which self-consciousness involves. Hitherto we have been dealing with it on the objective side—with the attempt to know knowledge as a result of experience received through the senses—and have found the supposed source of thought already charged with its creations; with the relations of inner

---

[1] As becomes apparent on examination of such passages, as Book II. chap. i. sec. 1, sub. fin.; and Book II. chap. i. sec. 23.

[2] See above, paragraphs 11, 12, 13

and outer, of substance and attribute, of cause and effect, of appearance and reality. The supposed 'outward' turns out to have its outwardness constituted by thought, and thus to be inward. The 'outer sense' is only an outer sense at all so far as feelings, by themselves neither outward nor inward, are by the mind referred to a thing or cause which 'the mind supposes;' and only thus have its reports a prerogative of reality over the 'fantasies,' supposed merely of the mind. Meanwhile, unable to ignore the subjective side of self-consciousness, Locke has to put an inward experience as a separate, but co-ordinate, source of knowledge alongside of the outer. But this inward experience, simply as a succession of feelings, does not differ from the outer : it only so differs as referred to that very 'thinking thing,' called the mind, which by its supposition of causal substance has converted feeling into an experience of an outer thing. 'Mind' thus, by the relations which it 'invents,' constitutes both the inner and outer, and yet is treated as itself the inner 'substratum which it accustoms itself to suppose.' It thus becomes the creature of its own suppositions. Nor is this all. This, indeed, is no more than the fate which it must suffer at the hands of every philosopher who, in Kantian language, brings the source of the Categories under the Categories. But with Locke the constitution of the outer world by mental supposition, however uniformly implied, is always ignored; and thus mind, as the inward substance, is not only the creature of its own suppositions, but stands over against a real existence, of which the reality is held to consist just in its being the opposite of all such suppositions : while, after all, the effect of these mutually exclusive causes is one and the same experience, one and the same system of sequent and co-existent ideas.

130. Is it then a case of *joint*-effect ? Do the outer and inner substances combine, like mechanical forces, to produce the psychical result ? Against such a supposition a follower of Locke would find not only the language of his master, with whom perception appears *indifferently* as the result of the outer or inner cause, but the inherent impossibility of analysing the effect into separate elements. The 'Law of Parcimony,' then, will dictate to him that one or other of the causes must be dispensed with ; nor, so long as he takes Locke's identification of the outward with the real for

granted, will he have much doubt as to which of the two must go. To get rid of the causality of mind, however, though it might not be untrue to the tendency of Locke, would be to lose sight of his essential merit as a formulator of what everyone thinks, which is that, at whatever cost of confusion or contradiction, he at least formulates it fully. In him the ' Dialectic,' which popular belief implicitly involves, goes on under our eyes. If the primacy of self-conscious thought is never recognized, if it remains the victim of its own misunderstood creations, there is at least no attempt to disguise the unrest which attaches to it in this self-imposed subjection.

131. We have already noticed how the inner ' tablet,' on which the outer thing is supposed to act, is with Locke perpetually receding.[1] It is first the brain, to which the ' motion of the outward parts ' must be continued in order to constitute sensation (Book II. chap. ix. sec. 3). Then perception is distinguished from sensation, and the brain itself, as the subject of sensation, becomes the outward in contrast with the understanding as the subject of perception.[2] Then perception, from being simply a reception, is converted into an ' operation,' and thus into an efficient of ideas. The ' understanding' itself, as perceptive, is now the outward which makes on the ' mind,' as the inner ' tablet,' that impression of its own operation in perception which is called an idea of reflection.[3] Nor does the regressive process—the process of finding a mind within the mind—stop here, though the distinction of inner and outer is not any further so explicitly employed in it. From mind, as receptive of, and operative about, ideas, *i. e.* consciousness, is distinguished mind as the ' substance within us ' of which consciousness is an ' operation' that it sometimes exercises, sometimes (*e. g.* when it sleeps) does not (Book II. chap. i. secs. 10–12) ; and from this thinking substance again is distinguished the man who ' finds it in himself' and carries it about with him in a coach or on horseback (Book II. chap. xxiii. sec. 20)—the person, ' consisting of soul and body,' who is prone to sleep and in sound sleep is unconscious, but whose personal identity

---

[1] See above, paragraph 14.

[2] Book II., chap. i. sec. 23. 'Sensation is such an impression made in some part of the body, as produces some perception in the understanding.'

[3] Locke speaks indifferently of the mind impressing the understanding, and of the understanding impressing the mind, with ideas of reflection, but as he specially defines ' understanding' as the ' perceptive power' (Book II. chap. 21, sec. 25.), I have written as above.

strangely consists in sameness of consciousness, sameness of
an occasional operation of part of himself.[1]

132. In the history of subsequent philosophy two typical
methods have appeared of dealing with this chaos of anti-
nomies. One, which we shall have to treat at large in
writing of Hume, affects to dispose of both the outward and the
inward synthesis—both of the unity of feelings in a subject
matter and of their unity in a subject mind—as 'fictions of
thought.' This method at once suggests the vital question whether a mind which thus invents has been effectively
suppressed—whether, indeed, the theory can be so much as
stated without a covert assumption of that which it claims
to have destroyed. The other method, of which Kant is the
parent, does not attempt to efface the apparent contradictions which beset the 'relation between mind and matter;'
but regarding them as in a certain sense inevitable, traces
them to their source in the application to the thinking Ego
itself of conceptions, which it does indeed constitute in virtue
of its presence to phenomena given under conditions of time,
but under which for that very reason it cannot itself be
known. It is in virtue of the presence of the self-conscious
unit to the manifold of feeling, according to this doctrine,
that the latter becomes an order of definite things, each external to the other; and it is only by a false inclusion within
this order of that which constitutes it that the Ego itself
becomes a 'thinking thing' with other things outside it. The
result of such inclusion is that the real world, which it in
the proper sense makes, becomes a reality external to it, yet
apart from which it would not be actually anything. Thus
with Locke, though the mind has a potential existence of its
own, it is experience of 'things without it' that 'furnishes' it
or makes it what it actually is. But the relation of such
outer things to the mind cannot be spoken of without contradiction. If supposed outward as bodies, they have to be
brought within consciousness as objects of sensation; if supposed outward as sensation, they have to be brought within
consciousness—to find a home in the understanding—as ideas
of sensation. Meanwhile the consideration returns that after

[1] Cf. II. chap. i. secs. 11 and 14, with
II. chap. xxvii. sec. 9. It is difficult
to see what ingenuity could reconcile the
doctrine stated in Book II. chap. xxvii.
sec. 9, that personal identity is identity
of consciousness, with the doctrine implied in Book II. chap. i. sec. 11, that
the waking Socrates is the same person
with Socrates asleep, i.e. (according to
Locke) not conscious at all.

all the ' thinking thing ' contributes something to that which it thinks about ; and, this once admitted, it is as impossible to limit its work on one side as that of the outer thing on the other. Each usurps the place of its opposite. Thus with Locke the understanding produces effects on itself, but the product is one and the same ' perception' otherwise treated as an effect of the outer world. One and the same self-consciousness, in short,[1] involving the correlation of subject and object, becomes the result of two separate ' things,' each exclusive of the other, into which the opposite poles of this relation have been converted—the extended thing or ' body ' on the one side, and the thinking thing or ' mind ' on the other.

133. To each of these supposed ' things ' thought transfers its own unity and self-containedness, and thereupon finds itself in new difficulties. These, so far as they concern the outward thing, have already been sufficiently noticed. We have seen how the single self-contained thing on the one hand attenuates itself to the bare atom, presented in a moment of time, which in its exclusiveness is actually nothing :[2] how, on the other, it spreads itself, as everything which for one moment we regard as independent turns out in the next to be a 'retainer' to something else, into a series that cannot be summed.[3] A like consequence follows when the individual man, conceiving of the thought, which is not mine but me, and which is no less the world without which I am not I, as a thinking thing within him, limited by the limitations of his animal nature, seeks in this thinking thing, exclusive of other things, that unity and self-containedness, which only belong to the universal ' I.' He finds that he ' thinks not always ;' that during a fourth part of his time he neither thinks nor perceives at all; and that even in his waking hours his consciousness consists of a succession of separate feelings, whose recurrence he cannot command.[4] Thought being thus broken and dependent, substantiality is not to be found in it. It is next sought in the ' thing ' of which thought is an occasional operation—a thing of which it may readily be admitted that its nature cannot be known,[5] since it has no nature, being merely that which remains of the thinking thing upon ab-

[1] For the equivalence of perception with self-consciousness in Locke, see above, paragraph 24, et infra.

[2] See above, paragraph 94 and the following.

[3] See above, paragraph 125.

[4] Locke, Essay ii. chap. i. sec. 10, etc.

[5] Book ii. chap. xxiii. sec. 29, etc.

straction of its sole determination. It is in principle nothing else than the supposed basis of sensible qualities remaining after these have been abstracted—the 'parcel of matter' which has no essence—with which accordingly Locke sometimes himself tends to identify it.[1] But meanwhile, behind this unknown substance, whether of spirit or of body, the self-consciousness, which has been treated as its occasional unessential operation, re-asserts itself as the self which claims both body and spirit, the immaterial no less than the material substance, as its own, and throughout whatever diversity in these maintains its own identity.

134. Just, then, as Locke's conception of outward reality grows under his hands into a conception of nature as a system of relations which breaks through the limitations of reality as constituted by mere *individua*, so it is with the self, as he conceived it. It is not a simple idea. It is not one of the train that is for ever passing, 'one going and another coming,' for it looks on this succession as that which it experiences, being itself the same throughout the successive differences (Book II. chap. vii. sec. 9, and chap. xxvii. sec. 9). As little can it be adjusted to any of the conditions of real 'things,' thinking or unthinking, which he ordinarily recognises. It has no 'particularity in space and time.' That which is past in 'reality' is to it present. It is 'in its nature indifferent to any parcel of matter.' It is the same with itself yesterday and to-day, here and there. That 'with which its consciousness can join itself is one self with it,' and it can so join itself with substances apart in space and remote in time (Book II. chap. xxvii. secs. 9, 13, 14, 17). For speaking of it as eternal, indeed, we could find no warrant in Locke. He does not so clearly distinguish it from the 'thinking thing' supposed to be within each man, that has 'had its determinate time and place of beginning to exist, relation to which determines its identity so long as it exists' (Book II. chap. xxvii. sec. 2). Hence he supposed an actual limit to the past which it could make present—a limit seemingly fixed for each man at the farthest by the date of his birth—though he talks vaguely of the possibility of its range being extended (Book II. chap. xxvii. sec. 16). In the discussion of personal identity, however, the distinction gradually forces itself upon him, and he at last expressly says (sec. 16), that if the same Socrates,

---

[1] See above, paragraph 106, near the end.

sleeping and waking, do not partake of the same consciousness (as according to Book II. chap. i. sec. 11 he certainly does not), 'Socrates sleeping and waking is not the same person;' whereas the 'thinking thing'—the substance of which consciousness is a power sometimes exercised, sometimes not—is the same in the sleeping as in the waking Socrates. This is a pregnant admission, but it brings nothing to the birth in Locke himself. The inference which it suggests to his reader, that a self which does not slumber or sleep is not one which is born or dies, does not seem to have occurred to him. Taking for his method the imaginary process of 'looking into his own breast,' instead of the analysis of knowledge and morality, he could not find the eternal self which knowledge and morality pre-suppose, but only the contradiction of a person whose consciousness is not the same for two moments together, and often ceases altogether, but who yet, in virtue of an identity of this very consciousness, is the same in childhood and in old age.

135. Here as elsewhere we have to be thankful that the contradiction had not been brought home so strongly to Locke as to make him seek the suppression of either of its alternatives. He was aware neither of the burden which his philosophy tended to put upon the self which 'can consider itself as itself in different times and places'—the burden of replacing the stable world, when 'the new way of ideas' should have resolved the outward thing into a succession of feelings —nor of the hopelessness of such a burden being borne by a 'perishing' consciousness, 'of which no two parts exist together, but follow each other in succession.'[1] When he 'looked into himself,' he found consciousness to consist in the succession of ideas, 'one coming and another going:' he also found that 'consciousness alone makes what we call self,' and that he was the same self at any different points in the succession. He noted the two 'facts of consciousness' at different stages of his enquiry, and was apparently not struck by their contradiction. He could describe them both, and whatever he could describe seemed to him to be explained.

[1] Cf. II. chap. xiv. sec. 32—'by observing what passes in our minds, how our ideas there in train constantly some vanish and others begin to appear, we come by the idea of succession; and by observing a distance in the parts of this succession, we get the idea of duration' —with chap. xv. sec. 12. 'Duration is the idea we have of perishing distance, of which no two parts exist together, but follow each other in succession.'

Hence they did not suggest to him any question either as to the nature of the observed object or as to the possibility of observing it, such as might have diverted philosophy from the method of self-observation. He left them side by side, and, far from disguising either, put alongside of them another fact—the presence among the perpetually perishing ideas of that of a consciousness identical with itself, not merely in different times and places, but in all times and places. Such an idea, under the designation of an eternal wise Being, he was 'sure he had' (Book II. chap. xvii. sec. 14).

136. The remark will at once occur that the question concerning the relation between our consciousness, as in succession, and the idea of God, is essentially different from that concerning the relation between this consciousness and the self identical throughout it, inasmuch as the relation in the one case is between a fact and an idea, in the other between conflicting facts. The identity of the self, which Locke asserts, is one of ' real being,' and this is found to lie in consciousness, in apparent conflict with the fact that consciousness is a succession, of which 'no two parts exist together.' There is no such conflict, it will be said, between the *idea* of a conscious being, who is the same yesterday, to-day, and for ever—the correspondence to which of any reality is a farther question—and the *fact* of our consciousness being in succession. Allowing for the moment the validity of this distinction, we will consider first the difficulties that attach to Locke's account of the idea of God, as an idea.

137. This idea, with him, is a ' complex idea of substance.' It is the idea each man has of the 'thinking thing within him, enlarged to infinity.' It is beset then in the first place with all the difficulties which we have found to belong to his doctrine of substance generally and of the thinking substance in particular.[1] These need not be recalled in detail. When God is the thinking substance they become more obvious. It is the antithesis to ' material substance,' as the source of ideas of sensation, that alone with Locke gives a meaning to 'thinking substance,' as the source of ideas of reflection : and if, as we have seen, the antithesis is untenable when it is merely the source of human ideas that is in question, much more must it be so in regard to God, to whom any opposition of material substance must be a limitation of his perfect

[1] See above, paragraph 35 and the following, and 127 and the following.

nature. Of the generic element in the above definition, then, no more need here be said. It is the qualification of 'enlargement to infinity,' by which the idea of man as a thinking substance is represented as becoming the idea of God, that is the special difficulty now before us. Of this Locke writes as follows :—' The complex idea we have of God is made up of the simple ones we receive from reflection. If I find that I know some few things, and some of them, or all perhaps, imperfectly, I can frame an idea of knowing twice as many : which I can double again as often as I can add to number, and thus enlarge my ideas of knowledge by extending its comprehension to all things existing or possible. The same I can do of knowing them more perfectly, *i.e.* all their quali- ties, powers, causes, consequences, and relations; and thus frame the idea of infinite or boundless knowledge. The same also may be done of power till we come to that we call infinite; and also of the duration of existence without beginning or end; and so frame the idea of an eternal being. . . All which is done by enlarging the simple ideas we have taken from the operation of our own minds by reflection, or by our senses from exterior things, to that vastness to which infinity can extend them. For it is infinity which joined to our ideas of existence, power, knowledge, &c., makes that complex idea whereby we represent to ourselves the supreme being' (Book II. chap. xxiii. sec. 33—35). What is meant by this 'joining of infinity' to our ideas?

138. 'Finite and infinite,' says Locke, 'are looked upon by the mind as the modes of quantity, and are to be attributed primarily only to those things that have parts and are capable of increase by the addition of any the least part' (Book II. chap. xvii. sec. 1). Such are 'duration and expansion.' The applicability then of the term 'infinite' in its proper sense to God implies that he has expansion or duration; and it is characteristic of Locke that though he was clear about the divisibility of expansion and duration, as the above passage shows, he has no scruple about speaking of them as attributes of God, of whom as being 'in his own essence simple and uncompounded' he would never have spoken as 'having parts.' 'Duration is the idea we have of perishing distance, of which no parts exist together but follow each other in succession; as expansion is the idea of lasting

distance, all whose parts exist together.' Yet of duration
and expansion, thus defined, he says that 'in their full extent' (*i. e.* as severally 'eternity and immensity') 'they
belong only to the Deity' (Book II. chap. xv. secs. 8 and 12).
'A full extent' of them, however, is in the nature of the case
impossible. With a last moment duration would cease to be
duration; without another space beyond it space would not
be space. Locke is quite aware of this. When his conception of infinity is not embarrassed by reference to God, it
is simply that of unlimited 'addibility'—a juxta-position of
space to space, a succession of time upon time, to which we
can suppose no limit so long as we consider space and time
'as having parts, and thus capable of increase by the addition of parts,' and which therefore excludes the very possibility of a totality or 'full extent' (Book II. chap. xvi. sec. 8,
and xvii. sec. 13). The question, then, whether infinity of
expansion and duration in this, its only proper, sense can be
predicated of the perfect God, has only to be asked in order
to be answered in the negative. Nor do we mend the matter
if, instead of ascribing such infinity to God, we substitute
another phrase of Locke's, and say that He 'fills eternity
and immensity' (Book II. chap. xv. sec. 3). Put for eternity
and immensity their proper equivalents according to Locke,
viz. unlimited 'addibility' of times and spaces, and the
essential unmeaningness of the phrase becomes apparent.

139. In regard to any other attributes of God than those
of his duration and expansion,[1] Locke admits that the term
'infinite' is applied 'figuratively' (Book II. chap. xvii. sec.
1). 'When we call them (*e. g.* His power, wisdom, and
goodness) infinite, we have no other idea of this infinity
but what carries with it some reflection on, or intimation of,
that number or extent of the acts or objects of God's wisdom,
&c., which can never be supposed so great or so many which
these attributes will not always surmount, let us multiply
them in our thoughts as far as we can with all the infinity
of endless number.' What determination, then, according to
this passage, of our conception of God's goodness is repre-

---

[1] In the passages referred to, Locke
speaks of 'duration and *ubiquity*.' The
proper counterpart, however, of 'duration' according to him is 'expansion'—
this being to space what duration is
to time. Under the embarrassment,
however, which necessarily attends the
ascription of expansion to God, he tacitly
substitutes for it 'ubiquity,' a term
which does not match 'duration,' and
can only mean presence throughout the
whole of expansion, presence throughout
the whole of that which does not admit
of a whole.

sented by calling it infinite ? Simply its relation to a number
of acts and objects of which the sum can always be increased,
and which, just for that reason, cannot represent the perfect
God.   Is it then, it may be asked, of mere perversity that
when thinking of God under attributes that are not quantitative, and therefore do not carry with them the necessity of
incompleteness, we yet go out of our way by this epithet 'infinite' to subject them to the conditions of quantity and its
'progressus ad infinitum ?'

140. Retaining Locke's point of view, our answer of course
must be that our ideas of the Divine attributes, being
primarily our own ideas of reflection, are either ideas of the
single successive acts that constitute our inward experience
or formed from these by abstraction and combination. In
parts our experience is given, in parts only can we recall it.
Our complex or abstract ideas are symbols which only take
a meaning so far as we resolve them into the detached impressions which in the sum they represent, or recall the
objects, each with its own before and after, from which they
were originally taken. So it is with the ideas of wisdom,
power, and goodness, which from ourselves we transfer to
God.   They represent an experience given in succession and
piece-meal—a numerable series of acts and events, which like
every other number is already infinite in the only sense of
the word of which Locke can give a clear account, as susceptible of indefinite repetition (Book II. chap. vi. sec. 8.) When
we 'join infinity' to these ideas, then, unless some other
meaning is given to infinity, we merely state explicitly what
was originally predicable of the experience they embody.
Nor will it avail us much to shift the meaning of infinite,
as Locke does when he applies it to the divine attributes,
from that of indefinite 'addibility' to that of exceeding any
sum which indefinite multiplication can yield us. Let us
suppose an act of consciousness, from which we have taken
an abstract idea of an attribute—say of wisdom—to be a
million times repeated ; our idea of the attribute will not
vary with the repetition.   Nor if, having supposed a limit
to the repetition, we then suppose the act indefinitely repeated beyond this limit and accordingly speak of the attribute as infinite, will our idea of the attribute vary at all
from what it was to begin with. Its content will be the same.
There will be nothing to be said of it which could not have

been said of the experience from which it was originally
abstracted, and of which the essential characteristic—that
it is one of a series of events of which no two can be present
together—is incompatible with divine perfection.

141. It appears then that it is the subjection of our experience to the form of time which unfits the ideas derived
from it for any combination into an idea of God; nor by
being 'joined with an infinity,' which itself merely means
the absence of limit to succession in time, is their unfitness
in any way modified. On the contrary, by such conjunction
from being latent it becomes patent. In one important
passage Locke becomes so far aware of this that, though
continuing to ascribe infinite duration to God, he does it
under qualifications inconsistent with the very notion of
duration. 'Though we cannot conceive any duration without succession, nor put it together in our thoughts that any
being does now exist to-morrow or possess at once more than
the present moment of duration; yet we can conceive the
eternal duration of the Almighty far different from that of
man, or any other finite being: because man comprehends
not in his knowledge or power all past and future things
. . . . what is once past he can never recall, and what
is yet to come he cannot make present. . . . God's infinite
duration being accompanied with infinite knowledge and
power, he sees all things past and to come' (Book II. chap.
xv. sec 12). It is clear that in this passage 'infinite'
changes its meaning; that it is used in one sense—the
proper sense according to Locke—when applied to duration, and in some wholly different sense, not a figurative
one derived from the former, when applied to knowledge
and power; and that the infinite duration of God, as 'accompanied by infinite power and knowledge,' is no longer in
any intelligible sense duration at all. It is no longer 'the
idea we have of perishing distance,' derived from our fleeting
consciousness in which 'what is once past can never be recalled,' but the attribute of a consciousness of which, if it is
to be described in terms of time at all, in virtue of its 'seeing all things past and to come' at once, it can only be
said that it 'does now exist to-morrow.' If it be asked,
What meaning can we have in speaking of such a consciousness? into what simple ideas can it be resolved when
all our ideas are determined by a before and after?—the

answer must be, Just as much or as little meaning as we have when, in like contradiction to the successive presentation of ideas, we speak of a self, constituted by consciousness, as identical with itself throughout the years of our life.

142. A more positive answer it is not our present business to give. Our concern is to show that 'eternity and immensity,' according to any meaning that Locke recognises, or that the observation of our ideas could justify, do not express any conception that can carry us beyond the perpetual incompleteness of our experience; but that in his doctrine of personal identity he does admit a conception which no observation of our ideas of reflection—since these are in succession and could not be observed if they were not —can account for; and that it is just this conception, the conception of a constant presence of consciousness to itself incompatible with conditions of space and time, that can alone give such meaning to 'eternal and infinite' as can render them significant epithets of God. Such a conception (we say it with respect) Locke admits when it is wanted without knowing it. It must indeed always underlie the idea of God, however alien to it may be attempted adaptations of the other ' infinite '—the *progressus ad indefinitum* in space and time—by which, as with Locke, the idea is explained. But it is one for which the psychological method of observing what happens in oneself cannot account, and which therefore this method, just so far as it is thoroughly carried out, must tend to discard. That which happens, whether we reckon it an inward or an outward, a physical or a psychical event—and nothing but an event can, properly speaking, be observed—is as such in time. But the presence of consciousness to itself, though, as the true ' punctum stans,' [1] it is the condition of the observation of events in time, is not such an event itself. In the ordinary and proper sense of ' fact,' it is not a fact at all, nor yet a possible abstraction from facts. To the method, then, which deals with phrases about the mind by ascertaining the observable ' mental phenomena ' which they represent, it must remain a mere phrase, to be explained as the offspring of other phrases whose real import has been misunderstood.

<hr>

[1] Locke, Essay II. chap. xvii. sec. 16.

It can only recover a significance when this method, as with Hume, has done its worst, and is found to leave the possibility of knowledge, without such 'punctum stans,' still unaccounted for.

143. We have finally to notice the way in which Locke maintains our knowledge of the 'real existence' of thinking substance, both as that which 'we call our mind,' and as God. Of the former first. 'Experience convinces us that we have an intuitive knowledge of our own existence.. . . If I know I feel pain, it is evident I have as certain perception of my own existence as of the pain I feel. If I know I doubt, I have as certain perception of the existence of the thing doubting as of that thought which I call doubt' (Book IV. chap. ix. sec. 3). Upon this the remark must occur that the existence of a painful feeling is one thing; the existence of a permanent subject, remaining the same with itself, when the feeling is over, and through the succession of other feelings, quite another. The latter is what is meant by my own existence, of which undoubtedly there is a 'certain perception,' if the feeling of pain has become the 'knowledge that I feel pain,' and if by the 'I' is understood such a permanent subject. That the feeling, as 'simple idea,' is taken to begin with by Locke for the knowledge that I feel something, we have sufficiently seen.[1] Just as, in virtue of this conversion, it gives us 'assurance' of the real existence of the outer thing or material substance on the one side, so of the thinking substance on the other. It carries with it the certainty at once that I have a feeling, and that something makes me feel. But whereas, after the conversion of feeling into a felt thing has been throughout assumed—as indeed otherwise feeling could not be spoken of—a further question is raised, which causes much embarrassment, as to the real existence of such thing; on the contrary, the reference of the feeling to the *thinking* thing is taken as carrying with it the real existence of such thing. The question whether it really exists or no is only once raised, and then summarily settled by the sentence we have quoted, while the reality whether of existence or of essence on the part of the outward thing, as we have found to our cost, is the main burden of the Third and Fourth Books.

---

[1] See above, paragraphs 26 and following, and 59 and following.

144. In principle, indeed, the answer to both questions, as given by Locke, is the same : for the reasons which he alleges for being assured of the 'existence of a thing without us corresponding to the idea of sensation' reduce themselves, as we have seen, to the reiteration of that reference of the idea to a thing, which according to him is originally involved in it, and which is but the correlative of its reference to a subject. This, however, is what he was not himself aware of. To him the outer and the inner substance were separate and independent things, for each of which the question of real existence had to be separately settled. To us, according to the view already indicated, it is the presence of self-consciousness, or thought as an object-to-itself, to feeling that converts it into a relation between feeling thing and felt thing, between ' cogitative and incogitative substance.' The source of substantiation upon each side being the same, the question as to the real existence of either substance must be the same, and equally so the answer to it. It is an answer that must be preceded by a counter question.—Does real existence mean existence independent of thought ? To suppose such existence is to suppose an impossibility—one which is not the less so though the existence be supposed material, if 'material' means in ' space' and space itself is a relation constituted by the mind, ' bringing things to and setting them by one another.' Yet is the supposition itself but a mode of the logical substantiation we have explained, followed by an imaginary abstraction of the work of the mind from this, its own creation. Does real existence mean a possible feeling ? If so, it is as clear that what converts feeling into a relation between felt thing and feeling subject cannot in this sense be real, as it is that without such conversion no distinction between real and fantastic would be possible. Does it, finally, mean individuality, in such a sense that unless I can say this or that is substance, thinking or material, substance does not really exist ? If it does, the answer is that substance, being constituted by a relation by which self-conscious thought is for ever determining feelings, and which every predication represents, cannot be identified with any 'this or that,' though without it there could be no ' this or that' at all.

145. We have already found that Locke accepts each of the above as determinations of real existence, and that, though in spite of them he labours to maintain the real existence of

outward things, he is so far faithful to them as to declare real essence unknowable. In answering the question as to 'his own existence' he wholly ignores them. He does not ask how the real existence of the thinking Ego sorts with his ordinary doctrine that the real is what would be in the world whether there were a mind or no ; or its real identity, present throughout the particulars of experience, with his ordinary doctrine of the fictitiousness of 'generals.' A real existence of the mind, however, founded on the logical necessity of substantiation, rests on a shifting basis, so long as by the mind is understood a thinking thing, different in each man, to which his inner experience is referred as accidents to a substance. The same law of thought which compels such reference requires that the thinking thing in its turn, as that which is born grows and dies, be referred as an accident to some ulterior substance. 'A fever or fall may take away my reason or memory, or both; and an apoplexy leave neither sense nor understanding, no, nor life.'[1] Just as each outer thing turns out to be a 'retainer to something else,' so is it with the inner thing. Such a dependent being cannot be an ultimate substance ; nor can any natural agents to which we may trace its dependence really be so either. The logical necessity of further substantiation would affect them equally, appearing in the supposition of an unknown something beyond, which makes them what they are. It is under such logical necessity that Locke, in regard to all the substances which he commonly speaks of as ultimate — God, spirit, body—from time to time gives warning of something still ulterior and unknowable, whether under the designation of substance or real essence (Book II. chap. xxiii. secs. 30 and 36). If, then, it will be said, substance is but the constantly-shifting result of a necessity of thought—so shifting that there is nothing of which we can finally say, ' This is substance, not accident'—there can be no evidence of the 'real existence' of a permanent Ego in the necessary substantiation therein of my inner experience.

146. The first result of such a consideration in a reader of Locke will naturally be an attempt to treat the inner synthesis as a fiction of thought or figure of speech, and to confine real existence to single feelings in the moments of their occurrence. This, it will seem, is to be faithful to

---

[1] Locke, Book III. chap. vi. sec. 4.

Locke's own clearer mind, as it frequently emerges from the still-returning cloud of scholasticism.   The final result will rather be the discovery that the single feeling is nothing real, but that the synthesis of appearances, which alone for us constitutes reality, is never final or complete : that thus absolute reality, like ultimate substance, is never to be found by us— in a thinking as little as in a material thing—belonging as it does only to that divine self-consciousness, of which the presence in us is the source and bond of the ever-growing synthesis called knowledge, but which, because it is the source of that synthesis and not one of its partial results, is neither real nor knowable in the same sense as is any other object.   It is this presence which alone gives meaning to ' proofs of the being of God ;' to Locke's among the rest. For it is in a sense true, as he held, that ' my own real existence ' is evidence of the existence of God, since the self, in the only sense in which it is absolutely real or an ultimate subject, is already God.[1]

147.   Our knowledge of God's existence, according to him, is ' demonstrative,' based on the ' intuitive ' knowledge of our own.   Strictly taken, according to his definitions, this must mean that the agreement of the idea of God with existence is perceived mediately through the agreement of the idea of self with existence, which is perceived immediately ; that thus the idea of God and the idea of self ' agree.' [2] We need not, however, further dwell either on the contradiction implied in the knowledge of real existence, if knowledge is a perception of agreement between ideas and if real existence is the antithesis of ideas ; or on the embarrassments which follow when a definition of reasoning, only really applicable to the comparison of quantities, is extended to other regions of knowledge.   Locke virtually ignores his definitions in the passage before us.   ' If we know there is some real being ' (as we do know in the knowledge of our own existence) ' and that non-entity cannot produce any real being, it is an evident demonstration that from eternity there has been something ; since what was not from eternity had a beginning, and what had a beginning must be produced by something else ' (Book IV. chap. x. sec. 3).   Next as to the qualities of this something else.   ' What had its being and beginning from another must also have all that which

---

[1] See below, paragraph 152.   [2] See above, paragraphs 25 and 24.

is in, and belongs to, its being from another too' (Ibid.
sec. 4.). From this is deduced the supreme power and
perfect knowledge of the eternal being upon the principle
that whatever is in the effect must also be in the cause
—a principle, however, which has to be subjected to
awkward limitations in order that, while proving enough,
it may not prove too much. It might seem that, according to it, since the real being, from which as effect the
eternal being as cause is demonstrated, is ' both material and
cogitative' or ' made up of body and spirit,' matter as well
as thought must belong to the eternal being too. That
thought must belong to him, Locke is quite clear. It is as
impossible, he holds, that thought should be derived from
matter, or from matter and motion together, as that something should be derived from nothing. ' If we will suppose
nothing first or eternal, matter can never begin to be : if we
suppose bare matter without motion eternal, motion can
never begin to be : if we suppose only matter and motion
first or eternal, thought can never begin to be' (Book IV.
chap. x. sec. 10). The objection which is sure to occur, that
it must be equally impossible for matter to be derived from
thought, he can scarcely be said to face. He takes refuge in
the supreme power of the eternal being, as that which is able
to create matter out of nothing. He does not anticipate the
rejoinder to which he thus lays himself open, that this power
in the eternal being to produce one effect not homogeneous
with itself, viz. matter, may extend to another effect, viz.
thought, and that thus the argument from thought in the
effect to thought in the cause becomes invalid, and nothing
but blind power, we know not what, remains as the attribute
of the eternal being. Nor does he remember, when he meets
the objection drawn from the inconceivability of matter being
made out of nothing by saying that what is inconceivable is
not therefore impossible (*ibid*. sec. 19), that it is simply the
inconceivability of a sequence of something upon nothing
that has given him his 'evident demonstration' of an eternal
being.

148. The value of the first step in Locke's argument—the
inference, namely, from there being something now to there
having been something from eternity—must be differently
estimated according to the meaning attached to 'something'
and ' from eternity.' If the existence of something means
the occurrence of an event, of this undoubtedly it can always

be said that it follows another event, nor to this sequence can any limit be supposed, for a first event would not be an event at all. It would be a contingency contingent upon nothing. Thus understood, the argument from a something now to a something from eternity is merely a statement of the infinity of time according to that notion of infinity, as a 'progressus ad indefinitum,' which we have already seen to be Locke's.[1] It is the exact reverse of an argument to a creation or a first cause. If we try to change its character by a supplementary consideration that infinity in the series of events is inconceivable, the rejoinder will be that a first event is not for that reason any less of a contradiction, and that the infinity which Locke speaks of only professes to be a negative idea, representing the impossibility of conceiving a first event (Book II. chap. xvii. sec. 13, &c.). In truth, however, when Locke speaks of 'something from eternity' he does not mean—what would clearly be no God at all—a series of events to which, because *of events*, and therefore in time, no limit 'can be supposed; but a being which is neither event nor series of events, to which there is no before or after. The inference to such a being is not of a kind with the transition from one event to another habitually associated with it; and if this be the true account of reasoning from effect to cause, no such reasoning can yield the result which Locke requires. As we have seen, however, this is not his account of it,[2] however legitimately it may follow from his general doctrine.

149. The inference of cause with him is the inference from a change to something having power to produce it.[3] The value of this definition lies not in the notion of efficient power, but in that of an order of nature, which it involves. If instead of 'something having power to produce it' we read 'something that accounts for the change,' it expresses the inference on which all science rests, but which is as far as possible from being merely a transition from one event to another that usually precedes it. An event, interpreted as a change of something that remains constant, is no longer a mere event. It is no longer merely in time, a present which next moment becomes a past. It takes its character from relation to the thing or system of things of which it is an altered appearance, but which in itself is always the same.

[1] See above, paragraph 138.
[2] See above, paragraph 68.
[3] Cf. II. chap. xxvi. sec. 1, and chap. xxi. sec. 1.

Only in virtue of such a relation does it require to be accounted for, to be referred to a 'cause,' which is in truth the conception that holds together or reconciles the endless flux of events with eternal unity. The cause of a 'phenomenon,' even according to the authoritative exponent of the Logic which believes itself to follow Hume, is the 'sum total of its conditions.' In its fulness, that is, it is simply that system of things, conceived explicitly, of which there must already have been an implicit conception in order that the event might be regarded as a change and thus start the search for a cause. An event in time, apart from reference to something not in time, could suggest no enquiry into the sum of its conditions. Upon occurrence of a certain feeling there might indeed be spontaneous recollection of a feeling usually precedent, spontaneous expectation of another usually sequent. But such association of feelings can never explain that conception of cause in virtue of which, when accounting for a phenomenon, we set aside the event which in our actual experience has usually preceded it, for one which we only find to precede it in the single case of a crucial experiment. That we do so shows that it is not because of antecedence in time, however apparently uniform, that an educated man reckons a certain event to be the cause of another, but that, because of its sole sufficiency under the sum of known conditions to account for the given event, he decides it to be its uniform antecedent, however much ordinary appearances may tell to the contrary. Thus, though he may still strangely define cause as a uniformly antecedent event (in spite of its being a definition that would prevent him from speaking of gravity as the cause of the fall of a stone), it is clear that by such event he means one determined by a complex of conditions in an unchanging universe. These conditions, again, he may speak of as contingencies, i.e. as events contingent upon other events in endless series, but he must add 'contingent in accordance with the uniformity of nature '—in other words, he must determine the contingencies by relation to what is not contingent; he must suppose nature unchanging, though our experience of it through sensation be a 'progressus ad indefinitum'—if he is to allow a possibility of knowledge at all. In short, if events were merely events, feelings that happen to me now and next moment are over, no 'law of causation'

and therefore no knowledge would be possible. If the knowledge founded on this law actually exists, then the ' argumentum a contingentiâ mundi ' rightly understood—the ' inference ' from nature to a being neither in time nor
contingent but self-dependent and eternal, that constant
reality of which events are the changing appearances—is
valid because the conception of nature, of a world to be
known, already implies such a being. To the rejoinder that
implication in the conception of nature does not prove real
existence, the answer must be the question, What meaning
has real existence, the antithesis of illusion, except such as
is equivalent to this conception?

150. The value, then, of Locke's demonstration of the
existence of God, as an argument from there being something
now to an eternal being from which the real existence that
we know ' has all which is in and belongs to it,' depends
on our converting it into the ' argumentum a contingentiâ
mundi,' stated as above. In other words, it depends on our
interpreting it in a manner which may be warranted by his
rough account of causation, and by one of the incompatible
views of the real that we have found in him,[1] but which is
inconsistent with his opposition of reality to the work of the
mind, and his reduction of it to ' particular existence,' as well
as with his ordinary view that ' infinite' and ' eternal' can
represent only a ' progressus ad indefinitum.' If by ' real
existence corresponding to an idea' is meant its presentation
in a particular ' here and now,' an attempt to find a real
existence of God can bring us to nothing but such a contradiction in terms as a first event. To prove it from the real
existence of the self is to prove one impossibility from another.
If, on the other hand, real existence implies the determination
of our ideas by an order of nature—if it means ideas ' in ordine
ad universum ' (to use a Baconian phrase), in distinction from
' in ordine ad nos '—then the argument from a present to an
eternal real existence is valid, but simply in the sense that
the present is already real, and ' has all that is in and belongs
to it,' only in virtue of the relation to the eternal.

151. This, it may be said, is to vindicate Locke's ' proof'
only by making it Pantheistic. It gives us an eternity of
nature, but not God. Our present concern, however, is not
with the distinction between Pantheism and true Theism,

---

[1] See above, paragraphs 49 and 91.

but with the exposition of Locke's doctrine according to the only development by which it can be made to show the real existence of an eternal being at all.   It is only by making the most of certain Cartesian elements that appear in his doctrine, irreconcileable with its general purport, that we can find fair room in it for such a being, even as the system of nature. Any attempt to exhibit (in Hegelian phrase) 'Spirit as the truth of nature,' would be to go wholly beyond our record; yet without this the 'ens realissimum' cannot be the God whose existence Locke believes himself to prove—a *thinking* being from whom matter and motion are derived, but in whom they are not.   It is true that, according to the context, it is the real existence of the self from which that of the eternal being is proved.   This is because, in the Fourth Book, where the 'proof' occurs, following the new train of enquiry started by the definition of knowledge, Locke has for the time left in abeyance his fundamental doctrine that all simple ideas are types of reality, and is writing as if 'my own real existence' were the only one known with intuitive certainty.   This, however, makes no essential difference in the effect of his argument.   The given existence, from which the divine is proved, is treated expressly as *both* 'material and cogitative:' nor, since according to Locke the world is both and man is both, and even the 'thinking thing' takes its content from impressions made by matter, could it be otherwise.   To have taken thought by itself·as the basis of the proof would have been to leave the other part of the world, as he conceived it, to be referred to another God. The difficulty then arises, either that there is no inference possible from the nature of the effect to the nature of the eternal being, its cause; in which case no attribute whatever can be asserted of the latter: or that to it too, like the effect, matter as well as thought must belong.

152. As we have seen, neither of these alternative views is really met by Locke.   To the former we may reply that the relation between two events, of which neither has anything in common with the other, but which we improperly speak of as effect and cause (*e.g.* death and a sunstroke), has no likeness to that which we have explained between the world in its contingency and the world as an eternal system—a relation according to which the cause is the effect in unity. Whatever is part of the reality of the world must belong, it

would seem, to the 'ens realissimum,' its cause. We are thus thrown back on the other horn of the dilemma. Is not matter part of the reality of the world? This is a question to which the method of observing the individual consciousness can give none but a delusive answer. A true answer cannot be given till for this method has been substituted the enquiry, How knowledge is possible, and it has been found that it is only possible as the progressive actualisation in us of a self-consciousness in itself complete, and which in its completeness includes the world as its object. From the point of view thus attained the question as to matter will be, How is it related to this self-consciousness?—a question to which the answer must vary according to what is understood by 'matter.' If it means the abstract opposite of thought—that which is supposed void of all determination that comes of thinking—we must pronounce it simply a delusion, the creation of self-consciousness in one stage of its communication to us. If it means the world as in space and time, this we may allow to be real enough as a stage in the process by which self-consciousness constitutes reality. Thus understood, we may speak of it roughly as part of the 'ens realissimum' which the complete self-consciousness, or God, includes as its object, without any limitation of the divine perfectness. The limitation only seems to arise so far as we, being ourselves (as our knowledge and morality testify), though formally self-conscious, yet parts of this partial world, interpret it amiss and ascribe to it a reality, in abstraction from the self-conscious subject, which it only derives from relation to it. Thus while on the one hand it is the presence in us of God, as the self-conscious source of reality, that at once gives us the idea of God and of an eternal self, and renders superfluous the further question as to their real existence; on the other hand it is because, for all this presence, we are but emerging from nature, of which as animals we are parts, that to us there must seem an incompatibility of existence between God and matter, between the self and the flux of events which makes our life. This necessary illusion is our bondage, but when the source of illusion is known, the bondage is already being broken.

153. We have now sufficiently explored the system which it was Hume's mission to try to make consistent with itself. We have found that it is governed throughout by the anti-

thesis between what is given to consciousness—that in regard to which the mind is passive—as the supposed real on the one side, and what is 'invented,' 'created,' 'superinduced' by the mind on the other: while yet this 'real' in all its forms, as described by Locke, has turned out to be constituted by such ideas as, according to him, are not given but invented. Stripped of these superinductions, nothing has been found to remain of it but that of which nothing can be said—a chaos of unrelated, and therefore unmeaning, *individua*. Turning to the theory of the mind itself, the source of the superinduction, we have found this to be a reduplication of the prolonged inconsistency which forms the theory of the 'real.' It impresses itself with that which, according to the other theory, is the impress of matter, and it really exists as that which it itself invents. The value of Hume's philosophy lies in its being an attempt to carry out the antithesis more rigorously—to clear the real, whether under the designation of mind or of its object, of all that could not be reckoned as given in feelings which occur to us 'whether we will or no.' The consequence is a splendid failure, a failure which it might have been hoped would have been taken as a sufficient proof that a theory, which starts from that antithesis, cannot even be stated without implicitly contradicting itself.

154. Such a doctrine—a doctrine founded on the testimony of the senses, which ends by showing that the senses testify to nothing—cannot be criticised step by step according to the order in which its author puts it, for its characteristic is that, in order to state itself, it has to take for granted popular notions which it afterwards shows to be unmeaning. Its power over ordinary thinkers lies just in this, that it arrives at its destructive result by means of propositions which every one believes, but to the validity of which its result is really fatal. An account of our primitive consciousness, which derives its plausibility from availing itself of the conceptions of cause and substance, is the basis of the argument which reduces these conceptions to words misunderstood. It cannot, therefore, be treated by itself, as it stands in the first part of the Treatise on the Understanding, but must be taken in connection with Part IV., especially with the section on 'Scepticism with regard to the Senses;' not upon the plan of discrediting a principle by reference to the 'dangerous' nature

of its consequences, but because the final doctrine brings out the inconsistencies lurking in that assumed to begin with. On this side of his scepticism Hume mainly followed the orthodox Berkeley, of whose criticism of Locke, made with a very different purpose, some account must first be given. The connection between the two authors is instructive in many ways; not least as showing that when the most pious theological purpose expresses itself in a doctrine resting on an inadequate philosophical principle, it is the principle and not the purpose that will regulate the permanent effect of the doctrine.

155. Berkeley's treatises, we must remember, though professedly philosophical, really form a theological polemic. He wrote as the champion of orthodox Christianity against 'mathematical atheism,' and, like others of his order, content with the demolition of the rival stronghold, did not stay to enquire whether his own untempered mortar could really hold together the fabric of knowledge and rational religion which he sought to maintain. He found practical ungodliness and immorality excusing themselves by a theory of 'materialism '—a theory which made the whole conscious experience of man dependent upon 'unperceiving matter.' This, whatever it might be, was not an object which man could love or reverence, or to which he could think of himself as accountable. Berkeley, full of devout zeal for God and man, and not without a tincture of clerical party-spirit (as appears in his heat against Shaftesbury, whom he ought to have regarded as a philosophical yoke-fellow), felt that it must be got rid of. He saw, or thought he saw, that the 'new way of ideas' had only to be made consistent with itself, and the oppressive shadow must vanish. Ideas, according to that new way (or, to speak less ambiguously, feelings) make up our experience, and they are not matter. Let us get rid, then, of the self-contradictory assumption that they are either copies of matter—copies of that, of which it is the sole and simple differentia that it is not an idea, or its effects— effects of that which can only be described as the unknown opposite of the only efficient power with which we are acquainted—and what becomes of the philosopher's blind and dead substitute for the living and knowing God? It was one thing, however, to show the contradictions involved in Locke's doctrine of matter, another effectively to replace

it. To the latter end Berkeley cannot be said to have made any permanent contribution. That explicit reduction of ideas to feelings ' particular in time,' which was his great weapon of destruction, was incompatible with his doing so. He adds nothing to the philosophy, which he makes consistent with itself, while by making it consistent he empties it of three parts of its suggestiveness. His doctrine, in short, is merely Locke purged, and Locke purged is no Locke.

156. The question which he mainly dealt with may be stated in general terms as that of the relation between the mind and the external world. Under this general statement, however, are covered several distinct questions, the confusion between which has been a great snare for philosophers—questions as to the relations (a) between a sensitive and non-sensitive body, (b) between thought and its object, (c) between thought and something only qualified as the negation of thought. The last question, it will be observed, is what the second becomes upon a certain notion being formed of what the object of thought must be. Upon this notion being discarded a further question (d), also covered by the above general statement, must still remain as to the relation between thought, as in each man, and the world which he does not make, but which, in some sort, makes him what he is. In what follows, these questions, for the sake of brevity, will be referred to symbolically.

157. Locke's doctrine of matter, as we have seen, involves a confusion between (a) and (b). The feeling of touch in virtue of an intellectual interpretation—*intellectual* because implying the action of the mind as (according to Locke) the source of ideas of relation—becomes the idea of solidity, *i.e.* the idea of a relation between bodies in the way of impulse and resistance. But the function of the intellect in constituting the relation is ignored. Under cover of the ambiguous ' idea,' which stands alike for a nervous irritation and the intellectual interpretation thereof, the feeling of touch and conception of solidity are treated as one and the same. Thus the true *conceived* outwardness of body to body —an outwardness which thought, as the source of relations, can alone constitute—becomes first an imaginary *felt* outwardness of body to the organs of touch, and then, by a further fallacy—these organs being confused with the mind —an outwardness of body to mind, which we need only kick

a stone to be sure of. Meanwhile the consideration of question (d) necessitates the belief that the real world does not come and go with each man's fleeting consciousness, and no distinction being recognised between consciousness as fleeting and consciousness as permanent, or between feeling and thought, the real world comes to be regarded as the absolute opposite of thought and its work. This opposition combines with the supposed externality of body to mind to give the notion that body is the real. The qualities which ' the mind finds inseparable from body ' thus become qualities which would exist all the same ' whether there were a perceiving mind or no,' and are primarily real; while such as consist in our feelings, though real in so far as, ' not being of our own making, they imply the action of things without us,' are yet only secondarily so because this action is relative to something which is not body. Then, finally, by a renewed confusion of the relation between thought and its object with that between body and body, qualities, which are credited with a primary reality as independent of and antithetical to the mind, are brought within it again as ideas. They are supposed to copy themselves upon it by impact and impression; and that not in touch merely, but (visual feelings being interpreted by help of the same conception) in sight also.

158. Such ' materialism ' invites two different methods of attack. On the one hand its recognised principle, that all intellectual ' superinduction ' upon simple feeling is a departure from the real, may be insisted on, and it may be shown that it is only by such superinduction that simple feeling becomes a feeling of body. Matter, then, with all its qualities, is a fiction except so far as these can be reduced to simple feelings. Such in substance was Berkeley's short method with the materialists. In his early life it seemed to him sufficient for the purposes of orthodox ' spiritualism,' because, having posed the materialist, he took the moral and spiritual attributes of God as ' revealed,' without enquiring into the possibility of such revelation to a merely sensitive consciousness. As he advanced, other questions, fatal to the constructive value of his original method, began to force themselves upon him. Granting that intellectual superinduction = fiction, how is the fiction possible to a mind which cannot originate? Exclude from

reality all that such fiction constitutes, and what remains to
be real? These questions, however, though their effect on
his mind appears in the later sections of his 'Siris,' he never
systematically pursued. He thus missed the true method
of attack on materialism—the only one that does not build
again that which it destroys—the method which allows that
matter is real but only so in virtue of that intellectual superinduction upon feeling without which there could be for us
no reality at all: that thus it is indeed opposed to thought,
but only by a position which is thought's own act. For the
development of such views Berkeley had not patience in his
youth nor leisure in his middle life. Whatever he may have
suggested, all that he logically achieved was an exposure of
the equivocation between feeling and felt body; and of this
the next result, as appears in Hume, was a doctrine which
indeed delivers mind from dependence on matter, but only
by reducing it in effect to a succession of feelings which
cannot know themselves.

159. It was upon the extension of the metaphor of impression to sight as well as touch, and the consequent notion
that body, with its inseparable qualities, revealed itself
through both senses, that Berkeley first fastened. Is it
evident, as Locke supposed it to be, that men 'perceive by
their sight' not colours merely, but 'a distance between
bodies of different colours and between parts of the same
body';[1] in other words, situation and magnitude? To
show that they do not is the purpose of Berkeley's 'Essay
towards a new Theory of Vision.' He starts from two
principles which he takes as recognised: one, that the
'proper and immediate object of sight is colour'; the other,
that distance from the eye, or distance in the line of vision,
is not immediately seen. If, then, situation and magnitude
are 'properly and immediately' seen, they must be qualities
of colour. Now in one sense, according to Berkeley, they are
so: in other words, there is such a thing as *visible* extension.
We see lights and colours in 'sundry situations' as well as
'in degrees of faintness and clearness, confusion and distinctness.' (*Theory of Vision*, sec. 77.) We also see objects
as made up of certain 'quantities of coloured points,' *i.e.*
as having visible magnitude. (Ibid. sec. 54.) But situation

---

[1] Locke, Essay II. chap. xiii. sec. 2.

and magnitude *as visible* are not external, not ' qualities of body,' nor do they represent by any *necessary* connection the situation and magnitude that are truly qualities of body, ' without the mind and at a distance.' These are tangible. Distance in all its forms—as distance from the eye; as distance between parts of the same body, or magnitude; and as distance of body from body, or situation—is tangible. What a man means when he says that ' he sees this or that thing at a distance ' is that ' what he sees suggests to his under-standing that after having passed a certain distance, to be measured by the motion of his body which is perceivable by touch, he shall come to perceive such and such tangible ideas which have been usually connected with such and such visible ideas ' (Ibid. sec. 45). On the same principle we are said to see the magnitude and situation of bodies. Owing to long experience of the connection of these tangible ideas with visible ones, the magnitude of the latter and their degrees of faintness and clearness, of confusion and distinct-ness, enable us to form a ' sudden and true ' estimate of the magnitude of the former (*i.e.* of bodies) ; even as visible situation enables us to form a like estimate of the ' situa-tion of things outward and tangible' (Ibid. secs. 56 and 99). The connection, however, between the two sets of ideas, Berkeley insists, is habitual only, not necessary. As Hume afterwards said of the relation of cause and effect, it is not constituted by the nature of the ideas related.[1] The visible ideas, that as a matter of fact ' suggest to us the various magnitudes of external objects before we touch them, might have suggested no such thing.' That would really have been the case had our eyes been so framed as that the *maximum visibile* should be less than the *minimum tangibile*; and, as a matter of constant experience, the greater visible extension suggests sometimes a greater, sometimes a less, tangible ex-tension according to the degree of its strength or faintness, ' being in its own nature equally fitted to bring into our minds the idea of small or great or no size at all, just as the words of a language are in their own nature indifferent to signify this or that thing, or nothing at all.'   (Ibid. secs. 62–64.)

160. So far, then, the conclusion merely is that body as external, and space as a relation between bodies or parts of a body, are not both seen and felt, but felt only ; in other

[1] See below, paragraph 283.

words, that it is only through the organs of touch that we receive, strictly speaking, impressions from without. This is all that the Essay on Vision goes to show; but according to the 'Principles of Human Knowledge' this conclusion was merely provisional. The object of touch does not, any more than the object of sight, 'exist without the mind,' nor is it 'the image of an external thing.' 'In strict truth the ideas of sight, when by them we apprehend distance and things placed at a distance, do not suggest or mark out to us things actually existing at a distance, but only admonish us what ideas of touch will be imprinted in our minds at such and such distances of time, and in consequence of such and such actions' ('Principles of H. K.' sec. 44). Whether, then, we speak of visible or tangible objects, the object *is* the idea, its 'esse is the percipi.' Body is not a thing separate from the idea of touch, yet revealed by it; so far as it exists at all, it must either be that idea or be a succession of ideas of which that idea is suggestive. It follows that the notion of the real which identifies it with matter, as something external to and independent of consciousness, and which derives the reality of ideas from their relation to body as thus outward, must disappear. Must not, then, the distinction between the real and fantastic, between dreams and facts, disappear with it? What meaning is there in asking whether any given idea is real or not, unless a reference is implied to something other than the idea itself?

170. Berkeley's theory, no less than Locke's, requires such reference. He insists, as much as Locke does, on the difference between ideas of imagination which do, and those of sense which do not, depend on our own will. 'It is no more than willing, and straightway this or that idea arises in my fancy; and by the same power it is obliterated and makes way for another.' But 'when in broad daylight I open my eyes, it is not in my power to choose whether I shall see or no, or to determine what particular objects shall present themselves to my view.' Moreover 'the ideas of sense are more strong, lively, and distinct than those of the imagination; they have likewise a steadiness, order, and coherence, and are not excited at random as those which are the effects of human wills often are, but in a regular train and series' (Ibid. secs. 28–30). These characteristics of ideas of sense, however, do not with Berkeley, any more than

with Locke, properly speaking, *constitute* their reality. This lies in their relation to something else, of which these characteristics are the tests. The difference between the two writers lies in their several views as to what this 'something else' is. With Locke it was body or matter, as proximately, though in subordination to the Divine Will, the 'imprinter' of those most lively ideas which we cannot make for ourselves. His followers insisted on the proximate, while they ignored the ultimate, reference. Hence, as Berkeley conceived, their Atheism, which he could cut from under their feet by the simple plan of eliminating the proximate reference altogether, and thus showing that God, not matter, is the immediate 'imprinter' of ideas on the senses and the suggester of such ideas of imagination as the ideas of sense, in virtue of habitual association, constantly introduce (Ibid. sec. 33).

171. To eliminate the reference to matter might seem to be more easy than to substitute for it a reference to God. If the object of the idea is only the idea itself, does not all determination by relation logically disappear from the idea, except (perhaps) such as consists in the fact of its sequence or antecedence to other ideas? This issue was afterwards to be tried by Hume—with what consequences to science and religion we shall see. Berkeley avoids it by insisting that the 'percipi,' to which 'esse' is equivalent, implies reference to a mind. At first sight this reference, as common to all ideas alike, would not seem to avail much as a basis either for a distinction between the real and fantastic or for any Theism except such as would 'entitle God to all our fancies.' If it is to serve Berkeley's purpose, we must suppose the idea to carry with it not merely a relation to mind but a relation to it as its effect, and the conscious subject to carry with him such a distinction between his own mind and God's as leads him to refer his ideas to God's mind as their cause when they are lively, distinct and coherent, but when they are otherwise, to his own. And this, in substance, is Berkeley's supposition. To show the efficient power of mind he appeals to our consciousness of ability to produce at will ideas of imagination; to show that there is a divine mind, distinct from our own, he appeals to our consciousness of inability to produce ideas of sense.

172. Even those least disposed to 'vanquish Berkeley with a grin' have found his doctrine of the real, which is also his

doctrine of God, 'unsatisfactory.' By the real world they are accustomed to understand something which—at least in respect of its 'elements' or 'conditions' or 'laws'—permanently is; though the combinations of the elements, the events which flow from the conditions, the manifestations of the laws, may never be at one time what they will be at the next. But according to the Berkeleian doctrine the permanent seems to disappear: the 'is' gives place to a 'has been' and 'will be.' If I say (δεικτικῶς) 'there is a body,' I must mean according to it that a feeling has just occurred to me, which has been so constantly followed by certain other feelings that it suggests a lively expectation of these. The suggestive feeling alone *is*, and it is ceasing to be. If this is the true account of propositions suggested by everyone's constantly-recurrent experience, what are we to make of scientific truths, *e.g.* 'a body will change its place sooner than let another enter it,' 'planets move in ellipses,' 'the square on the hypotheneuse is equal to the squares on the sides.' In these cases, too, does the present reality lie merely in a feeling experienced by this or that scientific man, and to him suggestive of other feelings? Does the proposition that 'planets move in ellipses' mean that to some watcher of the skies, who understands Kepler's laws, a certain perception of 'visible extension' (*i.e.* of colour or light and shade) not only suggests, as to others, a particular expectation of other feelings, which expectation is called a planet, but a further expectation, not shared by the multitude, of feelings suggesting successive situations of the visible extension, which further expectation is called elliptical motion? Such an explanation of general propositions would be a form of the doctrine conveniently named after Protagoras—'ἀληθὲς ὃ ἑκάστῳ ἑκάστοτε δοκεῖ'—a doctrine which the vindicators of Berkeley are careful to tell us we must not confound with his. The question, however, is not whether Berkeley himself admits the doctrine, but whether or no it is the logical consequence of the method which he uses for the overthrow of materialists and 'mathematical Atheists'?

173. His purpose was the maintenance of Theism, and a true instinct told him that pure Theism, as distinct from nature-worship and dæmonism, has no philosophical foundation, unless it can be shown that there is nothing real apart from thought. But in the hurry of theological advocacy,

and under the influence of a misleading terminology, he failed to distinguish this true proposition—there is nothing real apart from thought—from this false one, its virtual contradictory—there is nothing other than feeling. The confusion was covered, if not caused, by the ambiguity, often noticed, in the use of the term 'idea.' This to Berkeley's generation stood alike for feeling proper, which to the subject that merely feels is neither outer nor inner, because not referring itself to either mind or thing, and for conception, or an object thought of under relations. According to Locke, pain, colour, solidity, are all ideas equally with each other and equally with the *idea of* pain, *idea of* colour, *idea of* solidity. If all alike, however, were feelings proper, there would be no world either to exist or be spoken of. Locke virtually saves it by two suppositions, each incompatible with the equivalence of idea to feeling, and implying the conversion of it into conception as above defined. One is that there are abstract ideas; the other that there are primary qualities of which ideas are copies, but which do not come and go with our feelings. The latter supposition gives a world that 'really exists,' the former a world that may be known and spoken of; but neither can maintain itself without a theory of conception which is not forthcoming in Locke himself. We need not traverse again the contradictions which according to his statement they involve—contradictions which, under whatever disguise, must attach to every philosophy that admits a reality either in things as apart from thought or in thought as apart from things, and only disappear when the thing as thought of, and through thought individualised by the relations which constitute its community with the universe, is recognised as alone the real. Misled by the phrase 'idea of a thing,' we fancy that idea and thing have each a separate reality of their own, and then puzzle ourselves with questions as to how the idea can represent the thing—how the ideas of primary qualities can be copies of them, and how, if the real thing of experience be merely individual, a general idea can be abstracted from it. These questions Berkeley asked and found unanswerable. There were then two ways of dealing with them before him. One was to supersede them by a truer view of thought and its object, as together in essential correlation constituting the real; but this way he did not take. The other was to avoid them by merging both thing and idea in the indifference of simple feeling. For a merely sentient being, it is true—for one who did not think upon his feelings—the oppositions of inner and outer, of subjective and objective, of fantastic and real, would not exist; but neither would knowledge or a world to be known. That such oppositions, misunderstood, may be a heavy burden on the human spirit, the experience of current controversy and its spiritual effects might alone suffice to convince us; but the philosophical deliverance can only lie in the recognition of thought as their author, not in the attempt to obliterate them by the reduction of thought and its world to feeling—an attempt which contradicts itself, since it virtually admits their existence while it renders them unaccountable.

174. That Berkeley's was such an attempt, looking merely to his treatment of primary qualities and abstract ideas, we certainly could not doubt: though, since language does not allow of its consistent statement, and Berkeley was quite ready to turn the exigencies of language to account, passages logically incompatible with it may easily be found in him. The hasty reader, when he is told that body or distance are suggested by feelings of sight and touch rather than immediately seen, accepts the doctrine without scruple, because he supposes that which is suggested to be a present reality, though not at present felt. But if not at present felt it is not according to Berkeley an idea, therefore 'without the mind,' therefore an impossibility.[1] That which is suggested, then, must itself be a feeling which consists in the expectation of other feelings. Distance, and body, *as suggested*, can be no more than such an expectation; and as *actually existing*, no more than the actual succession of the expected feelings— a succession of which, as of every succession, 'no two parts exist together.'[2] There is no time, then, at which it can be said that distance and body exist.

175. This, it may seem, however inconsistent with the doctrine of primary qualities, is little more than the result which Locke himself comes to in his Fourth Book; since, if 'actual present succession' forms our only knowledge of real existence, there could be no time at which distance and body might be *known* as really existing. But Locke, as we have

---

[1] Reference is here merely made to the doctrine by which Berkeley disposes of 'matter,' the consideration of its reconcilability with his doctrine of 'spirits' and 'relations' as objects of knowledge being postponed.

[2] Locke, Book II. chap. xv. sec. 1.

seen, is able to save mathematical, though not physical, knowledge from the consequences of this admission by his doctrine
of abstract ideas—'ideas removed in our thoughts from particular existence'—whose agreement or disagreement is stated
in propositions which 'concern not existence,' and for that
reason may be general without becoming either uncertain or
uninstructive. This doctrine Berkeley expressly rejects on
the ground that he could not perceive separately that which
could not exist separately ('Principles of Human Knowledge,'
Introduction, sec. 10); a ground which to the ordinary reader
seems satisfactory because he has no doubt, and Berkeley's
instances do not suggest a doubt, as to the present existence
of 'individual objects'—this man, this horse, this body. But
with Berkeley to exist means to be felt ('Principles of Human
Knowledge,' sec. 3), and the feelings, which I name a body,
being successive, its existence must be in succession likewise.
The limitation, then, of possibility of 'conception' by possibility of existence, means that 'conception,' too, is reduced
to a succession of feelings.

176. Berkeley, then, as a consequence of the methods by
which he disposes at once of the 'real existence' and 'abstract
idea of matter,' has to meet the following questions :—How
are either reality or knowledge possible without permanent
relations? and, How can feelings, of which one is over before
the next begins, constitute or represent a world of permanent
relations?   The difficulty becomes more obvious, though not
more serious, when the relations in question are not merely
themselves permanent, as are those between natural phenomena, but are relations between permanent parts like those of
space. It is for this reason that its doctrine of geometry is the
most easily assailable point of the 'sensational' philosophy.
Locke distinguishes the ideas of space and of duration as
got, the one from the permanent parts of space, the other
'from the fleeting and perpetually perishing parts of succession.' [1] He afterwards prefers to oppose the term 'expansion'
to 'duration,' as bringing out more clearly than 'space' the
opposition of relation between permanent facts to that between 'fleeting successive facts which never exist together.'
How, then, can a consciousness, consisting simply of 'fleeting
successive facts,' either be or represent that of which the
differentia is that its facts are permanent and co-exist?

[1] Book ii. chap. xiv. sec. 1.

177. This crucial question in regard to extension does not seem even to have suggested itself to Berkeley. The reason why is not far to seek. Professor Fraser, in his valuable edition, represents him as meaning by visible extension 'coloured experience in sense,' and by tangible extension 'resistent experience in sense.'[1] No fault can be found with this interpretation, but the essential question, which Berkeley does not fairly meet, is whether the experience in each case is complete in a single feeling or consists in a succession of feelings. If in a single feeling, it clearly is not extension, as a relation between parts, at all; if in a succession of feelings, it is only extension because a synthetic principle, which is not itself one of the feelings, but equally present to them all, transforms them into permanent parts of which each qualifies the other by outwardness to it. Berkeley does not see the necessity of such a principle, because he allows himself to suppose extension—at any rate visible extension—to be constituted by a single feeling. Having first pronounced that the proper object of sight is colour, he quietly substitutes for this *situations* of colour, degrees of strength and faintness in colour, and quantities of coloured points, as if these, interchangeably with mere colour, were properly objects of sight and perceived in single acts of vision. Now if by object of sight were meant something other than the sensation itself— something which to a thinking being it suggests as its cause —there would be no harm in this language, but neither would there be any ground for saying that the proper object of sight is colour, for distinguishing visible from tangible extension, or for denying that the outwardness of body to body is seen. Such restrictions and distinctions have no meaning, unless by sight is meant the nervous irritation, the affection of the visual organ, as it is to a merely feeling subject; yet in the very passages where he makes them, by saying that we see situations and degrees of colour, and quantities of coloured points, Berkeley converts sight into a judgment of extensive and intensive quantity. He thus fails to discern that the transition from colour to coloured extension cannot be made without on the one hand either the presen-

---

[1] See Fraser's Berkeley, 'Theory of Vision,' note 42. I may here say that I have gone into less detail in my account of Berkeley's system than I should otherwise have thought necessary, because Professor Fraser has supplied, in the way of explanation of it, all that a student can require.

tation of successive pictures or (which comes to the same) successive acts of attention to a single picture, and on the other hand a synthesis of the successive presentations as mutually qualified parts of a whole. In other words, he ignores the work of thought involved in the constitution alike of coloured and tangible extension, and in virtue of which alone either is extension at all.

178. But though he does not scruple to substitute for colour situations and quantities of coloured points, these do not with him constitute space, which he takes according to Locke's account of it to be 'distance between bodies or parts of the same body.' This, according to his 'Theory of Vision,' is *tangible* extension, and this again is alone the object of geometry. As in that treatise a difference is still supposed between tangible extension and the feeling of touch, the question does not there necessarily arise whether the tactual experience, that constitutes this extension, is complete in a single feeling or only in a succession of feelings; but when in the subsequent treatise the difference is effaced, it is decided by implication that the experience is successive :[1] and all received modifications of the theory, which assign to a locomotive or muscular sense the office which Berkeley roughly assigned to touch, make the same implication still more clearly. Now in the absence of any recognition of a synthetic principle, in relation to which the successive experience becomes what it is not in itself, this means nothing else than that space is a succession of feelings, which again means that space is not space, not a qualification of bodies or parts of body by mutual externality, since to such qualification it is necessary that bodies or their parts coexist. Thus, in his hurry to get rid of externality as independence of the mind, he has really got rid of it as a relation between bodies, and in so doing (however the result may be disguised) has logically made a clean sweep of geometry and physics.

179. Of this result he himself shows no suspicion. He professes to be able, without violence to his doctrine, to accept the sciences as they stand, except so far as they rest upon the needless and unmeaning assumptions (as he reckoned

[1] 'Principles of Human Knowledge,' sec. 44. It will be observed that in that passage Berkeley uses the term 'distance,' not 'space,' and though with him the terms are strictly interchangeable, this may have helped to disguise from him the full monstrosity of the doctrine, 'space is a succession of feelings,' which, stated in that form, must surely have scandalised him.

them) of *pure* space and its infinite divisibility. The truth seems to be that—at any rate in the state of mind represented by his earlier treatises—he was only able to work on the lines which Locke had laid. It did not occur to him to treat the primary qualities as relations constituted by thought, because Locke had not done so. Locke having treated them as external to the mind, Berkeley does so likewise, and for that reason feels that they must be got rid of. The mode of riddance, again, was virtually determined for him by Locke. Locke having admitted that they copied themselves in feelings, the untenable element in this supposition had only to be dropped and they became feelings simply. It is thus only so far as space is supposed to exist after a mode of which, according to Locke himself, sense could take no copy—*i.e.* as exclusive not merely of all colour but of all body, and as infinitely divisible—that Berkeley becomes aware of its incompatibility with his doctrine. Pure space, or 'vacuum,' to him means space that can not be touched—a tangible extension that is not tangible—and is therefore a contradiction in terms. The notion that, though not touched, it might be seen, he excludes,[1] apparently for the same reason which prevents him from allowing *visible* extension to be space at all; the reason, namely, that there is no 'outness' or relation of externality between the parts of such extension. The fact that there can be no such relation between the successive feelings which alone, according to him, constitute 'tangible extension,' he did not see to be equally fatal to the latter being in any true sense space. In other words, he did not see that the test of reduction to feeling, by which he disposed of the *vacuum*, disposed of space altogether. If he had, he would have understood that space and body were intelligible relations, which can be thought of apart from the feelings which through them become the world that we know, since it is they that are the conditions of these feelings becoming a knowledge, not the feelings that are the condition of the relations being known. Whether they can be thought of apart from each other—whether the simple relation of externality between parts of a whole can be thought of without the parts being considered as solid—is of course a further question, and one which Berkeley cannot be said properly to discuss at all, since the abstraction of space from body to him

---

[1] 'Principles of Human Knowledge,' sec. 116.

meant its abstraction from feelings of touch.   The answer to
it ceases to be difficult as soon as the question is properly
stated.

180. As with vacuum, so with infinite divisibility.   Once
let it be understood that extension is constituted by the relation of externality between homogeneous parts, and it follows
that there can be no *least* part of extension, none that does
not itself consist of parts; in other words, that it is infinitely
divisible : just as conversely it follows that there can be no
last part of it, not having another outside it; in other words,
that (to use Locke's phrase) it is infinitely addible.   Doubtless, as Berkeley held, there is a 'minimum visibile'; but this
means that there are conditions under which any seen colour
disappears, and disappearing, ceases to be known under the
relation of extension; but it is only through a confusion of
the relation with the colour that the disappearance of the
latter is thought to be a disappearance of so much extension.[1]
It was, in short, the same failure to recognise the true ideality
of space, as a relation constituted by thought, that on the one
hand made its ' purity ' and infinity unmeaning to Berkeley,
and on the other made him think that, if pure (*sc.* irreducible to
feelings) and infinite, it must limit the Divine perfection, either
as being itself God or as 'something beside God which is
eternal, uncreated, and infinite' ('Principles of Human Knowledge,' sec. 117).   Fear of this result set him upon that
method of resolving space, and with it the world of nature,
into sequent feelings, which, if it had been really susceptible
of logical expression, would at best have given him nothing
but a μέγα ζῶον for God.   If he had been in less of a hurry with
his philosophy, he might have found that the current tendency
to ' bind God in nature or diffuse in space ' required to be met
by a sounder than his boyish idealism—by an idealism which
gives space its due, but reflects that to make space God, or a
limitation on God, is to subject thought itself to the most
superficial of the relations by which it forms the world that
it knows.

181. So far we have only considered Berkeley's reduction
of primary qualities, supposed to be sensible, to sensations
as it affects the qualities themselves, rather than as it affects
the possibility of universal judgments about them.   If, indeed,

---

[1] The same remark of course applies, *mutatis mutandis*, to the ' minimum tangibile.' See below, paragraphs 265 and 266.

as we have found, such reduction really amounts to the absolute obliteration of the qualities, no further question can
remain as to the possibility of general knowledge concerning
them. As Berkeley, however, did not admit the obliteration,
the further question did remain for him : and the condition
of his plausibly answering it was that he should recognise
in the 'idea,' as subject of predication, that intelligible qualification by relation which he did not recognise in it simply as
'idea,' and which essentially differences it from feeling
proper. If any particular 'tangible extension,' *e.g.* a right-
angled triangle, is only a feeling, or in Berkeley's own
language, 'a fleeting perishable passion'[1] not existing at all,
even as an 'abstract idea,' except when some one's tactual
organs are being affected in a certain way—what are we
to make of such a general truth as that the square on its
base is always equal to the squares on its sides ? Omitting
all difficulties about the convertibility of a figure with a
feeling, we find two questions still remain—How such separation can be made of the figure from the other conditions
of the tactual experience as that propositions should be
possible which concern the figure simply ; and how a single
case of tactual experience—that in which the mathematician
finds a feeling called a right-angled triangle followed by
another which he calls equality between the squares, &c.—
leads in the absence of any 'necessary connexion' to the
expectation that the sequence will always be the same.[2] The
difficulty becomes the more striking when it is remembered
that though the geometrical proposition in question, according
to Berkeley, concerns the tangible, the experience which
suggests it is merely visual.

182. Berkeley's answer to these questions must be gathered
from his theory of general names. 'It is, I know,' he says,
'a point much insisted on, that all knowledge and demonstration are about universal notions, to which I fully agree : but
then it does not appear to me that those notions are formed
by abstraction—*universality*, so far as I can comprehend, not
consisting in the absolute positive nature or conception of
anything, but in the relation it bears to the particulars
signified or represented by it; by virtue whereof it is that
things, names, or notions, being in their own nature *particular*, are rendered universal. Thus, when I demonstrate

---

[1] 'Principles of Human Knowledge,' sec. 89.   [2] See above, paragraph 122.

any proposition concerning triangles, it is to be supposed that I have in view the universal idea of a triangle; which is not to be understood as if I could frame an idea of a triangle which was neither equilateral nor scalene nor equicrural; but only that the particular triangle I considered, whether of this or that sort it matters not, doth equally stand for and represent all rectilinear triangles whatsoever, and is in that sense universal.' Thus it is that 'a man may consider a figure merely as triangular.' ('Principles of Human Knowledge,' Introd. secs. 15 and 16.)

183. In this passage appear the beginnings of a process of thought which, if it had been systematically pursued by Berkeley, might have brought him to understand by the 'percipi,' to which he pronounced 'esse' equivalent, definitely the 'intelligi.' As it stands, the result of the passage merely is that the triangle (for instance) 'in its own nature,' because 'particular,' is not a possible subject of general predication or reasoning: that it is so only as 'considered' under a relation of resemblance to other triangles and by such consideration universalized. 'In its own nature,' or as a 'particular idea,' the triangle, we must suppose, is so much tangible (or visible, as symbolical of tangible) extension, and therefore according to Berkeley a feeling. But a relation, as he virtually admits,[1] is neither a feeling nor felt. The triangle, then, as considered under relation and thus a possible subject of general propositions, is quite other than the triangle in its own nature. This, of course, is so far merely a virtual repetition of Locke's embarrassing doctrine that real things are not the things which we speak of, and which are the subject of our sciences; but it is a repetition with two fruitful differences —one, that the thing in its 'absolute positive nature' is more explicitly identified with feeling; the other, that the process, by which the thing thought and spoken of is supposed to be derived from the real thing, is no longer one of 'abstraction,' but consists in consideration of relation. It is true that with Berkeley the mere feeling has a 'positive nature' apart from considered relations,[2] and that the considered relation, by which the feeling is universalised, is only that of resemblance between properties supposed to exist independently of it. The 'particular triangle,' reducible to feelings of touch, has its

[1] See 'Principles of Human Knowledge,' sec. 89. (2nd edit.)
[2] See below, paragraph 298.

triangularity (we must suppose) simply as a feeling. It is only the resemblance between the triangularity in this and other figures—not the triangularity itself—that is a relation, and, as a relation, not felt but considered ; or in Berkeley's language, something of which we have not properly an ' idea' but a ' notion.'[1]

184. But though Berkeley only renders explicit the difficulties implicit in Locke's doctrine of ideas, that is itself a great step taken towards disposing of them.   Once let the equivocation between sensible qualities and sensations be got rid of—once let it be admitted that the triangle in its absolute nature, as opposed to the triangle considered, is merely a feeling, and that relations are not feelings or felt—and the question must soon arise, What in the absence of all relation remains to be the absolute nature of the triangle ?   It is a question which ultimately admits of but one answer.   The triangularity of the given single figure must be allowed to be just as much a relation as the resemblance, consisting in triangularity, between it and other figures ; and if a relation, then not properly felt, but understood.   The ' particular' triangle, if by that is meant the triangle as subject of a singular proposition, is no more ' particular in time,' no more constituted by the occurrence of a feeling, than is the triangle as subject of a general proposition.   It really exists as constituted by relation, and therefore only as ' considered' or understood.   In its existence, as in the consideration of it, the relations indicated by the terms ' equilateral, equicrural and scalene,' presuppose the relation of triangularity, not it them ; and for that reason it can be considered apart from them, though not they apart from it, without any breach between that which is considered and that which really exists.   Thus, too, it becomes explicable that a single experiment should warrant a universal affirmation ; that the mathematician, having once found as the result of a certain comparison of magnitudes that the square on the hypothenuse is equal to the square on the sides, without waiting for repeated experience at once substitutes for the singular proposition, which states his discovery, a general one.   If the

[1] 'Principles of Human Knowledge,' *Ibid.* This perhaps is the best place for saying that it is not from any want of respect for Dr. Stirling that I habitually use 'notion' in the loose popular way which he counts 'barbarous,' but because the barbarism is so prevalent that it seems best to submit to it, and to use 'conception' as the equivalent of the German ' Begriff.'

singular proposition stated a sensible event or the occurrence of a feeling, such substitution would be inexplicable: for if that were the true account of the singular proposition, a general one could but express such expectation of the recurrence of the event as repeated experience of it can alone give. But a relation is not contingent with the contingency of feeling. It is permanent with the permanence of the combining and comparing thought which alone constitutes it; and for that reason, whether it be recognised as the result of a mathematical construction or of a crucial experiment in physics, the proposition which states it must already be virtually universal.

185. Of such a doctrine Berkeley is rather the unconscious forerunner than the intelligent prophet. It is precisely upon the question whether, or how far, he recognised the constitution of things by intelligible relations, that the interpretation of his early (which is his only developed) idealism rests. Is it such idealism as Hume's, or such idealism as that adumbrated in some passages of his own 'Siris'? Is the idea, which is real, according to him a feeling or a conception? Has it a nature of its own, consisting simply in its being felt, and which we afterwards for purposes of our own consider in various relations; or does the nature consist only in relations, which again imply the action of a mind that is eternal— present to that which is in succession, but not in succession itself? The truth seems to be that this question in its full significance never presented itself to Berkeley, at least during the period represented by his philosophical treatises. His early idealism, as we learn from the commonplace-book brought to light by Professor Fraser, was merely a cruder form of Hume's. By the time of the publication of the 'Principles of Human Knowledge' he had learnt that, unless this doctrine was to efface 'spirit' as well as 'matter,' he must modify it by the admission of a 'thing' that was not an 'idea,' and of which the 'esse' was 'percipere' not 'percipi.' This admission carried with it the distinction between the object felt and the object known, between 'idea' and 'notion'—a distinction which was more clearly marked in the 'Dialogues.' Of 'spirit' we could have a 'notion,' though not an 'idea.' But it was only in the second edition of the 'Principles' that 'relation' was put along with 'spirit,' as that which could be known but which was no 'idea;' and

then without any recognition of the fact that the whole reduction of primary qualities to mere ideas was thereby
invalidated. The objects, with which the mathematician
deals, are throughout treated as in their own nature 'particular ideas,' into the constitution of which relation does not
enter at all; in other words, as successive feelings.

186. If the truths of mathematics seemed to Berkeley explicable on this supposition, those of the physical sciences
were not likely to seem less so. As long as the relations
with which these sciences deal are relations between 'sensible
objects,' he does not notice that they *are* relations, and
therefore not feelings or felt, at all. He treats felt things as
if the same as feelings, and ignores the relations altogether.
Thus a so-called 'sensible' motion causes him no difficulty.
He would be content to say that it was a succession of ideas,
not perceiving that motion implies a relation between spaces
or moments as successively occupied by something that
remains one with itself—a relation which a mere sequence of
feelings could neither constitute nor of itself suggest. It is
only about a motion which does not profess to be 'seen,' such
as the motion of the earth, that any question is raised—a
question easily disposed of by the consideration that in a different position we should see it. 'The question whether the
earth moves or not amounts in reality to no more than this, to
wit, whether we have reason to conclude from what hath been
observed by astronomers, that if we were placed in such and
such circumstances, and such or such a position and distance
both from the earth and sun, we should perceive the former to
move among the choir of the planets, and appearing in all
respects like one of them: and this by the established rules
of nature, which we have no reason to mistrust, is reasonably
collected from the phenomena' ('Principles of Human Knowledge,' sec. 58).[1]

187. Now this passage clearly does not mean—as it ought
to mean if the '*esse*' of the motion were the '*percipi*' by us—
that the motion of the earth would begin as soon as we were
there to see it. It means that it is now going on as an 'established law of nature,' which may be 'collected from the
phenomena.' In other words, it means that our successive
feelings are so related to each other as determined by one
present and permanent system, on which not they only but

[1] Cf. 'Dialogues,' page 147, in Prof. Fraser's edition.

all possible feelings depend, that by a certain set of them we are led—not to expect a recurrence of them in like order according to the laws of association, but, what is the exact reverse of this—to infer that certain other feelings, of which we have no experience, would now occur to us if certain conditions of situation on our part were fulfilled, because the 'ordo ad universum,' of which these feelings would be the 'ordo ad nos,' does now obtain. But though Berkeley's words mean this for us, they did not mean it for him. That such relation—merely intelligible, or according to his phraseology not an idea or object of an idea at all, as he must have admitted it to be—gives to our successive feelings the only 'nature' that they possess, he never recognised. By the relation of idea to idea, as he repeatedly tells us, he meant not a 'necessary connexion,' *i.e.* not a relation without which neither idea would be what it is, but such *de facto* sequence of one upon the other as renders the occurrence of one the unfailing but arbitrary sign that the other is coming. It is thus according to him (and here Hume merely followed suit) that feelings are symbolical—symbolical not of an order other than the feelings and which accounts for them, but simply of feelings to follow. To Berkeley, indeed, unlike Hume, the sequence of feelings symbolical of each other is also symbolical of something farther, viz. the mind of God : but when we examine what this 'mind' means, we find that it is not an intelligible order by which our feelings may be interpreted, or the spiritual subject of such an order, but simply the arbitrary will of a creator that this feeling shall follow that.

188. Such a doctrine could not help being at once confused in its account of reality, and insecure in its doctrine alike of the human spirit and of God. On the recognition of relations as constituting the *nature* of ideas rests the possibility of any tenable theory of their reality. An isolated idea could be neither real nor unreal. Apart from a definite order of relation we may suppose (if we like) that it would *be*, but it would certainly not be real; and as little could it be unreal, since unreality can only result from the confusion in our consciousness of one order of relation with another. It is diversity of relations that distinguishes, for instance, these letters as they now appear on paper from the same as I imagine them with my eyes shut, giving each sort its own reality : just as upon

confusion with the other each alike becomes unreal. Thus, though with Locke simple ideas are necessarily real, we soon find that even according to him they are not truly so in their simplicity, but only as related to an external thing producing them. He is right enough, however inconsistent with himself, in making relation constitute reality; wrong in limiting this prerogative to the one relation of externality. When he afterwards, in virtual contradiction to this limitation, finds the reality of moral and mathematical ideas just in that sole relation to the mind, as its products, which he had previously made the source of all unreality, he forces upon us the explanation which he does not himself give, that unreality does not lie in either relation as opposed to the other, but in the confusion of any relation with another. It is for lack of this explanation that Locke himself, as we have seen, finds in the liveliness and involuntariness of ideas the sole and sufficient tests (not *constituents*) of their reality; though they are obviously tests which put the dreams of a man in a fever upon the same footing with the 'impressions' of a man awake, and would often prove that unreal after dinner which had been proved real before. There is a well-known story of a man who in a certain state of health commonly saw a particular gory apparition, but who, knowing its origin, used to have himself bled till it disappeared. The reality of the apparition lay, he knew, in some relation between the circulation of his blood and his organs of sight, in distinction from the reality existing in the normal relations of his visual organs to the light : and in his idea, accordingly, there was nothing unreal, because he did not confuse the one relation with the other. Locke's doctrine, however, would allow of no distinction between the apparition as it was for such a man and as it would be for one who interpreted it as an actual 'ghost.' However interpreted, the liveliness and the involuntariness of the idea remain the same, as does its relation to an efficient cause. If in order to its reality the cause must be an 'outward body,' then it is no more real when rightly, than when wrongly, interpreted; while on the ground of liveliness and involuntariness it is as real when taken for a ghost as when referred to an excess of blood in the head.

189. As has been pointed out above, it is in respect not of the 'ratio cognoscendi' but of the 'ratio essendi' that Berkeley's doctrine of reality differs from Locke's. With him

it is not as an effect of an outward body, but as an immediate effect of God, that an 'idea of sense' is real. Just as with Locke real ideas and matter serve each to explain the other, so with Berkeley do real ideas and God. If he is asked, What is God? the answer is, He is the efficient cause of real ideas; if he is asked, What are real ideas? the answer is, Those which God produces, as opposed to those which we make for ourselves. To the inevitable objection, that this is a logical see-saw, no effective answer can be extracted from Berkeley but this—that we have subjective tests of the reality of ideas apart from a knowledge of their cause. In his account of these Berkeley only differs from Locke in adding to the qualifications of liveliness and involuntariness those of 'steadiness, order, and coherence' in the ideas. This addition may mean either a great deal or very little. To us it may mean that the distinction of real and unreal is one that applies not to feelings but to the conceived relations of feelings; not to events as such, but to the intellectual interpretation of them. The occurrence of a feeling taken by itself (it may be truly said) is neither coherent nor incoherent; nor can the sequence of feelings one upon another with any significance be called coherence, since in that case an incoherence would be as impossible as any failure in the sequence. As little can we mean by such coherence an usual, by incoherence an unusual, sequence of feelings. If we did, every sequence not before experienced—such, for instance, as is exhibited by a new scientific experiment—being unusual, would have to be pronounced incoherent, and therefore unreal. Coherence, in short, we may conclude, is only predicable of a system of relations, not felt but conceived; while incoherence arises from the attempt of an imperfect intelligence to think an object under relations which cannot ultimately be held together in thought. The qualification then of 'ideas' as coherent has in truth no meaning unless 'idea' be taken to mean not *feeling* but *conception*: and thus understood, the doctrine that coherent ideas *are* (Berkeley happily excludes the notion that they merely *represent*) the real, amounts to a clear identification of the real with the world of conception.

190. If such idealism were Berkeley's, his inference from the 'ideality' of the real to spirit and God would be more valid than it is. To have got rid of the notion that the

world first exists and then is thought of—to have seen that
it only really exists as thought of—is to have taken the first
step in the only possible 'proof of the being of God,' as the
self-conscious subject in relation to which alone an intelligible world can exist, and the presence of which in us is the
condition of our knowing it.[1] But there is nothing to show
that in adopting coherence as one test, among others, of the
reality of ideas, he attached to it any of the significance
exhibited above. He adopted it from ordinary language
without considering how it affected his view of the world as
a succession of feelings. That still remained to him a sufficient account of the world, even when he treated it as affording
intuitive certainty of a soul 'naturally immortal,' and demonstrative certainty of God. He is not aware, while he
takes his doctrine of such certainty from Locke, that he has
left out, and not replaced, the only solid ground for it which
Locke's system suggested.

191. The soul or self, as he describes it, does not differ
from Locke's 'thinking substance,' except that, having got
rid of 'extended matter' altogether, he cannot admit with
Locke any possibility of the soul's being extended, and,
having satisfied himself that 'time was nothing abstracted
from the succession of ideas in the mind,'[2] he was clear that
'the soul always thinks'—since the time at which it did not
think, being abstracted from a succession of ideas, would be
no time at all. A soul which is necessarily unextended and
therefore 'indiscerptible,' and without which there would be
no time, he reckons 'naturally immortal.'

192. Upon this the remark must occur that, if the fact of
being unextended constituted immortality, all sounds and
smells must be immortal, and that the inseparability of time
from the succession of feelings may prove that succession
endless, but proves no immortality of a soul unless there be
one self-conscious subject of that succession, identical with
itself throughout it. To the supposition of there being such
a subject, which Berkeley virtually makes, his own mode of
disposing of matter suggested ready objections. In Locke,
as we have seen, the two opposite 'things,' thinking and
material, always appear in strict correlativity, each representing (though he was not aware of this) the same logical

[1] See above, paragraphs 146 and 149–152.

[2] 'Principles of Human Knowledge,' sec. 98.

necessity of substantiation. 'Sensation convinces us that there are solid extended substances, and reflection that there are thinking ones.' These are not two convictions, however, but one conviction, representing one and the same essential condition of knowledge. Such logical necessity indeed is misinterpreted when made a ground for believing the real existence either of a multitude of independent things, for everything is a 'retainer' to everything else;[1] or of a separation of the thinking from the material substance, since, according to Locke's own showing, they at least everywhere overlap;[2] or of an absolutely last substance, which because last would be unknowable: but it is evidence of the action of a synthetic principle of self-consciousness without which all reference of feelings to mutually-qualified subjects and objects, and therefore all knowledge, would be impossible. It is idle, however, with Berkeley so to ignore the action of this principle on the one side as to pronounce the material world a mere succession of feelings, and so to take it for granted on the other as to assert that every feeling implies relation to a conscious substance. Upon such a method the latter assertion has nothing to rest on but an appeal to the individual's consciousness—an appeal which avails as much or as little for material as for thinking substance, and, in face of the apparent fact that with a knock on the head the conscious independent substance may disappear altogether, cannot hold its own against the suggestion that the one substance no less than the other is reducible to a series of feelings, so closely and constantly sequent on each other as to seem to coalesce. We cannot substitute for this illusory appeal the valid method of an analysis of knowledge, without finding that substantiation in matter is just as necessary to knowledge as substantiation in mind. If this method had been Berkeley's he would have found a better plan for dealing with the 'materialism' in vogue. Instead of trying to show that material substance was a fiction, he would have shown that it was really a basis of intelligible relations, and that thus all that was fictitious about it was its supposed sensibility and consequent opposition to the work of thought. Then his doctrine of matter would itself have established the necessity of spirit, not indeed as substance but as the source of all substantiation. As it was, misunderstanding

---

[1] Above, paragraph 125.   [2] Above, paragraph 127.

the true nature of the antithesis between matter and mind, in his zeal against matter he took away the ground from under the spiritualism which he sought to maintain. He simply invited a successor in speculation, of colder blood than himself, to try the solution of spirit in the same crucible with matter.

193. His doctrine of God is not only open to the same objection as his doctrine of spiritual substance, but to others which arise from the illogical restrictions that have to be put upon his notion of such substance, if it is to represent at once the God of received theology and the God whose agency the Berkeleian system requires as the basis of distinction between the real and unreal. Admitting the supposition involved in his certainty of the 'natural immortality' of the soul—the supposition that the succession of feelings which constitutes the world, and which at no time was not, implies one feeling substance—that substance we should naturally conclude was God. Such a God, it is true (as has been already pointed out),[1] would merely be the μέγα ζῶον of the crudest Pantheism, but it is the only God logically admissible—if any be admissible—in an 'ideal' system of which the text is not ' the world really exists only as thought of,' but 'the world only exists as a succession of feelings.' It was other than a *feeling* substance, however, that Berkeley required not merely to satisfy his religious instincts, but to take the place held by ' outward body' with Locke as the efficient of real ideas. The reference to this feeling substance, if necessary for any idea, is necessary for all—for the 'fantastic' as well as for those of sense—and can therefore afford no ground for distinction between the real and unreal. Instead, however, of being thus led to a truer view of this distinction, as in truth a distinction between the complete and incomplete conception of an intelligible world, he simply puts the feeling substance, when he regards it as God, under an arbitrary limitation, making it relative only to those ideas of which with Locke 'matter' was the substance, as opposed to those which Locke had referred to the thinking thing. The direct consequence of this limitation, indeed, might seem to be merely to make God an animal of partial, instead of universal, susceptibility; but this consequence Berkeley avoids by dropping the ordinary notion of substance altogether, so as to represent the ideas of

sense not as subsisting in God but as effects of His power—
as related to Him, in short, just as with Locke ideas of sense
are related to the primary qualities of matter. 'There must
be an active power to produce our ideas, which is not to be
found in ideas themselves, for we are conscious that they are
inert, nor in matter, since that is but a name for a bundle of
ideas ; which must therefore be in spirit, since of that we are
conscious as active; yet not in the spirit of which we are
conscious, since then there would be no difference between
real and imaginary ideas; therefore in a Divine Spirit, to
whom, however, may forthwith be ascribed the attributes of
the spirit of which we are conscious.' Such is the sum
of Berkeley's natural theology.

194. From a follower of Hume it of course invites the reply
that he does not see the necessity of an active power at all,
to which, since, according to Berkeley's own showing, it is no
possible 'idea' or object of an idea, all his own polemic against
the 'absolute idea' of matter is equally applicable; that the
efficient power, of which we profess to be conscious in ourselves,
is itself only a name for a particular feeling or impression
which precedes certain other of our impressions; that, even
if it were more than this, the transition from the spiritual
efficiency of which we are conscious to another, of which it is
the special differentia that we are not conscious of it, would
be quite illegitimate, and that thus in saying that certain
feelings are real because, being lively and involuntary, they
must be the work of this unknown spirit, we in effect say
nothing more than that they are real because lively and
involuntary. Against a retort of this kind Berkeley's theistic
armour is even less proof than Locke's. His 'proof of the
being of God' is in fact Locke's with the sole *nervus probandi*
left out. The value of Locke's proof, as an argument from
their being something now to their having been something
from eternity, lay, we saw, in its convertibility into an argument from the world as a system of relations to a present
and eternal subject of those relations. For its being so convertible there was this to be said, that Locke, with whatever
inconsistency, at least recognised the constitution of reality
by permanent relations, though he treated the mere relation
of external efficiency—that in virtue of which we say of
nature that it consists of bodies outward to and acting on
each other—as if it alone constituted the reality of the world.

Berkeley's reduction of the 'primary qualities of matter' to a succession of feelings logically effaces this relation, and puts nothing intelligible, nothing but a name, in its place. The effacement of the distinction between the real and unreal, which would properly ensue, is only prevented by bringing back relation to something under the name of God, either wholly unknown and indeterminate, or else, under a thin disguise, determined by that very relation of external efficiency which, when ascribed to something only nominally different, had been pronounced a gratuitous fiction. If Berkeley had dealt with the opposition of reality to thought by showing the primary qualities to be conceived relations, and the distinction between the real and unreal to be one between the fully and the defectively conceived, the case would have been different. The real and God would alike have been logically saved. The peculiar embarrassment of Locke's doctrine we have found to be that it involves the unreality of every object, into the constitution of which there enters any idea of reflection, or any idea retained in the mind, as distinct from the present effect of a body acting upon us—*i.e.* of every object of which anything can be said. With the definite substitution of full intelligibility of relations for present sensibility, as the true account of the real, this embarrassment would have been got rid of. At the same time there would have been implied an intelligent subject of these relations; the ascription to whom, indeed, of moral attributes would have remained a further problem, but who, far from being a 'Great Unknown,' would be at least determined by relation to that order of nature which is as necessary to Him as He to it. But in fact, as we have seen, the notion of the reality of relations, not felt but understood, only appears in Berkeley's developed philosophy as an after-thought, and the notion of an order of nature, other than our feelings, which enables us to infer what feelings that have never been felt would be, is an unexplained intrusion in it. The same is true of the doctrine, which struggles to the surface in the Third Dialogue, that the 'sensible world' is to God not felt at all, but known; that to Him it is precisely not that which according to Berkeley's refutation of materialism it really is— a series or collection of sensations. These 'after-thoughts,' when thoroughly thought out, imply a complete departure from Berkeley's original interpretation of 'phenomena' as simple feelings; but with him, so far from being thought out, they merely suggested themselves incidentally as the conceptions of God and reality were found to require them. In other words, that interpretation of phenomena, which is necessary to any valid 'collection' from them of the existence of God, only appears in him as a consequence of that 'collection' having been made. To pursue the original interpretation, so that all might know what it left of reality, was the best way of deciding the question of its compatibility with a rational belief in God—a question of too momentous an interest to be fairly considered in itself. Thus to pursue it was the mission of Hume.

195. Hume begins with an account of the 'perceptions of the human mind,' which corresponds to Locke's account of ideas with two main qualifications, both tending to complete that dependence of thought on something other than itself which Locke had asserted, but not consistently maintained. He distinguishes 'perceptions' (equivalent to Locke's ideas) into 'impressions' and 'ideas' accordingly as they are originally produced in feeling or reproduced by memory and imagination, and he does not al.ow 'ideas of reflection' any place in the *original* 'furniture of the mind.' 'An impression first strikes upon the senses, and makes us perceive heat or cold, thirst or hunger, pleasure or pain, of some kind or other. Of this impression there is a copy taken by the mind, which remains after the impression ceases; and this we call an idea. This idea of pleasure or pain, when it returns upon the soul, produces the new impressions of desire and aversion, hope and fear, which may properly be called impressions of reflection, because derived from it. These, again, are copied by the memory and imagination, and become ideas; which, perhaps, in their turn give rise to other impressions and ideas; so that the impressions are only antecedent to their correspondent ideas, but posterior to those of sensation and derived from them' (Part I. §2). He is at the same time careful to explain that the causes from which the impressions of sensation arise are unknown (ibid.), and that by the term 'impression' he is not to be 'understood to express the manner in which our lively perceptions are produced in the soul, but merely the perceptions themselves' (p. 312, note). The distinction between impression and idea he treats as equivalent to that between feeling and thinking, which, again,

lies merely in the different degrees of 'force and liveliness' with which the perceptions, thus designated, severally 'strike upon the mind.'[1] Thus the rule which he emphasises (p. 310) 'that all our simple ideas in their first appearance are derived from simple impressions which are correspondent to them and which they exactly represent,' strictly taken, means no more than that a feeling must be more lively before it becomes less so. As the reproduced perception, or 'idea,' differs in this respect from the original one, so, according to the greater or less degree of secondary liveliness which it possesses, is it called 'idea of memory,' or 'idea of imagination.' The only other distinction noticed is that, as might be expected, the comparative faintness of the ideas of imagination is accompanied by a possibility of their being reproduced in a different order from that in which the corresponding ideas were originally presented. Memory, on the contrary, 'is in a manner tied down in this respect, without any power of variation' (p. 318) ; which must be understood to mean that, when the ideas are faint enough to allow of variation in the order of reproduction, they are not called 'ideas of memory.'

196. All, then, that Hume could find in his mind, when after Locke's example he 'looked into it,' were, according to his own statement, feelings with their copies, dividing themselves into two main orders—those of sensation and those of reflection, of which the latter, though results of the former, are not their copies. The question, then, that he had to deal with was, to what impressions he could reduce those conceptions of relation—of cause and effect, substance and attribute, and identity—which all knowledge involves. Failing the impressions of sensation he must try those of reflection, and failing both he must pronounce such conceptions to be no 'ideas' at all, but words misunderstood, and leave knowledge to take its chance. The vital nerve of his philosophy lies in his treatment of the 'association of ideas' as a sort of process of spontaneous generation, by which impressions of sensation issue in such impressions of reflection, in the shape of habitual propensities,[2] as will account, not indeed for there being— since there really are not—but for there seeming to be, those formal conceptions which Locke, to the embarrassment of

---

[1] See pp. 327 and 375.   [2] Pp. 460 and 496.

his philosophy, had treated as at once real and creations of the mind.

197. Such a method meets at the outset with the difficulty that the impressions of sensation and those of reflection, if Locke's determination of the former by reference to an impressive matter is excluded, are each determined only by reference to the other. What is an impression of reflection? It is one that can only come after an impression of sensation. What is an impression of sensation? It is one that comes before any impression of reflection. An apparent determination, indeed, is gained by speaking of the original impressions as ' conveyed to us by our senses;' but this really means determination by reference to the organs of our body as affected by outward bodies—in short, by a physical theory. But of the two essential terms of this theory, ' our own body,' and ' outward body,' neither, according to Hume, expresses anything present to the original consciousness. 'Properly speaking, it is not our body we perceive when we regard our limbs and members, but certain impressions which enter by the senses.' Nor do any of our impressions 'inform us of distance and outness (so to speak) immediately, and without a certain reasoning and experience ' (p. 481). In such admissions Hume is as much a Berkeleian as Berkeley himself, and they effectually exclude any reference to body from those original impressions, by reference to which all other modes of consciousness are to be explained.

198. He thus logically cuts off his psychology from the support which, according to popular conceptions, its primary truths derive from physiology. We have already noticed how with Locke metaphysic begs defence of physic;[1] how, having undertaken to answer by the impossible method of self-observation the question as to what consciousness is to itself at its beginning, he in fact tells us what it is to the natural philosopher, who accounts for the production of sensation by the impact of matter ' on the outward parts, continued to the brain.' To those, of course, who hold that the only possible theory of knowledge and of the human spirit is physical, it must seem that this was his greatest merit; that, an unmeaning question having been asked, it was the best thing to give an answer which indeed is no answer to

[1] See above, paragraph 17.

the question, but has some elementary truth of its own. According to them, though he may have been wrong in supposing consciousness to be to itself what the physiologist explains it to be—since any supposition at all about it except as a phenomenon, to which certain other phenomena are invariably antecedent, is at best superfluous—he was not wrong in taking the physiological explanation to be the true and sufficient one. To such persons we can but respectfully point out that they have not come in sight of the problem which Locke and his followers, on however false a method, sought to solve; that, however certain may be the correlation between the brain and thought, in the sense that the individual would be incapable of the processes of thought unless he had brain and nerves of a particular sort, yet it is equally certain that every theory of the correlation must presuppose a knowledge of the processes, and leave that knowledge exactly where it was before; that thus their science, valuable like every other science within its own department, takes for granted just what metaphysic, as a theory of knowledge, seeks to explain. When the origin, for instance, of the conception of body or of that of an organic structure is in question, it is in the strictest sense preposterous to be told that body makes the conception of body, and that unless the brain were organic to thought I should not now be thinking. 'The brain is organic to thought;' here is a proposition involving conceptions within conceptions—a whole hierarchy of ideas. How am I enabled to re-think these in order, to make my way from the simpler to the more complex, by any iteration or demonstration of the proposition, which no one disputes, or by the most precise examination of the details of the organic structure itself?

199. The quarrel of the physiologist with the metaphysician is, in fact, due to an *ignorantia elenchi* on the part of the former, for which the behaviour of English 'metaphysicians,' in attempting to assimilate their own procedure to that of the natural philosophers, and thus to win the popular acceptance which these alone can fairly look for, has afforded too much excuse. The question really at issue is not between two co-ordinate sciences, as if a theory of the human body were claiming also to be a theory of the human soul, and the theory of the soul were resisting the aggression. The question is, whether the conceptions which all the departmental

sciences alike presuppose shall have an account given of them or no. For dispensing with such an account altogether (life being short) there is much to be said, if only men would or could dispense with it; but the physiologist, when he claims that his science should supersede metaphysic, is not dispensing with it, but rendering it in a preposterous way. He accounts for the formal conceptions in question, in other words for thought as it is common to all the sciences, as sequent upon the antecedent facts which his science ascertains—the facts of the animal organisation. But these conceptions—the relations of cause and effect, &c.—are necessary to constitute the facts. They are not an *ex post facto* interpretation of them, but an interpretation without which there would be no ascertainable facts at all. To account for them, therefore, as the result of the facts is to proceed as a geologist would do, who should treat the present conformation of the earth as the result of a certain series of past events, and yet, in describing these, should assume the present conformation as a determining element in each.

200. 'Empirical psychology,' however, claims to have a way of its own for explaining thought, distinct from that of the physiologist, but yet founded on observation, though it is admitted that the observation takes place under difficulties. Its method consists in a history of consciousness, as a series of events or successive states observed in the individual by himself. By tracing such a chain of *de facto* sequence it undertakes to account for the elements common to all knowledge. Its first concern, then, must be, as we have previously put it, to ascertain what consciousness is to itself at its beginning. No one with Berkeley before him, and accepting Berkeley's negative results, could answer this question in Locke's simple way by making the primitive consciousness report itself as an effect of the operation of body. To do so is to transfer a later and highly complex form of consciousness, whose growth has to be traced, into the earlier and simple form from which the growth is supposed to begin. This, upon the supposition that the process of consciousness by which conceptions are formed is a series of psychical events—a supposition on which the whole method of empirical psychology rests—is in principle the same false procedure as that which we have imagined in the case of a

geologist above. But the question is whether, by any procedure not open to this condemnation, the theory could seem
to do what it professes to do—explain thought or ' cognition
by means of conceptions' as something which happens in
sequence upon previous psychical events. Does it not, however stated, carry with it an implication of the supposed
later state in the earlier, and is it not solely in virtue of this
implication that it seems to be able to trace the genesis of
the later? No one has pursued it with stricter promises, or
made a fairer show of being faithful to them, than Hume.
He will begin with simple feeling, as first experienced by the
individual—unqualified by complex conceptions, physical or
metaphysical, of matter or of mind—and trace the process
by which it generates the ' ideas of philosophical relation.'
If it can be shown, as we believe it can be, that, even when
thus pursued, its semblance of success is due to the fact that,
by interpreting the earliest consciousness in terms of the
latest, it puts the latter in place of the former, some suspicion
may perhaps be created that a natural history of self-consciousness, and of the conceptions by which it makes the
world its own, is impossible, since such a history must be of
events, and self-consciousness is not reducible to a series of
events ; being already at its beginning formally, or potentially, or implicitly all that it becomes actually or explicitly
in developed knowledge.

201. If Hume were consistent in allowing no other determination to the impression than that of its having the
maximum of vivacity, or to other modes of consciousness
than the several degrees of their removal from this maximum,
he would certainly have avoided the difficulties which attend
Locke's use of the metaphor of impression, while at the same
time he would have missed the convenience, involved in this
use, of being able to represent the primitive consciousness as
already a recognition of a thing impressing it, and thus an
' idea of a quality of body.' But at the outset he remarks
that ' the examination of our sensations ' (*i.e.* our impressions
of sensation) ' belongs more to anatomists and natural philosophers than to moral,' and that for that reason he shall
begin not with them but with ideas (p. 317). Now this virtually means that he will begin, indeed, with the feelings he
finds in himself, but with these as determined by the notion
that they are results of something else, of which the nature

is not for the present explained. Thus, while he does not, like Locke, identify our earliest consciousness with a rough and ready physical theory of its cause, he gains the advantage of this identification in the mind of his reader, who from sensation, thus apparently defined, transfers a definiteness to the ideas and secondary impressions as derived from it, though in the sequel the theory turns out, if possible at all, to be at best a remote result of custom and association. We shall see this more clearly if we look back to the general account of impressions and ideas quoted above. 'An impression first strikes upon the senses and makes us perceive pleasure or pain, of which a copy is taken by the mind,' called an idea. Now if we set aside the notion of a body making impact upon a sensuous, and through it upon a mental, tablet, pleasure or pain *is* the impression, which, again, is as much or as little in the mind as the idea. Thus the statement might be re-written as follows :—' Pleasure or pain makes the mind perceive pleasure or pain, of which a copy is taken by the mind.' This, of course, is nonsense; but between this nonsense and the plausibility of the statement as it stands, the difference depends on the double distinction understood in the latter—the distinction (*a*) between the producing cause of the impression and the impression produced ; and (*b*) between the impression as produced on the senses, and the idea as preserved by the mind. This passage, as we shall see, is only a sample of many of the same sort. Throughout, however explicitly Hume may give warning that the difference between impression and idea is only one of liveliness, however little he may scruple in the sequel to reduce body and mind alike to the succession of feelings, his system gains the benefit of the contrary assumption which the uncritical reader is ready to make for him. As often as the question returns whether a phrase, purporting to express an ' abstract conception,' expresses any actual idea or no, his test is, ' Point out the impression from which the idea, if there be any, is derived '—a test which has clearly no significance if the impression is merely the idea itself at a livelier stage (for a person, claiming to have the idea, would merely have to say that he had never known it more lively, and that, therefore, it was itself an impression, and the force of the test would be gone), but which seems so satisfactory because the impres-

sion is regarded as the direct effect of outward things, and
thus as having a prerogative of reality over any perception
to which the mind contributes anything of its own. By
availing himself alternately of this popular conception of the
impression of sensation and of his own account of it, he gains
a double means of suppressing any claim of thought to originate. Every idea, by being supposed in a more lively state,
can be represented as derived from an impression, and thus
(according to the popular notion) as an effect of something
which, whatever it is, is not thought. If thereupon it is
pointed out that this outward something is a form of
substance which, according to Hume's own showing, is a
fiction of thought, there is an easy refuge open in the reply
that 'impression' is only meant to express a lively feeling, not any dependence upon matter of which we know
nothing.

202. Thus the way is prepared for the juggle which the
modern popular logic performs with the word 'phenomenon'
—a term which gains acceptance for the theory that turns
upon it because it conveys the notion of a relation between
a real order and a perceiving mind, and thus gives to those
who avail themselves of it the benefit of an implication of the
'noumena' which they affect to ignore. Hume's inconsistency, however, stops far short of that of his later disciples.
For the purpose of detraction from the work of thought he
availed himself, indeed, of that work as embodied in language, but only so far as was necessary to his destructive
purpose. He did not seriously affect to be reconstructing
the fabric of knowledge on a basis of fact.   There occasionally appears in him, indeed, something of the charla-
tanry of common sense in passages, more worthy of Boling-
broke than himself, where he writes as a champion of facts
against metaphysical jargon. But when we get behind the
mask of concession to popular prejudice, partly ironical,
partly due to his undoubted vanity, we find much more of
the ancient sceptic than of the 'positive philosopher.'

203. The ancient sceptic (at least as represented by the
ancient philosophers), finding knowledge on the basis of distinction between the real and apparent to be impossible,
discarded the enterprise of arriving at general truth in opposition to what appears to the individual at any particular
instant, and satisfied himself with noting such general tendencies of expectation and desire as would guide men in the

conduct of life and enable them to get what they wanted by contrivance and persuasion.[1] Such a state of mind excludes all motive to the 'interrogation of nature,' for it recognises no 'nature' but the present appearance to the individual; and this does not admit of being interrogated. The 'positive philosopher' has nothing in common with it but the use, in a different sense, of the word 'apparent.' He plumes himself, indeed, on not going in quest of any ' thing-in-itself' other than what appears to the senses; but he distinguishes between a real and apparent in the order of appearance, and considers the real order of appearance, having a permanence and uniformity which belong to no feeling as the individual feels it, to be the true object of knowledge. No one is more severe upon 'propensities to believe,' however spontaneously suggested by the ordinary sequence of appearances, if they are found to conflict with the order of nature as ascertained by experimental interrogation; i.e. with a sequence observed (it may be) in but a single instance. Which of the two attitudes of thought is the more nearly Hume's, will come out as we proceed. It was just with the distinction between the 'real and fantastic,' as Locke had left it, that he had to deal; and, as will appear, it is finally by a 'propensity to feign,' not by a uniform order of natural phenomena, that he replaces the real which Locke, according to his first mind, had found in archetypal things and their operations on us.

204. We have seen that Berkeley, having reduced 'simple ideas' to their simplicity by showing the illegitimacy of the assumption that they report qualities of a matter which is itself a complex idea, is only able to make his constructive theory march by the supposition of the reality and knowability of 'spirit' and relations. 'Ideas' are 'fleeting, perishable passions;' but the relations between them are uniform, and in virtue of this uniformity the fleeting idea may be interpreted as a symbol of a real order. But such relations, as real, imply the presence of the ideas to the constant mind of God, and, as knowable, their presence to a like mind in us. We have further seen how little Berkeley, according to the method by which he disposed of ' abstract general ideas,' was entitled to such a supposition. Hume sets it aside; but the

---

[1] Cf. Plato's 'Protagoras,' 323, and 'Theætetus,' 167, with the concluding paragraphs of the last part of the first book of Hume's 'Treatise on Human Nature.'

question is, whether without a supposition virtually the same he can represent the association of ideas as doing the work that he assigned to it.

205. His exclusion of Berkeley's supposition with regard to 'spirit' is stated without disguise, though unfortunately not till towards the end of the first book of the 'Treatise on Human Nature,' which could not have run so smoothly if the statement had been made at the beginning. It follows legitimately from the method, which he inherited, of 'looking into his mind to see how it wrought.' 'From what impression,' he asks, ' could the idea of self be derived? It must be some one impression that gives rise to every real idea. But self or person is not any impression, but that to which our several impressions and ideas are supposed to have a reference. If any impression gives rise to the idea of self, that impression must continue invariably the same through the whole course of our lives, since self is supposed to exist after that manner. But there is no impression constant and invariable. Pain and pleasure, grief and joy, passions and sensations succeed each other, and never all exist at the same time. It cannot, therefore, be from any of these impressions, or from any other, that the idea of self is derived ; and, consequently, there is no such idea.' Again: ' When I enter most intimately into what is called myself, I always stumble on some particular perception of heat or cold, light or shade, love or hatred, pain or pleasure. I never can catch myself at any time without a perception, and never can observe anything but the perception. When my perceptions are removed for any time, as by sound sleep, so long am I insensible of myself, and may truly be said not to exist.' Thus ' men are nothing but a bundle or collection of different perceptions that succeed each other with inconceivable rapidity, and are in a perpetual flux or movement. Our eyes cannot turn in their sockets without varying our perceptions. Our thought is still more variable than our sight. . . . nor is there any single power of the soul which remains unalterably the same perhaps for one moment. . . . There is properly no simplicity in the mind at one time nor identity at different' (pp. 533 and 534).

206. His position in regard to ideas of relation cannot be so summarily exhibited. It is from its ambiguity, indeed, that his system derives at once its plausibility and its weak-

ness. In the first place, it is necessary, according to him, to distinguish between 'natural' and 'philosophical relation.' The latter is one of which the idea is acquired by the comparison of objects, as distinct from natural relation or 'the quality by which two ideas are connected together in the imagination, and the one naturally' (*i.e.* according to the principle of association) 'introduces the other' (p. 322). Of philosophical relation—or, according to another form of expression, of 'qualities by which the ideas of philosophical relation are produced'—seven kinds are enumerated; viz. 'resemblance, identity, relations of time and place, proportion in quantity and number, degrees in quality, contrariety, and causation' (ibid., and p. 372). Some of these do, some do not, *apparently* correspond to the qualities by which the mind is *naturally* 'conveyed from one idea to another;' or which, in other words, constitute the 'gentle force' that determines the order in which the imagination habitually puts together ideas. Freedom in the conjunction of ideas, indeed, is implied in the term 'imagination,' which is only thus differenced from 'memory;' but, as a matter of fact, it commonly only connects ideas which are related to each other in the way either of resemblance, or of contiguity in time and place, or of cause and effect. Other relations of the philosophical sort are the opposite of *natural*. Thus, 'distance will be allowed by philosophers to be a true relation, because we acquire an idea of it by the comparing of objects; but in a common way we say, " that nothing can be more distant than such or such things from each other; nothing can have less relation "' (ibid.).

207. Hume's classification of philosophical relations evidently serves the same purpose as Locke's, of the 'four sorts of agreement or disagreement between ideas,' in the perception of which knowledge consists;[1] but there are some important discrepancies. Locke's second sort, which he awkwardly describes as 'agreement or disagreement in the way of relation,' may fairly be taken to cover three of Hume's kinds; viz. relations of time and place, proportion in quantity or number, and degrees in any quality. About Locke's first sort, 'identity and diversity,' there is more difficulty. Under 'identity,' as was pointed out above, he includes the

---

[1] See above, paragraph 25 and the passages from Locke there referred to.

relations which Hume distinguishes as 'identity proper' and 'resemblance.' 'Diversity' at first sight might seem to correspond to 'contrariety;' but the latter, according to Hume's usage, is much more restricted in meaning. Difference of number and difference of kind, which he distinguishes as the opposites severally of identity and resemblance, though they come under Locke's 'diversity,' are not by Hume considered relations at all, on the principle that 'no relation of any kind can subsist without some degree of resemblance.' They are 'rather a negation of relation than anything real and positive.' 'Contrariety' he reckons only to obtain between ideas of existence and non-existence, 'which are plainly resembling as implying both of them an idea of the object; though the latter excludes the object from all times and places in which it is supposed not to exist' (p. 323). There remain 'cause and effect' in Hume's list; 'co-existence' and 'real existence' in Locke's. 'Co-existence' is not expressly identified by Locke with the relation of cause and effect, but it is with 'necessary connection.' It means specially, it will be remembered,[1] the co-existence of ideas, not as constituents of a 'nominal essence,' but as qualities of real substances in nature; and our knowledge of this depends on our knowledge of necessary connection between the qualities, either as one supposing the other (which is the form of necessary connection between primary qualities), or as one being the effect of the other (which is the form of necessary connection between the ideas of secondary qualities and the primary ones). Having no knowledge of necessary connection as in real substances, we have none of 'co-existence' in the above sense, but only of the present union of ideas in any particular experiment.[2] The parallel between this doctrine of Locke's and Hume's of cause and effect will appear as we proceed. To 'real existence,' since the knowledge of it according to Locke's account is not a perception of agreement between ideas at all, it is not strange that nothing should correspond in Hume's list of relations.

208. It is his method of dealing with these ideas of philosophical relation that is specially characteristic of Hume. Let us, then, consider how the notion of relation altogether is affected by his reduction of the world of consciousness to

[1] See above, paragraph 122.
[2] Locke, Book IV. sec. iii. chap. xiv.; and above, paragraph 121 and 122.

impressions and ideas. What is an impression? To this, as we have seen, the only direct answer given by him is that it is a feeling which must be more lively before it becomes less so.[1] For a further account of what is to be understood by it we must look to the passages where the governing terms of 'school-metaphysics' are, one after the other, shown to be unmeaning, because not taken from impressions. Thus, when the idea of substance is to be reduced to an 'unintelligible chimæra,' it is asked whether it 'be derived from the impressions of sensation or reflection? If it be conveyed to us by our senses, I ask, which of them, and after what manner? If it be perceived by the eyes, it must be a colour; if by the ears, a sound; if by the palate, a taste; and so of the other senses. But I believe none will assert that substance is either a colour, or a sound, or a taste. The idea of substance must therefore be derived from an impression of reflection, if it really exist. But the impressions of reflection resolve themselves into our passions and emotions' (p. 324). From the polemic against abstract ideas we learn further that 'the appearance of an object to the senses' is the same thing as an 'impression becoming present to the mind' (p. 327). That is to say, when we talk of an impression of an object, it is not to be understood that the feeling is determined by reference to anything other than itself: it is itself the object. To the same purpose, in the criticism of the notion of an external world, we are told that 'the senses are incapable of giving rise to the notion of the continued existence of their objects, after they no longer appear to the senses; for that is a contradiction in terms' (since the appearance *is* the object); and that 'they offer not their impressions as the images of something distinct, or independent, or external, because they convey to us nothing but a single perception, and never give us the least intimation of anything beyond' (p. 479). The distinction between impression of sensation and impression of reflection, then, cannot, any more than that between impression and idea, be regarded as either really or apparently a distinction between outer and inner. 'All impressions are internal and perishing existences' (p. 483); and, 'everything that enters the mind being in reality as the impression, 'tis impossible anything should to feeling appear different' (p. 480).

[1] See above, paragraphs 195 and 197.

209. This amounts to a full acceptance of Berkeley's doctrine of sense; and the question necessarily arises—such being the impression, and all ideas being impressions grown weaker, can there be an idea of relation at all ? Is it not open to the same challenge which Hume offers to those who talk of an idea of substance or of spirit ? ' It is from some one impression that every real idea is derived.' What, then, is the one impression from which the idea of relation is derived ? ' If it be perceived by the eyes, it must be a colour; if by the ears, a sound; if by the palate, a taste; and so of the other senses.' There remain ' our passions and emotions;' but what passion or emotion is a resemblance, or a proportion, or a relation of cause and effect ?

210. Respect for Hume's thoroughness as a philosopher must be qualified by the observation that he does not attempt to meet this difficulty in its generality, but only as it affects the relations of identity and causation. The truth seems to be that he wrote with Berkeley steadily before his mind; and it was Berkeley's treatment of these two relations in particular as not sensible but intelligible, and his assertion of a philosophic Theism on the strength of their mere intelligibility, that determined Hume, since it would have been an anachronism any longer to treat them as sensible, to dispose of them altogether. The condition of his doing so with success was that, however unwarrantably, he should treat the other relations as sensible. The language, which seems to express ideas of the two questionable relations, he has to account for as the result of certain impressions of reflection, called ' propensities to feign,' which in their turn have to be accounted for as resulting from the *natural* relations of ideas according to the definition of these quoted above,[1] as ' the qualities by which one idea habitually introduces another.' Among these, as we saw, he included not only resemblance and contiguity in time or place, but ' cause and effect.' ' There is no relation,' he says, ' which produces a stronger connection in the fancy than this.' But in this, as in much of the language which gives the first two Parts their plausibility, he is taking advantage of received notions on the part of the reader, which it is the work of the rest of the book to set aside. In any sense, according to him, in which it differs

[1] See above, paragraph 206.

from usual contiguity, the relation of cause and effect is itself reducible to a 'propensity to feign,' arising from the other natural relations ; but when the reader is told of its producing ' a strong connection in the fancy,' he is not apt to think of it as itself nothing more than the product of such a connection. For the present, however, we have only to point out that Hume, when he co-ordinates it with the other natural relations, must be understood to do so provisionally. According to him it is derived, while they are primary. Upon them, then, rested the possibility of filling the gap between the occurrence of single impressions, none ' determined by reference to anything other than itself,' and what we are pleased to call our knowledge, with its fictions of mind and thing, of real and apparent, of necessary as distinct from usual connection.

211. We will begin with Resemblance. As to this, it will be said, it is an affectation of subtlety to question whether there can be an impression of it or no. The difficulty only arises from our regarding the perception of resemblance as different from, and subsequent to, the resembling sensations ; whereas, in fact, the occurrence of two impressions of sense, such as (let us say) yellow and red, is itself the impression of their likeness and unlikeness. Hume himself, it may be further urged, at any rate in regard to resemblance, anticipates this solution of an imaginary difficulty by his important division of philosophical relations into two classes (p. 372)— such as depend entirely on the ideas which we compare together, and such as may be changed without any change in the ideas '—and by his inclusion of resemblance in the former class.

212. Now we gladly admit the mistake of supposing that sensations undetermined by relation first occur, and that afterwards we become conscious of their relation in the way of likeness or unlikeness. Apart from such relation, it is true, the sensations would be nothing. But this admission involves an important qualification of the doctrine that impressions are single, and that the mind (according to Hume's awkward figure) is a 'bundle or collection of these,' succeeding each other 'in a perpetual flux or movement.' It implies that the single impression in its singleness is what it is through relation to another, which must there-

fore be present along with it; and that thus, though they
may occur in a perpetual flux of succession—every turn of
the eyes in their sockets, as Hume truly says, giving a new
one—yet, just so far as they are qualified by likeness or unlikeness to each other, they must be taken out of that succession by something which is not itself in it, but is indivisibly
present to every moment of it. This we may call soul, or
mind, or what we will; but we must not identify it with the
brain[1] either directly or by implication (as we do when we
'refer to the anatomist' for an account of it), since by the
brain is meant something material, *i.e.* divisible, which the
unifying subject spoken of, as feeling no less than as thinking,
cannot be. In short, any such modification of Hume's doctrine of the singleness and successiveness of impressions as
will entitle us to speak of their carrying with them, though
single and successive, the consciousness of their resemblance
to each other, will also entitle us to speak of their carrying
with them a reference to that which is not itself any single
impression, but is permanent throughout the impressions;
and the whole ground of Hume's polemic against the idea
of self or spirit is removed.[2]

213. The above admission, however, does not dispose of
the question about ideas of resemblance. A feeling qualified
by relation of resemblance to other feelings is a different
thing from an idea of that relation—different with all the
difference which Hume ignores between feeling and thought,
between consciousness and self-consciousness. The qualification of successive feelings by mutual relation implies,
indeed, the presence to them of a subject permanent and
immaterial (*i. e.* not in time or space); but it does not imply
that this subject presents them to itself as related objects,
permanent with its own permanence, which abide and may
be considered apart from 'the circumstances in time' of their
occurrence. Yet such presentation is supposed by all language
other than interjectional. It is it alone which can give us
names of things, as distinct from noises prompted by the
feelings as they occur. Of course it is open to any one to
say that by an idea of resemblance he does not mean any
thought involving the self-conscious presentation spoken of,
but merely a feeling qualified by resemblance, and not at its

---

[1] It is, of course, quite a different
thing to say that the brain (or, more
properly, the whole body) is organic to it.

[2] See above, paragraph 205.

liveliest stage. Thus Hume tells us that by 'idea' he merely means a feeling less lively than it has been, and that by idea *of anything* he implies no reference to anything other than the idea,[1] but means just a related idea, *i.e.* a feeling qualified by 'natural relation' to other feelings. It is by this thought-ful abnegation of thought, as we shall find, that he arrives at his sceptical result. But language (for the reason mentioned) would not allow him to be faithful to the abnegation. He could not make such a profession without being false to it. This appears already in his account of 'complex' and 'ab-stract' ideas.

214. His account of the idea of a substance (p. 324) is simply Locke's, as Locke's would become upon elimination of the notion that there is a real 'something' in which the col-lection of ideas subsist, and from which they result. It thus avoids all difficulties about the relation between nominal and real essence. Just as Locke says that in the case of a 'mixed mode' the nominal essence *is* the real, so Hume would say of a substance. The only difference is that while the collection of ideas, called a mixed mode, does not admit of addition without a change of its name, that called a substance does. Upon discovery of the solubility of gold in aqua regia we add that idea to the collection, to which the name 'gold' has pre-viously been assigned, without disturbance in the use of the name, because the name already covers not only the ideas of certain qualities, but also the idea of a 'principle of union' between them, which will extend to any ideas presented along with them. As this principle of union, however, is not itself any 'real essence,' but 'part of the complex idea,' the question, so troublesome to Locke, whether a proposition about gold asserts real co-existence or only the inclusion of an idea in a nominal essence, will be superfluous. How the 'principle of union' is to be explained, will appear below.[2]

215. There are names, then, which represent 'collections of ideas.' How can we explain such collection if ideas are merely related feelings grown fainter? Do we, when we use one of these names significantly, recall, though in a fainter form, a series of feelings that we have experienced in the process of collection? Does the chemist, when he says that gold is soluble in aqua regia, recall the visual and tactual

---

feeling which he experienced when he found it soluble? If so, as that feeling took its character from relation to a multitude of other ' complex ideas,' he must on the same principle recall in endless series the sensible occurrences from which each constituent of each constituent of these was derived; and a like process must be gone through when gold is pronounced ductile, malleable, &c. But this would be, according to the figure which Hume himself adopts, to recall a 'perpetual flux.' The very term ' collection of ideas,' indeed, if this be the meaning of ideas, is an absurdity, for how can a perpetual flux be collected? If we turn for a solution of the difficulty to the chapter where Hume expressly discusses the significance of general names, we shall find that it is not the question we have here put, and which flows directly from his account of ideas, that he is there treating, but an entirely different one, and one that could not be raised till for related feeling had been substituted the thought of an object under relations.

216. The chapter mentioned concerns the question which arises out of Locke's pregnant statement that words and ideas are ' particular in their existence ' even when ' general in their signification.' From this statement we saw[1] that Berkeley derived his explanation of the apparent generality of ideas—the explanation, namely, which reduces it to a relation, yet not such a one as would affect the nature of the idea itself, which is and remains ' particular,' but a symbolical relation between it and other particular ideas for which it is taken to stand. An idea, however, that carries with it a consciousness of symbolical relation to other ideas, cannot but be qualified by this relation. The generality must become part of its ' nature,' and, accordingly, the distinction between idea and thing being obliterated, of the nature of things. Thus Berkeley virtually arrives at a result which renders unmeaning his preliminary exclusion of universality from 'the absolute, positive nature or conception of anything.' Hume seeks to avoid it by putting ' custom ' in the place of the consciousness of symbolical relation. True to his vocation of explaining away all functions of thought that will not sort with the treatment of it as ' decaying sense,' he would resolve that idea of a relation between certain ideas, in virtue of which one is taken to stand for the rest, into the *de facto*

---

[1] Above, paragraphs 182 and 183.

sequence upon one of them of the rest. Here, as everywhere else, he would make related feelings do instead of relations of ideas ; but whether the related feelings, as he is obliged to describe them, do not already presuppose relations of ideas in distinction from feelings, remains to be seen.

217. The question about 'generality of signification,' as he puts it, comes to this. In every proposition, though its subject be a common noun, we necessarily present to our-selves some one individual object 'with all its particular circumstances and proportions.' How then can the propo-sition be general in denotation and connotation ? How can it be made with reference to a multitude of individual objects other than that presented to the mind, and how can it con-cern only such of the qualities of the latter as are common to the multitude ? The first part of the question is answered as follows :—' When we have found a resemblance among several objects that often occur to us, we apply the same name to all of them . . . whatever differences may appear among them. After we have acquired a custom of this kind, the hearing of that name revives the idea of one of these objects, and makes the imagination conceive it with all its particular circumstances and proportions. But as the same word is supposed to have been frequently applied to other individuals, that are different in many respects from that idea which is immediately present to the mind, the word not being able to revive the idea of all these individuals, only touches the soul and revives that custom which we have acquired by surveying them. They are not really and in fact present to the mind, but only in power. . . . The word raises up an individual idea along with a certain custom, and that custom produces any other individual one for which we may have occasion. . . . Thus, should we mention the word triangle and form the idea of a particular equilateral one to correspond to it, and should we afterwards assert *that the three angles of a triangle are equal to each other*, the other individuals of a scalenum and isosceles, which we over-looked at first, immediately crowd in upon us and make us perceive the falsehood of this proposition, though it be true with relation to that idea which we had formed' (p. 328).

218. Next, as to the question concerning connotation :—
'The mind would never have dreamed of distinguishing a figure from the body figured, as being in reality neither distin-

guishable nor different nor separable, did it not observe that even in this simplicity there might be contained many different resemblances and relations. Thus, when a globe of white marble is presented, we receive only the impression of a white colour disposed in a certain form, nor are we able to distinguish and separate the colour from the form. But observing afterwards a globe of black marble and a cube of white, and comparing them with our former object, we find two separate resemblances in what formerly seemed, and really is, perfectly inseparable. After a little more practice of this kind, we begin to distinguish the figure from the colour by a *distinction of reason*;—*i.e.* we consider the figure and colour together, since they are, in effect, the same and indistinguishable; but still view them in different aspects according to the resemblances of which they are susceptible. . . . A person who desires us to consider the figure of a globe of white marble without thinking on its colour, desires an impossibility; but his meaning is, that we should consider the colour and figure together, but still keep in our eye the resemblance to the globe of black marble or that to any other globe whatever' (p. 333).

219. It is clear that the process described in these passages supposes 'ab initio' the conversion of a feeling into a conception; in other words, the substitution of the definite individuality of a thing, thought of under attributes, for the mere singleness in time of a feeling that occurs after another and before a third. The 'finding of resemblances and differences among objects that often occur to us' implies that each object is distinguished as one and abiding from manifold occurrences, in the way of related feelings, in which it is presented to us, and that these accordingly are regarded as representing permanent relations or qualities of the object. Thus from being related feelings, whether more or less 'vivacious,' they have become, in the proper sense, ideas of relation. The difficulty about the use of general names, as Hume puts it, really arises just from the extent to which this process of determination by ideas of relation, and with it the removal of the object of thought from simple feeling, is supposed to have gone. It is because the idea is so complex in its individuality, and because this qualification is not understood to be the work of thought, by comparison and

contrast accumulating attributes on an object which it itself constitutes, but is regarded as given ready-made in an impression (*i.e.* a feeling), that the question arises whether a general proposition is really possible or no. To all intents and purposes Hume decides that it is not. The mind is so tied down to the particular collection of qualities which is given to it or which it 'finds,' that it cannot present one of them to itself without presenting all. Having never found a triangle that is not equilateral or isosceles or scalene, we cannot imagine one, for ideas can only be copies of impressions, and the imagination, though it has a certain freedom in combining what it finds, can invent nothing that it does not find. Thus the idea, represented by a general name and of which an assertion, general in form, is made, must always have a multitude of other qualities besides those common to it with the other individuals to which the name is applicable. If any of these, however, were included in the predicate of the proposition, the sleeping custom, which determines the mind to pass from the idea present to it to the others to which the name has been applied, would be awakened, and it would be seen at once that the predicate is not true of them. When I make a general statement about ' the horse,' there must be present to my mind some particular horse of my acquaintance, but if on the strength of this I asserted that ' the horse is a grey-haired animal,' the custom of applying the name without reference to colour would return upon me and correct me—as it would not if the predicate were ' four-footed.'

220. It would seem then that the predicate may, though the subject cannot, represent either a single quality, or a set of qualities which falls far short even of those common to the class, much more of those which characterise any individual. If I can think these apart, or have an idea of them, as the predicate of a proposition, why not (it may be asked) as the subject? It may be said, indeed, with truth, that it is a mistake to think of the subject as representing one idea and the predicate another; that the proposition as a whole represents one idea, in the sense of a conception of relation between attributes, and that at bottom this account of it is consistent with Locke's definition of knowledge as a perception of relation between ' ideas,' since with him ' ideas ' and

'qualities' are used interchangeably.[1] It is no less true, however, that the relation between attributes, which the proposition states, is a relation between them in an individual subject. It is the nature of the individuality of this subject, then, that is really in question. Must it, as Hume supposed, be 'considered' under other qualities than those to which the predicate relates? When the proposition only concerns the relation between certain qualities of a spherical figure, must the figure still be considered as of a certain colour and material?

221. The possibility of such a question being raised implies that the step has been already taken, which Hume ignored, from feeling to thought. His doctrine on the matter arises from that mental equivocation, of which the effects on Locke have been already noticed,[2] between the mere singleness of a feeling in time and the individuality of the object of thought as a complex of relations. If the impression is the single feeling which disappears with a turn of the head, and the idea a weaker impression, every idea must indeed be in one sense 'individual,' but in a sense that renders all predication impossible because it empties the idea of all content. Really, according to Hume's doctrine of general names, it is individual in a sense which is the most remote opposite of this, as a multitude of 'different resemblances and relations' in 'simplicity.' It is just such an individual as Locke supposed to be found (so to speak) ready-made in nature, and from which he supposed the mind successively to abstract ideas less and less determinate. Such an object Hume, coming after Berkeley, could not regard in Locke's fashion as a separate material existence outside consciousness. The idea with him is a 'copy' not of a thing but of an 'impression,' but to the impression he transfers all that individualization by qualities which Locke had ascribed to the substance found in nature ; and from the impression again transfers it to the idea which 'is but the weaker impression.' Thus the singleness in time of the impression becomes the 'simplicity' of an object 'containing many different resemblances and relations,' and the individuality of the subject of a proposition, instead of being regarded in its true light as a temporary isolation from other relations of those for the time under view—an individuality

---

[1] See above, paragraph 17.
[2] See above, paragraphs 47, 95, &c.

which is perpetually shifting its limits as thought proceeds—becomes an individuality fixed once for all by what is given in the impression. Because, as is supposed, I can only ' see ' a globe as of a certain colour and material, I can only think of it as such. If the ' sight ' of it had been rightly interpreted as itself a complex work of thought, successively detaching felt things from the ' flux ' of feelings and determining these by relations similarly detached, the difficulty of thinking certain of these—*e.g.* those designated as ' figure '—apart from the rest would have disappeared. It would have been seen that this was merely to separate in reflective analysis what had been gradually put together in the successive synthesis of perception. But such an interpretation of the supposed *datum* of sense would have been to elevate thought from the position which Hume assigned to it, as a ' decaying sense,' to that of being itself the organizer of the world which it knows.[1]

222. Here, then, as elsewhere, the embarrassment of Hume's doctrine is nothing which a better statement of it could avoid. Nay, so dexterous is his statement, that only upon a close scrutiny does the embarrassment disclose itself. To be faithful at once to his reduction of the impression to simple feeling, and to his account of the idea as a mere copy of the impression, was really impossible. If he had kept his word in regard to the impression, he must have found thought filling the void left by the disappearance, under Berkeley's criticism, of that outward system of things which Locke had commonly taken for granted. He preferred fidelity to his account of the idea, and thus virtually restores the fiction which represents the real world as consisting of so many, materially separate, bundles of qualities—a fiction which even Locke in his better moments was beginning to outgrow—with only the difference that for the separation of ' substances ' in space he substitutes a separation of ' impressions ' in time. That thought (the ' idea ') can but faintly copy feeling (the ' impression ') he consistently maintains, but he avails himself of the actual determination of feeling by reference to an object of thought—the determination expressed by such phrases as impression of a man, impression of a globe, &c.—to charge the feeling with a content which it only derives from

[1] The phrase ' decaying sense ' belongs to Hobbes, but its meaning is adopted by Hume.

such determination, while yet he denies it. By this means predication can be accounted for, as it could not be if our consciousness consisted of mere feelings and their copies, but only in the form of the singular proposition; because the object of thought determined by relations, being identified with a single feeling, must be limited by the ' this ' or ' that ' which expresses this singleness of feeling. It is really *this* or *that* globe, *this* or *that* man, that is the subject of the proposition, according to Hume, even when in form it is general. It is true that the general name ' globe ' or ' man ' not merely represents a ' particular ' globe or man, though that is all that is presented to the mind, but also ' raises up a custom which produces any other individual idea for which we may have occasion.' As this custom, however, is neither itself an idea nor affects the singleness of the subject idea, it does not constitute any distinction between singular and general propositions, but only between two sorts of the singular proposition according as it does, or does not, suggest an indefinite series of other singular propositions, in which the same qualities are affirmed of different individual ideas to which the subject-name has been applied.

223. A customary sequence, then, of individual ideas upon each other is the reality, which through the delusion of words (as we must suppose) has given rise to the fiction of there being such a thing as general knowledge. We say ' fiction,' for with the possibility of general propositions, as the Greek philosophers once for all pointed out, stands or falls the possibility of science. Locke was so far aware of this that, upon the same principle which led him to deny the possibility of general propositions concerning real existence, he ' suspected' a science of nature to be impossible, and only found an exemption for moral and mathematical truth from this condemnation in its ' bare ideality.' Hume does away with the exemption. He applies to all propositions alike the same limitation which Locke applies to those concerning real existence. With Locke there may very well be a proposition which to the mind, as well as in form, is general—one of which the subject is an ' abstract general idea '—but such proposition ' concerns not existence.' As knowledge of real existence is limited to the ' actual present sensation,' so a proposition about such existence is limited to what is given in such sensation. It is a real truth that this piece of gold

is now being dissolved in aqua regia, when the 'particular experiment' is going on under our eyes, but the general proposition 'gold is soluble' is only an analysis of a nominal essence. With Hume the distinction between propositions that do, and those that do not, 'concern existence' disappears. Every proposition is on the same footing in this respect, since it must needs be a statement about an ' idea,' and every idea exists. 'Every object that is presented must necessarily be existent. . . . Whatever we conceive, we conceive to be existent. Any idea we please to form is the idea of a being ; and the idea of a being is any idea we please to form ' (p. 370). But since, according to him, the idea cannot be separated, as Locke supposed it could, from the conditions ' that determine it to this or that particular existence,' propositions of the sort which Locke understood by 'general propositions concerning substances,' though if they were possible they would 'concern existence' as much as any, are simply impossible. Hume, in short, though he identifies the real and nominal essences which Locke had distinguished, yet limits the nominal essence by the same 'particularity in space and time' by which Locke had limited the real.

224. A great advance in simplification has been made when the false sort of ' conceptualism ' has thus been got rid of— that conceptualism which opposes knowing and being under the notion that things, though merely individual in reality, may be known as general. This riddance having been achieved, as it was by Hume, the import of the proposition becomes the central question of philosophy, the answer to which must determine our theory of real existence just as much as of the mind. The issue may be taken on the proposition in its singular no less than in its general form. The weakness of Hume's opponents, indeed, has lain primarily in their allowing that his doctrine would account for any significant predication whatever, as distinct from exclamations prompted by feelings as they occur. This has been the inch, which once yielded, the full ell of his nominalism has been easily won ; just as Locke's empiricism becomes invincible as soon as it is admitted that qualified things are 'found in nature' without any constitutive action of the mind. As the only effective way of dealing with Locke is to ask,—After abstraction of all that he himself admitted to be the creation of thought, what remains to be merely

found ?—so Hume must be met *in limine* by the question
whether, apart from such ideas of relation as according to
his own showing are not simple impressions, so much as the
singular proposition is possible. If not, then the singularity
of such proposition does not consist in any singleness of
presentation to sense ; it is not the ' particularity in time ' of
a present feeling ; and the exclusion of generality, whether
in thoughts or in things, as following from the supposed
necessity of such singleness or particularity, is quite ground-
less.

225. Hitherto the idea of relation which we have had
specially in view has been that of relation in the way of
resemblance, and the propositions have been such as represent the most obvious ' facts of observation '—facts about
this or that ' body,' man or horse or ball. We have seen
that these already suppose the thought of an object qualified,
not transitory as are feelings, but one to which feelings are
referred on their occurrence as resemblances or differences
between it and other objects ; but that by an equivocation,
which unexamined phraseology covers, between the thought
of such an object and feeling proper—as if because we talk
of seeing a man, therefore a man were a feeling of colour
—Hume is able to represent them as mere data of sense,
and thus to ignore the difference between related feelings
and ideas of relation. Thus the first step has been taken
towards transferring to the sensitive subject, as merely sensitive, the power of thought and significant speech. The
next is to transfer to it ideas of those other relations [1] which
Hume classifies as ' relations of time and place, proportion
in quantity or number, degrees in any quality ' (p. 368). This
done, it is sufficiently equipped for achieving its deliverance
from metaphysics. An animal, capable of experiments

[1] The course which our examination
of Hume should take was marked out,
it will be remembered, by his enumeration of the '*natural*' relations that regulate the association of ideas. It
might seem a departure from this
course to proceed, as in the text, from
the relation of resemblance to ' relations
of time and place, proportion in quantity or number, and degrees of any
quality,' since these appear in Hume's
enumeration, not of '*natural*,' but of
' *philosophical*' relations. Such departure, however, is the consequence of

Hume's own procedure. Whether he
considered these relations merely equivalent to the ' natural ones ' of resemblance and contiguity, he does not expressly say ; but his reduction of the
principles of mathematics to data of
sense implies that he did so. The
treatment of degrees in quality and
proportions in quantity as sensible implies that the difference between resemblance and measured resemblance, between contiguity and measured contiguity, is ignored.

concerning matter of fact, and of reasoning concerning
quantity and number, would certainly have some excuse for
throwing into the fire all books which sought to make it
ashamed of its animality.[1]

226. In thus leaving mathematics and a limited sort of
experimental physics (limited by the exclusion of all general
inference from the experiment) out of the reach of his
scepticism, and in making them his basis of attack upon
what he conceived to be the more pretentious claims of
knowledge, Hume was again following the course marked out
for him by Locke. It will be remembered that Locke, even
when his ' suspicion' of knowledge is at its strongest, still
finds solid ground (a) in ' particular experiments ' upon
nature, expressed in singular propositions as opposed to
assertions of universal or necessary connexion, and (b) in
mathematical truths which are at once general, certain, and
instructive, because 'barely ideal.' All speculative propositions
that do not fall under one or other of these heads are either
' trifling' or merely ' probable.' Hume draws the line between
certainty and probability at the same point, nor in regard to
the ground of certainty as to 'matter of fact or existence '
is there any essential difference between him and his master.
As this ground is the ' actual present sensation ' with the
one, so it is the ' impression ' with the other; and it is only
when the proposition becomes universal or asserts a necessary connection, that the certainty, thus given, is by either
supposed to fail. It is true that with Locke this authority
of the sensation is a derived authority, depending on its
reference to a ' body now operating upon us,' while with
Hume, so far as he is faithful to his profession of discarding
such reference, it is original. But with each alike the fundamental notion is that a feeling must be 'true *while it
lasts*,' and that in regard to real existence or matter of fact
no other truth can be known but this. Neither perceives
that a truth thus restricted is no truth at all—nothing that
can be stated even in a singular proposition ; that the ' particularity in time,' on which is supposed to depend the real

---

[1] ' If we take in our hand any volume
of divinity or school-metaphysics, for
instance, let us ask, *Does it contain any
abstract reasoning for quantity or number?* No. *Does it contain any experimental reasoning concerning matter of*
fact and resistance? No. Commit it
then to the flames, for it can contain
nothing but sophistry and illusion.'—
' Inquiry concerning the Human Understanding,' at the end.

certainty of the simple feeling, is just that which deprives
it of significance [1]—because neither is really faithful to the
restriction. Each allows himself to substitute for the momentary feeling an object qualified by relations, which are
the exact opposite of momentary feelings. 'If I myself
see a man walk on the ice,' says Locke (IV, xv. 5), 'it is
past probability, it is knowledge : ' nor would Hume, though
ready enough on occasion to point out that what is seen
must be a colour, have any scruple in assuming that such a
complex judgment as the above so-called 'sight' has the
certainty of a simple impression. It is only in bringing to
bear upon the characteristic admission of Locke's Fourth Book,
that no general knowledge of nature can be more than probable, a more definite notion of what probability is, and in
exhibiting the latent inconsistency of this admission with
Locke's own doctrine of ideas as effects of a causative substance, that he modifies the theory of *physical* certainty
which he inherited. In their treatment of mathematical
truths on the other hand, of propositions involving relations
of distance, quantity and degree, a fundamental discrepancy appears between the two writers. The ground of
certainty, which Hume admits in regard to propositions of
this order, must be examined before we can appreciate his
theory of probability as it affects the relations of cause and
substance.

227. It has been shown [2] that Locke's opposition of
mathematical to physical certainty, with his ascription to
the former of instructive generality on the ground of its bare
ideality—the 'ideal' in this regard being opposed to what is
found in sensation—strikes at the very root of his system.
It implies that thought can originate, and that what it originates is in some sort real—nay, as being nothing else than
the 'primary qualities of matter,' is the source of all other
reality. Here was an alien element which 'empiricism' could
not assimilate without changing its character. Carrying
such a conception along with it, it was already charged with
an influence which must ultimately work its complete transmutation by compelling, not the admission of an ideal world
of guess and aspiration alongside of the empirical, but the
recognition of the empirical as itself ideal. The time for

---

[1] See above, paragraphs 45 and 97.   [2] See above, paragraphs 117 and 125.

this transmutation, however, was not yet.   Berkeley, in over-hasty zeal for God, had missed that only true way of finding God in the world which lies in the discovery that the world is Thought.   Having taken fright at the ' mathematical Atheism,' which seemed to grow out of the current doctrines about primary qualities of matter, instead of applying Locke's own admissions to show that these were intelligible and merely intelligible, he fancied that he had won the battle for Theism by making out that they were merely feelings or sequences of feelings.   From him Hume got the text for all he had to say against the metaphysical mathematicians; but, for the reason that Hume applied it with no theological interest, its true import becomes more apparent with him than with Berkeley.

228. His account of mathematical truths, as contained in Part II. of the First Book of the ' Treatise on Human Nature,' cannot be fairly read except in connection with the chapters in Part IV. on ' Scepticism with regard to the Senses,' and on ' the Modern Philosophy.'   The latter chapter is expressly a polemic against Locke's doctrine of primary qualities, and its drift is to reverse the relations which Locke had asserted between them and sensations, making the primary qualities depend on sensations, instead of sensations on the primary qualities.   In Locke himself we have found that two inconsistent views on the subject perpetually cross each other.[1] According to one, momentary sensation is the sole conveyance to us of reality ; according to the other, the real is constituted by qualities of bodies which not only ' are in them whether we perceive them or not,' but which only complex ideas of relation can represent.   The unconscious device which covered this inconsistency lay, we found,[2] in the conversion of the mere feeling of touch into the touch *of a body*, and thus into an experience of solidity.   By this conversion, since solidity according to Locke's account carries with it all the primary qualities, these too become data of sensation, while yet, by the retention of the opposition between them and ideas, the advantage is gained of apparently avoiding that identification of what is real with simple feeling, which science and common sense alike repel.

229. Hume makes a show of getting rid of this see-saw.

Instead of assuming at once the reality of sensation on the strength of its relation to the primary qualities and the reality of these on the strength of their being given in tactual experience, he pronounces sensations alone the real, to which the primary qualities must be reduced, if they are not to disappear altogether. 'If colours, sounds, tastes, and smells be merely perceptions, nothing we can conceive is possessed of a real, continued, and independent existence' (513). That they are perceptions is of course undoubted. The question is, whether there is a real something beside and beyond them, contrast with which is implied in speaking of them as '*merely* perceptions.' The supposed qualities of such a real are 'motion, extension, and solidity' (Ibid.). To modes of these the other primary qualities enumerated by Locke are reducible; and of these again motion and extension, according to Locke's account no less than Hume's own, presuppose solidity. What then do we assert of the real, in contrast with which we talk of perception, as *mere* perception, when we say that it is solid? 'In order to form an idea of solidity we must conceive two bodies pressing on each other without any penetration. . . . . . Now, what idea do we form of these bodies? . . . . . To say that we conceive them as solid is to run on *ad infinitum*. To affirm that we paint them out to ourselves as extended, either resolves them all into a false idea or returns in a circle; extension must necessarily be conceived either as coloured, which is a false idea,[1] or as solid, which brings us back to the first question.' Of solidity, then, the ultimate determination of the supposed real, there is 'no idea to be formed' apart from those perceptions to which, as independent of our senses, it is opposed. 'After exclusion of colours, sounds, heat and cold from the rank of external existences, there remains nothing which can afford us a just and consistent idea of body.'

230. Our examination of Locke has shown us how it is that his interpretation of ideas by reference to body is fairly open to this attack. It is so because, in thus interpreting them, he did not know what he was really about. He thought he was explaining ideas of sense according to the only method of explanation which he recognises—the method of resolving

---

[1] 'A false idea,' that is, according to the doctrine that extension is a primary quality, while colour is only an idea of a secondary quality, not resembling the quality as it is in the thing.

complex into simple ideas, and of 'sending a man to his senses' for a knowledge of the simple. In fact, however, when he explained ideas of sense as derived from the qualities of body, he was explaining simple ideas by reference to that which, according to his own showing, is a complex idea. To say that, as Locke understood the derivation in question, the primary qualities are an αἴτιον γενέσεως to the ideas of secondary qualities, but not an αἴτιον γνώσεως—that without our having ideas of them they cause those ideas of sense from which afterwards our ideas of the primary qualities are formed—is to suppose an order of reality other than the order of our sensitive experience, and thus to contradict Locke's fundamental doctrine that the genesis of ideas is to be found by observing their succession in 'our own breasts.' It is not thus that Locke himself escapes the difficulty. As we have seen, he supposes our ideas of sense to be from the beginning ideas of the qualities of bodies, and virtually justifies the supposition by sending the reader to his sense of touch for that idea of solidity in which, as he defines it, all the primary qualities are involved. That the sense in question does not really yield the idea is what Hume points out when he says that, 'though bodies are felt by means of their solidity, yet the feeling is quite a different thing from the solidity, nor have they the least resemblance to each other.' In other words, having come to suppose that there are solid bodies, we explain our feeling as due to their solidity; but we may not at once interpret feeling as the result of solidity, and treat solidity as itself a feeling. It was by allowing himself so to treat it that Locke disguised from himself the objection to his interpretation of feeling. Hume tears off the disguise, and in effect gives him the choice of being convicted either of reasoning in a circle or of explaining the simple idea by reference to the complex. The solidity, which is to explain feeling, can itself only be explained by reference to body. If body is only a complex of ideas of sense, in referring tactual feeling to it we are explaining a simple idea by reference to a compound one. If it is not, how is it to be defined except in the 'circular' way, which Locke in fact adopts when he makes body a 'texture of solid parts' and solidity a relation of bodies ?[1]

---

[1] See above, paragraph 101.

231. This 'vicious circle' was nothing of which Locke need have been ashamed, if only he had understood and avowed its necessity. Body is to solidity and to the primary qualities in general simply as a substance to the relations that determine it; and the 'circle' in question merely represents the logical impossibility of defining a substance except by relations, and of defining these relations without presupposing a substance. It was only Locke's confusion of the order of logical correlation with the sequence of feelings in time, that laid him open to the charge of making body and the ideas of primary qualities, and again the latter ideas and those of secondary qualities, at once precede and follow each other. To avoid this confusion by recognising the logical order—the order of intellectual 'fictions'—as that apart from which the sequence of feelings would be no order of knowable reality at all, would be of course impossible for one who took Locke's antithesis of thought and fact for granted. The time for that was not yet. A way of escape had first to be sought in a more strict adherence to Locke's identification of the sequence of feelings with the order of reality. Hence Hume's attempt, reversing Locke's derivation of ideas of sense from primary qualities of body, to derive what with Locke had been primary qualities, as compound impressions of sense, from simple impressions and to reduce body itself to a name not for any 'just and consistent idea,' but for a ' propensity to feign,' the gradual product of custom and imagination. The question by which the value of such derivation and reduction is to be tried is our old one, whether it is not a tacit conversion of the supposed original impressions into qualities of body that alone makes them seem to yield the result required of them. If the Fourth Book of the ' Treatise on Human Nature,' with its elimination of the idea of body, had come before the second, would not the plausibility of the account of mathematical ideas contained in the latter have disappeared? And conversely, if these ideas had been reduced to that which upon elimination of the idea of body they properly become, would not that ' propensity to feign,' which is to take the place of the excluded idea, be itself unaccountable ?

232. ' After exclusion of colours, sounds, heat and cold, from the rank of external existences, there remains nothing which can afford us a just and consistent idea of body.'

Now, no one can 'exclude them from the rank of external existences' more decisively than Hume. They are impressions, and 'all impressions are internal and perishing existences, and appear as such.' Nor does he shirk the consequence, that we have no 'just and consistent idea of body.' It is true that we cannot avoid a ' belief in its existence '— a belief which according to Hume consists in the supposition of ' a continued existence of objects when they no longer appear to the senses, and of their existence as distinct from the mind and perceptions;' in other words, as 'external to and independent of us.' This belief, however, as he shows, is not given by the senses. That we should feel the existence of an object to be continued when we no longer feel it, is a contradiction in terms; nor is it less so, that we should feel it to be distinct from the feeling. We cannot, then, have an impression of body; and, since we cannot have an idea which does not correspond to an impression or collection of impressions, it follows that we can have no idea of it. How the 'belief in its existence' is accounted for by Hume in the absence of any idea of it, is a question to be considered later.[1] Our present concern is to know whether the idea of extension can hold its ground when the idea of body is excluded.

233. 'The first notion of space and extension,' he says, ' is derived solely from the senses of sight and feeling: nor is there anything but what is coloured or tangible that has parts disposed after such a manner as to convey the idea.' Now, there may be a meaning of ' derivation,' according to which no one would care to dispute the first clause of this sentence. Those who hold that *really*, i.e. *for a consciousness to which the distinction between real and unreal is possible*, there is no feeling except such as is determined by thought, are yet far from holding that the determination is arbitrary; that any and every feeling is potentially any and every conception. Of the feelings to which the visual and tactual nerves are organic, as they would be for a merely feeling consciousness, nothing, they hold, can be said; in that sense they are an ἄπειρον; but for the thinking consciousness, or (which is the same) as they *really* are, these feelings do, while those to which other nerves are organic do not, form the specific possibility of the conception of space. Ac-

<hr />

[1] See below, paragraph 303, and foll.

cording to this meaning of the words, all must admit that
'the first notion of space and extension is derived from the
senses of sight and feeling;' though it does not follow that
a repeated or continued activity of either sense is necessary
to the continued presence of the notion.   With Hume, however, the derivation spoken of must mean that the notion of
space is, to begin with, simply a visual or tactual feeling,
and that such it remains, though with indefinite abatement
and revival in the liveliness of the feeling, according to the
amount of which it is called 'impression' or 'idea.'   If we
supposed him to mean, not that the notion of space was
either a visual or tactual feeling indifferently, but that it was
a compound result of both,[1] we should merely have to meet a
further difficulty as to the possibility of such composition of
feelings when their inward synthesis in a soul, and the outward in a body, have been alike excluded.   In the next clause
of the sentence, however, we find that for visual and tactual
feelings there are quietly substituted 'coloured and tangible
objects, having parts so disposed as to convey the idea of
extension.'   It is in the light of this latter clause that the
uncritical reader interprets the former.   He reads back the
plausibility of the one into the other, and, having done so,
finds the whole plausible.   Now this plausibility of the latter
clause arises from its implying a three-fold distinction—a
distinction of colour or tangibility on the one side from the
disposition of the parts on the other; a distinction of the
colour, tangibility and disposition of parts alike from an
object to which they belong ; and a distinction of this object
from the idea that it conveys.   In other words, it supposes
a negative answer to the three following questions :—Is the
idea of extension the same as that of colour or tangibility?
Is it possible without reference to something other than a
possible impression?   Is the idea of extension itself extended?   Yet to the two latter questions, according to
Hume's express statements, the answer must be affirmative ;
nor can he avoid the affirmative answer to the first, to which
he would properly be brought, except by equivocation.

234. The *pièces justificatives* for this assertion are not
far to seek.   Some of them have been adduced already.   The
idea of space, like every other idea, must be a 'copy of an

---

[1] It is not really in this sense that
the impression of space according to
Hume is a 'compound' one, as will appear below.

impression.'[1] To speak of a feeling in its fainter stage as an 'image' of what it was in its livelier stage may, indeed, seem a curious use of terms; but in this sense only, according to Hume's strict doctrine, can the idea of space be spoken of as an 'image' of anything at all. The impression from which it is derived, *i.e.* the feeling at its liveliest, cannot properly be so spoken of, for 'no impression is presented by the senses as the image of anything distinct, or external, or independent.'[2] If no impression is so presented, neither can any idea, which copies the impression, be so. It can involve no reference to anything which does not come and go with the impression. Accordingly no distinction is possible between space on the one hand, and either the impression or idea of it on the other. All impressions and ideas that can be said to be of extension must be themselves extended; and conversely, as Hume puts it, ' all the qualities of extension are qualities of a perception.' It should follow that space is either a colour or feeling of touch. In the terms which Hume himself uses with reference to 'substance,' 'if it be perceived by the eyes, it must be colour; if by the ears, a sound; and so on, of the other senses.' As he expressly tells us that it is 'perceived by the eyes,' the conclusion is inevitable.

235. Hume does not attempt to reject the conclusion directly. He had too much eye to the appearance of consistency for that. But, in professing to admit it, he wholly alters its significance. The passage in question must be quoted at length. 'The table, which just now appears to me, is only a perception, and all its qualities are qualities of a perception. Now, the most obvious of all its qualities is extension. The perception consists of parts. These parts are so situated as to afford us the notion of distance and contiguity, of length, breadth, and thickness. The termination of these three dimensions is what we call figure. The figure is moveable, separable, and divisible. Mobility and separability are the distinguishing properties of extended objects. And, to cut short all disputes, the very idea of extension is copied from nothing but an impression, and consequently must perfectly agree to it. To say the idea of extension agrees to anything is to say it is extended.' Thus ' there are impressions and ideas that are really extended.'[3]

236. In order to a proper appreciation of this passage it is essential to bear in mind that Hume, so far as the usages of language would allow him, ignores all such differences in modes of consciousness as the Germans indicate by the distinction between 'Empfindung' and 'Vorstellung,' and by that between 'Anschauung' and 'Begriff;' or, more properly, that he expressly merges them in a mode of consciousness for which, according to the most consistent account that can be gathered from him, the most natural term would be 'feeling.'[1] It is true that Hume himself, admitting a distinction in the degree of vivacity with which this consciousness is at different times presented, inclines to restrict the term 'feeling' to its more vivacious stage, and to use 'perception' as the more general term, applicable whatever the degree of vivacity may be.[2] We must not allow him, however, in using this term to gain the advantage of a meaning which popular theory does, but his does not, attach to it. 'Perception' with him covers 'idea' as well as 'impression;' but nothing can be said of idea that cannot be said of impression, save that it is less lively, nor of impression that cannot be said of idea, save that it is more so. It is this explicit reduction of all consciousness virtually, if not in name, to feeling that brings to the surface the difficulties latent in Locke's 'idealism.' These we have already traced at large; but they may be summed up in the question, How can feelings, as 'particular in time' or (which is the same) in 'perpetual flux,' constitute or represent a world of permanent relations?[3] The difficulty becomes more obvious, though not more real, when the relations in question are not merely themselves permanent, like those between natural phenomena, but are 'relations between permanent parts,' like those of space. It is for this reason that its doctrine about geometry has always been found the most easily assailable point of the 'sensational' philosophy. Locke distinguishes the ideas of space and of duration as got, the one 'from the permanent parts of space,' the other 'from the fleeting and perpetually perishing parts of succession.'[4] He afterwards prefers the term 'expan-

---

[1] As implying no distinction from, or reference to, a thing causing and a subject experiencing it. See above, paragraphs 195 and 208, and the passages there referred to.

[2] 'To hate, to love, to think, to feel, to see; all this is nothing but to per-

ceive.' P. 371.

'When I shut my eyes and *think* of my chamber, the ideas I form are exact representations of the impressions I *felt*.' P. 312.

[3] See above, paragraphs 172 & 176.

[4] Essay II. chap. XIV. sec. 1.

sion' to space, as the opposite of duration, because it brings
out more clearly the distinction of a relation between permanent parts from that between 'fleeting successive parts which
never exist together.' How, then, can a consciousness consisting simply of 'fleeting successive parts' either be or
represent that of which the differentia is that its parts are
permanent and co-exist ?

237. If this crux had been fairly faced by Hume, he must
have seen that the only way in which he could consistently
deal with it was by radically altering, with whatever consequence to the sciences, Locke's account of space. As it was,
he did not face it, but—whether intentionally or only in effect
—disguised it by availing himself of the received usages of
language, which roughly represent a theory the exact opposite of his own, to cover the incompatibility between the
established view of the nature of space, and his own reduction
of it to feeling. A very little examination of the passage,
quoted at large above, will show that while in it a profession
is made of identifying extension and a certain sort of perception with each other, its effect is not really to reduce extension to such a perception as Hume elsewhere explains all
perceptions to be, but to transfer the recognised properties of
extension which with such reduction would disappear, to something which for the time he chooses to reckon a perception,
but which he can only so reckon at the cost of contradicting
his whole method of dealing with the ideas of God, the soul,
and the world. The passage, in fact, is merely one sample
of the continued shuffle by which Hume on the one hand
ascribes to feeling that intelligible content which it only derives from relation to objects of thought, and on the other
disposes of these objects because they are not feelings.

238. 'The table, which just now appears to me, is only a
perception, and all its qualities are qualities of a perception.
Now, the most obvious of all its qualities is extension. The
perception consists of parts. These parts are so situated as
to afford us the notion of distance and contiguity, of length,
breadth, and thickness,' &c., &c. If, now, throughout this
statement (as according to Hume's doctrine we are entitled
to do) we write *feeling* for 'perception' and 'notion,' it will
appear that this table is a feeling, which has another feeling,
called extension, as one of its qualities ; and that this latter
feeling consists of parts. These, in turn, must be themselves

feelings, since the parts of which a perception consists must be themselves perceived, and, being perceived, must, according to Hume, be themselves perceptions which = feelings. These feelings, again, afford us other feelings of certain relations —distance and contiguity, &c.—feelings which, as Hume's doctrine allows of no distinction between the feeling and that of which it is the feeling, must be themselves relations. Thus it would seem that a feeling may have another feeling as one of its qualities; that the feeling, which is thus a quality, has other feelings as its co-existent parts; and that the feelings which are parts 'afford us' other feelings which are relations. Is that sense or nonsense?

239. To this a follower of Hume, if he could be brought to admit the legitimacy of depriving his master of the benefit of synonyms, might probably reply, that the apparent non-sense only arises from our being unaccustomed to such use of the term 'feeling;' that the table is a 'bundle of feelings,' actual and possible, of which the actual one of sight suggests a lively expectation, easily confused with the presence, of the others belonging to the other senses; that any one of these may be considered a quality of the total impression formed by all; that the feeling thus considered, if it happens to be visual, may not improperly be said to consist of other feelings, as a whole consists of parts, since it is the result of impressions on different parts of the retina, and from a different point of view even itself to be the relation between the parts, just as naturally as a mutual feeling of friendship may be said either to consist of the loves of the two parties to the friendship, or to constitute the relation between them. Such language represents those modern adaptations of Hume, which retain his identification of the real with the felt but ignore his restrictions on the felt. Undoubtedly, if Hume allowed us to drop the distinction between feeling as it might be for a merely feeling consciousness, and feeling as it is for a thinking consciousness, the objection to his speaking of feeling in those terms, in which it must be spoken of if extension is to be a feeling, would disappear; but so, likewise, would the objection to speaking of thought as constitutive of reality. To appreciate his view we must take feeling not as we really know it—for we cannot know it except under those conditions of self-consciousness, the logical categories, which in his attempt to get at feeling, pure and simple, Hume is consistent

enough to exclude—but as it becomes upon exclusion of all determination by objects which Hume reckons fictitious. What it would thus become *positively* we of course cannot say, for of the unknowable nothing can be said; but we can decide *negatively* what it cannot be. Can that in any case be said of it, which must be said of it if a feeling may be extended, and if extension is a feeling? Can it be such a quality of an object, so consisting of parts, and such a relation, as we have found that Hume takes it to be in his account of the perception of this table?

240. After having taken leave throughout the earlier part of the 'Treatise on Human Nature' to speak in the ordinary way of objects and their qualities—and otherwise of course he could not have spoken at all—in the fourth book he seems for the first time to become aware that his doctrine did not authorise such language. To perceive qualities of an object is to be conscious of relation between a subject and object, of which neither perishes with the moment of perception. Such consciousness is self-consciousness, and cannot be reduced to any natural observable event, since it is consciousness of that of which we cannot say 'Lo, here,' or 'Lo, there,' 'it is now but was not then,' or 'it was then but is not now.' It is therefore something which the spirit of the Lockeian philosophy cannot assimilate, and which Hume, as the most consistent exponent of that spirit, most consistently tried to get rid of. The subject as self, the object as body, he professes to reduce to figures of speech, to be accounted for as the result of certain 'propensities to feign:' nor will he allow that any impression or idea (and impressions and ideas with him, be it remembered, exhaust our consciousness) carries with it a reference to an object other than itself, any more than do pleasure or pain to which 'in their nature' all perceptions correspond.[1] He cannot, indeed, avoid speaking of the consciousness thus reduced to the level of simple pain and pleasure, as being that which in fact it can only be when determined by relation to a self-conscious subject, *i.e.* as

[1] 'Every impression, external and internal, passions, affections, sensations, pains, and pleasures, are originally on the same footing; and, whatever other differences we may observe among them, appear, all of them, in their true colours, as impressions or perceptions.' P. 480.

'All sensations are felt by the mind such as they really are; and, when we doubt whether they present themselves as distinct objects or as mere impressions, the difficulty is not concerning their nature, but concerning their relations and situation.' P. 480.

itself an object; but he is so far faithful in his attempt to
avoid such determination, that he does not reckon the object
more permanent than the impression. It, too, is a 'perishing existence.' As the impression disappears with a 'turn
of the eye in its socket,' so does the object, which really is
the impression, and cannot appear other than it is any more
than a feeling can be felt to be what it is not.[1]

241. Such being the only possible object, how can
qualities of it be perceived? We cannot here find refuge
in any such propensity to feign as that which, according to
Hume, leads us to 'endow objects with a continued existence, distinct from our perceptions.' If such propensities
can give rise to impressions at all, it can only be to impressions of reflection, and it cannot be in virtue of them that
extension, an impression of sensation, is given as a quality
of an object. Now if there is any meaning in the phrase
'qualities of an object,' it implies that the qualities co-exist
with each other and the object. Feelings, then, which are felt
as qualities of another feeling must co-exist with, *i.e.* (according to Hume) be felt at the same time as, it and each other.
Thus, if an impression of sight be the supposed object, no
feeling that occurs after this impression has disappeared can
be a quality of it. Accordingly, when Hume speaks of extension being seen as one of the qualities of this table, he is
only entitled to mean that it is one among several feelings,
experienced at one and the same time, which together constitute the table. Whatever is not so experienced, whether
extension or anything else, can be no quality of that 'perception.' How much of the perception, then, will survive?
Can any feelings, strictly speaking, be cotemporaneous?
Those received through different senses, as Hume is careful
to show, may be; *e.g.* the smell, taste, and colour of a
fruit.[2] In regard to them, therefore, we may waive the
difficulty, How can feelings successive to each other be yet
co-existent qualities? but only to find ourselves in another
as to what the object may be of which the cotemporaneous
feelings are qualities. It cannot, according to Hume, be

[1] See above, paragraph 208, with
the passages there cited.

[2] 'The taste and smell of any fruit are
inseparable from its other qualities of
colour and tangibility, and . . . .
'tis certain they are always co-existent.

Nor are they only co-existent in general,
but also cotemporary in their appearance in the mind.' P. 521. (Contrast
p. 370, where existence and appearance
are identified.)

other than one or all of the cotemporaneous feelings. Is, then, the taste of an apple a quality of its colour or of its smell, or of colour, smell, and taste put together ? It will not help us to speak of the several feelings as qualities of the 'total impression;' for the 'total impression' either merely means the several feelings put together, or else covertly implies just that reference to an object other than these, which Hume expressly excludes.

242. In fact, however, when he speaks of the feeling, which is called extension, as a quality of the feeling, which is called sight, of the table, he has not even the excuse that he might have had if the feelings in question, being of different senses, might be cotemporary. According to him they are feelings of the same sense. The extension of the table he took to be a datum of sight just as properly as its colour ; yet he cannot call it the same as colour, but only ' a quality of the coloured object.' As the ' coloured object,' however, apart from ' propensities to feign,' can, according to him, be no other than the feeling of colour, his doctrine can only mean that, colour and extension being feelings of the same sense, the latter is a quality of the former. Is this any more possible than that red should be a quality of blue, or a sour taste of a bitter one ? Must not the two feelings be successive, however closely successive, so that the one which is object will have disappeared before the other, which is to be its quality, will have occurred ? [1]

243. If we look to the detailed account which Hume gives of the relation between extension and colour, we find that he avoids the appearance of making one feeling a quality of another, by in fact substituting for colour a superficies of coloured points, in which it is very easy to find extension as a quality because it already is extension as an object. To speak of extension, though a feeling, as made up of parts is just as legitimate or illegitimate as to speak of the feeling of colour being made up of coloured points. The legitimacy of this once admitted, there remains, indeed, a logical question as to how it is that a quality should be spoken of in terms that seem proper to a substance—as is done when it is said

---

[1] It should be needless to point out that by taking extension to be a quality of ' tangibility ' or muscular effort we merely change the difficulty. The question as to its relation to such feelings will be simply a repetition of that, put in the text, as to its relation to the feeling of colour.

to consist of parts—and yet, again, should be pronounced a
relation of these parts; but to one who professed to merge
all logical distinctions in the indifference of simple feeling,
such a question could have no recognised meaning. It is,
then, upon the question whether, according to Hume's doctrine of perception, the perception of an object made up of
coloured points may be used interchangeably with the perception of colour, that the consistency of his doctrine of
extension must finally be tried.

244. The detailed account is to the following effect:—
' Upon opening my eyes and turning them to the surround-
ing objects, I perceive many visible bodies; and upon shut-
ting them again and considering the distance betwixt these
bodies, I acquire the idea of extension.' From what impression, Hume proceeds to ask, is this idea derived? ' Internal impressions' being excluded, ' there remain nothing
but the senses which can convey to us this original impression.' . . . ' The table before me is alone sufficient by its
view to give me the idea of extension. This idea, then, is
borrowed from and represents some impression which this
moment appears to the senses. But my senses convey to me
only the impressions of coloured points, disposed in a certain
manner. . . . We may conclude that the idea of extension
is nothing but a copy of these coloured points and of the
manner of their appearance.' [1]

245. If the first sentence of the above had been found by
Hume in an author whom he was criticising, he would
scarcely have been slow to pronounce it tautological. As it
stands, it simply tells us that having seen things extended we
consider their extension, and upon considering it acquire an
idea of it. It is a fair sample enough of those ' natural his-
tories' of the soul in vogue among us, which by the help of a
varied nomenclature seem able to explain a supposed later
state of consciousness as the result of a supposed earlier one,
because the terms in which the earlier is described in effect
assume the later. It may be said, however, that it is only by
a misinterpretation of a carelessly written sentence that
Hume can be represented as deriving the idea of extension
from the consideration of distance; that, as the sequel shows,
he regarded the ' consideration' and the ' idea' in question

---

[1] Pp. 340 and 341.

as equivalent, and derived from the same impression of sense. It is undoubtedly upon his account of this impression that his doctrine of extension depends. It is described as 'an impression of coloured points disposed in a certain manner.' To it the idea of extension is related simply as a copy; which, we have seen, properly means with Hume, as a feeling in a less lively stage is related to the same feeling in a more lively stage. It is itself, we must note, the *impression* of extension; and it is an impression of sense, about which, accordingly, no further question can properly be raised. Hume, indeed, allows himself to speak as if it were included in a 'perception of visible bodies' other than itself; just as in the passage from the fourth book previously examined, he speaks as if the perception, called extension, were a quality of some other perception. This we must regard as an exercise of the privilege which he claims of 'speaking with the vulgar while he thought with the learned;' since, according to him, 'visible body,' in any other sense than that of the impression of coloured points, is properly a name for a 'propensity to feign' resulting from a process posterior to all impressions of sense. The question remains whether, in speaking of an impression as one of 'coloured points disposed in a certain manner,' he is not introducing a 'fiction of thought' into the impression just as much as in calling it a 'perception of body.'

246. An impression, we know, can, according to Hume, never be *of* an object in the sense of involving a reference to anything other than itself. When one is said, then, to be *of* coloured points, &c., this can only mean that itself *is*, or consists of, such points. Thus the question we have to answer is only a more definite form of the one previously put, Can a feeling consist of parts? In answering it we must remember that the parts, here supposed to be coloured points, must, according to Hume's doctrine, be themselves impressions or they are nothing. Consistently with this he speaks of extension as 'a compound impression, consisting of parts or lesser impressions, that are indivisible to the eye or feeling, and may be called impressions of atoms or corpuscles, endowed with colour and solidity.'[1] Now, unless we suppose that a multitude of feelings of one and the same

sense can be present together, these 'lesser impressions' must follow each other and precede the 'compound impression.' That is to say, none of the parts of which extension consists will be in existence at the same time, and all will have ceased to exist before extension itself comes into being. Can we, then, adopt the alternative supposition that a multitude of feelings of one and the same sense can be present together? In answering this question according to Hume's premisses we may not help ourselves by saying that in a case of vision there really are impressions on different parts of the retina. To say that it *really* is so, is to say that it is so for the *thinking* consciousness—for a consciousness that distinguishes between what it feels and what it knows. To a man, as simply seeing and while he sees, his sight is not an impression on the retina at all, much less a combination of impressions on different parts of the retina. It is so for him only as thinking on the organs of his sight; or, if we like, as 'seeing' them in another, but 'seeing' them in a way determined by sundry suppositions (bodies, rays, and the like) which are not feelings, and therefore with Hume not possible 'perceptions,' at all. But it is the impression of sight, as it would be for one simply seeing and while he sees, undetermined by reference to anything other than itself, whether subject or object—an impression as it would be for a merely feeling consciousness or (in Hume's language) 'on the same footing with pain and pleasure'—that we have to do with when, from Hume's point of view, we ask whether a multitude of such impressions can be present at once, *i.e.* as one impression.

247. If this question had been brought home to Hume, he could scarcely have avoided the admission that to answer it affirmatively involved just as much of a contradiction as that which he recognises between the 'interrupted' and 'continuous' existence of objects;[1] and just as in the latter case he gets over the contradiction by taking the interrupted existence, because the datum of sense, to be the reality, and the continued existence to be a belief resulting from 'propensities to feign,' so in the case before us he must have taken the multiplicity of successive impressions to be the reality, and their co-existence as related parts to be a

[1] P. 483 and following, and p. 486.

figure of speech, which he must account for as best he could.
As it is, he so plays fast and loose with the meaning of ' impression ' as to hide the contradiction which is involved in
the notion of a ' compound impression ' if impression is interpreted as feeling—the contradiction, namely, that a single
feeling should be felt to be manifold—and in consequence loses
the chance of being brought to that truer interpretation of the
compound impression, as the thought of an object under relations, which a more honest trial of its reduction to feeling
might have shown to be necessary.   To convict so skilful a
writer of a contradiction in terms can never be an easy
task.   He does not in so many words tell us that all impressions of sight must be successive, but he does tell us
that ' the impressions of touch,' which, indifferently with
those of sight, he holds to constitute the compound impression of extension, ' change every moment upon us.'[1]   And
in the immediate sequel of the passage where he has made
out extension to be a compound of co-existent impressions,
he derives the idea of time ' from the succession of our
perceptions *of every kind*, ideas as well as impressions, and
impressions of reflection as well as of sensation.'   The
parts of time, he goes on to say, cannot be co-existent; and,
since ' time itself is nothing but different ideas and impressions succeeding each other,' these parts, we must conclude, are those ' perceptions of every kind ' from which
the idea of time is derived.[2]   It is only, in fact, by availing
himself of the distinction, which he yet expressly rejects,
between the impression and its object, that he disguises the
contradiction in terms of first pronouncing certain impressions, as parts of space, co-existent, and then pronouncing all
impressions, as parts of time, successive.   A statement that
' as from the coexistence of visual, and also of tactual, perceptions we receive the idea of extension, so from the succession of perceptions of every kind we form the idea of
time,' would arouse the suspicion of the most casual reader;
while Hume's version of the same,—' as 'tis from the disposition of visible and tangible objects we receive the idea of
space, so from the succession of ideas and impressions we
form the idea of time '[3]—has the full ring of empirical
plausibility.

[1] P. 516.   [2] Pp. 342, 343.   [3] P. 342.

248. This plausibility depends chiefly on our reading into Hume's doctrine a physical theory which, as implying a distinction between feeling and its real but unfelt cause, is strictly incompatible with it. Is it not an undoubted fact, the reader asks, that two colours may combine to produce a third different from both—that red and yellow, for instance, together produce orange? Is not this already an instance of a compound impression? Why may not a like composition of unextended impressions of colour constitute an impression different from any one of the component impressions, viz. extended colour? A moment's consideration, however, will show that no one has a conscious sensation at once of red and yellow, and of orange as a compound of the two. The elements which combine to produce the colour called orange are not—as they ought to be if it is to be a case of compound impression in Hume's sense—feelings of the person who sees the orange colour, but certain known causes of feeling, confused in language with the feelings, which separately they might produce, but which in fact they do not produce when they combine to give the sensation of orange; and to such causes of feeling, which are not themselves feelings, Hume properly can have nothing to say.

249. So far we have been considering the composition of impressions generally, without special reference to extension. The contradiction pointed out arises from the confusion between impressions as felt and impressions as thought of; between feelings as they are in themselves, presented successively in time, and feelings as determined by relation to the thinking subject, which takes them out of the flux of time and converts them into members of a permanent whole. It is in this form that the confusion is most apt to elude us. When the conceived object is one of which the qualities can really be felt, *e.g.* colour, we readily forget that a felt quality is no longer simply a feeling. But the case is different when the object is one, like extension, which forces on us the question whether its qualities can be felt, or presented in feeling, at all. A compound of impressions of colour, to adopt Hume's phraseology, even if such composition were possible, would still be nothing else than an impression of colour. In more accurate language, the conception, which results from the action of thought upon feelings of colour, can only be a conception of colour. Is extension, then, the

same as colour? To say that it was would imply that geometry was a science of colour; and Hume, though ready enough to outrage 'Metaphysics and School Divinity,' always stops reverently short of direct offence to the mathematical sciences. As has been said above, of the three main questions about the idea of extension which his doctrine raises—Is it itself extended? Is it possible without reference to something other than a possible impression? Is it the same as the idea of colour or tangibility?—the last is the only one which he can scarcely even profess to answer in the affirmative.[1] Even when he has gone so far as to speak of the parts of a perception, a sound instinct compels him, instead of identifying the perception directly with extension, to speak of it as 'affording through the situation of its parts the notion of' extension.[2] In like manner, when he has asserted extension to be a compound of impressions, he avoids the proper consequence of the assertion by speaking of the component impressions as those, not of colour but, of coloured points, 'atoms or corpuscles endowed with colour and solidity;' and, again, does not call extension the compound of these simply, but the compound of them as 'disposed in a certain manner.' When the idea which is a copy of this impression has to be spoken of, the expression is varied again. It is an 'idea of the coloured points *and of the manner of their appearance*,' or of their 'disposition.' The disposition of the parts having been thus virtually distinguished from their colour, it is easy to suppose that, finding a likeness in the disposition of points under every unlikeness of their colour, 'we omit the peculiarities of colour, as far as possible, and found an abstract idea merely on that disposition of points, or manner of appearance, in which they agree. Nay, even when the resemblance is carried beyond the objects of one sense, and the impressions of touch are found to be similar to those of sight in the disposition of their parts, this does not hinder the abstract idea from representing both on account of their resemblance.'[3]

250. If words have any meaning, the above must imply that the disposition of points is at least a different idea from either colour or tangibility, however impossible it may be for

---

[1] Above, paragraph 233. Though, as we shall see, he does so in one passage.

[2] Above, paragraph 235.

[3] P. 341.

us to experience it without one or other of the latter. Nor
can we suppose that this impression, other than colour, is one
that first results from the composition of colours, even if we
admit that such composition could yield a result different
from colour. According to Hume, the components of the
compound impression are already impressions of coloured
'points, atoms, or corpuscles,' and such points imply just that
limitation by mutual externality, which is already the disposition in question. Is this 'disposition,' then, an impression
of sensation? If so, 'through which of the senses is it
received? If it be perceived by the eyes it must be a colour,'
&c. &c.; [1] but from colour, the impression with which Hume
would have identified it if he could, he yet finds himself obliged
virtually to distinguish it. It is a relation, and not even
one of those relations, such as resemblance, which in Hume's
language, 'depending on the nature of the impressions related,'[2] may plausibly be reckoned to be themselves impressions.
The 'disposition' of parts and their 'situation' he uses interchangeably, and the situation of impressions he expressly
opposes to their 'nature'[3]—that nature in respect of which
all impressions, call them what we like, are 'originally on
the same footing' with pain and pleasure. Consistently
with this he pronounces the 'external position' of objects—
their position as bodies external to each other and to our
body—to be no datum of sense, no impression or idea, at all.[4]
Our belief in it has to be accounted for as a complex result
of 'propensities to feign.' How, then, can there be an impression of that which does not belong to the nature of any
impression? What difference is there between 'bodies' and
'corpuscles endowed with colour and solidity,' that the
outwardness of the latter to each other—also called their

---

[1] Above, paragraph 208.

[2] P. 372, 'Philosophical relations
may be divided into two classes : into
such as depend entirely on the ideas
which we compare together; and such
as may be changed without any change
in the ideas. . . . The relations
of contiguity and distance between
two objects may be changed without
any change in the objects themselves
or their ideas.'

[3] P. 480. 'When we doubt whether
sensations present themselves as distinct objects or as mere impressions,
the difficulty is not concerning their

nature, but concerning their relations
and situation.'

[4] P. 481. In there showing that
the senses alone cannot convince us
of the external existence of body, he
remarks that 'sounds, tastes, and
smells appear not to have any existence
in extension;' and (p. 483) 'as far as
the senses are judges, all perceptions
are the same in the manner of their
existence.' Therefore perceptions of
sight cannot have 'an existence in
extension' any more than 'sounds,
tastes, and smells;' and if so, how can
'existence in extension' be a perception?

'distance' from each other [1]—should be an impression, while it is admitted that the same relation between 'bodies' cannot be so?

251. To have plainly admitted that it was not an impression must have compelled Hume either to discard the 'abstract idea' with which geometry deals, or to admit the possibility of ideas other than 'fainter impressions.' It is a principle on which he insists with much emphasis and repetition, that whatever 'objects,' 'impressions,' or 'ideas' are distinguishable are also separable.[2] Now if there is an abstract idea of extension, it can scarcely be other than distinguishable, and consequently (according to Hume's account of the relation of idea to impression) derived from a distinguishable and therefore separable impression. It would seem then that Hume cannot escape conviction of one of two inconsistencies; either that of supposing a separate impression of extension, which yet is not of the nature of any assignable sensation; or that of supposing an abstract idea of it in the absence of any such impression. We shall find that he does not directly face either horn of the dilemma, but evades both of them. He admits that 'the ideas of space and time are no separate and distinct ideas, but merely those of the manner or order in which objects' (sc. impressions) 'exist.'[3] In the Fourth Book, where the equivalence of impression to feeling is more consistently carried out, the fact that what is commonly reckoned an impression is really a judgment about the 'manner of existence,' as opposed to the 'nature,' of impressions, is taken as sufficient proof that it is no impression at all; and if not an impression, therefore not an idea.[4] He thus involuntarily recognized the true difference between feeling and thought, between the mere occurrence of feelings and the presentation of that occurrence by the self-conscious subject to itself; and, if only he had known what he was about in the recognition, might have anticipated Kant's distinction between the matter and form of sensation. In the Second Book, however, he will neither say explicitly that space is an impression of colour or a compound of colours—that would be to extinguish geometry; nor yet that it is impression of sense separate from that of colour—that would lay him open to the retort that he was

---

[1] Above, paragraphs 235 and 244.
[2] P. 319, 326, 332, 335 518.
[3] P. 346.
[4] P. 480.

virtually introducing a sixth sense; nor on the other hand will he boldly avow of it, as he afterwards does of body, that it is a fiction. He denies that it is a separate impression, so far as that is necessary for avoiding the challenge to specify the sense through which it is received; he distinguishes it from a mere impression of sight, when it is necessary to avoid its simple identification with colour. By speaking of it as ' the manner in which objects exist '—so long as he is not confronted with the declarations of the Fourth Book or with the question how, the objects being impressions, their order of existence can be at once that of succession in time and of co-existence in space—he gains the credit for it of being a datum of sight, yet so far distinct from colour as to be a possible 'foundation for an abstract idea,' representative also of objects not coloured at all but tangible. At the same time, if pressed with the question how it could be an impression of sight and yet not interchangeable with colour, he could put off the questioner by reminding him that he never made it a ' separate or distinct impression, but one of the manner in which objects exist.'

252. Disguise it as he might, however, the admission that there was in some sense an abstract idea of space, which the existence of geometry required of him, really carried with it the admission either of a distinct impression of the same, or of some transmuting process by which the idea may become what the impression is not. His way of evading this consequence has been already noticed in our examination of his doctrine of ' abstract ideas ' generally, though without special reference to extension.[1] It consists in asserting figure and colour to be ' really,' or as an impression, ' the same and indistinguishable,' but different as ' relations and resemblances' of the impression; in other words, different according to the 'light in which the impression is considered' or ' the aspect in which it is viewed.' Of these ' separate resemblances and relations,' however, are there ideas or are there not? If there are not, they are according to Hume nothing of which we are conscious at all; if there are, there must be distinguishable, and therefore separable, impressions corresponding. To say then that figure and colour form one and the same indistinguishable impression, and yet that they constitute

---

[1] Above, paragraph 218.

'different resemblances and relations,' without such explanation as Hume cannot consistently give, is in fact a contradiction in terms. The true explanation is that the 'impression' has a different meaning, when figure and colour are said to be inseparable in the impression, from that which it has when spoken of as a subject of different resemblances and relations. In the former sense it is the feeling pure and simple—*one* as presented singly in time, after another and before a third. In this sense it is doubtless insusceptible of distinction into qualities of figure and colour, because (for reasons already stated) it can have no qualities at all. But the 'simplicity in which many different resemblances and relations may be contained' is quite other than this singleness. It is the unity of an object thought of under manifold relations—a unity of which Hume, reducing all consciousness to 'impression' and impression to feeling, has no consistent account to give. Failing such an account, the unity of the intelligible object, and the singleness of the feeling in time, are simply confused with each other. It is only an object as thought of, not a feeling as felt, that can properly be said to have qualities at all; while it is only because it is still regarded as a feeling that qualities of it, which cannot be referred to separate impressions, are pronounced the same and indistinguishable. If the idea of space is other than a feeling grown fainter, the sole reason for regarding it as originally an impression of colour disappears; if it *is* such a feeling, it cannot contain such 'different resemblances and relations' as render it representative of objects not only coloured in every possible way, but not coloured at all.

253. It is thus by playing fast and loose with the difference between feeling and conception that Hume is able, when the character of extension as an intelligible relation is urged, to reply that it is the same with the feeling of colour; and on the other hand, when asked how there then can be an abstract idea of it, to reply that this does not mean a separate idea, but coloured objects considered under a certain relation, viz. under that which consists in the disposition of their parts. The most effective way of meeting him on his own ground is to ask him how it is, since 'consideration' can only mean a succession of ideas, and ideas are fainter impressions, that extension, being one and the same impression with colour, can by any 'consideration'

become so different from it as to constitute a resemblance to objects that are not coloured at all. The true explanation, according to his own terminology, would be that the resemblance between the white globe and all other globes, being a resemblance not of impressions but of such relations between impressions as do not 'depend on the nature of the impressions' related, is unaffected by the presence or absence of colour or any other sensation. Of such relations, however, there can properly, if ideas are fainter impressions, be no ideas at all. In regard to those of cause and identity Hume virtually admits this; but the 'propensities to feign,' by which in the case of these latter relations he tries to account for the appearance of there being ideas of them, cannot plausibly be applied to relations in space and time, of which, as we shall see, ideas must be assumed in order to account for the 'fictions' of body and necessary connexion. Since then they cannot be derived from any separate impression without the introduction in effect of a sixth sense, and since all constitutive action of thought as distinct from feeling is denied by Hume, the only way to save appearances is to treat the order in which a multitude of impressions present themselves as the same with each impression, even though immediately afterwards it may have to be confessed, that it is so independent of the nature of any or all of the impressions as to be the foundation of an abstract idea, which is representative of other impressions having nothing whatever in common with them but the order of appearance. This once allowed—an abstract idea having been somehow arrived at which is not really the copy of any impression—it is easy to argue back from the abstract idea to an impression, and because there is an idea of the composition of points to substitute a 'composition of coloured points' for colour as the original impression. From such impression, being already extension, the idea of extension can undoubtedly be abstracted.

254. We now know what becomes of 'extended matter' when the doctrine, which has only to be stated to find acceptance, that we cannot 'look for anything anywhere but in our ideas'—in other words that for us there is no world but consciousness—is fairly carried out. Its position must become more and more equivocal, as the assumption, that consciousness reveals to us an alien matter, has in one after

another of its details to be rejected, until a principle of synthesis within consciousness is found to explain it. In default of this, the feeling consciousness has to be made to take its place as best it may; which means that what is said of it as feeling has to be unsaid of it as extended, and *vice versâ.* As *feeling,* it carries no reference to anything other than itself, to an object of which it is a quality; as *extended,* it is a qualified object. As *extended* again, its qualities are relations of coexistent parts; as *feeling,* it is an unlimited succession, and therefore, not being a possible whole, can have no parts at all. Finally as *feeling,* it must in each moment of existence either be 'on the same footing' with pain and pleasure or else—a distinction between impressions of sensation and reflection being unwarrantably admitted—be a colour, a taste, a sound, a smell, or 'tangibility;' as *extended,* it is an 'order of appearance' or 'disposition of corpuscles,' which, being predicable indifferently at any rate of two of these sensations, can no more be the same with either than either can be the same with the other. It is not the fault of Hume but his merit that, in undertaking to maintain more strictly than others the identification of extension with feeling, he brought its impossibility more clearly into view. The pity is that having carried his speculative enterprise so far before he was thirty, he allowed literary vanity to interfere with its consistent pursuit, caring only to think out the philosophy which he inherited so far as it enabled him to pose with advantage against Mystics and Dogmatists, but not to that further issue which is the entrance to the philosophy of Kant.

255. As it was, he never came fairly to ask himself the fruitful question, How the sciences of quantity 'continuous and discreet,' which undoubtedly do exist, are possible to a merely feeling consciousness, because, while professedly reducing all consciousness to this form, he still allowed himself to interpret it in the terms of these sciences and, having done so, could easily account for their apparent 'abstraction' from it. If colour is already for feeling a magnitude, as is implied in calling it a 'composition of coloured points,' the question, how a knowledge of magnitude is possible, is of course superfluous. It only remains to deal, as Hume professes to do, with the apparent abstraction

in mathematics of magnitude from colour and the consequent suppositions of pure space and infinite divisibility. Any ulterior problem he ignores. That magnitude is not any the more a feeling for being 'endowed with colour' he shows no suspicion. He pursues his 'sensationalism' in short, in its bearing on mathematics, just as far as Berkeley did and no further. The question at issue, as he conceived it, was not as to the possibility of magnitude altogether, but only as to the existence of a vacuum; not as to the possibility of number altogether, but only as to the infinity of its parts. Just as he takes magnitude for granted as found in extension, and extension as equivalent to the feeling of colour, so he takes number for granted, without indeed any explicit account of the impression in which it is to be found, but apparently as found in time, which again is identified with the succession of impressions. In the second part of the Treatise, though the idea of number is assumed and an account is given of it which is supposed to be fatal to the infinite divisibility of extension, we are told nothing of the impression or impressions from which it is derived. In the Fourth Part, however, there is a passage in which a certain consideration of time is spoken of as its source.

256. In the latter passage, in order to account for the idea of identity, he is supposing 'a single object placed before us and surveyed for any time without our discovering in it any variation or interruption.' 'When we consider any two points of this time,' he proceeds, 'we may place them in different lights. We may either survey them at the very same instant; in which case they give us the idea of number, both by themselves and by the object, which must be multiplied in order to be conceived at once, as existent in these two different points of time: or, on the other hand, we may trace the succession of time by a like succession of ideas, and conceiving first one moment, along with the object then existent, imagine afterwards a change in the time without any variation or interruption in the object; in which case it gives us the idea of unity.' [1]

257. A slight scrutiny of this passage will show that it is a prolonged tautology. The difference is merely verbal between the processes by which the ideas of number and unity

are severally supposed to be given, except that in the former
process it is the moment of surveying the times that is
supposed to be one, while the times themselves are many;
in the latter it is the object that is supposed to be one, but
the times many. According to the second version of the
former process—that according to which the different times
surveyed together are said to give the idea of number 'by
their object'—even this difference disappears. The only remaining distinction is that in the one case the object is
supposed to be given as one, 'without interruption or
variation,' but to become multiple as conceived to exist in
different moments; in the other the objects are supposed to
be given as manifold, being ideas presented in successive
times, but to become one through the imaginary restriction
of the multiplicity to the times in distinction from the
object. Undoubtedly any one of these verbally distinct
processes will yield indifferently the ideas of number and of
unity, since these ideas in strict correlativity are presupposed
by each of them. 'Two points of time surveyed at the same
time' will give us the idea of number because, being a
duality in unity, they are already a number. So, too, and
for the same reason, will the object, one in itself but multiple
as existent at different times. Nor does the idea given by
imagining ideas, successively presented, to be 'one uninterrupted object,' differ from the above more than many-in-one
differs from one-in-many. The real questions of course are,
How two times can be surveyed at one time; how a single
object can be multiplied or become many; how a succession of ideas can be imagined to be an unvaried and uninterrupted object. To these questions Hume has no answer
to give. His reduction of thought to feeling logically excluded an answer, and the only alternative for him was to
ignore or disguise them.

258. In the passage from part II. of the Treatise, already
referred to, he distinctly tells us that the unity to which
existence belongs excludes multiplicity. 'Existence itself
belongs to unity, and is never applicable to number but on
account of the unites of which the number is composed.
Twenty men may be said to exist, but 'tis only because one,
two, three, four, &c., are existent. . . . . A unite, consisting of a number of fractions, is merely a fictitious denomination, which the mind may apply to any quantity of

objects it collects together; nor can such an unity any more exist alone than number can, as being in reality a true number. But the unity which can exist alone, and whose existence is necessary to that of all number, is of another kind and must be perfectly indivisible and incapable of being resolved into any lesser unity.' [1] What then is the ' unity which can exist alone '? The answer, according to Hume, must be that it is an impression separately felt and not resoluble into any other impressions. But then the question arises, how a succession of such impressions can form a number or sum; and if they cannot, how the so-called real unity or separate impression can in any sense be a unite, since a unite is only so as one of a sum. To put the question otherwise, Is it not the case that a unite has no more meaning without number than number without unites, and that every number is not only just such a ' fictitious denomination,' as Hume pronounces a 'unite consisting of a number of fractions ' to be, but a fiction impossible for our consciousness according to Hume's account of it? It will not do to say that such a question touches only the fiction of ' abstract number,' but not the existence of numbered objects; that (to take Hume's instance) twenty men exist with the existence of each individual man, each real unit, of the lot. It is precisely the numerability of objects—not indeed their existence, if that only means their successive appearance, but their existence *as a sum*—that is in question. If such numerability is possible for such a consciousness as Hume makes ours to be; in other words, if he can explain the fact that we count; ' abstract number ' may no doubt be left to take care of itself. Is it then possible ? ' Separate impressions ' mean impressions felt at different times, which accordingly can no more co-exist than, to use Hume's expression, ' the year 1737 can concur with the year 1738 ;' whereas the constituents of a sum must, as such, co-exist. Thus when we are told that 'twenty may be said to exist because one, two, three, &c., are existent,' the alleged reason, understood as Hume was bound to understand it, is incompatible with the supposed consequence. The existence of an object would, to him, mean no more than the occurrence of an impression ; but that one impression should occur, and then another and then another, is the exact opposite of their co-existence as a sum of impressions, and it is such co-existence that is implied when the impressions are counted and pronounced so many. Thus when Hume tells us that a single object, by being 'multiplied in order to be conceived at once as existent in different points of time,' gives us the idea of number, we are forced to ask him what precisely it is which thus, being one, can become manifold. Is it a 'unite that can exist alone'? That, having no parts, cannot become manifold by resolution. 'But it may by repetition?' No, for it is a separate impression, and the repetition of an impression cannot co-exist, so as to form one sum, with its former occurrence. 'But it may be *thought of* as doing so?' No, for that, according to Hume, could only mean that feelings might concur in a fainter stage though they could not in a livelier. Is the single object then a unite which already consists of parts? But that is a 'fictitious denomination,' and presupposes the very idea of number that has to be accounted for.

259. The impossibility of getting number, as a many-in-one, out of the succession of feelings, so long as the self is treated as only another name for that succession, is less easy to disguise when the supposed units are not merely given in succession, but are actually the moments of the succession; in other words, when time is the many-in-one to be accounted for. How can a multitude of feelings of which no two are present together, undetermined by relation to anything other than the feelings, be at the same time a consciousness of the relation between the moments in which the feelings are given, or of a sum which these moments form? How can there be a relation between 'objects' of which one has ceased before the other has begun to exist? 'For the same reason,' says Hume, 'that the year 1737 cannot concur with the present year 1738, every moment must be distinct from, and posterior or antecedent to, another.'[1] How then can the present moment form one sum with all past moments, the present year with all past years; the sum which we indicate by the number 1738? The answer of common sense of course will be that, though the feeling of one moment is really past before that of another begins, yet thought retains the former, and combining it with the latter, gets the idea of time both

[1] P. 338.

as a relation and as a sum. Such an answer, however, implies that the retaining and combining thought is other
than the succession of the feelings, and while it takes this
succession to be the reality, imports into it that determination by the relations of past and present which it can only
derive from the retaining and combining thought opposed to
it. It is thus both inconsistent with Hume's doctrine,
which allows no such distinction between thought, *i.e.* the
succession of ideas, and the succession of impressions, and
inconsistent with itself. Yet Hume by disguising both inconsistencies contrives to avail himself of it. By tacitly
assuming that a conception of 'the manner in which impressions appear to the mind' is given in and with the occurrence
of the impressions, he imports the consciousness of time,
both as relation and as numerable quantity, into the sequence
of impressions. He thus gains the advantage of being able
to speak of this sequence indifferently under predicates which
properly exclude each other. He can make it now a consciousness in time, now a consciousness of itself as in time;
now a series that cannot be summed, now a conception of the
sum of the series. The sequence of feelings, then, having
been so dealt with as to make it appear in effect that time
can be *felt*, that it should be *thought of* can involve no further
difficulty. The conception, smuggled into sensitive experience as an 'impression,' can be extracted from it again as
'idea,' without ostensible departure from the principle that
the idea is only the weaker impression.

260. 'The idea of time is not derived from a particular
impression mixed up with others and plainly distinguishable
from them, but arises altogether from the manner in which
impressions appear to the mind, without making one of the
number. Five notes played on the flute give us the impression
and idea of time, though time be not a sixth impression
which presents itself to the hearing or any other of the
senses. Nor is it a sixth impression which the mind by
reflection finds in itself. These five sounds, making their
appearance in this particular manner, excite no emotion or
affection in the mind, which being observed by it can give
rise to a new idea. For *that* is necessary to produce a new
idea of reflection; nor can the mind, by revolving over a
thousand times all its ideas of sensation, ever extract from
them any new original idea, unless nature has so framed its

faculties that it feels some new original impression arise from such a contemplation. But here it only takes notice of the *manner* in which the different sounds make their appearance, and that it may afterwards consider without considering these particular sounds, but may conjoin it with any other objects. The ideas of some objects it certainly must have, nor is it possible for it without these ever to arrive at any conception of time; which, since it appears not as any primary distinct impression, can plainly be nothing but different ideas or impressions or objects disposed in a certain manner, *i.e.* succeeding each other.' [1]

261. In this passage the equivocation between 'impression' as feeling, and 'impression' as conception of the manner in which feelings occur, is less successfully disguised than is the like equivocation in the account of extension—not indeed from any failure in Hume's power of statement, but from the nature of the case. In truth the mere reproduction of impressions can as little account for the one conception as for the other. Just as, in order to account for the 'impression' from which the abstract idea of space may be derived, we have to suppose first that the feeling of colour, through being presented by the self-conscious subject to itself, becomes a coloured thing, and next, that this thing is viewed as a whole of parts limiting each other; so, in order to account for the 'impression' from which the idea of time may be abstracted, we have to suppose the presentation of the succession of feelings to a consciousness not in succession, and the consequent view of such presented succession as a sum of numerable parts. It is a relation only possible for a thinking consciousness—a relation, in Hume's language, not depending on the nature of the impressions related—that has in each case to be introduced into experience in order to be extracted from it again by 'consideration:' but there is this difference, that in one case the relation is not really between feelings at all, but between things or parts of a thing; while in the other it is just that relation between feelings, the introduction of which excludes the possibility that any feeling should be the consciousness of the relation. Thus to speak of a feeling of extension does not involve so direct a contradiction as to speak in the same way of time. The reader gives Hume the benefit of a way of thinking which Hume's

[1] P. 343.

own theory excludes. Himself distinguishing between feeling and felt thing, and regarding extension as a relation between parts of a thing, he does not reflect that for Hume there is no such distinction; that a 'feeling of extension' means that feeling is extended, which again means that it has co-existent parts; and that what is thus said of feeling as *extended* is incompatible with what is said of it as *feeling*. But when it comes to a 'feeling of time'—a feeling of the successiveness of all feelings—the incompatibility between what is said of feeling as the object and what is implied of it as the subject is less easy to disguise. In like manner because we cannot really think of extension as being that which yet according to Hume it is, it does not strike us, when he speaks of it as coloured or of colour as extended, that he is making one feeling a quality of another. But it would be otherwise if any specific feeling were taken as a quality of what is ostensibly a relation between all feelings. There is thus no 'sensible quality' with which time can be said to be 'endowed,' as extension with 'colour and solidity;' none that can be made to do the same duty in regard to it as these do in regard to extension, 'giving the idea' of it without actually being it.

262. Hence, as the passage last quoted shows, in the case of time the alternative between ascribing it to a sixth sense, and confessing that it is not an impression at all, is very hard to avoid. It would seem that there is an impression of 'the manner in which impressions appear to the mind,' which yet is no 'distinct impression.' What, then, is it? It cannot be any one of the impressions of sense, for then it would be a distinct impression. It cannot be a 'compound impression,' for such composition is incompatible with that successiveness of all feelings to each other which is the object of the supposed impression. It cannot be any 'new original impression' arising from the contemplation of other impressions, for then, according to Hume, it would be 'an affection or emotion.' But after the exclusion of impressions of sense, compound impressions, and impressions of reflection, Hume's inventory of the possible sources of ideas is exhausted. To have been consistent, he ought to have dealt with the relation of time as he afterwards does with that of cause and effect, and, in default of an impression from which it could be derived, have reduced it to a figure of speech. But since the possibility

of accounting for the propensities to feign, which our language about cause and effect according to him represents, required the consciousness of relation in time, this course could not be taken. Accordingly after the possibility of time being an impression has been excluded as plainly as it can be by anything short of a direct negation, by a device singularly *naïf* it is made to appear as an impression after all. On being told that the consciousness of time is not a 'new original impression of reflection,' since in that case it would be an emotion or affection, but '*only* the notice which the mind takes of the manner in which impressions appear to it,' the reader must be supposed to forget the previous admission that it is no distinct impression at all, and to interpret this 'notice which the mind takes,' because it is not an impression of reflection, as an impression of sense. To make such interpretation easier, the account given of time earlier in the paragraph quoted is judiciously altered at its close, so that instead of having to ascribe to feeling a consciousness of 'the manner in which impressions appear to the mind,' we have only to ascribe to it the impressions so appearing. But this alteration admitted, what becomes of the 'abstractness' of the idea of time, *i.e.* of the possibility of its being 'conjoined with any objects' indifferently? It is the essential condition of such indifferent conjunction, as Hume puts it, that time should be only the manner of appearance as distinct from the impressions themselves. If time *is* the impressions, it must have the specific sensuous character which belongs to these. It must be a multitude of sounds, a multitude of tastes, a multitude of smells—these one after the other in endless series. How then can such a series of impressions become such an idea, *i.e.* so grow fainter as to be 'conjoined' indifferently 'with any impressions whatever'?

263. The case then between Hume and the conceptions which the exact sciences presuppose, as we have so far examined it, stands thus. Of the idea of quantity, as such, he gives no account whatever. We are told, indeed, that there are 'unites which can exist alone,' *i.e.* can be felt separately, and which are indivisible; but how such unites, being separate impressions, can form a sum or number, or what meaning a unite can have except as one of a number—how again a sum formed of separate unites can be a continuous whole or magnitude—we are not told at all. Of the ideas of space

and time we do find an account. They are said to be given in impressions, but, to justify this account of them, each impression has to be taken to be at the same time a consciousness of the manner of its own existence, as determined by relation to other impressions not felt along with it and as interpreted in a way that presupposes the unexplained idea of quantity. With this supposed origin of the ideas the sciences resting on them have to be adjusted. They may take the relations of number and magnitude, time and space, for granted, as 'qualities of perceptions,' and no question will be asked as to how the perceptions come to assume qualities confessed to be 'independent of their own nature.' It is only when they treat them in a way incompatible not merely with their being feelings—that must always be the case—but with their being relations between felt things, that they are supposed to cross the line which separates experimental knowledge from metaphysical jargon. So long then as space is considered merely as the relation of externality between objects of the 'outer,' time as that of succession between objects of the 'inner,' sense—in other words, so long as they remain what they are to the earliest self-consciousness and do not become the subject matter of any science of quantity— if we sink the difference between feelings and relations of felt things, and ask no questions about the origin of the distinction between outer and inner sense, they may be taken as data of sensitive experience. It is otherwise when they are treated as quantities, and it is their susceptibility of being so treated that, rightly understood, brings out their true character as the intelligible element in sensitive experience. But Hume contrives at once to treat them as quantities, thus seeming to give the exact sciences their due, and yet to appeal to their supposed origin in sense as evidence of their not having properties which, if they are quantities, they certainly must have. Having thus seemingly disposed of the purely intelligible character of quantity in its application to space and time, he can more safely ignore what he could not so plausibly dispose of—its pure intelligibility as number.

264. The condition of such a method being acquiesced in is, that quantity in all its forms should be found reducible to ultimate unites or indivisible parts in the shape of separate impressions. Should it be found so, the whole question indeed, how ideas of relation are possible for a merely feeling

consciousness, would still remain, but mathematics would stand on the same footing with the experimental sciences, as a science of relations between impressions. Upon this reducibility, then, we find Hume constantly insisting. In regard to number indeed he could not ignore the fact that the science which deals with it recognizes no ultimate unite, but only such a one as ' is itself a true number.' But he passes lightly over this difficulty with the remark that the divisible unite of actual arithmetic is a ' fictitious denomination '— leaving his reader to guess how the fiction can be possible if the real unite is a separate indivisible impression—and proceeds with the more hopeful task of resolving space into such impressions. He is well aware that the constitution of space by impressions and its constitution by indivisible parts stand or fall together. If space is a compound impression, it is made up of indivisible parts, for there is a ' minimum visibile ' and by consequence a minimum of imagination; and conversely, if its parts are indivisible, they can be nothing but impressions; for, being indivisible, they cannot be extended, and, not being extended, they must be either simple impressions or nothing. With that instinct of literary strategy which never fails him, Hume feels that the case against infinite divisibility, from its apparent implication of an infinite capacity in the mind, is more effective than that in favour of space being a compound impression, and accordingly puts that to the front in the Second Part of the Treatise, in order, having found credit for establishing it, to argue back to the constitution of space by impressions. In fact, however, it is on the supposed composition of all quantity from separate impressions that his argument against its infinite divisibility rests.

265. The essence of his doctrine is contained in the following passages : ' 'Tis certain that the imagination reaches a *minimum*, and may raise up to itself an idea, of which it cannot conceive any subdivision, and which cannot be diminished without a total annihilation. When you tell me of the thousandth and ten thousandth part of a grain of sand, I have a distinct idea of these numbers and of their several proportions, but the images which I form in my mind to represent the things themselves are nothing different from each other nor inferior to that image by which I represent the grain of sand itself, which is supposed so vastly to

exceed them. What consists of parts is distinguishable into them, and what is distinguishable is separable. But whatever we may imagine of the thing, the idea of a grain of sand is not distinguishable nor separable into twenty, much less into a thousand, ten thousand, or an infinite number of different ideas. 'Tis the same case with the impressions of the senses as with the ideas of the imagination. Put a spot of ink upon paper, fix your eye upon that spot, and retire to such a distance that at last you lose sight of it; 'tis plain that the moment before it vanished the image or impression was perfectly indivisible. 'Tis not for want of rays of light striking on our eyes that the minute parts of distant bodies convey not any sensible impression; but because they are removed beyond that distance at which their impressions were reduced to a *minimum*, and were incapable of any further diminution. A microscope or telescope, which renders them visible, produces not any new rays of light, but only spreads those which always flowed from them; and by that means both gives parts to impressions, which to the naked eye appear simple and uncompounded, and advances to a minimum what was formerly imperceptible.' [1] (Part II. § 1.)

266. In this passage it will be seen that Hume virtually yields the point as regards number. When he is told of the thousandth or ten thousandth part of a grain of sand he has ' a distinct idea of these numbers and of their different proportions,' though to this idea no distinct ' image ' corresponds; in other words, though the idea is not a copy of any impression. It is of such parts *as parts of the grain of sand*—as parts of a ' compound impression '—that he can form no idea, and for the reason given in the sequel, that they are less than any possible impression, less than the ' minimum visibile.' This, it would seem, is a fixed quantity. That which is the least possible impression once is so always. Telescopes and microscopes do not alter it, but present it under conditions under which it could not be presented to the naked eye. Their effect, according to Hume, could not be to render that visible which existed unseen before, nor to reveal parts in that which previously had, though it seemed not to have, them—that would imply that an impression was ' an image of something distinct and external '—but either to

present a simple impression of sight where previously there was none or to substitute a compound impression for one that was simple.[1] It is then because all divisibility is supposed to be into impressions, *i.e.* into feelings, and because there are conditions under which every feeling disappears, that an infinite divisibility is pronounced impossible. But the question is whether a finite divisibility into feelings is not just as impossible as an infinite one. Just as for the reasons stated above[2] a 'compound feeling' is impossible, so is the division of a compound into feelings. Undoubtedly if the 'minimum visibile' were a feeling it would not be divisible, but for the same reason it would not be a quantity. But if it is not a quantity, with what meaning is it called a minimum, and how can a quantity be supposed to be made up of such 'visibilia' as have themselves no quantity? In truth the 'minimum visibile' is not a feeling at all but a felt thing, conceived under attributes of quantity; in particular, as the term 'minimum' implies, under a relation of proportion to other quantities of which, if expressed numerically, Hume himself, according to the admission above noticed, would have to confess there was an idea which was an image of no impression. That which thought thus presents to itself as a thing doubtless has been a feeling; but, as thus presented, it is already other than and independent of feeling. With a step backward or a turn of the head, the feeling may cease, 'the spot of ink may vanish;' but the thing does not therefore cease to be a thing or to have quantity, which implies the possibility of continuous division.

267. It is thus the confusion between feeling and conception that is at the bottom of the difficulty about divisibility. For a consciousness formed merely by the succession of feelings, as there would be no *thing* at all, so there would be no parts of a thing—no addibility or divisibility. But Hume is forced by the exigencies of his theory to hold together, as best he may, the reduction of all consciousness to feeling and the existence for it of divisible objects. The consequence is his supposition of 'compound impressions' or feelings having parts, divisible into separate impressions

---

[1] It will be noticed that in the last sentence of the passage quoted, Hume assumes the convenient privilege of 'speaking with the vulgar,' and treats the 'minimum visibile' presented by telescope or microscope as representing something other than itself, which previously existed, though it was imperceptible.

[2] See above, §§ 241 & 246.

but divisible no further when these separate impressions have been reached. We find, however, that in all the instances he gives it is not really a feeling that is divided into feelings, but a thing into other things. It is the heap of sand, for instance, that is divided into grains, not the feeling which, by intellectual interpretation, represents to me a heap of sand that is divided into lesser feelings. I may feel the heap and feel the grain, but it is not a feeling that is the heap nor a feeling that is the grain. Hume would not offend common sense by saying that it was so, but his theory really required that he should, for the supposition that the grain is no further divisible when there are no separate impressions into which it may be divided, implies that in that case it is itself a separate impression, even as the heap is a compound one. But what difference, it may be asked, does it make to say that the heap and the grain are not feelings, but things conceived of, if it is admitted, as since Berkeley it must be, that the thing is nothing outside or independent of consciousness? Do we not by such a statement merely change names and invite the question how a thought can have parts, in place of the question how a feeling can have them?

268. If thought were no more than Hume takes feeling to be, this objection would be valid. But if by thought we understand the self-conscious principle which, present to all feelings, forms out of them a world of mutually related objects, permanent with its own permanence, we shall also understand that the relations by which thought qualifies its object are not qualities of itself—that, in thinking of its object as made up of parts, it does not become itself a quantum. We shall also be on the way to understand how thought, detaching that relation of simple distinctness by which it has qualified its objects, finds before it a multitude of units of which each, as combining in itself distinctions from all the other units, is at the same time itself a multitude; in other words, finds a quantum of which each part, being the same in kind with the whole and all other parts, is also a quantum; *i.e.* which is infinitely divisible. When once it is understood, in short, that quantity is simply the most elementary of the relations by which thought constitutes the real world, as detached from this world and presented by thought to itself as a separate object, then infinite

divisibility becomes a matter of course. It is real just in so far as quantity, of which it is a necessary attribute, is real. If quantity, though not feeling, is yet real, that its parts should not be feelings can be nothing against their reality. This once admitted, the objections to infinite divisibility disappear; but so likewise does that mysterious dignity supposed to attach to it, or to its correlative, the infinitely addible, as implying an infinite capacity in the mind. From Hume's point of view, the mind being 'a bundle of impressions'—though how impressions, being successive, should form a bundle is not explained—its capacity must mean the number of its impressions, and, all divisibility being into impressions, it follows that infinite divisibility means an infinite capacity in the mind. This notion however arises, as we have shown, from a confusion between a *felt* division of an impossible 'compound feeling,' and that conceived divisibility of an object which constitutes but a single attribute of the object and represents a single relation of the mind towards it. There may be a sense in which all conception implies infinity in the conceiving mind, but so far from this doing so in any special way, it arises, as we have seen, from the presentation of objects under that very condition of endless, unremoved, distinction which constitutes the true limitation of our thought.

269. When, as with Hume, it is only in its application to space and time that the question of infinite divisibility is treated, its true nature is more easily disguised, for the reason already indicated, that space and time are not necessarily considered as quanta. When Hume, indeed, speaks of space as a 'composition of parts' or 'made up of points,' he is of course treating it as a quantum; but we shall find that in seeking to avoid the necessary consequence of its being a quantum—the consequence, namely, that it is infinitely divisible—he can take advantage of the possibility of treating it as the simple, unquantified, relation of externality. We have already spoken of the dexterity with which, having shown that all divisibility, because into impressions, is into simple parts, he turns this into an argument in favour of the composition of space by impressions. 'Our idea of space is compounded of parts which are indivisible.' Let us take one of these parts, then, and ask what sort of idea it is: 'let us form a judgment of its nature and qualities.' ''Tis plain it

is not an idea of extension: for the idea of extension consists of parts; and this idea, according to the supposition, is perfectly simple and indivisible. Is it therefore nothing? That is impossible,' for it would imply that a real idea was composed of nonentities. The way out of the difficulty is to 'endow the simple parts with colour and solidity.' In words already quoted, 'that compound impression, which represents extension, consists of several lesser impressions, that are indivisible to the eye or feeling, and may be called impressions of atoms or corpuscles endowed with colour and solidity.' (Part II. § 3, near the end.)

270. It is very plain that in this passage Hume is riding two horses at once. He is trying so to combine the notion of the constitution of space by impressions with that of its constitution by points, as to disguise the real meaning of each. In what lies the difference between the feelings of colour, of which we have shown that they cannot without contradiction be supposed to 'make up extension,' and 'coloured points or corpuscles'? Unless the points, as points, mean something, the substitution of coloured points for colours means nothing. But according to Hume the point is nothing except as an impression of sight or touch. If then we refuse his words the benefit of an interpretation which his doctrine excludes, we find that there remains simply the impossible supposition that space consists of feelings. This result cannot be avoided, unless in speaking of space as composed of points, we understand by the point that which is definitely other than an impression. Thus the question which Hume puts—If extension is made up of parts, and these, being indivisible, are unextended, what are they?—really remains untouched by his ostensible answer. Such a question indeed to a philosophy like Locke's, which, ignoring the constitution of reality by relations, supposed real things to be first found and then relations to be superinduced by the mind—much more to one like Hume's, which left no mind to superinduce them—was necessarily unanswerable.

271. In truth, extension is the relation of mutual externality. The constituents of this relation have not, as such, any nature but what is given by the relation. If in Hume's language we 'separate each from the others and, considering it apart, from a judgment of its nature and qualities,' by the very way we put the problem we render it insoluble or, more

properly, destroy it; for, thus separated, they have no nature. It is this that we express by the proposition which would otherwise be tautological, that extension is a relation between extended points. The 'points' are the simplest expression for those coefficients to the relation of mutual externality, which, as determined by that relation and no otherwise, have themselves the attribute of being extended and that only. If it is asked whether the points, being extended, are therefore divisible, the answer must be twofold. *Separately* they are not divisible, for separately they are nothing. Whether, as determined by mutual relation, they are divisible or no, depends on whether they are treated as forming a quantum or no. If they are not so treated, we cannot with propriety pronounce them to be either further divisible or not so, for the question of divisibility has no application to them. But being perfectly homogeneous with each other and with that which together they constitute, they are susceptible of being so treated, and *are* so treated when, with Hume in the passage before us, we speak of them as the parts of which extended matter consists. Thus considered as parts of a quantum and therefore themselves quanta, the infinite divisibility which belongs to all quantity belongs also to them.

272. In this lies the answer to the most really cogent argument which Hume offers against infinite divisibility. 'A surface terminates a solid; a line terminates a surface; a point terminates a line; but I assert that if the *ideas* of a point, line, or surface were not indivisible, 'tis impossible we should ever conceive these terminations. For let these ideas be supposed infinitely divisible, and then let the fancy endeavour to fix itself on the idea of the last surface, line, or point, it immediately finds this idea to break into parts; and upon its seizing the last of these parts it loses its hold by a new division, and so on *ad infinitum*, without any possibility of its arriving at a concluding idea.'[1] If 'point,' 'line,' or 'surface' were really names for 'ideas' either in Hume's sense, as feelings grown fainter, or in Locke's, as definite imprints made by outward things, this passage would be perplexing. In truth they represent objects determined by certain conceived relations, and the relation under which the object is considered may vary without a corresponding variation in the name. When a 'point' is considered simply as the

[1] P. 345.

'termination of a line,' it is not considered as a quantum. It represents the abstraction of the relation of externality, as existing between *two lines*. It is these lines, not the point, that in this case are the constituents of the relation, and thus it is they alone that are for the time considered as extended, therefore as quanta, therefore as divisible. So when the line in turn is considered as the 'termination of a sur-face.' It then represents the relation of externality *as between surfaces*, and for the time it is the surfaces, not the line, that are considered to have extension and its consequences. The same applies to the view of a surface as the termination of a solid. Just as the line, though not a quantum when considered simply as a relation between surfaces, becomes so when considered in relation to another line, so the point, though it 'has no magnitude' when considered as the termination of a line, yet acquires parts, or becomes divisible, so soon as it is considered in relation to other points as a constituent of extended matter; and it is thus that Hume considers it, ἑκὼν ἢ ἄκων, when he talks of extension as 'made up of coloured points.'

273. It is the necessity then, according to his theory, of making space an impression that throughout underlies Hume's argument against its infinite divisibility; and, as we have seen, the same theory which excludes its infinite divisibility logically extinguishes it as a quantity, divisible and measurable, altogether. He of course does not recognize this consequence. He is obliged indeed to admit that in regard to the proportions of 'greater, equal and less,' and the relations of different parts of space to each other, no judgments of universality or exactness are possible. We may judge of them, however, he holds, with various approximations to exactness, whereas upon the supposition of infinite divisibility, as he ingeniously makes out, we could not judge of them at all. He 'asks the mathematicians, what they mean when they say that one line or surface is equal to, or greater or less than, another.' If they 'maintain the composition of extension by indivisible points,' their answer, he supposes, will be that 'lines or surfaces are equal when the numbers of points in each are equal.' This answer he reckons 'just,' but the standard of equality given is entirely useless. 'For as the points which enter into the composition of any line or surface, whether perceived by the sight or touch, are so

minute and so confounded with each other that 'tis utterly
impossible for the mind to compute their number, such a
computation will never afford us a standard by which we
may judge of proportions.' The opposite sect of mathematicians, however, are in worse case, having no standard of
equality whatever to assign. ' For since, according to their
hypothesis, the least as well as greatest figures contain an
infinite number of parts, and since infinite numbers, properly
speaking, can neither be equal nor unequal with respect to
each other, the equality or inequality of any portion of space
can never depend on any proportion in the number of their
parts.' His own doctrine is 'that the only useful notion of
equality or inequality is derived from the whole united
appearance, and the comparison of, particular objects.' The
judgments thus derived are in many cases certain and infallible. 'When the measure of a yard and that of a foot are
presented, the mind can no more question that the first is
longer than the second than it can doubt of those principles
which are most clear and self-evident.' Such judgments,
however, though 'sometimes infallible, are not always so.'
Upon a 'review and reflection' we often ' pronounce those
objects equal which at first we esteemed unequal,' and *vice
versâ*. Often also ' we discover our error by a juxtaposition
of the objects; or, where that is impracticable, by the use of
some common and invariable measure which, being successively applied to each, informs us of their different proportions. And even this correction is susceptible of a new
correction, and of different degrees of exactness, according to
the nature of the instrument by which we measure the
bodies, and the care which we employ in the comparison.'
(Pp. 351–53.)

274. Such indefinite approach to exactness is all that
Hume can allow to the mathematician. But it is undoubtedly
another and an absolute sort of exactness that the mathematician himself supposes when he pronounces all right angles
equal. Such perfect equality ' beyond what we have instru-
ments and art' to ascertain, Hume boldly calls a ' mere
fiction of the mind, useless as well as incomprehensible.'[1]
Thus when the mathematician talks of certain angles as
always equal, of certain lines as never meeting, he is either

[1] P. 353.

making statements that are untrue or speaking of nonentities. If his 'lines' and 'angles' mean ideas that we can possibly have, his universal propositions are untrue; if they do not, according to Hume they can mean nothing. He says, for instance, that 'two right lines cannot have a common segment;' but of such ideas of right lines as we can possibly have this is only true 'where the right lines incline upon each other with a sensible angle.'[1] It is not true when they 'approach at the rate of an inch in 20 leagues.' According to the 'original standard of a right line,' which is 'nothing but a certain general appearance, 'tis evident right lines may be made to concur with each other.'[2] Any other standard is a 'useless and incomprehensible fiction.' Strictly speaking, according to Hume, we have it not, but only a tendency to suppose that we have it arising from the progressive correction of our actual measurements.[3]

275. Now it is obvious that what Hume accounts for by means of this tendency to feign, even if the tendency did not presuppose conditions incompatible with his theory, is not mathematical science as it exists. It has even less appearance of being so than (to anticipate) has that which is accounted for by those propensities to feign, which he substitutes for the ideas of cause and substance, of being natural science as it exists. In the latter case, when the idea of necessary connexion has been disposed of, an impression of reflection can with some plausibility be made to do duty instead; but there is no impression of reflection in Hume's sense of the word, no 'propensity,' that can be the subject of mathematical reasoning. He speaks, indeed, of our *supposing* some imaginary standard—of our having 'an obscure and implicit notion '—of perfect equality, but such language is only a way of saving appearances; for according to him, a 'supposition' or 'notion' which is neither impression nor idea, cannot be anything. A hasty reader, catching at the term 'supposition,' may find his statement plausible with all the plausibility of the modern doctrine, which accounts for the universality and exactness of mathematical truths as 'hypothetical '—the doctrine that we suppose figures exactly corresponding to our definitions, though such do

---

[1] Cf. Aristotle, *Metaph.* 998 a, on a corresponding view ascribed to Pro-   tagoras.
[2] P. 356.   [3] P. 354.

not really exist. With those who take this view, however, it is always understood that the definitions represent ideas, though not ideas to which real objects can be found exactly answering. Perhaps, if pressed about their distinction between idea and reality, they might find it hard consistently to maintain it, but it is by this practically that they keep their theory afloat. Hume can admit no such distinction. The real with him is the impression, and the idea the fainter impression. There can be no idea of a straight line, a curve, a circle, a right angle, a plane, other than the impression, other than the 'appearance to the eye,' and there are no appearances exactly answering to the mathematical definitions. If they do not *exactly* answer, they might as well for the purposes of mathematical demonstration not answer at all. The Geometrician, having found that the angles at the base of *this* isosceles triangle are equal to each other, at once takes the equality to be true of all isosceles triangles, as being exactly like the original one, and on the strength of this establishes many other propositions. But, according to Hume, no idea that we could have would be one of which the sides were precisely equal. The Fifth Proposition of Euclid then is not precisely true of the particular idea that we have before us when we follow the demonstration. Much less can it be true of the ideas, *i.e.* the several appearances of colour, indefinitely varying from this, which we have before us when we follow the other demonstrations in which the equality of the angles at the base of an isosceles is taken for granted.

276. Here, as elsewhere, what we have to lament is not that Hume 'pushed his doctrine too far,' so far as to exclude ideas of those exact proportions in space with which geometry purports to deal, but that he did not carry it far enough to see that it excluded all ideas of quantitative relations whatever. He thus pays the penalty for his equivocation between a feeling of colour and a disposition of coloured points. Even alongside of his admission that ' relations of space and time' are independent of the nature of the ideas so related, which amounts to the admission that of space and time there are no ideas at all in his sense of the word, he allows himself to treat 'proportions between spaces ' as depending entirely on our ideas of the spaces— depending on ideas which in the context he by implication

admits that we have not.[1] If, instead of thus equivocating, he had asked himself how sensations of colour and touch could be added or divided, how one could serve as a measure of the size of another, he might have seen that only in virtue of that in the 'general appearance' of objects which, in his own language, is 'independent of the nature of the ideas themselves'—*i.e.* which does not belong to them as feelings, but is added by the comparing and combining thought—are the proportions of greater, less, and equal predicable of them at all; that what thought has thus added, viz. limitation by mutual externality, it can abstract; and that by such abstraction of the limit it obtains those several terminations, as Hume well calls them — the surface terminating bodies, the line terminating surfaces, the point terminating lines—from which it constructs the world of pure space : that thus the same action of thought in sense, which alone renders appearances measurable, gives an object matter which, because the pure construction of thought, we can measure exactly and with the certainty that the judgment based on a comparison of magnitudes in a single case is true of all possible cases, because in none of these can any other conditions be present than those which we have consciously put there.

277. To have arrived at this conclusion Hume had only to extend to proportions in space the principle upon which the impossibility of sensualizing arithmetic compels him to deal with proportions in number. 'We are possessed,' he says, ' of a precise standard by which we can judge of the equality and proportion of numbers; and according as they correspond or not to that standard we determine their relations without any possibility of error. When two numbers are so combined, as that the one has always an unite answering to every unite of the other, we pronounce them equal.'[2] Now what are the unites here spoken of? If they were those single impressions which he elsewhere[3] seems to regard as alone properly unites, the point of the passage would be gone, for combinations of such unites could at any rate only yield those 'general appearances' of whose proportions we have been previously told there can be no precise standard. They can be no other than those

unites which, not being impressions, he has to call 'fictitious denominations'—unites which are nothing except in relation to each other and of which each, being in turn divisible, is itself a true number. We can easily retort upon Hume, then, when he argues that the supposition of infinite divisibility is incompatible with any comparison of quantities because with any unite of measurement, that, according to his own virtual admission, in the only case where such comparison is exact the ultimate unite of measurement is still itself divisible; which, indeed, is no more than saying that whatever measures quantity must itself be a quantity, and that therefore quantity is infinitely divisible. If Hume, instead of slurring over this characteristic of the science of number, had set himself to explain it, he would have found that the only possible explanation of it was one equally applicable to the science of space—that what is true of the unite, as the abstraction of distinctness, is true also of the abstraction of externality. As the unite, because constituted by relation to other unites, so soon as considered breaks into multiplicity, and only for that reason is a quantity by which other quantities can be measured; so is it also with the limit in whatever form abstracted, whether as point, line, or surface. If the fact that number can have no least part since each part is itself a number or nothing, so far from being incompatible with the finiteness of number, is the consequence of that finiteness, neither can the like attribute in spaces be incompatible with their being definite magnitudes, that can be compared with and measured by each other. The real difference, which is also the rationale of Hume's different procedure in the two cases, is that the conception of space is more easily confused than that of number with the feelings to which it is applied, and which through such application become sensible spaces. Hence the liability to the supposition, which is at bottom Hume's, that the last feeling in the process of diminution before such sensible space disappears (being the 'minimum visibile') is the least possible portion of space.

278. Just as that reduction of consciousness to feeling, which really excludes the idea of quantity altogether, is by Hume only recognised as incompatible with its infinite divisibility, so it is not recognised as extinguishing space altogether, but only space as a vacuum. If it be true, he says, 'that the

idea of space is nothing but the idea of visible or tangible points distributed in a certain order, it follows that we can form no idea of vacuum, or space where there is nothing visible or tangible.'[1] Here as elsewhere the acceptability of his statement lies in its being taken in a sense which according to his principles cannot properly belong to it. It is one doctrine that the ideas of space and body are essentially correlative, and quite another that the idea of space is equivalent to a feeling of sight or touch. It is of the latter doctrine that Hume's denial of a vacuum is the corollary; but it is the former that gains acceptance for this denial in the mind of his reader. Space we have already spoken of as the relation of externality. If, abstracting this relation from the world of which it is the uniform but most elementary determination, we regard it as a relation between objects having no other determination, these become spaces and nothing but spaces—space pure and simple, *vacuum*. But we have known the world in confused fulness before we detach its constituent relations in the clearness of unreal abstraction. We have known bodies συγκεχυμένως, before we think their limits apart and out of these construct a world of pure space. It is thus in a sense true that in the development of our consciousness an idea of body precedes that of space, though the *abstraction* of space—the detachment of the relation so-called from the real complex of relations—precedes that of body; and it is this fact that, in the face of geometry, strengthens common sense in its position that an idea of vacuum is impossible. It is not, however, the inseparability of space from body whether in reality or for our consciousness, but its identity with a certain sort of feeling, that is implied in Hume's exclusion of the idea of vacuum. 'Body,' as other than feeling, is with him as much a fiction as vacuum. That there can be no idea of vacuum, is thus in fact merely his negative way of putting that proposition of which the positive form is, that space is a compound impression of sight and touch. Having examined that proposition in the positive, we need not examine it again in the negative form. It will be more to the purpose to enquire whether the 'tendency to suppose' or 'propensity to feign' by which, in the absence of any such idea, our language about 'pure space' has to be accounted

for, does not according to Hume's own showing presuppose
such an idea.

279. By vacuum he understands invisible and intangible
extension. If an idea of vacuum, then, is possible at all, he
argues, it must be possible for darkness and mere motion to
convey it. That they cannot do so *alone* is clear from the
consideration that darkness is 'no positive idea' and that an
'invariable motion,' such as that of a 'man supported in the
air and softly conveyed along by some invisible power,' gives
no idea at all. Neither can they do so when 'attended with
visible and tangible objects.' 'When two bodies present
themselves where there was formerly an entire darkness, the
only change that is discoverable is in the appearance of these
two objects: all the rest continues to be, as before, a perfect
negation of light and of every coloured or tangible object.'[1]
'Such dark and indistinguishable distance between two bodies
can never produce the idea of extension,' any more than
blindness can. Neither can a like 'imaginary distance between tangible and solid bodies.' 'Suppose two cases, viz.
that of a man supported in the air, and moving his limbs to
and fro without meeting anything tangible; and that of a
man who, feeling something tangible, leaves it, and after a
motion of which he is sensible perceives another tangible
object. Wherein consists the difference between these two
cases? No one will scruple to affirm that it consists merely
in the perceiving those objects, and that the sensation which
arises from the motion is in both cases the same; and as
that sensation is not capable of conveying to us an idea of
extension, when unaccompanied with some other perception,
it can no more give us that idea, when mixed with the impressions of tangible objects, since that mixture produces no
alteration upon it.'[2] But though a 'distance not filled with
any coloured or solid object' cannot give us an idea of vacuum,
it is the cause why we falsely imagine that we can form such
an idea. There are 'three relations'—*natural* relations according to Hume's phraseology[3]—between it and that distance
which really 'conveys the idea of extension.' 'The distant
objects affect the senses in the same manner, whether separated by the one distance or the other; the former species
of distance is found capable of receiving the latter; and they

both equally diminish the force of every quality. These relations betwixt the two kinds of distance will afford us an easy reason why the one has so often been taken for the other, and why we imagine we have an idea of extension without the idea of any object either of the sight or feeling.'[1]

280. It appears then that we have an idea of 'distance unfilled with any coloured or solid object.' To speak of this distance as 'imaginary' or fictitious can according to Hume's principles make no difference, so long as he admits, which he is obliged to do, that we actually have an idea of it; for every idea, being derived from an impression, is as much or as little imaginary as every other. And not only have we such an idea, but Hume's account of the 'relations' between it and the idea of extension implies that, *as ideas of distance*, they do not differ at all. But the idea of 'distance unfilled with any coloured or solid object' *is* the idea of vacuum. It follows that the idea of extension does not differ from that of vacuum, except so far as it is other than the idea of distance. But it is from the consideration of distance that Hume himself expressly derives it;[2] and so derived, it can no more differ from distance than an idea from a corresponding impression. Thus, after all, he has to all intents and purposes to admit the idea of vacuum, but saves appearances by refusing to call it extension—the sole reason for such refusal being the supposition that every idea, and therefore the idea of extension, must be a datum of sense, which the admission of an idea of 'invisible and intangible distance' already contradicts.

281. We now know the nature of that preliminary manipulation which 'impressions and ideas' have to undergo, if their association is to yield the result which Hume requires —if through it the succession of feelings is to become a knowledge of things and their relations. Such a result was required as the only means of maintaining together the two characteristic positions of Locke's philosophy; that, namely, the only world we can know is the world of 'ideas,' and that thought cannot originate ideas. Those relations, which Locke had inconsistently treated at once as intellectual superinductions and as ultimate conditions of reality, must be dealt with by one of two methods. They must be reduced to

impressions where that could plausibly be done : where it could not, it must be admitted that we have no ideas of them, but only ' tendencies to suppose ' that we have such, arising from the association, through 'natural relations,' of the ideas that we have. So dexterously does Hume work the former method that, of all the ' philosophical relations which he recognizes, only Identity and Causation remain to be disposed of by the latter ; and if the other relations— resemblance, time and space, proportion in quantity and degree in quality—could really be admitted as data of sense, there would at least be a possible basis for those ' tendencies to suppose ' which, in the absence of any corresponding ideas, the terms ' Identity ' and ' Causation ' must be taken to represent. But, as we have shown, they can only be claimed for sense, if sense is so far one with thought—one not by conversion of thought into sense but by taking of sense into thought—as that Hume's favourite appeals to sense against the reality of intelligible relations become unmeaning. They may be ' impressions,' there may be ' impressions of them,' but only if we deny of the impression what Hume asserts of it, and assert of it what he denies—only if we understand by ' impression ' *not* an ' internal and perishing existence ;' *not* that which, if other than taste, colour, sound, smell or touch, must be a ' passion or emotion '; *not* that which carries no reference to an object other than itself, and which must *either* be single *or* compound ; but something permanent and constituted by permanently coexisting parts ; something that may ' be conjoined with ' any feeling, because it is none ; that always carries with it a reference to a subject which it is not but of which it is a quality ; and that is both many and one, since ' in its simplicity it contains many different resemblances and relations.'

282. In the account just adduced of vacuum, the effect of that double dealing with ' impressions,' which we shall have to trace at large in Hume's explanation of our language about Causation and Identity, is already exhibited in little. Just as, after the idea of pure space has been excluded because not a copy of any possible impression, we yet find an ' idea.' only differing from it in name, introduced as the basis of that tendency to suppose which is to take the place of the excluded idea, so we shall find ideas of relation in the way of Identity and Causation—ideas which according to Hume we

have not—presupposed as the source of those 'propensities to feign' by which he accounts for the appearance of our having them.

283. The primary characteristic of these relations according to Hume, which they share with those of space and time, and which in fact vitiates that definition of 'philosophical relation,' as depending on comparison, which he adopts, is that they 'depend not on the ideas compared together, but may be changed without any change in the ideas.' [1] It follows that they are not objects of knowledge, according to the definition of knowledge which Hume inherited, as 'the perception of agreement or disagreement between ideas.' A partial recognition of this consequence in regard to cause and effect we found in Locke's suspicion that a science of nature was impossible—impossible because, however often a certain 'idea of quality and substance' may have followed or accompanied another, such sequence or accompaniment never amounts to agreement or 'necessary connexion' between the ideas, and therefore never can warrant a general assertion, but only the particular one, that the ideas in question have so many times occurred in such an order. 'Matters of fact,' however, which no more consist in agreement of ideas than does causation, are by Locke treated without scruple as matter of knowledge when they can be regarded as relations between present sensations. Thus the 'particular experiment' in Physics constitutes knowledge—the knowledge, for instance, that a piece of gold is now dissolved in aqua regia; and when 'I myself see a man walk on the ice, it is knowledge.' In such cases it does not occur to him to ask, either what are the ideas that agree or how much of the experiment is a present sensation. [2] Nor does Hume commonly carry his analysis further. After admitting that the relations called 'identity and situation in time and place' do not depend on the nature of the ideas related, he proceeds: 'When both the objects are present to the senses along with the relation, we call *this* perception rather than reasoning; nor is there in this case any exercise of the thought or any action, properly speaking, but a mere passive admission of the impressions through the organs of sensation. According to this way of thinking, we ought not

[1] P. 372. [2] Above, §§ 122 & 123.

to receive as reasoning any of the observations we may make concerning *identity* and the *relations* of *time* and *place*; since in none of them the mind can go beyond what is immediately present to the senses, either to discover the real existence or the relations of objects.' [1]

284. This passage points out the way which Hume's doctrine of causation was to follow. That in any case ' the mind should go beyond a present feeling, either to discover the real existence or the relations of objects' other than present feelings, was what he could not consistently admit. In the judgment of causation, however, it seems to do so. ' From the existence or action of one object,' seen or remembered, it seems to be assured of the existence or action of another, not seen or remembered, on the ground of a necessary connection between the two.[2] It is such assurance that is reckoned to constitute reasoning in the distinctive sense of the term, as different at once from the analysis of complex ideas and the simple succession of ideas—such reasoning as, in the language of a later philosophy, can yield synthetic propositions. What Hume has to do, then, is to explain this ' assurance' away by showing that it is not essentially different from that judgment of relation in time and place which, because the related objects are ' present to the senses along with the relation,' is called ' perception rather than reasoning,' and to which no ' exercise of the thought' is necessary, but a ' mere passive admission of impressions through the organs of sensation.' Nor, for the assimilation of reasoning to perception, is anything further needed than a reference to the connection of ideas with impressions and of the ideas of imagination with those of memory, as originally stated by Hume. When both of the objects compared are present to the senses, we call the comparison perception; when neither, or only one, is so present, we call it reasoning. But the difference between the object that is present to sense, and that which is not, is merely the difference between impression and idea, which again is merely the difference between the more and the less lively feeling.[3] To feeling, whether with more or with less vivacity, every object, whether of perception or reasoning, must alike be present. Is it then a sufficient account of the matter, according to Hume, to say that when we are conscious of contiguity and succession

---

[1] P. 376.   [2] Pp. 376, 384.   [3] Pp. 327, 375.

between objects of which both are impressions we call it perception; but that when both objects are ideas, or one an impression and the other an idea, we call it reasoning? Not quite so. Suppose that I 'have seen that species of object we call flame, and have afterwards felt that species of sensation we call heat.' If I afterwards remembered the succession of the feeling upon the sight, both objects (according to Hume's original usage of terms [1]) would be ideas as distinct from the impressions; or, if upon seeing the flame I remembered the previous experience of heat, one object would be an idea; but we should not reckon it a case of reasoning. 'In all cases wherein we reason concerning objects, there is only one either perceived or *remembered*, and the other is supplied in conformity to our past experience' —supplied by the only other faculty than memory that can 'supply an idea,' viz. imagination.[2]

285. This being the only account of 'inference from the known to the unknown,' which Hume could consistently admit, his view of the relation of cause and effect must be adjusted to it. It could not be other than a relation either between impression and impression, or between impression and idea, or between idea and idea; and all these relations are equally between feelings that we experience. Thus, instead of being the 'objective basis' on which inference from the known to the unknown rests, it is itself the inference; or, more properly, it and the inference alike disappear into a particular sort of transition from feeling to feeling. The problem, then, is to account for its seeming to be other than this. 'There is nothing in any objects to persuade us that they are always *remote* or always *contiguous*; and when from experience and observation we discover that the relation in this particular is invariable, we always conclude that there is some secret *cause* which separates or unites them.'[3] It would *seem*, then, that the relation of cause and effect is something which we infer from experience, from the connection of impressions and ideas, but which is not itself impression or idea. And it would *seem* further, that, as we infer such an unexperienced relation, so likewise we make inferences from it. In regard to identity 'we readily suppose an object may continue individually the same, though several times absent from and present to the senses; and

---

[1] Above, par. 195. [2] Pp. 384, 388. [3] P. 376.

ascribe to it an identity, notwithstanding the interruption of the perception, whenever we conclude that if we had kept our hand or eye constantly upon it, it would have conveyed an invariable and uninterrupted perception. But this conclusion beyond the impressions of our senses can be founded only on the connection of *cause and effect*; nor can we otherwise have any security that the object is not changed upon us, however much the new object may resemble that which was formerly present to the senses.'

286. This relation which, going beyond our actual experience, we seem to infer as the explanation of invariable contiguity in place or time of certain impressions, and from which again we seem to infer the identity of an object of which the perception has been interrupted, is what we call necessary connection. It is their supposed necessary connection which distinguishes objects related as cause and effect from those related merely in the way of contiguity and succession,[1] and it is a like supposition that leads us to infer what we do not see or remember from what we do. If then the reduction of thought and the intelligible world to feeling was to be made good, this supposition, not being an impression of sense or a copy of such, must be shown to be an 'impression of reflection,' according to Hume's sense of the term, *i.e.* a tendency of the soul, analogous to desire and aversion, hope and fear, derived from impressions of sense but not copied from them;[2] and the inference which it determines must be shown to be the work of imagination, as affected by such impression of reflection. This in brief is the purport of Hume's doctrine of causation.

287. After his manner, however, he will go about with his reader. The supposed 'objective basis' of knowledge is to be made to disappear, but in such a way that no one shall miss it. So dexterously, indeed, is this done, that perhaps to this day the ordinary student of Hume is scarcely conscious of the disappearance. Hume merely announces to begin with that he will 'postpone the direct survey of this question concerning the nature of necessary connection,' and deal first with these other two questions, viz. (1) 'For what reason we pronounce it *necessary* that everything whose existence has a beginning, should also have a cause?' and (2) 'Why we conclude that such particular causes must *necessarily* have

[1] P. 376.   [2] Above, par. 195.

such particular effects; and what is the nature of that *inference* we draw from the one to the other, and of the *belief* we repose in it?' That is to say, he will consider the inference from cause or effect, before he considers cause and effect as a relation between objects, on which the inference is supposed to depend. Meanwhile necessary connection, as a relation between objects, is naturally supposed in some sense or other to survive. In *what* sense, the reader expects to find when these two preliminary questions have been answered. But when they have been answered, necessary connection, as a relation between objects, turns out to have vanished.

288. With the first of the above questions Hume only concerns himself so far as to show that we cannot know either intuitively or demonstratively, in Locke's sense of the words, that 'everything whose existence has a beginning also has a cause.' Locke's own argument for the necessity of causation—that 'something cannot be produced by nothing'—as well as Clarke's—that 'if anything wanted a cause it would produce itself, *i.e.* exist before it existed'—are merely different ways, as Hume shows, of assuming the point in question. 'If everything must have a cause, it follows that upon exclusion of other causes we must accept of the object itself, or of nothing, as causes. But 'tis the very point in question, whether everything must have a cause or not.'[1] On that point, according to Locke's own showing, there can be no certainty, intuitive or demonstrative; for between the idea of beginning to exist and the idea of cause there is clearly no agreement, mediate or immediate. They are not similar feelings, they are not quantities that can be measured against each other, and to these alone can the definition of knowledge and reasoning, which Hume retained, apply. There thus disappears that last remnant of 'knowledge' in regard to nature which Locke had allowed to survive—the knowledge that there is a necessary connection, though one which we cannot find out.[2]

289. Having thus shown, as he conceives, what the true answer to the first of the above questions is not, Hume proceeds to show what it is by answering the second. 'Since it is not from knowledge or any scientific reasoning that we derive the opinion of the necessity of a cause to every new

---

[1] P. 382.   [2] Cf. Locke IV. 3, 29, and Introduc., par. 121.

production,' it must be from experience; and every general opinion derived from experience is merely the summary of a multitude of particular ones. Accordingly when it has been explained why we infer particular causes from particular effects (and *vice versa*), the inference from every event to a cause will have explained itself. Now 'all our arguments concerning causes and effects consist both of an impression of the memory or senses, and of the idea of that existence which produces the object of the impression or is produced by it. Here, therefore, we have three things to explain, viz. *first*, the original impression; *secondly*, the transition to the idea of the connected cause or effect; *thirdly*, the nature and qualities of that idea.'[2]

290. As to the original impression we must notice that there is a certain inconsistency with Hume's previous usage of terms in speaking of an *impression* of memory at all.[3] This, however, will be excused when we reflect that according to him impression and idea only differ in liveliness, and that he is consistent in claiming for the ideas of memory, not indeed the maximum, but a high degree of vivacity, superior to that which belongs to ideas of imagination. All that can be said, then, of that 'original impression,' whether of the memory or senses, which is necessary to any 'reasoning from cause or effect,' is that it is highly vivacious. That the transition from it to the 'idea of the connected cause or effect' is not determined by reason, has already been settled. It could only be so determined, according to the received account of reason, if there were some agreement in respect of quantity or quality between the idea of cause and that of the effect, to be ascertained by the interposition of other ideas.[4] But when we examine any particular objects that we hold to be related as cause and effect, *e.g.* the sight of flame and the feeling of heat, we find no such agreement. What we *do* find is their 'constant conjunction' in experience, and 'conjunction' is equivalent to that 'contiguity in time and place,' which has already been pointed out as one of those 'natural relations' which act as 'principles of union' between ideas.[5] Because the impression of flame has always been found to be followed by the impression of heat, the idea

[1] P. 383.
[2] P. 385.
[3] Above, par. 195.
[4] Cf. Locke IV. 17, 2.
[5] Above, par. 206.

of flame always suggests the idea of heat. It is simple custom then that determines the transition from the one to the other, or renders 'necessary' the connection between them. In order that the transition, however, may constitute an inference from cause to effect (or *vice versâ*), one of the two objects thus naturally related, but not both, must be presented as an impression. If both were impressions it would be a case of 'sensation, not reasoning;' if both were ideas, no belief would attend the transition. This brings us to the question as to the 'nature and qualities' of the inferred idea.

2`1. ''Tis evident that all reasonings from causes or effects terminate in conclusions concerning matter of fact, *i. e.* concerning the existence of objects or of their qualities';[1] in other words, in belief. If this meant a new idea, an idea that we have not previously had, it would follow that inference could really carry us beyond sense, that there could be an idea not copied from any prior impression. But according to Hume it does not mean this. 'The idea of existence is the very same with the idea of what we conceive to be existent;'[2] and not only so, ' the *belief* of existence joins no new ideas to those which compose the idea of the object. When I think of God, when I think of him as existent, and when I believe him to be existent, my idea of him neither increases nor diminishes.'[3] In what then lies the difference between incredulity and belief; between an 'idea assented to,' or an object believed to exist, and a fictitious object or idea from which we dissent? The answer is, 'not in the parts or composition of the idea, but in the manner of conceiving it,' which must be understood to mean the manner of 'feeling' it; and this difference is further explained to lie in 'the superior force, or vivacity, or steadiness' with which it is felt.[4] We are thus brought to the further question, how it is that this 'superior vivacity' belongs to the inferred idea when we 'reason' from cause to effect or from effect to cause. The answer here is that the 'impression of the memory or senses,' which in virtue of a 'natural relation' suggests the idea, also 'communicates to it a share of its force or vivacity.'

292. Thus it appears that in order to the conclusion that any particular cause must have any particular effect, there is

[1] P. 394.
[2] P. 370.
[3] P. 395.

[4] P. 398. Cf. above, par. 170, for the corresponding view in Berkeley.

needed first the presence of an impression, and secondly the joint action of those two 'principles of union among ideas,' resemblance and contiguity. In virtue of the former principle the given impression calls up the image of a like impression previously experienced, which again in virtue of the latter calls up the image of its usual attendant, and the liveliness of the given impression so communicates itself to the recalled ideas as to constitute belief in their existence. If this is the true account of the matter, the question as to the nature of necessary connexion has answered itself. 'The necessary connexion betwixt causes and effects is the foundation of our inference from one to the other. The foundation of the inference is the transition arising from the accustomed union. These are therefore the same.'[1] We may thus understand how it is that there seems to be an idea of such connexion to which no impression of the senses, or (to use an equivalent phrase of Hume's) no 'quality in objects' corresponds. If the first presentation of two objects, of which one is cause, the other effect, (*i. e.* of which we afterwards come to consider one the cause, the other the effect) gives no idea of a connexion between them, as it clearly does not, neither can it do so however often repeated. It would not do so, unless the repetition ' either discovered or produced something new' in the objects; and it does neither. But it does 'produce a new impression in the mind.' After observing a ' constant conjunction of the objects, and an uninterrupted resemblance of their relations of contiguity and succession, we immediately feel a determination of the mind to pass from one of the objects to its usual attendant, and to conceive it in a stronger light on account of that relation.' It is of this 'internal impression,' this 'propensity which custom produces,' that the idea of necessary connexion is the copy.[2]

293. The sequence of ideas, which this propensity determines, clearly does not involve any inference ' beyond sense,' 'from the known to the unknown,' ' from instances of which we have had experience, to those of which we have had none,' any more than does any other ' recurrence of an idea '—which, as we have seen, merely means, according to Hume, the return of a feeling at a lower level of intensity after it has been felt at a higher. The idea which we speak of as an inferred cause or effect is only an 'instance of which we have no ex-

perience' in the sense of being *numerically different* from the similar ideas, whose previous constant association with an impression like the given one, determines the 'inference;' but in the same sense the 'impression' which I now feel on putting my hand to the fire is different from the impressions previously felt under the same circumstances, and I do not for that reason speak of this impression as an instance of which I have had no experience. Thus Hume, though retaining the received phraseology in reference to the 'conclusion from any particular cause to any particular effect'— phraseology which implies that prior to the inference the object inferred is in some sense unknown or unexperienced— yet deprives it of meaning by a doctrine which makes inference, as he himself puts it, 'a species of sensation,' 'an unintelligible instinct of our souls,' 'more properly an act of the sensitive than of the cogitative part of our natures'[1]— which in fact leaves no 'part of our natures' to be cogitative at all.

294. We are not entitled then, it would seem, to say that any inference to matter of fact, any proof of an 'instructive proposition,'—as distinct from the conclusion of a syllogism, which is simply derived from the analysis of a proposition already conceded,—rests on the relation of cause and effect. Such language implies that the relation is other than the inference, whereas, in fact, they are one and the same, each being merely a particular sort of sequence of feeling upon feeling—that sort of which the characteristic is that, when the former feeling only has the maximum of vivacity, it still, owing to the frequency with which it has been attended by the other, imparts to it a large, though less, amount of vivacity. This is the naked result to which Hume's doctrine leads—a result which, thus put, might have set men upon reconsidering the first principles of the Lockeian philosophy. But he wished to find acceptance, and would not so put it. A consideration of the points in which he had to sacrifice consistency to plausibility—since he was always consistent where he decently could be—will lead us to the true αἴτιον τοῦ ψευδοῦς, the impossibility on his principles of explaining the world of knowledge.

295. As the outcome of his doctrine, he submits two definitions of the relation of cause and effect. Considering

---

[1] Pp. 404, 475, and 471.

it as ' a *philosophical* relation or comparison of two ideas,
we may define a *cause* to be an object precedent and contiguous to another, and where all objects resembling the
former are placed in like relations of precedency and contiguity to those objects that resemble the latter.' Considering the relation as ' a *natural* one, or as an association
between ideas,' we may say that ' a *cause* is an object
precedent and contiguous to another, and so united with it
that the idea of one determines the mind to form the idea
of the other, and the impression of the one to form a more
lively idea of the other.' [1]

296. Our first enquiry must be how far these definitions
are really consistent with the theory from which they are
derived. At the outset, it is a surprise to find that the
' philosophical relation ' of cause and effect, as distinct from
the natural one, should still appear to survive. Such a
distinction has no meaning unless it implies a conceived
relation of objects other than the *de facto* sequence of
feelings, of which one 'naturally' introduces the other. It
is the characteristic of Locke's doctrine of knowledge that
in it this distinction is still latent. His language constantly
implies that knowledge, as a perception of relations, is other
than the sequence of feelings; but by confining his view
chiefly to relation in the way of likeness and unlikeness—a
relation that exists between feelings merely as felt, or as they
are for the feeling consciousness—he avoids the necessity of
deciding what the ' ideas ' are in the connection of which
knowledge and reasoning consist, whether objects constituted by conceived relations or feelings suggestive of each
other. But when once attention had been fixed, as it was
by Hume, on an ostensible relation between objects, like
that of cause and effect, which, if it exist at all, is clearly not
one in the way of resemblance between feelings, the distinction spoken of becomes patent. If the colour red had not the
likeness and unlikeness which it has to the colour blue, the
colours would be different feelings from what they are ; but
if the flame of fire and its heat were not regarded severally as
cause and effect, it would make no difference to them as
feelings; or, to put it conversely, it is not upon any comparison of two feelings with each other that we regard them
as related in the way of cause and effect. In what sense

[1] P. 464.

then can the relation between flame and heat be a philosophical relation, as defined by Hume—a relation in virtue
of which we compare objects, or an idea that we acquire
upon comparison?

297. This definition, indeed, is not stated so exactly or so
uniformly as might be wished. In different passages 'philosophical relation' appears as that in respect of which we
compare any two ideas; as that of which we acquire the
idea by comparing objects,[1] and finally (in the context of the
passage last quoted) as itself the comparison.[2] The real
source of this ambiguity lies in that impossibility of regarding an object as anything apart from its relations, which
compels any theory that does not recognize it to be inconsistent with itself. It is Locke's cardinal doctrine that real
'objects' are first given as simple ideas, and that their
relations, unreal in contrast with the simple ideas, are
superinduced by the mind—a doctrine which Hume completes by excluding all ideas that are not either copies of
simple feelings or compounds of these, and by consequence
ideas of relation altogether. The three statements of the
nature of philosophical relation, given above, mark three
stages of departure from, or approach to, consistency with
this doctrine. The first, implying as it does that relation is
not merely a subjective result in our minds from the comparison of ideas, but belongs to the ideas themselves, is most
obviously inconsistent with it according to the form in which
it is presented by Locke; but the second is equally incompatible with Hume's completion of the doctrine, for it implies
that we so compare ideas as to acquire an idea of relation
other than the ideas put together—an idea at once open to
Hume's own challenge, 'Is it a colour, sound, smell, &c.; or
is it a passion or emotion?'

298. We are thus brought to the third statement, according to which philosophical relation, instead of being
an idea acquired upon comparison, is itself the comparison. A comparison of ideas may seem not far removed
from the simple sequence of resembling ideas; but if we
examine the definition of cause, as stated above, which
with Hume corresponds to the view of the relation of cause
and effect as a '*philosophical*' one, we find that the relation
in question is neither a comparison of the related objects

---

[1] Cf. Part I. 5.   [2] P. 464.

nor an idea which arises upon such comparison. According to his statement a comparison is indeed necessary to give us an idea of the relation—a comparison, however, not of the objects which we reckon severally cause and effect with each other, but (a) of each of the two objects with other like objects, and (b) of the relation of precedency and contiguity between the two objects with that previously observed between the like objects. Now, unless the idea of relation between objects in the way of cause and effect is one that consists in, or is acquired by, comparison *of those objects*, the fact that another sort of comparison is necessary to constitute it does not touch the question of its possibility. However we come to have it, however reducible to impressions the objects may be, it is not only other than the idea of either object taken singly; it is not, as an idea of resemblance might be supposed to be, constituted by the joint presence or immediate sequence upon each other of the objects. Here, then, is an idea which is not taken either from an impression or from a compound of impressions (if such composition be possible), and this idea is ' the source of all our reasonings concerning matters of fact.'

299. The modern followers of Hume may perhaps seek refuge in the consideration that though the relation of cause and effect between objects is not one in the way of resemblance or one of which the idea is given by comparison of the objects, it yet results from comparisons, which may be supposed to act like chemical substances whose combination produces a substance with properties quite different from those of the combined substances, whether taken separately or together. Some anticipation of such a solution, it may be said, we find in Hume himself, who is aware that from the repetition of impressions of sense and their ideas new, heterogeneous, impressions—those of ' reflection '—are formed. Of this more will be said when we come to Hume's treatment of cause and effect as a ' natural relation.' For the present we have to enquire what exactly is implied in the comparisons from which this heterogeneous idea of relation is derived. If we look closely we shall find that they presuppose a consciousness of relations as little reducible to resemblance, *i. e.* as little the result of comparison, as that of cause and effect itself. It has been already noticed how Hume treats the judgment of proportion between figures as a mere affair of

sense, because such relation depends entirely on the ideas
compared, without reflecting that the existence of the figures
presupposes those relations of space to which, because (as he
admits) they do not depend on the comparison of ideas, the
only excuse for reckoning any relation sensible does not apply. In the same way he contents himself with the fact that
the judgment of cause and effect implies a comparison of
present with past experience, and may thus be brought under
his definition of 'philosophical relation,' without observing
that the experiences compared are themselves by no means
reducible to comparison. We judge that an object, which
we now find to be precedent and contiguous to another, is its
cause when, comparing present experience with past, we find
that it always has been so. That in effect is Hume's account
of the relation, 'considered as a philosophical one:' and it
implies that the constitution of the several experiences compared involves two sorts of relation which Hume admits not
to be derived from comparison, (a) relation in time and place,
(b) relation in the way of identity.

300. As to relations in time and space, we have already
traced out the inconsistencies which attend Hume's attempt
to represent them as compound ideas. The statement at the
beginning of Part III., that they are relations not dependent
on the nature of compared ideas, is itself a confession that
such representation is erroneous. If the difficulty about the
synthesis of successive feelings in a consciousness that consists merely of the succession could be overcome, we might
admit that the putting together of ideas might constitute
such an idea of relation as depends on the nature of the combined ideas. But no combination of ideas can yield a relation
which remains the same while the ideas change, and changes
while they remain the same. Thus, when Hume tells us that
'in none of the observations we may make concerning relations of time and place can the mind go beyond what is
immediately present to the senses, to discover the relations
of objects,'[1] the statement contradicts itself. Either we can
make no observation concerning relation in time and place
at all, or in making it we already 'go beyond what is immediately present to the senses,' since we observe what is
neither a feeling nor several feelings put together. If then
Hume had succeeded in his reduction of reasoning from

[1] P. 376.

cause or effect to observation of this kind, as modified in a certain way by habit, the purpose for which the reduction is attempted would not have been attained. The separation between perception and inference, between 'intuition' and 'discourse,' would have been got rid of, but inference and discourse would not therefore have been brought nearer to the mere succession of feelings, for the separation between feeling and perception would remain complete; and that being so, the question would inevitably recur—If the 'observation' of objects as related in space and time already involves a transition from the felt to the unfelt, what greater difficulty is there about the interpretation of a feeling as a change to be accounted for (which is what is meant by inference to a cause), that we should do violence to the sciences by reducing it to repeated observation lest it should seem that in it we 'go beyond' present feeling?

301. Relation in the way of identity is treated by Hume in the third part of the Treatise[1] pretty much as he treats contiguity and distance. He admits that it does not depend on the nature of any ideas so related—in other words, that it is not constituted by feelings as they would be for a merely feeling consciousness—yet he denies that the mind 'in any observations we may make concerning it' can go beyond what is immediately present to the senses. Directly afterwards, however, we find that there *is* a judgment of identity which involves a 'conclusion beyond the impressions of our senses'—the judgment, namely, that an object of which the perception is interrupted continues individually the same notwithstanding the interruption. Such a judgment, we are told, is a supposition founded only on the connection of cause and effect. How any 'observation concerning identity' can be made without it is not there explained, and, pending such explanation, observations concerning identity are freely taken for granted as elements given by sense in the experience from which the judgment of cause and effect is derived. In the second chapter of Part IV., however, where 'belief in an external world' first comes to be explicitly discussed by Hume, we find that 'propensities to feign' are as necessary to account for the judgment of identity as for that of necessary connection. If that chapter had preceded, instead of following, the theory of cause and effect as given in Part III.,

[1] P. 376.

the latter would have seemed much less plain sailing than to most readers it has done. It is probably because nothing corresponding to it appears in that later redaction of his theory by which Hume sought popular acceptance, that the true suggestiveness of his speculation was ignored, and the scepticism, which awakened Kant, reduced to the commonplaces of inductive logic. To examine its purport is the next step to be taken in the process of testing the possibility of a 'natural history' of knowledge. Its bearing on the doctrine of cause will appear as we proceed.

302. The problem of identity necessarily arises from the fusion of reality and feeling. We must once again recall the propositions in which Hume represents this fusion—that 'everything which enters the mind is both in reality and appearance as the perception;' that 'so far as the senses are judges, all perceptions are the same in the manner of their existence;' that 'perceptions' are either impressions, or ideas which are 'fainter impressions;' and 'impressions are internal and perishing existences, and appear as such.' If these propositions are true—and the 'new way of ideas' inevitably leads to them—how is it that we *believe* in 'a *continued* existence of objects even when they are not present to the senses,' and an existence 'distinct from the mind and perception'? They are the same questions from which Berkeley derived his demonstration of an eternal mind—a demonstration premature because, till the doctrine of 'ideas,' and of mind as their subject, had been definitely altered in a way that Berkeley did not attempt, it was explaining a belief difficult to account for by one wholly unaccountable. Before Theism could be exhibited with the necessity which Locke claimed for it, it was requisite to try what could be done with association of ideas and 'propensities to feign' in the way of accounting for the world of knowledge, in order that upon their failure another point of departure than Locke's might be found necessary. The experiment was made by Hume. He has the merit, to begin with, of stating the nature of identity with a precision which we found wanting in Locke. 'In that proposition, *an object is the same with itself*, if the idea expressed by the word *object* were no ways distinguished from that meant by *itself*, we really should mean nothing.' 'On the other hand, a multiplicity of objects can never convey the idea of identity, however resembling

they may be supposed. . . . Since then both number and unity are incompatible with the relation of identity, it must lie in something that is neither of them. But at first sight this seems impossible.' The explanation is that when ' we say that an object is the same with itself, we mean that the object existent at one time is the same with itself existent at another. By this means we make a difference betwixt the idea meant by the word *object* and that meant by *itself* without going the length of number, and at the same time without restraining ourselves to a strict and absolute unity.' In other words, identity means the unity of a thing through a multiplicity of times; or, as Hume puts it, ' the invariableness and uninterruptedness of any object through a supposed variation of time.'[1]

303. Now that ' an object exists ' can with Hume mean no more than that an ' impression ' is felt, and without succession of feelings according to him there is no time.[2] It follows that unity in the existence of the object, being incompatible with *succession* of feelings, is incompatible also with existence in time. Either then the unity of the object or its existence at manifold times—both being involved in the conception of identity—must be a fiction; and since ' all impressions are perishing existences,' perishing with a turn of the head or the eyes, it cannot be doubted which it is that is the fiction. That the existence of an object, which we call the same with itself, is broken by as many intervals of time as there are successive and different, however resembling, ' perceptions,' must be the fact; that it should yet be one throughout the intervals is a fiction to be accounted for. Hume accounts for it by supposing that when the separate ' perceptions ' have a strong ' natural relation ' to each other in the way of resemblance, the transition from one to the other is so ' smooth and easy ' that we are apt to take it for the ' same disposition of mind with which we consider one constant and uninterrupted perception; ' and that, as a consequence of this mistake, we make the further one of taking the successive resembling perceptions for an identical, *i.e.* uninterrupted as well as invariable object.[3] But we cannot mistake one object for another unless we have an idea of that other object. If then we ' mistake the succession of our

[1] Pp. 489, 490.
[2] 'Wherever we have no successive

perceptions, we have no notion of time.' (p. 342).   [3] P. 492.

interrupted perceptions for an identical object,' it follows
that we have an idea of such an object—of a thing one with
itself throughout the succession of impressions—an idea
which can be a copy neither of any one of the impressions
nor, even if successive impressions could put themselves
together, of all so put together. Such an idea being according to Hume's principles impossible, the appearance of our
having it was the fiction he had to account for; and he accounts for it, as we find, by a 'habit of mind' which already
presupposes it. His procedure here is just the same as in
dealing with the idea of vacuum. In that case, as we saw,
having to account for the appearance of there being the impossible idea of pure space, he does so by showing, that having
'an idea of distance not filled with any coloured or tangible
object,' we mistake this for an idea of extension, and hence
suppose that the latter may be invisible and intangible. He
thus admits an idea, virtually the same with the one excluded, as the source of the 'tendency to suppose' which is
to replace the excluded idea. So in his account of identity.
Either the habit, in virtue of which we convert resembling
perceptions into an identical object, is what Hume admits to
be a contradiction, 'a habit acquired by what was never
present to the mind;'[1] or the idea of identity must be present
to the mind in order to render the habit possible.

304. The device by which this *petitio principii* is covered
is one already familiar to us in Hume. In this case it is so
palpable that it is difficult to believe he was unconscious of
it. As he has 'to account for the belief of the vulgar with
regard to the existence of body,' he will 'entirely conform
himself to their manner of thinking and expressing themselves;' in other words, he will assume the fiction in question
as the beginning of a process by which its formation is to be
accounted for. The vulgar make no distinction between
thing and appearance. 'Those very sensations which enter
by the eye or ear are with them the true objects, nor can they
readily conceive that this pen or this paper, which is immediately perceived, represents another which is different
from, but resembling it. In order therefore to accommodate
myself to their notions, I shall at first suppose that there is
only a single existence, which I shall call indifferently *object*
and *perception*, according as it shall seem best to suit my

[1] P. 487.

purpose, understanding by both of them what any common man may mean by a hat, or shoe, or stone, or any other impression conveyed to him by his senses.'[1] Now it is of course true that the vulgar are innocent of the doctrine of representative ideas. They do not suppose that this pen or this paper, which is immediately perceived, represents another which is different from, but resembling, it; but neither do they suppose that this pen or this paper is a sensation. It is the intellectual transition from this, that, and the other successive sensations to this pen or this paper, as the identical object to which the sensations are referred as qualities, that is unaccountable if, according to Hume's doctrine, the succession of feelings constitutes our consciousness. In the passage quoted he quietly ignores it, covering his own reduction of felt thing to feeling under the popular identification of the real thing with the perceived. With 'the vulgar' that which is 'immediately perceived' is the real thing, just because it is not the mere feeling which with Hume it is. But under pretence of provisionally adopting the vulgar view, he entitles himself to treat the mere feeling, because according to him it is that which is immediately perceived, as if it were the permanent identical thing, which according to the vulgar is what is immediately perceived.

305. Thus without professedly admitting into consciousness anything but the succession of feelings he gets such individual objects as Locke would have called objects of 'actual present sensation.' When 'I survey the furniture of my chamber,' according to him, I see sundry 'identical objects '—this chair, this table, this inkstand, &c.[2] So far there is no fiction to be accounted for. It is only when, having left my chamber for an interval and returned to it, I suppose the objects which I see to be identical with those I saw before, that the 'propensity to feign' comes into play, which has to be explained as above. But in fact the original 'survey' during which, seeing the objects, I suppose them to continue the same with themselves, involves precisely the same fiction. In that case, says Hume, I 'suppose the change' (which is necessary to constitute the idea of identity) 'to lie only in the time.' But without 'succession of perceptions,' different however resembling, there could according to him be no change of time. The continuous survey of this table, or this

chair, then, involves the notion of its remaining the same
with itself throughout a succession of different perceptions—
i.e. the full-grown fiction of identity—just as much as does
the supposition that the table I see now is identical with the
one I saw before. The 'reality,' confusion with which of 'a
smooth passage along resembling ideas' is supposed to constitute the 'fiction,' is already itself the fiction—the fiction
of an object which must be other than our feelings, since it
is permanent while they are successive, yet so related to them
that in virtue of reference to it, instead of being merely different from each other, they become changes of a thing.

306. Having thus in effect imported all three 'fictions of
imagination'—identity, continued existence, and existence
distinct from perception—into the original 'perception,'
Hume, we may think, might have saved himself the trouble
of treating them as separate and successive formations.
Unless he had so treated them, however, his 'natural
history' of consciousness would have been far less imposing
than it is. The device, by which he represents the 'vulgar'
belief in the reality of the felt thing as a belief that the
mere feeling is the real object, enables him also to represent
the identity, which a smooth transition along closely resembling sensations leads us to suppose, as still merely identity of
a *perception.* 'The very image which is present to the senses
is with us the real body; and 'tis to these interrupted images
we ascribe a perfect identity.'[1] The identity lying thus in
the images or appearances, not in anything to which they
are referred, a further fiction seems to be required by which
we may overcome the contradiction between the interruption
of the appearances and their identity—the fiction of 'a continued being which may fill the intervals' between the
appearances.[2] That a 'propension' towards such a fiction
would naturally arise from the uneasiness caused by such a
contradiction, we may readily admit. The question is how
the propension can be satisfied by a supposition which is
merely another expression for one of the contradictory
beliefs. What difference is there between the appearance
of a perception and its existence, that interruption of the
perception, though incompatible with uninterruptedness in
its appearance, should not be so with uninterruptedness in
its existence? It may be answered that there is just the

difference between relation to a feeling subject and relation to a thinking one—between relation to a consciousness which is in time, or successive, and relation to a thinking subject which, not being itself in time, is the source of that determination by permanent conditions, which is what is meant by the real existence of a perceived thing. But to Hume, who expressly excludes such a subject—with whom 'it exists' = 'it is felt'—such an answer is inadmissible. He can, in fact, only meet the difficulty by supposing the existence of unfelt feelings, of unperceived perceptions. The appearance of a perception is its presence to ' what we call a mind,' which ' is nothing but a heap or collection of different perceptions, united together by certain relations, and supposed, though falsely, to be endowed with a perfect simplicity and identity.' [1] To consider a perception, then, as existing though not appearing is merely to consider it as detached from this ' heap ' of other perceptions, which, on Hume's principle that whatever is distinguishable is separable, is no more impossible than to distinguish one perception from all others.[2] In fact, however, it is obvious that the supposed detachment is the very opposite of such distinction. A perception distinguished from all others is determined by that distinction in the fullest possible measure. A perception *detached* from all others, left out of the 'heap which we call a mind,' being out of all relation, has no qualities—is simply nothing. We can no more ' consider ' it than we can see vacancy. Yet it is by the consideration of such nonentity, by supposing a world of unperceived perceptions, of ' existences ' without relation or quality, that the mind, according to Hume—itself only ' a heap of perceptions '— arrives at that fiction of a continued being which, as involved in the supposition of identity, is the condition of our believing in a world of real things at all.

307. It is implied, then, in the process by which, according to Hume, the fiction of a continued being is arrived at, that this being is supposed to be not only continued but ' distinct from the mind ' and ' independent ' of it. With Hume, however, the supposition of a distinct and ' independent ' existence of the *perception* is quite different from that of a distinct and independent object other than the perception. The former is the 'vulgar hypothesis,' and though a fiction,

it is also a universal belief: the latter is the 'philosophical hypothesis,' which, if it has a tendency to obtain belief at all, at any rate derives that tendency, in other words 'acquires all its influence over the imagination,' from the vulgar one.[1] Just as the belief in the independent and continued existence of perceptions results from an instinctive effort to escape the uneasiness, caused by the contradiction between the interruption of resembling perceptions and their imagined identity, so the contradiction between this belief and the evident dependence of all perceptions 'on our organs and the disposition of our nerves and animal spirits' leads to the doctrine of representative ideas or 'the double existence of perceptions and objects.' 'This philosophical system, therefore, is the monstrous offspring of two principles which are contrary to each other, which are both at once embraced by the mind and which are unable mutually to destroy each other. The imagination tells us that our resembling perceptions have a continued and uninterrupted existence, and are not annihilated by their absence. Reflection tells us that even our resembling perceptions are interrupted in their existence and different from each other. The contradiction betwixt these opinions we elude by a new fiction which is conformable to the hypotheses both of reflection and fancy, by ascribing these contrary qualities to different existences; the interruption to *perceptions*, and the continuance to *objects*.'[2]

308. Here, again, we find that the contradictory announcements, which it is the object of this new fiction to elude, are virtually the same as those implied in that judgment of identity which is necessary to the 'perception' of this pen or this paper. That 'interruption of our resembling perceptions,' of which 'reflection' (in the immediate context 'Reason') is here said to 'tell us,' is merely that difference in time, or succession, which Hume everywhere else treats as a datum of sense, and which, as he points out, is as necessary a factor in the idea of identity, as is the imagination of an existence continued throughout the succession. Thus the contradiction, which suggests this philosophical fiction of double existence, has been already present and overcome in every perception of a qualified object. Nor does the fiction itself, by which the contradiction is eluded, differ except verbally from that suggested by the contradiction between

[1] P. 500.   [2] P. 502.

the interruption and the identity of perceptions. What power is there in the word 'object' that the supposition of an unperceived existence of perceptions, continued while their appearance is broken, should be an unavoidable fiction of the imagination, while that of 'the double existence of perceptions and objects' is a gratuitous fiction of philosophers, of which 'vulgar' thinking is entirely innocent?

309. That it is gratuitous we may readily admit, but only because a recognition of the function of the Ego in the primary constitution of the qualified individual object—this pen or this paper—renders it superfluous. To the philosophy, however, in which Hume was bred, the perception of a qualified object was simply a feeling. No intellectual synthesis of successive feelings was recognized as involved in it. It was only so far as the dependence of the feeling on our organs, in the absence of any clear distinction between feeling and felt thing, seemed to imply a dependent and broken existence of the thing, that any difficulty arose—a difficulty met by the supposition that the felt thing, whose existence was thus broken and dependent, represented an unfelt and permanent thing of which it is a copy or effect. To the Berkeleian objections, already fatal to this supposition, Hume has his own to add, viz. that we can have no idea of relation in the way of cause and effect except as between objects which we have observed, and therefore can have no idea of it as existing between a perception and an object of which we can only say that it is not a perception. Is all existence then 'broken and dependent'? That is the 'sceptical' conclusion which Hume professes to adopt—subject, however, to the condition of accounting for the contrary supposition (without which, as he has to admit, we could not think or speak, and which alone gives a meaning to his own phraseology about impressions and ideas) as a fiction of the imagination. He does this, as we have seen, by tracing a series of contradictions, with corresponding hypotheses invented, either instinctively or upon reflection, in order to escape the uneasiness which they cause, all ultimately due to our mistaking similar successive feelings for an identical object. Of such an object, then, we must have an idea to begin with, and it is an object permanent throughout a variation of time, which means a succession of feelings; in other words, it is a felt thing, as distinct from feelings but to which feelings are referred as

its qualities. Thus the most primary perception—that in
default of which Hume would have no reality to oppose to
fiction, nor any point of departure for the supposed construction of fictions—already implies that transformation of feelings into changing relations of a thing which, preventing
any incompatibility between the perpetual brokenness of the
feeling and the permanence of the thing, ' eludes ' by anticipation all the contradictions which, according to Hume, we
only 'elude' by speaking as if we had ideas that we have not.

310. 'Ideas that we *have not*;' for no one of the fictions by
which we elude the contradictions, nor indeed any one of the
contradictory judgments themselves, can be taken to represent an ' idea' according to Hume's account of ideas.   He
allows himself indeed to speak of our having ideas of identical objects, such as *this table while I see or touch it*—though
in this case, as has been shown, either the object is not
identical or the idea of it cannot be copied from an impression—and of our transferring this idea to resembling but
interrupted perceptions.   But the supposition to which the
contradiction involved in this transference gives rise—the
supposition that the perception continues to exist when it is
not perceived—is shown by the very statement of it to be
no possible copy of an impression. Yet according to Hume it
is a ' belief,' and a belief is ' a lively idea associated with a
present impression.' What then is the impression and what
the associated idea ? ' As the propensity to feign the continued existence of sensible objects arises from some lively
impressions of the memory, it bestows a vivacity on that
fiction; or, in other words, makes us believe the continued
existence of body.' [1] Well and good: but this only answers
the first part of our question. It tells us what are the impressions in the supposed case of belief, but not what is the
associated idea to which their liveliness is communicated.
To say that it arises from a propensity to feign, strong in
proportion to the liveliness of the supposed impressions of
memory, does not tell us of what impression it is a copy.
Such a propensity indeed would be an ' impression of reflection,' but the fiction itself is neither the propensity nor a
copy of it. The only possible supposition left for Hume
would be that it is a 'compound idea;' but what combination

[1] P. 496.

of ' perceptions ' can amount to the existence of perceptions when they are not perceived ?

311. From this long excursion into Hume's doctrine of relation in the way of identity—having found him admitting explicitly that it is only by a ' fiction of the imagination ' that we identify this table as now seen with this table as seen an hour ago, and implicitly that the same fiction is involved in the perception of this table as an identical object even when hand or eye is kept upon it, while yet he says not a word to vindicate the possibility of such a fiction for a faculty which can merely reproduce and combine ' perishing impressions '—we return to consider its bearing upon his doctrine of relation in the way of cause and effect. According to him, as we saw,[1] that relation, ' considered as a philosophical ' one, is founded on a comparison of present experience with past, in the sense that we regard an object, precedent and contiguous to another, as its cause when all like objects have been found similarly related. The question then arises whether the experiences compared—the present and the past alike—do not involve the fiction of identity along with the whole family of other fictions which Hume affiliates to it? Does the relation of precedence and sequence, which, if constant, amounts to that of cause and effect, merely mean precedence and sequence of two feelings, indefinitely like an indefinite number of other feelings that have thus the one preceded and the other followed; or is it a relation between one qualified thing or definite fact always the same with itself, and another such thing or fact always the same with itself? The question carries its own answer. If in the definition quoted Hume used the phrase ' all like objects ' instead of the ' same object,' in order to avoid the appearance of introducing the ' fiction ' of identity into the definition of cause, the device does not avail him much. The effect of the ' like ' is neutralized by the ' all.' A *uniform* relation is impossible except between objects of which each has a definite identity.

312. When Hume has to describe the experience which gives the idea of cause and effect, he virtually admits this. ' The nature of experience,' he tells us, ' is this. We remember to have had frequent instances of the existence of

---

[1] Above, pars. 298 and 299.

one species of objects, and also remember that the individuals
of another species of objects have always attended them, and
have existed in a regular order of contiguity and succession
with regard to them.   Thus we remember to have seen that
species of object we call *flame*, and to have felt that species of
sensation we call *heat*.   We likewise call to mind their constant conjunction in all past instances.   Without any farther
ceremony we call the one cause, and the other effect, and
infer the existence of the one from the other.' [1]   It appears,
then, that upon experiencing certain sensations of sight and
touch, we recognize each as 'one of a species of objects' which
we remember to have observed in certain constant relations
before.   In virtue of the recognition the sensations become
severally this *flame* and this *heat*; and in virtue of the remembrance the objects thus recognized are held to be related in
the way of cause and effect.   Now it is clear that though the
recognition takes place upon occasion of a feeling, the object
recognized—this flame or this heat—is by no means the feeling as a 'perishing existence.'   Unless the feeling were
taken to represent a thing, conceived as permanently existing
under certain relations and attributes—in other words, unless
it were *identified* by thought—it would be no definite object,
not this *flame* or this *heat*, at all.   The moment it is named,
it has ceased to be a feeling and become a felt thing, or, in
Hume's language, an ' individual of *a species of objects*.'   And
just as the present ' perception ' is the recognition of such an
individual, so the remembrance which determines the recognition is one wholly different from the return with lessened
liveliness of a feeling more strongly felt before.   According
to Hume's own statement, it consists in recalling 'frequent
instances of the existence of a *species of objects*.'   It is remembrance of an experience in which every feeling, that has been
attended to, has been interpreted as a fresh appearance of
some qualified object that ' exists ' throughout its appearances—an experience which for that reason forms a connected whole.   If it were not so, there could be no such
comparison of the relations in which two objects are now
presented with those in which they have always been presented, as that which according to Hume determines us to
regard them as cause and effect.   The condition of our so

[1] P. 388.

regarding them is that we suppose the objects now presented to be *the same* with those of which we have had previous experience. It is only on supposition that a certain sensation of sight is not merely like a multitude of others, but represents the same object as that which I have previously known as flame, that I infer the sequence of heat and, when it does follow, regard it as an effect. If I thought that the sensation of sight, however like those previously referred to flame, did not represent the same object, I should not infer heat as effect; and conversely, if, having identified the sensation of sight as representative of flame, I found that the inferred heat was not actually felt, I should judge that I was mistaken in the identification. It follows that it is only an experience of identical, and by consequence related and qualified, objects, of which the memory can so determine a sequence of feelings as to constitute it an experience of cause and effect. Thus the perception and remembrance upon which, according to Hume, we judge one object to be the cause of another, alike rest on the 'fictions of identity and continued existence.' Without these no present experience would, in his language, be an instance of an individual of a certain species existing in a certain relation, nor would there be a past experience of individuals of the same species, by comparison with which the constancy of the relation might be ascertained.

313. Against this derivation of the conception of cause and effect, as implying that of identity, may be urged the fact that when we would ascertain the truth of any identification we do so by reference to causes and effects. As Hume himself puts it at the outset of his discussion of causation, an inference of identity 'beyond the impressions of our senses can be founded only on the connexion of cause and effect.' . . . 'Whenever we discover a perfect resemblance between a new object and one which was formerly present to the senses, we consider whether it be common in that species of objects; whether possibly or probably any cause could operate in producing the change and resemblance; and according as we determine concerning these causes and effects, we form our judgment concerning the identity of the object.' [1] This admission, it may be said, though it tells against Hume's own

subsequent explanation of identity as a fiction of the imagination, is equally inconsistent with any doctrine that would
treat identity as the presupposition of inference to cause or
effect. Now undoubtedly if the identity of interrupted perceptions is one fiction of the imagination and the relation of
cause and effect another, each resulting from 'custom,' to
say with Hume, that we must have the idea of cause in order to
arrive at the supposition of identity, is logically to exclude any
derivation of that idea from an experience which involves
the supposition of identity. The 'custom' which generates
the idea of cause must have done its work before that which
generates the supposition of identity can begin. Hume therefore, after the admission just quoted, was not entitled to treat
the inference to cause or effect as a habit derived from experience of identical things. But it is otherwise if the conceptions of causation and identity are correlative—not results
of experience of which one must be formed before the other,
but co-ordinate expressions of one and the same synthetic
principle, which renders experience possible. And this is
the real state of the case. It is true, as Hume points out,
that when we want to know whether a certain sensation,
precisely resembling one that we have previously experienced,
represents the same object, we do so by asking how otherwise it can be accounted for. If no difference appears in its
antecedents or sequents, we identify it—refer it to the same
thing—as that previously experienced; for its relations
(which, since it is an event in time, take the form of antecedence and sequence) *are* the thing. The conceptions of
identity and of relation in the way of cause and effect are thus
as strictly correlative and inseparable as those of the thing
and of its relations. Without the conception of identity experience would want a centre, without that of cause and effect it
would want a circumference. Without the supposition of
objects which 'existing at one time are the same with themselves as existing at other times'—a supposition which at
last, when through acquaintance with the endlessness of
orderly change we have learnt that there is but one object
for which such identity can be claimed without qualification,
becomes the conception of nature as a uniform whole—there
could be no such comparison of the relations in which an
object is now presented with those in which it has been
before presented, as determines us to reckon it the cause or

effect of another; but it is equally true that it is only by
such comparison of relations that the identity of any particular object can be ascertained.

314. Thus, though we may concede to Hume that neither
in the inference to the relation of cause and effect nor in the
conclusions we draw from it do we go 'beyond experience,'[1]
this will merely be, if his account of it as a 'philosophical
relation' be true, because in experience we already go beyond
sense. 'There is nothing,' says Hume, 'in any object considered in itself that can afford us a reason for drawing a
conclusion beyond it,'[2]—a statement which to him means
that, if the mind really passes from it to another, this is only
because as a matter of fact another feeling follows on the first.
But, in truth, if each feeling were merely 'considered in itself,'
the fact that one follows on another would be no fact *for the
subject of the feelings*, no starting-point of intelligent experience
at all; for the fact is the relation between the feelings—a
relation which only exists for a subject that considers neither
feeling 'in itself,' as a 'separate and perishing existence,'
but finds a reality in the determination of each by the other
which, as it is not either or both of them, so survives, while
they pass, as a permanent factor of experience. Thus in
order that any definite 'object' of experience may exist for
us, our feelings must have ceased to be what according to
Hume they are in themselves. They cease to be so in virtue
of the presence to them of the Ego, in common relation to
which they become related to each other as mutually qualified
members of a permanent system—a system which at first for
the individual consciousness exists only as a forecast or in
outline, and is gradually realized and filled up with the
accession of experience. It is quite true that nothing more
than the reference to such a system, already necessary to
constitute the simplest object of experience, is involved in
that interpretation of every event as a changed appearance
of an unchanging order, and therefore to be accounted for,
which we call inference to a cause or the inference of necessary connection; or, again, in the identification of the event,
the determination of its particular nature by the discovery
of its particular cause.

315. The supposed difference then between immediate and
mediate cognition is no absolute difference. It is not a

difference between experience and a process that goes
beyond experience, or between an experience unregulated
by a conception of a permanent system and one that is so
regulated. It lies merely in the degree of fullness and articulation which that conception has attained. If this had
been what Hume meant to convey in his assimilation of
inference to perception, he would have gone far to anticipate
the result of the enquiry which Kant started. And this is
what he might have come to mean if, instead of playing fast
and loose with 'impression' and 'object,' using each as
plausibility required on the principle of accommodation to the
'vulgar,' he had faced the consequence of his own implicit
admission, that every perception of an object as identical is a
'fiction' in which we go beyond present feeling. As it is,
his 'scepticism with regard to the senses' goes far enough
to empty their 'reports' of the content which the 'vulgar'
ascribe to them, and thus to put a breach between sense and
the processes of knowledge, but not far enough to replace
the 'sensible thing' by a function of reason. In default of
such replacement, there was no way of filling the breach but
to bring back the vulgar theory under the cover of habits
and 'tendencies to feign,' which all suppose a ready-made
knowledge of the sensible thing as their starting-point.
Hence the constant contradiction, which it is our thankless
task to trace, between his solution of the real world into a
succession of feelings and the devices by which he sought to
make room in his system for the actual procedure of the physical sciences. Conspicuous among these is his allowance
of that view of relation in the way of cause and effect as an
objective reality, which is represented by his definition of it
as a 'philosophical relation.' It is in the sense represented
by that definition that his doctrine has been understood and
retained by subsequent formulators of inductive logic; but
on examining it in the light of his own statements we have
found that the relation, as thus defined, is not that which
his theory required, and as which to represent it is the whole
motive of his disquisition on the subject. It is not a sequence of impression upon impression, distinguished merely
by its constancy; nor a sequence of idea upon impression,
distinguished merely by that transfer of liveliness to the idea
which arises from the constancy of its sequence upon the impression. It is a relation between 'objects' of which each

is what it is only as 'an instance of a species' that exists continuously, and therefore in distinction from our 'perishing impressions,' according to a regular order of 'contiguity and succession.' As such existence and order are by Hume's own showing no possible impressions, and by consequence no possible ideas, so neither are the 'objects' which derive their whole character from them.

316. It may be said, however, that wherever Hume admits a definition purporting to be of a 'philosophical relation,' he does so only as an accommodation, and under warning that every such relation is 'fictitious' except so far as it is equivalent to a natural one; that according to his express statement 'it is only so far as causation is a *natural* relation, and produces an union among our ideas, that we are able to reason upon it or draw any inference from it;'[1] and that therefore it is only by his definition of it as a 'natural relation' that he is to be judged. Such a vindication of Hume would be more true than effective. That with him the 'philosophical' relation of cause and effect is 'fictitious,' with all the fictitiousness of a 'continued existence distinct from perceptions,' is what it has been the object of the preceding paragraphs to show. But the fictitiousness of a relation can with him mean nothing else than that, instead of having an idea of it, we have only a 'tendency to suppose' that we have such an idea. Thus the designation of the philosophical relation of cause and effect carries with it two conditions, one negative, the other positive, on the observance of which the logical value of the designation depends. The 'tendency to suppose' must *not* after all be itself translated into the idea which it is to replace; and it *must* be accounted for as derived from a 'natural relation' which is not fictitious. That the negative condition is violated by Hume, we have sufficiently seen. He treats the 'philosophical relation' of cause and effect, in spite of the 'fictions' which it involves, not as a name for a tendency to suppose that we have an idea which we have not, but as itself a definite idea on which he founds various 'rules for judging what objects are really so related and what are not.'[2] That the positive condition is violated also—that the 'natural relation' of cause and effect, according to the sense in which his definition of it is meant to be understood, already itself involves 'fic-

tions,' and only for that reason is a possible source of the
' philosophical '—is what we have next to show.

317. That definition, it will be remembered, runs as
follows: ' A cause is an object precedent and contiguous
to another, and so united with it in the imagination that
the idea of the one determines the mind to form the idea
of the other, and the impression of the one to form a more
lively idea of the other.' Now, as has been sufficiently shown,
the object of an idea with Hume can properly mean nothing
but the impression from which the idea is derived, which
again is only the livelier idea, even as the idea is the fainter
impression. The idea and the object of it, then, only differ
as different stages in the vivacity of a feeling.[1] It must be
remembered, further, in regard to the ' determination of the
mind' spoken of in the definition, that the ' mind' according to Hume is merely a succession of impressions and ideas,
and that its ' determination' means no more than a certain
habitualness in this succession. Deprived of the benefit of
ambiguous phraseology, then, the definition would run thus :
'A cause is a lively feeling immediately precedent to another,[2]
and so united with it that when either of the two more
faintly recurs, the other follows with like faintness, and when
either occurs with the maximum of liveliness the other
follows with less, but still great, liveliness.' Thus stated, the
definition would correspond well enough to the process by
which Hume arrives at it, of which the whole drift, as we
have seen, is to merge the so-called objective relation of cause
and effect, with the so-called inference from it, in the mere
habitual transition from one feeling to another. But it is
only because not thus stated, and because the actual statement is understood to carry a meaning of which Hume's
doctrine does not consistently admit, that it has a chance of
finding acceptance. Its plausibility depends on ' object' and
' mind' and ' determination' being understood precisely in
the sense in which, according to Hume, they ought not to be
understood, so that it shall express not a sequence of feeling

[1] See above, paragraphs 195 and 208.
Cf. also, among other passages, one in
the chapter now under consideration
(p. 451)—'Ideas always represent their
objects or impressions.'

[2] The phrase 'immediately precedent'
would seem to convey Hume's meaning
better than his own phrase 'precedent

and contiguous.' Contiguity *in space*
(which is what we naturally understand
by 'contiguity,' when used absolutely)
he could not have deliberately taken to
be necessary to constitute the relation
of cause and effect, since the impressions
so related, as he elsewhere shows, may
often not be in space at all.

upon feeling, as this might be for a merely feeling subject, but that permanent relation or law of nature which to a subject that thinks upon its feelings, and only to such a subject, their sequence constitutes or on which it depends.

318. It is this essential distinction between the sequence of feeling upon feeling for a sentient subject and the relation which to a thinking subject this sequence constitutes—a distinction not less essential than that between the conditions, through which a man passes in sleep, as they are for the sleeping subject himself, and as they are for another thinking upon them—which it is the characteristic of Hume's doctrine of natural relation in all its forms to disguise. Only in virtue of the presence to feelings of a subject, which distinguishes itself from them, do they become related objects. Thus, with Hume's exclusion of such a subject, with his reduction of mind and world alike to the succession of feelings, relations and ideas of relation logically disappear. But by help of the phrase 'natural relation,' covering, as it does, two wholly different things—the involuntary sequence of one feeling upon another, and that determination of each by the other which can only take place for a synthetic self-consciousness—he is able on the one hand to deny that the relations which form the framework of knowledge are more than sequences of feeling, and on the other to clothe them with so much of the real character of relations as qualifies them for 'principles of union among ideas.' Thus the mere occurrence of similar feelings is with him already that relation in the way of resemblance, which in truth only exists for a subject that can contemplate them as permanent objects. In like manner the succession of feelings, which can only constitute time for a subject that contrasts the succession with its own unity, and which, if ideas were feelings, would exclude the possibility of an idea of time, is yet with him indifferently time and the idea of time, though ideas are feelings and there is no 'mind' but their succession.

319. The fallacy of Hume's doctrine of causation is merely an aggravated form of that which has generally passed muster in his doctrine of time. If time, because a relation between feelings, can be supposed to survive the exclusion of a thinking self and the reduction of the world and mind to a succession of feelings, the relation of cause and effect has only to be assimilated to that of time in order that its in-

compatibility with the desired reduction may disappear. The great obstacle to such assimilation lies in that opposition to the mere sequence of feelings which causation as ' matter of fact '—as that in discovering which we ' discover the real existence and relations of objects '—purports to carry with it. Why do we set aside our usual experience as delusive in contrast with the exceptional experience of the laboratory— why do we decide that an event which has seemed to happen cannot really have happened, because under the given conditions no adequate cause of it could have been operative—if the relation of cause and effect is itself merely a succession of seemings, repeated so often as to leave behind it a lively expectation of its recurrence ? This question, once fairly put, cannot be answered : it can only be evaded. It is Hume's method of evasion that we have now more particularly to notice.

320. In its detailed statement it is very different from the method adopted in those modern treatises of Logic which, beginning with the doctrine that facts are merely feelings in the constitution of which thought has no share, still contrive to make free use in their logical canon of the antithesis between the real and apparent. The key to this modern method is to be found in its ambiguous use of the term ' phenomenon,' alike for the feeling as it is felt, ' perishing ' when it ceases to be felt, and for the feeling as it is for a thinking subject—a qualifying and qualified element in a permanent world. Only if facts were ' phenomena ' in the former sense would the antithesis between facts and conceptions be valid ; only if ' phenomena ' are understood in the latter sense can causation be said to be a law of phenomena. So strong, however, is the charm which this ambiguous term has exercised, that to the ordinary modern logician the question above put may probably seem unmeaning. ' The appearance,' he will say, ' which we set aside as delusive does not consist in any of the reports of the senses—these are always true—but in some false supposition in regard to them due to an insufficient analysis of experience, in some reference of an actual sensation to a group of supposed possibilities of sensation, called a " thing," which are either unreal or with which it is not really connected. The correction of the false appearance by a discovery of causation is the replacement of a false supposition, as to the possibility of the antecedence or sequence

of one feeling to another, by the discovery, through analysis of experience, of what feelings do actually precede and follow each other. It implies no transition from feelings to things, but only from a supposed sequence of feelings to the actual one. Science in its farthest range leaves us among appearances still. It only teaches us what really appears.'

321. Now the presupposition of this answer is the existence of just that necessary connexion as between appearances, just that objective order, for which, because it is not a possible ' impression or idea,' Hume has to substitute a blind propensity produced by habit. Those who make it, indeed, would repel the imputation of believing in any ' necessary connexion,' which to them represents that ' mysterious tie ' in which they vaguely suppose ' metaphysicians ' to believe. They would say that necessary connexion is no more than uniformity of sequence. But sequence of what ? Not of feelings as the individual feels them, for then there would be no perfect uniformities, but only various degrees of approximation to uniformity, and the measure of approximation in each case would be the amount of the individual's experience in that particular direction. The procedure of the inductive logician shows that his belief in the uniformity of a sequence is irrespective of the number of instances in which it has been experienced. A single instance in which one feeling is felt after another, if it satisfy the requirements of the ' method of difference,' *i.e.* if it show exactly what it is that precedes and what it is that follows in that instance, suffices to establish a uniformity of sequence, on the principle that what is fact once is fact always. Now a uniformity that can be thus established is in the proper sense necessary. Its existence is not contingent on its being felt by anyone or everyone. It does not come into being with the experiment that shows it. It is felt because it is real, not real because it is felt. It may be objected indeed that the principle of the ' uniformity of nature,' the principle that what is fact once is fact always, itself gradually results from the observation of facts which are feelings, and that thus the principle which enables us to dispense with the repetition of a sensible experience is itself due to such repetition. The answer is, that feelings which are conceived as facts are already conceived as constituents of a nature. The same presence of the thinking subject to, and distinction of itself from, the feelings, which renders them

knowable *facts*, renders them members of a world which is one throughout its changes. In other words, the presence of facts from which the uniformity of nature, as an abstract rule, is to be inferred, is already the consciousness of that uniformity *in concreto.*

322. Hume himself makes a much more thorough attempt to avoid that pre-determination of feelings by the conception of a world, of things and relations, which is implied in the view of them as permanent facts. He will not, if he can help it, so openly depart from the original doctrine that thought is merely weaker sense. Such conceptions as those of the uniformity of nature and of reality, being no possible 'impressions or ideas,' he only professes to admit in a character wholly different from that in which they actually govern inductive philosophy. Just as by reality he understands not something to which liveliness of feeling may be an index, but simply that liveliness itself, and by an inferred or believed reality a feeling to which this liveliness has been communicated from one that already has it; so he is careful to tell us 'that the supposition that the future resembles the past is derived entirely from habit, by which we are determined to expect for the future the same train of objects to which we have been accustomed.' [1] The supposition then *is* this 'determination,' this 'propensity,' to expect. Any 'idea' derived from the propensity can only be the propensity itself at a fainter stage; and between such a propensity and the conception of 'nature,' whether as uniform or otherwise, there is a difference which only the most hasty reader can be liable to ignore. But if by any confusion an expectation of future feelings, determined by the remembrance of past feelings, could be made equivalent to any conception of nature, it would not be of nature as uniform. As is the 'habit' which determines the expectation, such must be the expectation itself; and as have been the sequences of feeling in each man's past, such must be the habit which results from them. Now no one's feelings have always occurred to him in the same relative order. There may be some pairs of feelings of which one has always been felt before the other and never after it, and between which there has never been an intervention of a third—although (to take Hume's favourite instance) even the feeling of heat

[1] P. 431.

may sometimes precede the sight of the flame—and in these cases upon occurrence of one there will be nothing to qualify the expectation of the other. But just so far as there are exceptions in our past experience to the immediate sequence of one feeling upon another, must there be a qualification of our expectation of the future, if it be undetermined by extraneous conceptions, with reference to those particular feelings.

323. Thus the expectation that 'the future will resemble the past,' if the past means to each man (and Hume could not allow of its meaning more) merely the succession of his own feelings, must be made up of a multitude of different expectations—some few of these being of that absolute and unqualified sort which alone, it would seem, can regulate the transition that we are pleased to call 'necessary connexion;' the rest as various in their strength and liveliness as there are possible differences between cases where the chances are evenly balanced and where they are all on one side. From Hume's point of view, as he himself says, 'every past experiment,' *i.e.* every instance in which feeling (*a*) has been found to follow feeling (*b*), 'may be considered a kind of chance.' [1] As are the instances of this kind to the instances in which some other feeling has followed (*b*), such are the chances or 'probability' that (*a*) will follow (*b*) again, and such upon the occurrence of (*b*) will be that liveliness in the expectation of (*a*), which alone with Hume is the reality of the connexion between them. In such an expectation, in an expectation made up of such expectations, there would be nothing to serve the purpose which the conception of the uniformity of nature actually serves in inductive science. It could never make us believe that a feeling felt before another—as when the motion of a bell is seen before the sound of it has been heard—represents the real antecedent. It could never set us upon that analysis of our experience by which we seek to get beyond sequences that are merely usual, and admit of indefinite exceptions, to such as are invariable; upon that 'interrogation of nature' by which, on the faith that there is a uniformity if only we could find it out, we wrest from her that confession of a law which she does not spontaneously offer. The fact that some sequences of feeling have been so uniform as

[1] P. 433.

to result in unqualified expectations (if it be so) could of itself
afford no motive for trying to compass other expectations of
a like character which do not naturally present themselves.
Nor could there be anything in the appearance of an exception to a sequence, hitherto found uniform, to lead us to change
our previous expectation for one which shall not be liable to
such modification. The previous expectation would be so far
weakened, but there is nothing in the mere weakening of our
expectations that should lead to the effort to place them beyond the possibility of being weakened. Much less could the
bundle of expectations come to conceive themselves as one
system so as that, through the interpretation of each exception to a supposed uniformity of sequence as an instance of a
real one, the changes of the parts should prove the unchangeableness of the whole.

324. That a doctrine which reduces the order of nature to
strength of expectation, and exactly reverses the positions
severally given to belief and reality in the actual procedure of
science,[1] should have been ostensibly adopted by scientific men
as their own—with every allowance for Hume's literary skill and

[1] It is by a curious fate that Hume
should have been remembered, at any
rate in the 'religious' world, chiefly by
the argument against miracles which
appears in the 'Essays'—an argument
which, however irrefragable in itself,
turns wholly upon that conception of
nature as other than our instinctive expectations and imaginations, which has
no proper place in his system (see
Vol. IV. page 89). If 'necessary connexion' were really no more than the
transition of imagination, as determined
by constant association, from an idea to
its usual attendant—if there were no
conception of an objective order to determine belief other than the belief
itself—the fact that such an event, as
the revival of one four-days-dead at
the command of a person, had been
believed, since it would show that the
imagination was at liberty to pass from
the idea of the revival to that of the
command (or vice versa) with that liveliness which constitutes reality, would
show also that no necessary connexion,
no law of nature in the only sense in
which Hume entitles himself to speak
of such, was violated by the sequence
of the revival on the command. At
the same time there would be nothing
'miraculous,' according to his definition
of the miraculous as distinct from
the extraordinary, in the case. Taken
strictly, indeed, his doctrine implies
that a belief in a miracle is a contradiction in terms. An event is not regarded as miraculous unless it is regarded as a 'transgression of a law of
nature by a particular volition of the
Deity or by the interposition of some
invisible agent' (page 93, note 1); but it
could not transgress a law of nature in
Hume's sense unless it were so inconsistent with the habitual association of
ideas as that it could not be believed.
Hume's only consistent way of attack-
ing miracles, then, would have been to
show that the events in question, as
miraculous, had never been believed.
Having been obliged to recognize the
belief in their having happened, he is
open to the retort 'ad hominem' that
according to his own showing the belief
in the events constitutes their reality.
Such a retort, however, would be of no
avail in the theological interest, which
requires not merely that the events
should have happened but that they
should have been miraculous, i. e.
'transgressions of a law of nature by
a particular volition of the Deity.'

1or the charm which the prospect of overcoming the separation between reason and instinct exercises over naturalists—would have been unaccountable if the doctrine had been thus nakedly put or consistently maintained. But it was not so. Hume's sense of consistency was satisfied when expectation determined by remembrance had been put in the place of necessary connexion, as the basis of 'inference to matters of fact.' It does not lead him to adjust his view of the fact inferred to his view of the basis on which the inference rests. Expectation is an 'impression of reflection,' and if the relation of cause and effect is no more than expectation, that which seemed most strongly to resist reduction to feeling has yet been so reduced. But if the expectation is to be no more than an impression of reflection, the object expected must itself be no more than an impression of some kind or other. The expectation must be expectation of a feeling, pure and simple. Nor does Hume in so many words allow that it is otherwise, but meanwhile though the expectation itself is not openly tampered with, the remembrance that determines it is so. This is being taken to be that, which it cannot be unless ideas unborrowed from impressions are operative in and upon it. It is being regarded, not as the recurrence of a multitude of feelings with a liveliness indefinitely less than that in virtue of which they are called impressions of sense, and indefinitely greater than that in virtue of which they are called ideas of imagination, but as the recognition of a world of experience, one, real and abiding. An expectation determined by such remembrance is governed by the same 'fictions' of identity and continued existence which are the formative conditions of the remembrance. Expectation and remembrance, in fact, are one and the same intellectual act, one and the same reference of feelings, given in time, to an order that is not in time, distinguished according to the two faces which, its 'matter' being in time, it has to present severally to past and future. The remembrance is the measure of the expectation, but as the remembrance carries with it the notion of a world whose existence does not depend on its being remembered, and whose laws do not vary according to the regularity or looseness with which our ideas are associated, so too does the expectation, and only as so doing becomes the mover and regulator of 'inference from the known to the unknown.'

325. In the passage already quoted, where Hume is speak-

ing of the expectation in question as depending simply on
habit, he yet speaks of it as an expectation 'of the *same
train of objects* to which we have been accustomed.' These
words in effect imply that it is *not* habit, as constituted
simply by the repetition of separate sequences of feelings,
that governs the expectation—in which case, as we have
seen, the expectation would be made up of expectations as
many and as various in strength as have been the sequences
and their several degrees of regularity—but, if habit in any
sense, habit as itself governed by conceptions of 'identity
and distinct continued existence,' in virtue of which, as past
experience is not an indefinite series of perishing impressions
of separate men but represents one world, so all fresh
experience becomes part 'of the same train of objects;' part
of a system of which, as a whole, 'the change lies only in the
time.' [1] If now we look back to the account given of the relation of memory to belief we shall find that it is just so far
as, without distinct avowal, and in violation of his principles,
he makes 'impressions of memory' carry with them the
conception of a real system, other than the consciousness of
their own liveliness, that he gains a meaning for belief which
makes it in any respect equivalent to the judgment, based on
inference, of actual science.

326. Any one who has carefully read the chapters on
inference and belief will have found himself frequently
doubting whether he has caught the author's meaning correctly.   A clear line of thought may be traced throughout,
as we have already tried to trace it [2]—one perfectly consistent with itself and leading properly to the conclusion that
'all reasonings are nothing but the effect of custom, and that
custom has no influence but by enlivening the imagination' [3]
—but its even tenour is disturbed by the exigency of showing that proven fact, after turning out to be no more than
enlivened imagination, is still what common sense and physical science take it to be.   According to the consistent
theory, ideas of memory are needed for inference to cause or
effect, simply because they are lively.   Such inference is
inference to a 'real existence,' that is to an 'idea assented
to,' that is to a feeling having such liveliness as, not being
itself one of sense or memory, it can only derive from one of

---

sense or memory through association with it. That the inferred idea is a cause or effect and, as such, has 'real existence,' merely means that it has this derived liveliness or is believed; just as the reality ascribed to the impression of memory lies merely in its having this abundant liveliness from which to communicate to its 'usual attendant.' But while the title of an idea to be reckoned a cause or effect is thus made to depend on its having the derived liveliness which constitutes belief,[1] on the other hand we find Hume from time to time making belief depend on causation, as on a relation of objects distinct from the lively suggestion of one by the others. 'Belief arises only from causation, and we can draw no inference from one object to another except they be connected by this relation.' 'The relation of cause and effect is requisite to persuade us of any real existence.'[2] In the context of these disturbing admissions we find a reconsideration of the doctrine of memory which explains them, but only throws back on that doctrine the inconsistency which they exhibit in the doctrine of belief.

327. This reconsideration arises out of an objection to his doctrine which Hume anticipates, to the effect that since, according to it, belief is a lively idea associated 'to a present impression,' any suggestion of an idea by a resembling or contiguous impression should constitute belief. How is it then that 'belief arises only from causation'? His answer, which must be quoted at length, is as follows :—' 'Tis evident that whatever is present to the memory, striking upon the mind with a vivacity which resembles an immediate impression, must become of considerable moment in all the operations of the mind and must easily distinguish itself above the mere fictions of the imagination. Of these impressions or ideas of the memory we form a kind of system, comprehending whatever we remember to have been present either to our internal perception or senses, and every particular of that system, joined to the present impressions, we are pleased to call a *reality*. But the mind stops not here.

---

[1] It may be as well here to point out the inconsistency in Hume's use of 'belief.' At the end of sec. 5 (Part III.) the term is extended to 'impressions of the senses and memory.' We are said to believe when 'we feel an *immediate impression* of the senses, or a repetition of that impression in the memory. But in the following section the characteristic of belief is placed in the *derived* liveliness of an *idea* as distinct from the immediate liveliness of an impression.

[2] Pp. 407 & 409.

For finding that with this system of perceptions there is
another connected by custom or, if you will, by the relation
of cause and effect, it proceeds to the consideration of their
ideas; and as it feels that 'tis in a manner necessarily determined to view these particular ideas, and that the custom or
relation by which it is determined admits not of the least
change, it forms them into a new system, which it likewise
dignifies with the title of *realities*. The first of these systems
is the object of the memory and senses; the second of the
judgment. 'Tis this latter principle which peoples the world,
and brings us acquainted which such existences as, by their
removal in time and place, lie beyond the reach of the senses
and memory.'[1]

328. From this it appears that 'what we are pleased to
call reality' belongs, not merely to a 'present impression,' but
to 'every particular of a system joined to the present impression' and 'comprehending whatever we remember to
have been present either to our internal perception or senses.'
This admission already amounts to an abandonment of the
doctrine that reality consists in liveliness of feeling. It cannot be that every particular of the system comprehending
all remembered facts, which is joined with the present impression, can have the vivacity of that impression either along
with it or by successive communication. We can only feel
one thing at a time, and by the time the vivacity had spread
far from the present impression along the particulars of the
system, it must have declined from that indefinite degree
which marks an impression of sense. It is not, then, the
derivation of vivacity from the present impression, to which
it is joined, that renders the 'remembered system' real; and
what other vivacity can it be? It may be said indeed that
each particular of the system had once the required vivacity,
was once a present impression; but if in ceasing to be so, it
did not cease to be real—if, on the contrary, it could not
become a 'particular of the system,' counted real, without
becoming other than the 'perishing existence' which an impression is—it is clear that there is a reality which lively
feeling does not constitute and which involves the 'fiction'
of an existence continued in the absence, not only of lively
feeling, but of all feelings whatsoever. So soon, in short,

[1] P. 408.

as reality is ascribed to a system, which cannot be an 'impression' and of which consequently there cannot be an 'idea,' the first principle of Hume's speculation is abandoned. The truth is implicitly recognized that the reality of an individual object consists in that system of its relations which only exists for a conceiving, as distinct from a feeling, subject, even as the unreal has no meaning except as a confused or inadequate conception of such relations; and that thus the 'present impression' is neither real nor unreal in itself, but may be equally one or the other according as the relations, under which it is conceived by the subject of it, correspond to those by which it is determined for a perfect intelligence.[1]

329. A clear recognition of this truth can alone explain the nature of belief as a result of inference from the known to the unknown, which is, at the same time, inference to a matter of fact. The popular notion, of course, is that certain facts are given by feeling without inference and then other facts inferred from them. But what is 'fact' taken to mean? If a feeling, then an inferred fact is a contradiction, for it is an unfelt feeling. If (as should be the case) it is taken to mean the relation of a feeling to something, then it already involves inference—the interpretation of the feeling by means of the conception of a universal, self or world, brought to it—an inference which is all inference *in posse*, for it implies that a universe of relations is there, which I must know if I would know the full reality of the individual object: so that no fact can be even partially known without compelling an inference to the unknown, nor can there be any inference to the unknown without modification of what already purports to be known. Hume, trying to carry out the equivalence of fact and feeling, and having clearer sight than his masters, finds himself in the presence of this difficulty about inference. Unless the inferred object is other than one of sense (outer or inner) or of memory, there is no reasoning, but only perception;[2] but if it is other, how can it be real or even an object of consciousness at all, since consciousness is only of impressions, stronger or fainter? The only consistent way out of the difficulty, as we have seen, is to explain inference as the expectation of the recur-

<hr>

[1] See above, paragraphs 184 & 186.   [2] Pp. 376 & 388.

rence of a feeling felt before, through which the unknown becomes known merely in the sense that from the repetition of the recurrence the expectation has come to amount to the fullest assurance. But according to this explanation the difference between the inferences of the savage and those of the man of science will lie, not in the objects inferred, but in the strength of the expectation that constitutes the inference. Meanwhile, if a semblance of explanation has been given for the inference from cause to effect, that from effect to cause remains quite in the dark. How can there be inference from a given feeling to that felt immediately before it?

330. From the avowal of such paradoxical results, Hume only saved himself by reverting, as in the passage before us, to the popular view—to the distinction between two 'systems of reality,' one perceived, the other inferred; one 'the object of the senses and memory,' the other 'of the judgment.' He sees that if the educated man erased from his knowledge of the world all 'facts' but those for which he has 'the evidence of his senses and memory,' his world would be unpeopled; but he has not the key to the true identity between the two systems. Not recognizing the inference already involved in a fact of sense or memory, he does not see that it is only a further articulation of this inference which gives the fact of judgment; that as the simplest fact for which we have the 'evidence of sense' is already not a feeling but an explanation of a feeling, which connects it by relations, that are not feelings, with an unfelt universe, so inferred causes and effects are explanations of these explanations, by which they are connected as mutually determinant in the one world whose presence the simplest fact, the most primary explanation of feeling, supposes no less than the most complete. Not seeing this, what is he to make of the system of merely inferred realities? He will represent the relation of cause and effect, which connects it with the 'system of memory,' as a habit derived from the constant *de facto* sequence of this or that 'inferred' upon this or that remembered idea. The mind, 'feeling' the unchangeableness of this habit, regards the idea, which in virtue of it follows upon the impression of memory, as equally real with that impression. In this he finds an answer to the two questions which he himself raises: (*a*) 'Why is it that we draw no

inference from one object to another, except they be connected by the relation of cause and effect;' or (which is the same, since inference to an object implies the ascription of reality to it), 'Why is this relation requisite to persuade us of any real existence?' and (b), 'How is it that the relations of resemblance and contiguity have not the same effect?' The answer to the first is, that we do not ascribe reality to an idea recalled by an impression, unless we find that, owing to its customary sequence upon the impression, we cannot help passing from the one to the other. The answer to the second corresponds. The contiguity of an idea to an impression, if it has been repeated often enough and without any 'arbitrary' action on our part, is the relation of cause and effect, and thus does 'persuade us of real existence.' A 'feigned' contiguity, on the other hand, because we are conscious that it is 'of our mere good-will and pleasure' that we give the idea that relation to the impression, can produce no belief. 'There is no reason why, upon the return of the same impression, we should be determined to place the same object in the same relation to it.'[1] In like manner we must suppose (though this is not so clearly stated) that when an impression—such as the sight of a picture—calls up a resembling idea (that of the man depicted) with much vivacity, it does not 'persuade us of his real existence' because we are conscious that it is by the 'mere good-will and pleasure' of some one that the likeness has been produced.

331. Now this account has the fault of being inconsistent with Hume's primary doctrine, inasmuch as it makes the real an object of thought in distinction from feeling, without the merit of explaining the extension of knowledge beyond the objects of sense and memory. It turns upon a conception of the real, as the unchangeable, which the succession of feelings, in endless variety, neither is nor could suggest. It implies that not in themselves, but as representing such an unchangeable, are the feelings which 'return on us whether we will or no,' regarded as real. The peculiar sequence of one idea on another, which is supposed to constitute the relation of cause and effect, is not, according to this description of it, a sequence of feelings simply; it is a

sequence reflected on, found to be unchangeable, and thus
to entitle the sequent idea to the prerogative of reality
previously awarded (but only by the admission as real of the
'fiction' of distinct continued existence) to the system of
memory. But while the identification of the real with
feeling is thus in effect abandoned, in saving the appearance
of retaining it, Hume makes his explanation of the 'system
of judgment' futile for its purpose. He saves the appearance by intimating that the relation of cause and effect, by
which the inferred idea is connected with the idea of memory
and derives reality from it, is only the repeated sequence of
the one idea upon the other, of the less lively feelings upon
the more lively, or a habit that results from such repetition.
But if the sequence of the inferred idea upon the other must
have been so often repeated in order to the existence of the
relation which renders the inference possible, the inferred
idea can be no new one, but must itself be an idea of memory,
and the question, how any one's knowledge comes to extend
beyond the range of his memory, remains unanswered.

332. What Hume himself seems to mean us to understand
is, that the inferred idea is one of imagination, as distinct
from memory; and that the characteristic of the relation of
cause and effect is that through it ideas of imagination
acquire the reality that would otherwise be confined to
impressions of sense and memory. But, according to him,
ideas of imagination only differ from those of memory in
respect of their less liveliness, and of the freedom with which
we can combine ideas in imagination that have not been
given together as impressions.[1] Now the latter difference
is in this case out of the question. A compound idea of
imagination, in which simple ideas are put together that
have never been felt together, can clearly never be connected
with an impression of sense or memory by a relation derived
from constant experience of the sequence of one upon the
other, and specially opposed to the creations of 'caprice.'[2]
We are left, then, to the supposition that the inferred idea,
as idea of imagination, is one originally given as an impression of sense, but of which the liveliness has faded and
requires to be revived by association in the way of cause and
effect with one that has retained the liveliness proper to an

idea of memory. Then the question recurs, how the restoration of its liveliness by association with an impression, on which it must have been constantly sequent in order that the association may be possible, is compatible with the fact that its liveliness has faded. And however this question may be dealt with, if the relation of cause and effect is merely custom, the extension of knowledge by means of it remains unaccounted for; the breach between the expectation of the recurrence of familiar feelings and inductive science remains unfilled; Locke's 'suspicion' that 'a science of nature is impossible,' instead of being overcome, is elaborated into a system.

333. Thus inference, according to Hume's account of it as originating in habit, suffers from a weakness quite as fatal as that which he supposes to attach to it if accounted for as the work of reason. 'The work of reason' to a follower of Locke meant either the mediate perception of likeness between ideas, which the discovery of cause or effect cannot be; or else syllogism, of which Locke had shown once for all that it could yield no 'instructive propositions.' But if an idea arrived at by that process could be neither new nor real—not new, because we must have been familiar with it before we put it into the compound idea from which we ' deduce ' it; not real, because it has not the liveliness either of sensation or of memory—the idea inferred according to Hume's process, however real with the reality of liveliness, is certainly not new. ' If this means ' (the modern logician may perhaps reply), ' that according to Hume no new phenomenon can be given by inference, he was quite right in thinking so. If the object of inference were a separate phenomenon, it would be quite true that it must have been repeatedly perceived before it could be inferred, and that thus inference would be nugatory. But inference is in fact not to such an object, but to a uniform relation of certain phenomena in the way of co-existence and sequence; and what Hume may be presumed to mean is not that every such relation must have been perceived before it can be inferred, much less that it must have been perceived so constantly that an appearance of the one phenomenon causes instinctive expectation of the other, but (a) that the phenomena themselves must have been given by immediate perception, and (b) that the conception of a law

of causation, in virtue of which a uniformity of relation between them is inferred from a single instance of it, is itself
the result of an "inductio per enumerationem simplicem," of
the accumulated experience of generations that the same
sequents follow the same antecedents.'

334. At the point which our discussion has reached, few
words should be wanted to show that thus to interpret
Hume is to read into him an essentially alien theory, which
has doubtless grown out of his, but only by a process of
adaptation which it needs a principle the opposite of his to
justify. Hume, according to his own profession, knows of
no objects but impressions and ideas—feelings stronger or
more faint—of no reality which it needs thought, as distinct
from feeling, to constitute. But a uniform relation between
phenomena is neither impression nor idea, and can only
exist for thought. He could not therefore admit inference
to such relation as to a real existence, without a double contradiction, nor does he ever explicitly do so. He never
allows that inference is other than a transition to a certain
sort of feeling, or that it is other than the work of imagination, the weakened sense, as enlivened by custom to a
degree that puts it *almost* on a level with sense; which implies that in every case of inference the inferred object is
not a uniform relation—for how can there be an image of
uniform relation?—and that it *is* something which has been
repeatedly and without exception perceived to follow another
before it can be inferred. Even when in violation of his
principle he has admitted a 'system of memory'—a system of
things which have been felt, but which are not feelings,
stronger or fainter, and which are what they are only
through relation—he still in effect, as we have seen, makes
the 'system of judgment,' which he speaks of as inferred
from it, only the double of it. To suppose that, on the
strength of a general inference, itself the result of habit, in
regard to the uniformity of nature, particular inferences may
be made which shall be other than repetitions of a sequence
already habitually repeated, is, if there can be degrees of
contradiction, even more incompatible with Hume's principles than to suppose such inferences without it. If a uniformity of relation between particular phenomena is neither
impression nor idea, even less so is the system of all
relations.

335. There is language, however, in the chapters on 'Probability of Chances and of Causes,' which at first sight might seem to warrant the ascription of such a supposition to Hume. According to the distinction which he inherited from Locke all inference to or from causes or effects, since it does not consist in any comparison of the related ideas, should be merely probable. And as such he often speaks of it. His originality lies in his effort to explain what Locke had named; in his treating that 'something not joined on both sides to, and so not showing the agreement or disagreement of, the ideas under consideration' which yet 'makes me believe,'[1] definitely as Habit. But 'in common discourse,' as he remarks, 'we readily affirm that many arguments from causation exceed probability;'[2] the explanation being that in these cases the habit which determines the transition from impression to idea is 'full and perfect.' There has been enough past experience of the immediate sequence of the one 'perception' on the other to form the habit, and there has been no exception to it. In these cases the 'assurance,' though distinct from knowledge, may be fitly styled 'proof,' the term 'probability' being confined to those in which the assurance is not complete. Hume thus comes to use 'probability' as equivalent to incompleteness of assurance, and in this sense speaks of it as 'derived either from imperfect experience, or from contrary causes, or from analogy.'[3] It is derived from analogy when the present impression, which is needed to give vivacity to the 'related idea,' is not perfectly like the impressions with which the idea has been previously found united; 'from contrary causes,' when there have been exceptions to the immediate sequence or antecedence of the one perception to the other; 'from imperfect experience' when, though there have been no exceptions, there has not been enough experience of the sequence to form a 'full and perfect habit of transition.' Of this last 'species of probability,' Hume says that it is a kind which, 'though it naturally takes place before any entire proof can exist, yet no one who is arrived at the age of maturity can any longer be acquainted with. 'Tis true, nothing is more common than for people of the most advanced knowledge to have attained only an imperfect experience of many

---

[1] Locke, 4, 15, 3.   [2] P. 423.   [3] P. 439.

particular events; which naturally produces only an imperfect habit and transition; but then we must consider that
the mind, having formed another observation concerning the
connexion of causes and effects, gives new force to its reasoning from that observation; and by means of it can build an
argument on one single experiment, when duly prepared and
examined. What we have found once to follow from any
object we conclude will for ever follow from it; and if this
maxim be not always built upon as certain, 'tis not for want
of a sufficient number of experiments, but because we frequently meet with instances to the contrary'—which give
rise to the other sort of weakened assurance or probability,
that from 'contrary causes.'[1]

336. There is a great difference between the meaning
which the above passage conveys when read in the light of
the accepted logic of science, and that which it conveys
when interpreted consistently with the theory in the statement of which it occurs. Whether Hume, in writing as he
does of that conclusion from a single experiment, which our
observation concerning the connexion of cause and effect
enables us to draw, understood himself to be expressing his
own theory or merely using the received language provisionally, one cannot be sure; but it is certain that such language
can only be justified by those 'maxims of philosophers'
which it is the purpose or effect of his doctrine to explain
away—in particular the maxims that 'the connexion between
all causes and effects is equally necessary and that its seeming uncertainty in some instances proceeds from the secret
opposition of contrary causes;' and that 'what the vulgar
call chance is but a concealed cause.'[2] These maxims represent the notion that the law of causation is objective and
universal; that all seeming limitations to it, all 'probable
and contingent matter,' are the reflections of our ignorance,
and exist merely *ex parte nostrâ*. In other words, they represent the notion of that 'continued existence distinct from
our perceptions,' which with Hume is a phrase generated by
'propensities to feign.' Yet he does not profess to reject
them; nay, he handles them as if they were his own, but
after a very little of his manipulation they are so 'translated'
that they would not know themselves. Because philosophers

---

[1] Pp. 429 & 430.   [2] Ibid.

'allow that what the vulgar call chance is nothing but a concealed cause,' 'probability of causes' and 'probability of chances' may be taken as equivalent. But chance, as 'merely negation of a cause,' has been previously explained, on the supposition that causation means a 'perfect habit of imagination,' to be the absence of such habit—the state in which imagination is perfectly indifferent in regard to the transition from a given impression to an idea, because the transition has not been repeated often enough to form even the beginning of a habit. Such being mere chance, 'probability of chances' means a state of imagination between the perfect indifference and that perfect habit of transition, which is 'necessary connexion.' 'Probability of causes' is the same thing. Its strength or weakness depends simply on the proportion between the number of experiments ('each experiment being a kind of chance') in which A has been found to immediately follow B, and the number of those in which it has not.[1] Mere chance, probability, and causation then are equally states of imagination. The 'equal necessity of the connexion between all causes and effects' means not that any 'law of causation pervades the universe,' but that, unless the habit of transition between any feelings is 'full and perfect,' we do not speak of these feelings as related in the way of cause and effect.

337. Interpreted consistently with this doctrine, the passage quoted in the last paragraph but one can only mean that, when a man has arrived at maturity, his experience of the sequence of feelings cannot fail in quantity. He must have had experience *enough* to form not only a perfect habit of transition from any impression to the idea of its usual attendant, but a habit which would act upon us even in the case of novel events, and lead us after a single experiment or a sequence confidently to expect its recurrence, if only the experience had been *uniform*. It is because it has not been so, that in many cases the habit of transition is still imperfect, and the sequence of A on B not 'proven,' but 'probable.' The probability then which affects the imagination of the matured man is of the sort that arises from 'contrary causes,' as distinct from 'imperfect experience.' This is all that the passage in question can fairly mean. Such 'proba-

---

[1] Pp. 424-428, 432-434.

bility' cannot become 'proof,' or the 'imperfect habit,'
perfect, by *discovery* of any necessary connexion or law of
causation, for the perfect habit of transition, the imagination
enlivened to the maximum by custom, *is* the law of causation.
The formation of the habit constitutes the law: to discover
it would be to discover what does not yet exist. The incompleteness of the habit in certain directions, the limitation of
our assurance to certain sequences as distinct from others,
must be equally a limitation to the universality of the law.
It is impossible then that on the faith of the universality
of the law we should seek to extend the range of that
assurance which is identical with it. Our 'observation concerning the connexion of causes and effects' merely means
the sum of our assured expectations, founded on habit, at
any given time, and that on the strength of this we should
'prepare an experiment,' with a view to assuring ourselves
of a universal sequence from a single instance, is as unaccountable as that, given the instance, the assurance should
follow.

338. The case then stands thus. In order to make the
required distinction between inference to real existence and
the lively suggestion of an idea, Hume has to graft on his
theory the alien notion of an objective system, an order of
nature, represented by ideas of memory, and on the strength
of such a notion to interpret a transition from these ideas to
others, because we cannot help making it, as an objective
necessity. Of such alien notion and interpretation he avails
himself in his definition (understood as he means it to be
understood) of cause as a 'natural relation.'[1] But he had
not the boldness of his later disciples. Though he could be
inconsistent so far, he could not be inconsistent far enough
to make his theory of inference fit the practice of natural
philosophers. Bound by his doctrine of ideas as copied from
impressions, he can give no account of inferred ideas that
shall explain the extension of knowledge beyond the expectation that we shall feel again what we have felt already. It
was not till another theory of experience was forthcoming
than that given by the philosophers who were most fond of
declaring their devotion to it, that the procedure of science
could be justified. The old philosophy, we are often truly

See above, paragraph 317.

told, had been barren for want of contact with fact. It sought truth by a process which really consisted in evolving the ' connotation' of general names. The new birth came when the mind had learnt to leave the idols of the tribe and cave, and to cleave solely to experience. If the old philosophy, however, was superseded by science, science itself required a new philosophy to answer the question, What constitutes experience? It was in effect to answer this question that Locke and Hume wrote, and it is the condemnation of their doctrine that, according to it, experience is not a possible parent of science. It is not those, we know, who cry ' Lord, Lord!' the loudest, that enter into the kingdom of heaven, nor does the strongest assertion of our dependence on experience imply a true insight into its nature. Hume has found acceptance with men of science as the great exponent of the doctrine that there can be no new knowledge without new experience. It has not been noticed that with him such ' new experience' could only mean a further repetition of familiar feelings, and that if it means more to his followers, it is only because they have been less faithful than he was to that antithesis between thought and reality which they are not less loud in asserting.

339. From the point that our enquiry has reached, we can anticipate the line which Hume could not but take in regard to Self and God. His scepticism lay ready to his hand in the incompatibility between the principles of Locke and that doctrine of ' thinking substance,' which Locke and Berkeley alike maintained. If the reader will revert to the previous part of this introduction, in which that doctrine was discussed,[1] he will find it equally a commentary upon those sections of the ' Treatise on Human Nature' which deal with ' immateriality of the soul' and 'personal identity.' Substance, we saw, alike as ' extended' and as 'thinking,' was a ' creation of the mind,' yet real; something of which there was an ' idea,' but of which nothing could be said but that it was not an ' idea.' The ' thinking' substance, moreover, was at a special disadvantage in contrast with the ' extended,' because, in the first place, it could not, like body, be represented as given to consciousness in the feeling of solidity, and secondly it was not wanted. It was a mere double of the

---

[1] Above, paragraphs 127–135, 144–146, & 192.

extended substance to which, as the 'something wherein they do subsist and from which they do result,' our ideas had already been referred. Having no conception, then, of Spirit or Self before him but that of the thinking substance, of which Berkeley had confessed that it was not a possible idea or object of an idea, Hume had only to apply the method, by which Berkeley himself had disposed of extended substance, to get rid of Spirit likewise. This could be done in a sentence,[1] but having done it, Hume is at further pains to show that immateriality, simplicity, and identity cannot be ascribed to the soul; as if there were a soul left to which anything could be ascribed.

340. There were two ways of conceiving the soul as immaterial, of which Hume was cognizant. One, current among the theologians and ordinary Cartesians and adopted by Locke, distinguishing extension and thought as severally divisible and indivisible, supposed separate substances—matter and the soul—to which these attributes, incapable of 'local conjunction,' severally belonged. The other, Berkeley's, having ostensibly reduced extended matter to a succession of feelings, took the exclusion of all 'matter' to which thought could be 'joined' as a proof that the soul was immaterial. Hume, with cool ingenuity, turns each doctrine to account against the other. From Berkeley he accepts the reduction of sensible things to sensations. Our feelings do not represent extended objects other than themselves; but we cannot admit this without acknowledging the consequence, as Berkeley himself implicitly did,[2] that certain of our impressions—those of sight and touch—are themselves extended. What then becomes of the doctrine, that the soul must be immaterial because thought is not extended, and cannot be joined to what is so? Thought means the succession of impressions. Of these some, though the smaller number, are actually extended; and those that are not so are united to those that are by the 'natural relations' of resemblance and of contiguity in time of appearance, and by the consequent relation of cause and effect.[5] The relation of local conjunction, it is true, can only obtain between impressions which are alike extended. The ascription of it to such as are unextended arises from the 'propensity in human

---

[1] P. 517. [2] See above, par. 177. [3] Pp. 520-521.

nature, when objects are united by any relation, to add some
new relation in order to complete the union.'[1] This admission, however, can yield no triumph to those who hold
that thought can only be joined to a 'simple and indivisible
substance.' If the existence of unextended impressions
requires the supposition of a thinking substance 'simple and
indivisible,' the existence of extended ones must equally
imply a thinking substance that has all the properties of
extended objects. If it is absurd to suppose that perceptions
which are unextended can belong to a substance which is
extended, it is equally absurd to suppose that perceptions
which are extended can belong to a substance that is not
so. Thus Berkeley's criticism has indeed prevailed against
the vulgar notion of a material substance as opposed to a
thinking one, but meanwhile he is himself 'hoist with his
own petard.' If that thinking substance, the survival of
which was the condition of his theory serving its theological
purpose,[2] is to survive at all, it can only be as equivalent
to Spinoza's substance, in which 'both matter and thought
were supposed to inhere.' The universe of our experience
—'the sun, moon, and stars; the earth, seas, plants, animals,
men, ships, houses, and other productions, either of art or
nature'—is the same universe when it is called 'the universe
of objects or of body,' and when it is called 'the universe of
thought, or of impressions and ideas;' but to hold, according
to Spinoza's 'hideous hypothesis,' that 'the universe of objects or of body' inheres in one simple uncompounded
substance, is to rouse 'a hundred voices of scorn and detes-
tation;' while the same hypothesis in regard to the 'universe
of impressions and ideas' is treated 'with applause and
veneration.' It was to save God and Immortality that the
'great philosopher,' who had found the true way out of
the scholastic absurdity of abstract ideas,[3] had yet clung to
the 'unintelligible chimæra' of thinking substance; and
after all, in doing so, he fell into a 'true atheism,' indistinguishable from that which had rendered the unbelieving
Jew 'so universally infamous.'[4]

341. The supposition of spiritual substance being thus
at once absurd, and of a tendency the very opposite of the

[1] P. 521.
[2] See above, paragraphs 191 and foll.
[3] See page 325
[4] Pp. 523-526.

purpose it was meant to serve, can anything better be said for the supposition of a spiritual cause? It was to the representation of spirit as cause rather than as substance, it will be remembered, that both Locke and Berkeley trusted for the establishment of a Theism which should not be Pantheism.[1] Locke, in his demonstration of the being of God, trusted for proof of a first cause to the inference from that which begins to exist to something having power to produce it, and to the principle of necessary connexion—connexion in the way of agreement of ideas—between cause and effect for proof that this first cause must be immaterial, even as its effect, viz. our thought, is. Hume's doctrine of causation, of course, renders both sides of the demonstration unmeaning. Inference being only the suggestion by a feeling of the image of its 'usual attendant,' there can be no inference to that which is not a possible image of an impression. Nor, since causation merely means the constant conjunction of impressions, and there is no such contrariety between the impression we call 'motion of matter' and that we call 'thought,' any more than between any other impressions,[2] as is incompatible with their constant conjunction, is there any reason why we should set aside the hourly experience, which tells us that bodily motions are the cause of thoughts and sentiments. If, however, there were that necessary connexion between effect and cause, by which Locke sought to show the spirituality of the first cause, it would really go to show just the reverse of infinite power in such cause. It is from our impressions and ideas that we are supposed to infer this cause; but in these—as Berkeley had shown, and shown as his way of proving the existence of God—there is no efficacy whatever. They are 'inert.' If then the cause must agree with the effect, the Supreme Being, as the cause of our impressions and ideas, must be 'inert' likewise. If, on the other hand, with Berkeley we cling to the notion that there must be efficient power somewhere, and having excluded it from the relation

---

[1] See above, §§ 147, 171, 193.

[2] There is no contrariety, according to Hume, except between existence and non-existence (p. 323) and as all impressions and ideas equally exist (p. 394), there can be no contrariety between any of them. He does indeed in certain leading passages allow himself to speak of contrariety between ideas (e.g. pp. 494 and 535), which is incidental evidence that the ideas there treated of are not so, according to his account of ideas, at all.

of ideas to each other or of matter to ideas, find it in the
direct relation of God to ideas, we fall 'into the grossest
impieties;' for it will follow that God 'is the author of all
our volitions and impressions.'[1]

342. Against the doctrine of a real 'identity of the self or
person' Hume had merely to exhibit the contradictions
which Locke's own statement of it involves.[2] To have
transferred this identity definitely from 'matter' to consciousness was in itself a great merit, but, so transferred, in
the absence of any other theory of consciousness than
Locke's, it only becomes more obviously a fiction. If there
is nothing real but the succession of feelings, identity of
body, it is true, disappears as inevitably as identity of mind;
and so we have already found it to do in Hume.[3] But
whereas the notion of a unity of body throughout the succession of perceptions only becomes contradictory through
the medium of a reduction of body to a succession of perceptions, the identity of a mind, which has been already
defined as a succession of perceptions, is a contradiction in
terms. There can be 'properly no simplicity in it at one
time, nor identity at different; it is a kind of theatre where
several perceptions successively make their appearance.' But
this comparison must not mislead us. 'They are the successive perceptions only, that constitute the mind; nor have
we the most distant notion of the place where these scenes
are represented, or of the materials of which it is composed.'
The problem for Hume then in regard to personal, as
it had been in regard to bodily, identity is to account for
that 'natural propension to imagine' it which language
implies.

343. The method of explanation in each case is the same.
He starts with two suppositions, to neither of which he is
logically entitled. One is that we have a 'distinct idea of
identity or sameness,' i.e. of an object that remains invariable and uninterrupted through a supposed variation of time'
—a supposition which, as we have seen, upon his principles
must mean that a feeling, which is one in a succession of
feelings, is yet all the successive feelings at once. The other

---

[1] Pp. 529-531, a commentary on
the argument here given has been in
effect supplied in paragraphs 148-152,
and 194.

[2] See above, §§ 134 and foll.
[3] See above, §§ 306 and foll.

is that we have an idea 'of several different objects existing in succession, and connected together by a close' (natural) 'relation'—which in like manner implies that a feeling, which is one among a succession of feelings, is at the same time a consciousness of these feelings as successive and under that qualification by mutual relation which implies their equal presence to it. These two ideas, which in truth are 'distinct and even contrary,'[1] we yet come to confuse with each other, because 'that action of the imagination, by which we consider the uninterrupted and invisible object, and that by which we reflect on the succession of related objects, are almost the same to the feeling.' Thus, though what we call our mind is really a 'succession of related objects,' we have a strong propensity to mistake it for an 'invariable and uninterrupted object.' To this propensity we at last so far yield as to assert our successive perceptions to be in effect the same, however interrupted and variable; and then, by way of 'justifying to ourselves this absurdity, feign the continued existence of the perceptions of our senses, to remove the interruption; and run into the notion of a *soul*, and *self*, and *substance*, to disguise the variation.'[2]

344. It will be seen that the theory, which we have just summarised, would merely be a briefer version of that given in the section on 'Scepticism with regard to the Senses,' if in the sentence, which states its conclusion, for 'the notion of a soul and self and substance' were written 'the notion of a double existence of perceptions and objects.'[3] To a reader who has not thoroughly entered into the fusion of being and feeling, which belongs to the 'new way of ideas,' it may seem strange that one and the same process of so-called confusion has to account for such apparently disparate results, as the notion of a permanently identical self and that of the distinct existence of body. If he bears in mind, however, that with Hume the universe of our experience is the same when it is called 'the universe of objects or of body' and when it is called the 'universe of thought or my impressions and ideas,'[4] he will see that on the score of consistency Hume is to be blamed, not for applying the same method to account for the fictions of material and spiritual identity, but for allowing himself, in his preference for physical, as

---

[1] See note to § 341.   [3] Above, §§ 306-310.
[2] Pp. 535-536.   [4] Above, § 340.

against theological, pretension, to write as if the supposition of spiritual were really distinct from that of material identity, and might be more contemptuously disposed of. The original 'mistake,' out of which according to him the two fictitious suppositions arise, is one and the same; and though it is a 'mistake' without which, as we have found[1] from Hume's own admissions, we could not speak even in singular propositions of the most ordinary 'objects of sense '—-this pen, this table, this chair—it is yet one that on his principles is logically impossible, since it consists in a confusion between ideas that we cannot have. Of this original 'mistake' the fictions of body and of its 'continued and distinct existence' are but altered expressions. They represent in truth the same logical category of substance and relation. And of the Self according to Locke's notion of it[2] (which was the only one that Hume had in view), as a 'thinking thing' within each man among a multitude of other thinking things, the same would have to be said. But in order to account for the 'mistake,' of which the suppositions of thinking and material substance are the correlative expressions, and which it is the net result of Hume's speculation to exhibit at once as necessary and as impossible, we have found another notion of the self forced upon us—not as a double of body, but as the source of that 'familiar theory' which body in truth is, and without which there would be no universe of objects, whether 'bodies' or 'impressions and ideas,' at all.

345. Thus the more strongly Hume insists that 'the identity which we ascribe to the mind of man is only a fictitious one,'[3] the more completely does his doctrine refute itself. If he had really succeeded in reducing those 'invented' relations, which Locke had implicitly recognised as the framework of the universe, to what he calls 'natural' ones—to mere sequences of feeling—the case would have been different. With the disappearance of the conception of the world as a system of related elements, the necessity of a thinking subject, without whose presence to feelings they could not become such elements, would have disappeared likewise. But he cannot so reduce them. In all his attempts to do so we find that the relation, which has to be explained away, is pre-supposed under some other expression, and that

---

it is 'fictitious' not in the sense which Hume's theory requires—the sense, namely, that there is no such thing either really or in imagination, either as impression or idea—but in the sense that it would not exist if we did not think about our feelings. Thus, whereas identity ought for Hume s purpose to be either a 'natural relation,' or a propensity arising from such relation, or nothing, we find that according to his account, though neither natural relation nor propensity, it yet exists both as idea and as reality. He saves appearances indeed by saying[1] that natural relations of ideas 'produce it,' but they do so, according to his detailed account of the matter, in the sense that, the idea of an identical object being given, we mistake our successive and resembling feelings for such an object. In other words, the existence of numerically identical things is a 'fiction,' not as if there were no such things, but because it implies a certain operation of thought upon our feelings, a certain interpretation of impressions under direction of an idea not derived from impressions. By a like equivocal use of 'fiction' Hume covers the admission of real identity in its more complex forms—the identity of a mass, whose parts undergo perpetual change of distribution; of a body whose form survives not merely the redistribution of its materials, but the substitution of others; of animals and vegetables, in which nothing but the 'common end' of the changing members remains the same. The reality of such identity of mass, of form, of organism, he quietly takes for granted.[2] He calls it 'fictitious' indeed, but only either in the sense above given or in the sense that it is mistaken for mere numerical identity.

346. After he has thus admitted, as constituents of the 'universe of objects,' a whole hierarchy of ideas of which the simplest must vanish before the demand to 'point out the impression from which it is derived,' we are the less surprised to find him pronouncing in conclusion 'that the true idea of the human mind is to consider it as a system of different perceptions or different existences, which are

[1] P. 543. 'Identity depends on the relations of ideas; and these relations produce identity by means of that easy transition they occasion.' Strictly it should be 'that easy transition in which they consist;' since, according to Hume, the 'easiness of transition' is not an effect of natural relation, but constitutes it. Cf. pp. 322 & 497, and above, § 318.

[2] Pp. 536–538.

linked together by the relation of cause and effect, and mutually produce, destroy, influence and modify each other.'[1] A better definition than this, as a *definition of nature*, or one more charged with 'fictions of thought,' could scarcely be desired.   If the idea of such a system is a true idea at all, which we are only wrong in confusing with mere numerical identity, we need be the less concerned that it should be adduced as the true idea not of nature but of the ' human mind.'   Having learnt, through the discipline which Hume himself furnishes, that the recognition of a system of nature logically carries with it that of a self-conscious subject, in relation to which alone 'different perceptions' become a system of nature, we know that we cannot naturalise the 'human mind' without presupposing that which is neither nature nor natural, though apart from it nature would not be —that of which the designation as 'mind,' as 'human,' as 'personal,' is of secondary importance, but which is eternal, self-determined, and thinks.

[1] P. 541.

INTRODUCTION II.

1. In his speculation on morals, no less than on knowledge, Hume follows the lines laid down by Locke. With each there is a precise correspondence between the doctrine of nature and the doctrine of the good. Each gives an account of reason consistent at least in this that, as it allows reason no place in the constitution of real objects, so it allows it none in the constitution of objects that determine desire and, through it, the will. With each, consequently, the 'moral faculty,' whether regarded as the source of the judgments 'ought and ought not,' or of acts to which these judgments are appropriate, can only be a certain faculty of feeling, a particular susceptibility of pleasure and pain. The originality of Hume lies in his systematic effort to account for those objects, apparently other than pleasure and pain, which determine desire, and which Locke had taken for granted without troubling himself about their adjustment to his theory, as resulting from the modification of primary feelings by 'associated ideas.' 'Natural relation,' the close and uniform sequence of certain impressions and ideas upon each other, is the solvent by which in the moral world, as in the world of knowledge, he disposes of those ostensibly necessary ideas that seem to regulate impressions without being copied from them ; and in regard to the one application of it as much as to the other, the question is whether the efficiency of the solvent does not depend on its secretly including the very ideas of which it seems to get rid.

2. The place held by the 'essay concerning Human Understanding,' as a sort of philosopher's Bible in the last century, is strikingly illustrated by the effect of doctrines that

only appear in it incidentally.   It does not profess to be an
ethical treatise at all, yet the moral psychology contained in
the chapter 'of Power' (II. 21), and the account of moral
good and evil contained in the chapter 'of other Relations'
(II. 28), furnished the text for most of the ethical speculation
that prevailed in England, France, and Scotland for a century
later.   If Locke's theory was essentially a reproduction of
Hobbes', it was yet in the form he gave it that it survived
while Hobbes was decried and forgotten.   The chapter on
Power is in effect an account of determination by motives.
More, perhaps, than any other part of the essay it bears the
marks of having been written 'currente calamo.'   In the
second edition a summary was annexed which differs somewhat in the use of terms, but not otherwise, from the original
draught.   The main course of thought, however, is clear
throughout.   Will and freedom are at first defined in all but
identical terms as each a 'power to begin or forbear action
barely by a preference of the mind' (§§ 5, 8, 71).   Nor is
this identification departed from, except that the term 'will'
is afterwards restricted to the 'preference' or 'power of
preference,' while freedom is confined to the power of acting
upon preference; in which sense it is pointed out that though
there cannot be freedom without will, there may be will
without freedom, as when, through the breaking of a bridge,
a man cannot help falling into the water, though he prefers
not to do so.   'Freedom' and 'will' being thus alike powers,
if not the same power, it is as improper to ask whether the
will is free as whether one power has another power.   The
proper question is whether man is free (§§ 14, 21), and the
answer to this question, according to Locke, is that within
certain limits he is free to act, but that he is not free to will.
When in any case he has the option of acting or forbearing
to act, he cannot help preferring, i.e. willing, one or other
alternative.   If it is further asked, What determines the will
or preference? the answer is that 'nothing sets us upon any
new action but some uneasiness' (§ 29), viz., the 'most
urgent uneasiness we at any time feel' (§ 40), which again
is always 'the uneasiness of desire fixed on some absent good,
either negative, as indolence to one in pain, or positive, as
enjoyment of pleasure.'   In one sense, indeed, it may be said
that the will often runs counter to desire, but this merely
means that we 'being in this world beset with sundry un-

easinesses, distressed with different desires,' the determination of the will by the most pressing desire often implies the counteraction of other desires which would, indeed, under other circumstances, be the most pressing, but at the particular time of the supposed action are not so.

3. So far Locke's doctrine amounts to no more than this, that action is always determined by the strongest motive ; and only those who strangely hold that human freedom is to be vindicated by disputing that truism will care to question it. To admit that the strongest desire always moves action (there being, in fact, no test of its strength but its effect on action) and that, since every desire causes uneasiness till it is satisfied, the strongest desire is also the most pressing uneasiness,[1] is compatible with the most opposite views as to the constitution of the objects which determine desire. To understand that it is this constitution of the desired object, not any possible intervention of unmotived willing between the presentation of a strongest motive and action, which forms the central question of ethics, is the condition of all clear thinking on the subject. It is a question, however, which Locke ignores, and popular philosophy, to its great confusion, has not only continued to do the same, but would probably resent as pedantic any attempt at more accurate analysis. When we hear of the strongest ' desire ' being the uniform motive to action, we have to ask, in the first place, whether the term is confined to impulses determined by a prior consciousness, or is taken to include those impulses, commonly called ' mere appetites,' which are not so determined, but depend directly and solely on the ' constitution of our bodily organs.' The *appetite* of hunger is obviously quite independent of any remembrance of the pleasure of eating, yet nothing is commoner than to identify with such simple

---

[1] Locke's language in regard to 'the most pressing uneasiness' will not be found uniformly consistent. His usual doctrine is that the strength of a desire, as evinced by the resulting action, and the uneasiness which it causes are in exact proportion to each other. According to this view, desire for future happiness can only become a prevalent motive when the uneasiness which it causes has come to outweigh every other (Cf. Chap. xxi., Secs. 43 and 45). On the other hand, he sometimes seems to distinguish the desire for future pleasure from present uneasiness, while at the same time implying that it may be a strongest motive (Cf. sec. 65). But if so, it follows that there may be a strongest desire which is not the most pressing uneasiness. (See below, sec. 13.) Hume, distinguishing strong from violent desires, and restricting 'uneasiness' to the latter, is able to hold that it is not alone the present uneasiness which determines action. (Book ii., part 3, sec. 3, sub fin.)

appetite the desire determined by consciousness of some sort, as when we say of a drunkard, who never drinks merely because he is thirsty, that he is governed by his appetite. Upon this distinction, however, since it is recognised by current psychology, it is less important to insist than on that between the kinds of prior consciousness which may determine desire proper. Does this prior consciousness consist simply in the return of an image of past pleasure with consequent hope of its renewal, or is it a conception—the thought of an object under relations to self or of self in relation to certain objects —in a word, self-consciousness as distinct from simple feeling?

4. Of desire determined in the former way we have experience, if at all, in those motives which actuate us, as we say, 'unconsciously'; which means, without our attending to them—feelings which we do not fix even momentarily by reference to self or to a thing. As we cannot set ourselves to recall such feelings without thinking them, without determining them by that reference to self which we suppose them to exclude, they cannot be described; but some of our actions (such as the instinctive recurrence to a sweet smell), seem only to be thus accounted for, and probably those actions of animals which do not proceed from appetite proper are to be accounted for in the same way. But whether such actions are facts in human experience or no, those which make us what we are as men are not so determined. The man whom we call the slave of his appetite, the enlightened pleasure-hunter, the man who lives for his family, the artist, the enthusiast for humanity, are alike in this, that the desire which moves their action is itself determined not by the recurring image of a past pleasure, but by the conception of self. The self may be conceived of simply as a subject to be pleased, or may be a subject of interests, which, indeed, when gratified, produce pleasure but are not produced by it—interests in persons, in beautiful things, in the order of nature and society—but self is still not less the 'punctum stans' whose presence to each passing pleasure renders it a constituent of a happiness which is to be permanently pursued, than it is the focus in which the influences of that world which only self-conscious reason could constitute—the world of science, of art, of human society—must be regathered in order to become the personal interests which move the actions of individuals. It is in this

self-consciousness involved in our motives, in that conversion into a conception by reference to self, which the image even of the merest animal pleasure must undergo before it can become an element in the formation of character, that the possibility of freedom lies. Without it we should be as sinless and as unprogressive, as free from remorse and aspiration, as incapable of selfishness and self-denial as the animals. Each pleasure would be taken as it came. We should have ' the greatest happiness of which our nature is capable,' without possibility of asking ourselves whether we might not have had more. It is only the conception of himself as a permanent subject to be pleased that can set man upon the invention of new pleasures, and then, making each pleasure a disappointment when it comes, produce the ' vicious ' temper; only this that can suggest the reflection how much more pleasure he might have had than he has had, and thus produce what the moralists know as ' cool selfishness '; only this, on the other hand, which, as ' enlightened self-love,' perpetually balances the attraction of imagined pleasure by the calculation whether it will be good for one as a whole. Nor less is it the conception of self, with a ' matter' more adequate to its ' form,' taking its content not from imagined pleasure, but from the work of reason in the world of nature and humanity, which determines that personal devotion to a work or a cause, to a state, a church, or mankind, which we call self-sacrifice.

5. If, now, we ask ourselves whether Locke recognised this function of reason, as self-consciousness, in the determination of the will, the answer must be yes and no. His cardinal doctrine, as we have sufficiently seen, forbade him to admit that reason or thought could originate an object. The only possible objects with him are either simple ideas or resoluble into these, and the simple idea, as that which we receive in pure passivity, is virtually feeling. Now no combination of feelings (supposing it possible [1]) can yield the conception of self as a permanent subject even of pleasure, much less as a subject of social claims. It cannot, therefore, yield the objects, ranging from sensual happiness to the moral law, humanity, and God, of which this conception is the correlative condition. Thus, strictly taken, Locke's doctrine excludes every motive to action, but appetite proper and such desire as is deter-

---

[1] Cf. Introduction to Vol. i., §§ 215 and 247.

mined by the imagination of animal pleasure or pain, and in
doing so renders vice as well as virtue unaccountable—the
excessive pursuit of pleasure as well as that dissatisfaction
with it which affords the possibility of ordinary reform. On
the other hand, the same happy intellectual unscrupulousness,
which we have traced in his theory of knowledge, attends
him also here.   Just as he is ready on occasion to treat any
conceived object that determines sense as if it were itself a
sensation, so he is ready to treat any object that determines
desire, without reference to the work of thought in its construction, as if it were itself the feeling of pleasure, or of
uneasiness removed, which arises upon satisfaction of the
desire.   In this way, without professedly admitting any
motive but remembered pleasure—a motive which, if it were
our only one, would leave 'man's life as cheap as beasts' '—
he can take for granted any objects of recognised interest as
accounting for the movement of human life, and as constituents of an utmost possible pleasure which it is his own fault
if every one does not pursue.

6. The term 'happiness' is the familiar cover for confusion between the animal imagination of pleasure and the
conception of personal well-being.   It is so when—having
raised the question, What moves desire?—Locke answers,
'happiness, and that alone.'   What, then, is happiness?
'Good and evil are nothing but pleasure and pain,' and
'happiness in its full extent is the utmost pleasure we are
capable of.' [1]   This is 'the proper object of desire in general,'
but Locke is careful to explain that the happiness which
'moves every particular man's desire' is not the full extent
of it, but 'so much of it as is considered and taken to make
a necessary part of his happiness.'   It is that 'wherewith he
in his present thoughts can satisfy himself.'   Happiness in
this sense 'every one constantly pursues,' and without possibility of error; for 'as to present pleasure the mind never
mistakes that which is really good or evil.'   Every one
'knows what best pleases him, and that he actually prefers.'
That which is the greater pleasure or the greater pain is
really just as it appears (Ibid. §§ 43, 58, 63).   Now in these
statements, if we look closely, we shall find that four different
meanings of happiness are mixed up, which we will take
leave to distinguish by letters—(a) happiness as an abstract

[1] Ibid., sec. 42, and cap. 28, sec. 5.

conception, the sum of possible pleasure; (b) happiness as equivalent to the pleasure which at any time survives most strongly in imagination; (c) happiness as the object of the self-conscious pleasure-seeker; (d) happiness as equivalent to any object at any time most strongly desired, not really a pleasure, but by Locke identified with happiness in sense (b) through the fallacy of supposing that the pleasure which arises on satisfaction of any desire, great in proportion to the strength of the desire, is itself the object which excites desire.

7. Happiness ' in its full extent,' as ' the utmost pleasure we are capable of,' is an unreal abstraction if ever there was one It is curious that those who are most forward to deny the reality of universals, in that sense in which they are the condition of all reality, viz., as relations, should yet, having pronounced these to be mere names, be found ascribing reality to a universal, which cannot without contradiction be supposed more than a name. Does this ' happiness in its full extent' mean the ' aggregate of possible enjoyments,' of which modern utilitarians tell us? Such a phrase simply represents the vain attempt to get a definite by addition of indefinites. It has no more meaning than ' the greatest possible quantity of time ' would have. Pleasant feelings are not quantities that can be added. Each is over before the next begins, and the man who has been pleased a million times is not really better off—has no more of the supposed chief good in possession—than the man who has only been pleased a thousand times. When we speak of pleasures, then, as forming a possible whole, we cannot mean pleasures as feelings, and what else do we mean ? Are we, then, by the 'happiness ' in question to understand pleasure *in general*, as might be inferred from Locke's speaking of it as the ' object of desire *in general*' ? But it is in its mere particularity that each pleasure has its being. It is a simple idea, and therefore, as Locke and Hume have themselves taught us, momentary, indefinable, in ' perpetual flux,' changing every moment upon us. Pleasure *in general*, therefore, is not pleasure, and it is nothing else. It is not a conceived reality, as a relation, or a thing determined by relations, is, since pleasure as feeling, in distinction from its conditions which are not feelings, for the same reason that it cannot be defined, cannot be conceived. It is a mere name which utilitarian philosophy

has mistaken for a thing; but for which—since no one, whatever his theory of the desirable, can actually desire either the abstraction of pleasure in general or the aggregate of possible pleasures—a practical substitute is apt to be found in any lust of the flesh that may for the time be the strongest.

8. Having begun by making this fiction 'the proper object of desire in general,' Locke saves the appearance of consistency by representing the particular pleasure or removal of uneasiness, which he in fact believed to be the object of every desire, as if it were a certain part of the 'full extent of happiness' which the individual, having this full extent before him, picked out as being what 'in his present thoughts would satisfy him.' Nor does he ever give up the notion of a 'happiness in general,' in distinction from the happiness of each man's actual choice, as a possible motive, which a man who finds himself wretched in consequence of his actions may be told that he ought to have adopted. His real notion, however, of the happiness which is motive to action is a confused result of the three other notions of happiness, distinguished above as (b), (c) and (d). As that about which no one can be mistaken, 'happiness' can only be so in sense (b), as the 'pleasure which survives most strongly in imagination.' Of this it can be said truly, and of this only, that 'it really is just as it appears,' and that 'a man never chooses amiss' since he must 'know what best pleases him.' But with this, almost in the same breath, Locke confuses 'happiness' in senses (c) and (d). So soon as it is said of an object that it is 'taken by the individual to make a necessary part of his happiness,' it is implied that it is determined by his conception of self. It is something which, as the result of the action of this conception on his past experience, he has come to present to himself as a constituent of his personal good. Unless he were conscious of himself as a permanent subject, he could have no conception of happiness as a whole from relation to which each present object takes its character as a part. Nor of the objects determined by this relation is it true, as Locke says, that they are always pleasures, or that they 'are really just as they appear.' Our readiness to accept his statements to this effect, is at bottom due to a confusion between the pleasure, or removal of uneasiness,

incidental to the satisfaction of a desire and the object which excites the desire. If having explained desire, as Locke does, by reference to the good, we then allow ourselves to explain the good by reference to desire, it will indeed be true that no man can be mistaken as to his present good, but only in the sense of the identical proposition that every man most desires what he does most desire ; and true also, that every attained good is pleasure, but only in the sense that what satisfies desire does satisfy it. The man of whom it could be truly said, in any other sense than that of the above identical proposition, that his only objects of desire— the only objects which he ' takes to make a necessary part of his happiness '—were pleasures, would be a man, as we say, of no interests. He would be a man who either lived simply for pleasures incidental to the satisfaction of animal appetite, or one who, having been interested in certain objects in which reason alone enables us to be interested— *e.g.*, persons, pursuits, or works of art—and having found consequent pleasure, afterwards vainly tries to get the pleasure without the interests. To the former type of character, of course, the approximations are numerous enough, though it may be doubted whether such an ideal of sensuality is often fully realised. The latter in its completeness, which would mean a perfect misery that could only issue in suicide, would seem to be an impossibility, though it is constantly being approached in proportion to the unworthiness and fleetingness of the interests by which men allow themselves to be governed, and which, after stimulating an indefinite hunger for good, leave it without an object to satisfy it ; in proportion, too, to the modern habit of hugging and poring over the pleasures which our higher interests cause us till these interests are vitiated, and we find ourselves in restless and hopeless pursuit of the pleasure when the interest which might alone produce it is gone.

9. Just as it is untrue, then, of the object of desire, as ' taken to be part of one's happiness ' or determined by the conception of self, that it is always a pleasure, so it is untrue that it is always really just as it appears, except in the trifling sense that what is most strongly desired is most strongly desired. Rather it is never really what it appears. It is least of all so to the professed pleasure-seeker. Obviously, to the man who seeks the pleasure incidental to

interests which he has lost, there is a contradiction in his quest which for ever prevents what seems to him desirable from satisfying his desire. And even the man who lives for merely animal pleasure, just because he seeks it as part of a happiness, never finds it to be that which he sought. There is no mistake about the pleasure, but he seeks it as that which shall satisfy him, and satisfy him, since he is not an animal, it cannot. Nor are our higher objects of desire ever what they seem. That is too old a topic with poets and moralizers to need enforcing. Each in its turn, we know, promises happiness when it shall have been attained, but when it is attained the happiness has not come. The craving for an object adequate to oneself, which is the source of the desire, is still not quenched; and because it is not, nor can be, even ' the joy of success ' has its own bitterness.

10. The case, then, stands thus. Locke, having too much ' common sense ' to reduce all objects of desire to the pleasures incidental to satisfactions of appetite, takes for granted any number of objects which only reason can constitute (or, in other words, which can only exist for a self-conscious subject) without any question as to their origin. It is enough for him that they are not conscious inventions of the individual, and that they are related to feeling—though related as determining it. This being so, they are to him no more the work of thought than are the satisfactions of appetite. The conception of them is of a kind with the simple remembrance or imagination of pleasures caused by such satisfactions. The question how, if only pleasure is the object of desire, they came to be desired before there had been experience of the pleasures incidental to their attainment, is virtually shelved by treating these latter pleasures as if they were themselves the objects originally desired. So far consistency at least is saved. No object but feeling, present or remembered, is ostensibly admitted within human experience. But meanwhile, alongside of this view, comes the account of the strongest motive as determined by the conception of self—as something which a man ' takes to be a necessary part of his happiness,' and which he is ' answerable to himself' for so taking. The inconsistency of such language with the view that every desired object must needs be a pleasure, would have been less noticeable if Locke himself had not frankly admitted, as the corollary of this view,

that the desired good 'is really just as it appears.' The necessity of this admission has always been the rock on which consistent Hedonism has broken. Locke himself has scarcely made it when he becomes aware of its dangerous consequences, and great part of the chapter on Power is taken up by awkward attempts to reconcile it with the distinction between true happiness and false, and with the existence of moral responsibility. If greatest pleasure is the only possible object, and the production of such pleasure the only possible criterion of action, and if 'as to present pleasure and pain the mind never mistakes that which is really good or evil,' with what propriety can any one be told that he might or that he ought to have chosen otherwise than he has done? 'He has missed the true good,' we say, 'which he might and should have found'; but 'good,' according to Locke, is only pleasure, and pleasure, as Locke in any other connexion would be eager to tell us, must mean either some actual present pleasure or a series of pleasures of which each in turn is present. If every one without possibility of mistake has on each occasion chosen the greatest present pleasure, how can the result for him at any time be other than the true good, *i.e.*, the series of greatest pleasures, each in its turn present, that have been hitherto possible for him?

11. A modern utilitarian, if faithful to the principle which excludes any test of pleasure but pleasure itself, will probably answer that every one does attain the maximum of pleasure possible for him, his character and circumstances being what they are; but that with a change in these his choice would be different. He would still choose on each occasion the greatest pleasure of which he was then capable, but this pleasure would be one 'truer'—in the sense of being more intense, more durable, and compatible with a greater quantity of other pleasures—than is that which he actually chooses. But admitting that this answer justifies us in speaking of any sort of pleasure as 'truer' than that at any time chosen by any one—which is a very large admission, for of the intensity of any pleasure we have no test but its being actually preferred, and of durability and compatibility with other pleasures the tests are so vague that a healthy and unrepentant voluptuary would always have the best of it in an attempt to strike the balance between the

pleasures he has actually chosen and any truer sort—it still only throws us back on a further question. With a better character, it is said, such as better education and improved circumstances might have produced, the actually greatest happiness of the individual—*i.e.*, the series of pleasures which, because he has chosen them, we know to have been the greatest possible for him—might have been greater or 'truer.' But the man's character is the result of his previous preferences; and if every one has always chosen the greatest pleasure of which he was at the time capable, and if no other motive is possible, how could any other than his actual character have been produced? How could that conception of a happiness truer than the actual, of something that should be most pleasant, and therefore preferred, though it is not—a conception which all education implies— have been a possible motive among mankind? To say that the individual is, to begin with, destitute of such a conception, but acquires it through education from others, does not remove the difficulty. How do the educators come by it? Common sense assumes them to have found out that more happiness might have been got by another than the merely natural course of living, and to wish to give others the benefit of their experience. But such experience implies that each has a conception of himself as other than the subject of a succession of pleasures, of which each has been the greatest possible at the time of its occurrence; and the wish to give another the benefit of the experience implies that this conception, which is no possible image of a feeling, can originate action. The assumption of common sense, then, contradicts the two cardinal principles of the Hedonistic philosophy; yet, however disguised in the terminology of development and evolution, it, or some equivalent supposition, is involved in every theory of the progress of mankind.

12. Such difficulties do not suggest themselves to Locke, because he is always ready to fall back on the language of common sense without asking whether it is reconcilable with his theory. Having asserted, without qualification, that the will in every case is determined by the strongest desire, that the strongest desire is desire for the greatest pleasure, and that ' pleasure is just so great, and no greater, than it is felt,' he finds a place for moral freedom and responsibility in the ' power a man has to suspend his desires

and stop them from determining his will to any action till he has examined whether it be really of a nature in itself and consequences to make him happy or no.'[1] But how does it happen that there is any need for such suspense, if as to pleasure and pain 'a man never chooses amiss,' and pleasure is the same with happiness or the good? To this Locke answers that it is only present pleasure which is just as it appears, and that in ' comparing present pleasure or pain with future we often make wrong judgments of them;' again, that not only present pleasure and pain, but 'things that draw after them pleasure and pain, are considered as good and evil,' and that of these consequences under the in- fluence of present pleasure or pain we may judge amiss.[2] By these wrong judgments, it will be observed, Locke does not mean mistakes in discovering the proper means to a desired end (Aristotle's ἀγνοία ἡ καθ᾽ ἕκαστα), which it is agreed are not a ground for blame or punishment, but wrong desires—desires for certain pleasures as being the greater, which are not really the greater. Regarding such desires as involving comparisons of one good with another, he counts them judgments, and (the comparison being incorrectly made) *wrong* judgments. A certain present pleasure, and a certain future one, are compared, and though the future would really be the greater, the present is preferred ; or a present pleasure, 'drawing after it' a certain amount of pain, is compared with a less amount of present pain, drawing after it a greater pleasure, and the present pleasure preferred. In such cases the man ' may justly incur punishment' for the wrong preference, because having ' the power to suspend his desire' for the present pleasure, he has not done so, but ' by too hasty choice of his own making has imposed on himself wrong measures of good and evil.' ' When he has once chosen it,' indeed, ' and thereby it is become part of his happiness, it raises desire, and that proportionately gives him uneasiness, which determines his will.' But the original wrong choice, having the ' power of suspending his desires,' he might have prevented. In not doing so he ' vitiated his own palate,' and must be ' answerable to himself' for the consequences.[3]

13. Responsibility for evil, then (with its conditions, blame, punishment, and remorse) supposes that a man has

[1] II. 21, Sec. 51 and 56.   [2] Ibid., Sec. 61, 63 67.   [3] Ibid., Sec. 56.

gone wrong in the comparison of present with future pleasure or pain, having had the chance of going right. Upon
this we must remark that as moving desire—and it is the
determination of desire that is here in question—NO pleasure can be present in the sense of actual enjoyment, or (in
Hume's language) as 'impression,' but only in memory or
imagination, as 'idea.' Otherwise desire would not be
desire. It would not be that uneasiness which, according
to Locke, implies the absence of good, and alone moves action.
On the other hand, to imagination EVERY pleasure must be
present that is to act as motive at all. In whatever sense,
then, pleasure, as pleasure, i.e. as undetermined by conceptions, can properly be said to move desire, every pleasure is
equally present and equally future.[1] For man, if he only
felt and retained his feelings in memory, or recalled them in
imagination, the only difference among the imagined pleasures which solicit his desires, other than difference of
intensity, would lie in the imagined pains with which each
may have become associated. One pleasure might be
imagined in association with a greater amount of the pain
of waiting than another. In that sense, and only in that,
could one be distinguished from the other as a future pleasure from a present one. According as the greater imagined
intensity of the future pleasure did or did not outweigh the
imagined pain of waiting for it, the scale of desire would
turn one way or the other. Or with one pleasure, imagined
as more intense than another, might be associated an expectation of a greater amount of pain to be 'drawn after it.'
Here, again, the question would be whether the greater
imagined intensity of pleasure would have the more effect in
exciting desire, or the greater amount of imagined sequent
pain in quenching it—a question only to be settled by the
action which results. In whatever sense it is true of the
'present pleasure or pain,' that it is really just as it appears,
it is equally true of the future. Whenever the determination of desire is in question, the statement that present
pleasure is just as it appears must mean that the pleasure
present in imagination is so, and in this sense all motive
pleasures are equally so present. Undoubtedly the pleasure

---

[1] It is noticeable that when Locke takes
to distinguishing the pleasures that
move desire into present and future, he
speaks as if the future pleasure alone
were an absent good, in contradiction
to his previous view that every object
of desire is an absent good. (Cf. sec.
65 with sec. 57 of cap. 21.)

associated with the pain of prolonged expectancy might turn out greater, and that associated with sequent pain less, than was imagined; but so might a pleasure not thus associated. Of every pleasure alike it is as true, that while it is imagined it is just as it is imagined, as that while felt it is just as it is felt; and if man only felt and imagined, there would be no more reason why he should hold himself accountable for his imaginations than for his feelings. Whatever pleasure was most attractive in imagination would determine desire, and, through it, action, which would be the only measure of the amount of the attraction. It would not indeed follow because an action was determined by the pleasure most attractive in imagination, that the ensuing pleasure in actual enjoyment would be greater than might have been attained by a different action—though it would be very hard to show the contrary—but it would follow that the man attained the greatest pleasure of which his nature was capable. There would be no reason why he should blame himself, or be blamed by others, for the result.

14. Thus on Locke's supposition, that desire is only moved by pleasure—which must mean *imagined* pleasure, since pleasure, determined by conceptions, is excluded by the supposition that pleasure alone is the ultimate motive, and pleasure in actual enjoyment is no longer desired—the 'suspense of desire,' that he speaks of, can only mean an interval, during which a competition of imagined pleasures (one associated with more, another with less, of sequent or antecedent pain) is still going on, and none has become finally the strongest motive. Of such suspense it is un-meaning to say that a man has 'the power of it,' or that, when it terminates in an action which does not produce so much pleasure as another might have done, it is because the man 'has vitiated his palate,' and that therefore he must be 'answerable to himself' for the consequences. This lan-guage really implies that pleasures, instead of being ultimate ends, are determined to be ends through reference to an object beyond them which the man himself constitutes; that it is only through his conception of self that every pleasure—not indeed best pleases him, or is most attractive in imagina-tion—but becomes his personal good. It may be that he identifies his personal good with the pleasure most attractive in imagination; but a pleasure so identified is quite a different

motive from a pleasure simply as imagined. It is no longer mere pleasure that the man seeks, but self-satisfaction through the pleasure. The same consciousness of self, which sets him on the act, continues through the act and its consequences, carrying with it the knowledge (commonly called the 'voice of conscience') that it is to himself, as the ultimate motive, that the act and its consequences, whether in the shape of natural pains or civil penalties, are due—a knowledge which breeds remorse, and, through it, the possibility of a better mind. Thus, when Locke finds the ground of responsibility in a man's power of suspending his desire till he has considered whether the act, to which it inclines him, is of a kind to make him happy or no, the value of the explanation lies in the distinction which it may be taken to imply, but which Locke could not consistently admit, between the imagination of pleasure and the conception of self as a permanent subject of happiness, by reference to which an imagined pleasure becomes a strongest motive. It is not really as involving a comparison between imagined pleasures, but as involving the consideration whether the greatest imagined pleasure will be the best for one in the long run, that the suspense of desire establishes the responsibility of man. Even if we admitted with Locke that nothing entered into the consideration but an estimate of 'future pleasures' —and Locke, it will be observed, by supposing the estimate to include 'pleasures of a sort we are unacquainted with,'[1] which is as much of a contradiction as to suppose a man influenced by unfelt feelings, renders this restriction unmeaning —still to be determined by the consideration whether something is good for me on the whole is to be determined, not by the imagination of pleasure, but by the conception of self, though it be of self only as a subject to be pleased.

15. The mischief is that, though his language implies this distinction, he does not himself understand it. 'The care of ourselves,' he tells us, 'that we mistake not imaginary for real happiness, is the necessary foundation of our liberty. The stronger ties we have to an unalterable pursuit of happiness in general, which is our greatest good, and which, as such, our desires always follow, the more are we free from

[1] Cap. 21, sec. 65. He has specially in view the pleasures of 'another life,' which 'being intended for a state of happiness, must certainly be agreeable to every one's wish and desire: could we suppose their relishes as different there as they are here, yet the manna in heaven will suit every one's palate.'

any necessary determination of our will to any particular action, till we have examined whether it has a tendency to, or is inconsistent with, our real happiness.'[1] But he does not see that the *rationale* of the freedom, thus paradoxically, though truly, placed in the strength of a tie, lies in that determination by the conception of self to which the ' unalterable pursuit of happiness' is really equivalent. To him it is not as one mode among others in which that self-determination appears, but simply in itself, that the consideration of what is for our real happiness is the ' foundation of our liberty,' and the consideration itself is no more than a comparison between imagined pleasures and pains. Hence to a reader who refuses to read into Locke an interpretation which he does not himself supply, the range of moral liberty must seem as narrow as its nature is ambiguous. As to its range, the greater part of our actions, and among them those which we are apt to think our best, are not and could not be preceded by any consideration whether they are for our real happiness or no. In truth, they result from a character which the conception of self has rendered possible, or express an interest in objects of which this conception is the condition, and for that reason they represent a will self-determined and free ; but they do not rest on the foundation which Locke calls ' the necessary foundation of our liberty.' As to the nature of this liberty, the reader, who takes Locke at his word, would find himself left to choose between the view of it as the condition of a mind 'suspended' between rival presentations of the pleasant, and the equally untenable view of it as that 'liberty of indifference,' which Locke himself is quite ready to deride—as consisting in a choice prior to desire, which determines what the desire shall be.[2]

16. This ambiguous deliverance about moral freedom, it must be observed, is the necessary result on a mind, having too strong a practical hold on life to tamper with human responsibility, of a doctrine which denies the originativeness of thought, and in consequence cannot consistently allow any motive to desire, but the image of a past pleasure or pain. The full logical effect of the doctrine, however, does not appear in Locke, because, with his way of taking any

[1] Cap. 21, sec. 51.
[2] Cf. the passage in sec. 56 : ' When he has once chosen it, and thereby it is become part of his happiness, it raises desire,' &c. (Cf. also sec. 43 sub fin.)

desire of which the satisfaction produces pleasure to have
pleasure for its object, he never comes in sight of the question how the manifold objects of actual human interest are
possible for a being who only feels and retains, or combines,
his feelings. An action moved by love of country, love of
fame, love of a friend, love of the beautiful, would cause him
no more difficulty than one moved by desire for the renewal
of some sensual enjoyment, or for that maintenance of
health which is the condition of such enjoyment in the
future. If pressed about them, we may suppose that—availing himself of the language probably current in the philosophic society in which he lived, though it first became
generally current in England through the writings of his
quasi-pupil, Shaftesbury—he would have said that he found
in his breast affections for public good, as well as for self-
good, the satisfaction of which gave pleasure, and to which
his doctrine, that pleasure is the 'object of desire in general,'
was accordingly applicable. The question—of what feelings
or combinations of feelings are the objects which excite
these several desires copies?—it does not occur to him to
ask. It is only when a class of actions presents itself for
which a motive in the way of desire or aversion is not
readily assignable that any difficulty arises, and then it is a
difficulty which the assignment of such a motive, without
any question asked as to its possibility for a merely feeling
and imagining subject, is thought sufficiently to dispose of.
Such a class of actions is that of which we say that we
'ought' to do them, even when we are not compelled and
had rather not. We ought, it is generally admitted, to keep
our promises, even when it is inconvenient to us to do so and
no punishment could overtake us if we did not. We ought
to be just even in ways that the law does not prescribe, and
when we are beyond its ken; and that, too, in dealing with
men towards whom we have no inclination to be generous.
We ought even—so at least Locke 'on the authority of
Revelation' would have said—to forgive injuries which we
cannot forget, and if not 'to love our enemies' in the literal
sense, which may be an impossibility, yet to act as if we did.
To what motive are such actions to be assigned?

17. 'To desire for pleasure or aversion from pain,' Locke
would answer, 'but a pleasure and pain other than the
natural consequences of acts and attached to them by some

law.' This is the result of his enquiry into ʿMoral Relations' (Book ɪɪ., chap. 28). Good and evil, he tells us, being ʿnothing but pleasure and pain, moral good or evil is only the conformity or disagreement of our actions to some law, whereby good or evil, *i.e.*, pleasure or pain, is drawn on us by the will and power of the law-maker.' All law according to its ʿtrue nature' is a rule set to the actions of others by an intelligent being, having ʿpower to reward the compliance with, and punish deviation from, his rule by some good and evil that is not the natural product and consequence of the action itself; for that, being a natural convenience or inconvenience, would operate of itself without a law.' Of such law there are three sorts. 1. Divine Law, ʿpromulgated to men by the light of nature or voice of revelation, by comparing their actions to which they judge whether, as duties or sins, they are like to procure them happiness or misery from the hands of the Almighty.' 2. Civil Law, ʿthe rule set by the Commonwealth to the actions of those who belong to it,' reference to which decides ʿwhether they be criminal or no.' 3. ʿThe law of opinion or reputation,' according to agreement or disagreement with which actions are reckoned ʿvirtues or vices.' This law may or may not coincide with the divine law. So far as it does, virtues and vices are really, what they are always supposed to be, actions ʿin their own nature' severally right or wrong. It is not as really right or wrong, however, but only as esteemed so, that an act is virtuous or vicious, and thus ʿthe common measure of virtue and vice is the approbation or dislike, praise or blame, which by a tacit consent establishes itself in the several societies, tribes, and clubs of men in the world, whereby several actions come to find credit or disgrace among them, according to the judgment, maxims, or fashions of the place.' Each sort of law has its own ʿenforcement in the way of good and evil.' That of the civil law is obvious. That of the Divine Law lies in the pleasures and pains of ʿanother world,' which (we have to suppose) render actions ʿin their own nature good and evil.' That of the third sort of law lies in those consequences of social reputation and dislike which are stronger motives to most men than are the rewards and punishments either of God or the magistrate (chap. 28, §§ 5–12).

18. ʿMoral goodness or evil,' Locke concludes, ʿis the

conformity or non-conformity of any action' to one or other
of the above rules (§ 14). But such conformity or non-conformity is not a feeling, pleasant or painful, at all. If, then,
the account of the good as consisting in pleasure, of which
the morally good is a particular form, is to be adhered to,
we must suppose that, when moral goodness is said to be
conformity to law, it is so called merely with reference to the
specific means of attaining that pleasure in which moral
good consists. Not the conception of conformity to law, but
the imagination of a certain pleasure, will determine the
desire that moves the moral act, as every other desire.
The distinction between the moral act and an act judiciously
done for the sake, let us say, of some pleasure of the palate,
will lie only in the channel through which comes the pleasure
that each is calculated to obtain. If the motive of an act
done for the sake of the pleasure of eating differs from the
motive of an act done for the sake of sexual pleasure on account of the difference of the channels through which the
pleasures are severally obtained, in that sense only can the
motive of either of these acts, upon Locke's principles, be
taken to differ from the motive of an act morally done. The
explanation, then, of the acts not readily assignable to
desire or aversion, of which we say that we only do them
because we ' ought,' has been found. They are so far of a kind
with all actions done to obtain or avoid what Locke calls
' future ' pleasures or pains that the difficulty of assigning
a motive for them only arises from the fact that their
immediate result is not an end but a means. They differ
from these, however, inasmuch as the pleasure they draw
after them is not their ' natural consequence,' any more than
the pain attaching to a contrary act would be, but is only
possible through the action of God, the magistrate, or
society in some of its forms.

19. After the above examination we can easily anticipate
the points on which a candid and clear-headed man, who
accepted the principles of Locke's doctrine, would see that
it needed explanation and development. If all action is
determined by impulse to remove the most pressing uneasiness, as consisting in desire for the greatest pleasure of which
the agent is at the time capable; if this, again, means
desire for the renewal of some ' impression ' previously experienced, and all impressions are either those of sense or

derived from them, how are we to account for those actual objects of human interest and pursuit which seem far removed from any combination of animal pleasures or of the means thereto, and specially for that class of actions determined, as Locke says, by expectation of pain or pleasure other than the 'natural consequence' of the act, to which the term 'moral' is properly applied? Hume, as we have seen,[1] in accepting Locke's principles, clothes them in a more precise terminology, marking the distinction between the feeling as originally felt and the same as returning in memory or imagination as that between 'impression and idea,' and excluding *original* ideas of reflection. 'An impression first strikes upon the senses, and makes us perceive heat or cold, thirst or hunger, pleasure or pain, of some kind or other. Of this impression there is a copy taken by the mind, which remains after the impression ceases; and this we call an idea. This idea of pleasure or pain, when it returns upon the soul, produces the new impressions of desire and aversion, hope and fear, which may properly be called impressions of reflection, because derived from it' (a). These, again, are copied by the memory and imagination, and become ideas; which perhaps in their turn give rise to other impressions' (b). Thus the impressions of reflection, marked (a), will be determined by ideas copied from impressions of sense. If desires, they will be desires for the renewal either of a pleasure incidental to the satisfaction of appetite, or of a pleasant sight or sound, a sweet taste or smell. These desires and their satisfactions will again be copied in ideas, but how can the impressions (b) to which these ideas give rise be other than desires for the renewal of the original animal pleasures? How do they come to be desires as unlike these as are the motives which actuate not merely the saint or the philanthropist, but the ordinary good neighbour or honest citizen or head of a family?

20. During the interval between the publication of Locke's essay and the 'Treatise on Human Nature' there had been much writing on ethical questions in English. The effect of this on Hume is plain enough. He writes with reference to current controversy, and in the moral part of the treatise probably had the views of Clarke, Shaftesbury, Butler, and Hutcheson more consciously before him than Locke's. This does not interfere, however, with the propriety of affiliating

[1] General Introd., vol. i., par. 195.

him in respect of his views on morals, no less than on knowledge, directly to Locke, whose principles and method were
in the main accepted by all the moralists of that age. His
characteristic lies in his more consistent application of these,
and the effect of current controversy upon him was chiefly
to show him the line which this application must take. It
was a controversy which turned almost wholly on two points ;
(a) the distinction between 'interested and disinterested,'
selfish and unselfish affections ; (b) the origin and nature of
that 'law,' relation to which, according to Locke, constitutes
our action 'virtuous or vicious.' In the absence of any notion
of thought but as a faculty which puts together simple ideas
into complex ones, of reason but as a faculty which calculates
means and perceives the agreement of ideas mediately, it
could have but one end.

21. By the generation in which Hume was bred the issue
as to the possible disinterestedness of action was supposed to
lie between the view of Hobbes and that of Shaftesbury.
Hobbes' moral doctrine had not been essentially different
from Locke's, but he had been offensively explicit on questions which Locke left open to more genial views than his
doctrine logically justified. Each started from the position
that the ultimate motive to every action can only be the
imagination of one's own pleasure or pain, and neither properly left room for the determination of desire by a conceived
object as distinct from remembered pleasure. But while
Locke, as we have seen, illogically took for granted desires
so determined, and thus made it possible for a disciple to
admit any benevolent desires as motives on the strength of
the pleasure which they produce when satisfied, Hobbes had
been more severe in his method, and had explained every
desire, of which the direct motive could not be taken to be
the renewal of some animal pleasure, as desire either for the
power in oneself to command such pleasure at will or for the
pleasure incidental to the contemplation of the signs of such
power. Hence his peculiar treatment of compassion and the
other 'social affections,' which it is easier to show to be untrue to the facts of the case than to be other than the
proper consequence of principles which Locke had rendered
orthodox.[1] The counter-doctrine of Shaftesbury holds water
just so far as it involves the rejection of the doctrine that

[1] See 'Leviathan,' part 1, chap. 6.

pleasure is the sole ultimate motive. It becomes confused just because its author had no definite theory of reason, as constitutive of objects, that could justify this rejection.

22. He begins with a doctrine that directly contradicts Locke's identification of the good with pleasure, and of the morally good with pleasure occurring in a particular way. 'In a sensible creature that which is not done through any affection at all makes neither good nor ill in the nature of that creature; who then only is supposed good, when the good or ill of the system to which he has relation is the immediate object of some passion or affection moving him.'[1] This, it will be seen, as against Locke, implies that the good of a man's action lies not in any pleasure sequent upon it to him, but in the nature of the affection from which it proceeds; and that the goodness of this affection depends on its being determined by an object wholly different from imagined pleasure—the *conceived* good of a system to which the man has relation, *i.e.*, of human society, which in Shaftesbury's language is the 'public' as distinct from the 'private' system. It is not enough that an action should result in good to this system; it must proceed from affection for it. 'Whatever is done which happens to be advantageous to the species through an affection merely towards self-good does not imply any more goodness in the creature than as the affection itself is good. Let him in any particular act ever so well; if at the bottom it be that selfish affection alone which moves him, he is in himself still vicious.'[2] Here, then, we seem to have a clear theory of moral evil as consisting in selfish, of moral good as consisting in unselfish affections. But what exactly constitutes a selfish affection, according to Shaftesbury? The answer that first suggests itself, is that as the unselfish affection is an affection for public good, so a selfish one is an affection for 'self-good,' the good of the 'private system.' Shaftesbury, however, does not give this answer. 'Affection for private good' with him is not, as such, selfish; it is so only when 'excessive' and 'inconsistent with the interest of the species or public.'[3] This qualification seems at once to efface the clear line of distinction previously drawn. It puts 'self-affection' on a level with public affection which, according

[1] 'Inquiry concerning Virtue,' BOOK I., part 2, sec. 1.

[2] Ibid., BOOK I., part 2, sec. 2.

[3] Ibid., BOOK II., part 1, sec. 3.

to Shaftesbury, may equally err on the side of excess. It implies that an affection for self-good, if only it be advantageous to the species, may be good; which is just what had been previously denied. And not only so; although, when the self-affections are under view, they are only allowed a qualified goodness in virtue of their indirect contribution to the good of the species, yet conversely, the superiority of the affections, which have this latter good for their object, is urged specially on the ground of the greater amount of happiness or 'self-good' which they produce.

23. The truth is that the notions which Shaftesbury attached to the terms 'affection for self-good' and 'affection for public good' were not such as allowed of a consistent opposition between them. They can only be so opposed if, on the one hand, self-good is identified with pleasure; and on the other, affection for public good is carefully distinguished from desire for that sort of pleasure of which the gratification of others is a condition. But with Shaftesbury, affections for self-good do not represent merely those desires for pleasure determined by self-consciousness—for pleasure presented as one's personal good—which can alone be properly reckoned sources of moral evil. They include equally mere natural appetites—hunger, the sexual impulse, &c.—which are morally neutral, and they do not clearly exclude any desire for an object which a man has so 'made his own' as to find his happiness—'self-enjoyment' or 'self-good,' according to Shaftesbury's language—in attaining it, though it be as remote from imagined pleasure as possible.[1] On the other hand, 'affections for public good,' as he describes them, are not restricted to such desires for the good of others as are irrespective of pleasure to self. They include not only such natural instincts as 'parental kindness and concern for the nurture and propagation of the young,' which, morally, at any rate, are not to be distinguished from the appetites reckoned as affections for self-good, but also desires for sympathetic pleasure—the pleasure to oneself which arises on consciousness that another is pleased. Shaftesbury's special antipathy, indeed, is the doctrine that benevolent affections are interested in the sense of having for their object a pleasure to oneself, apart from and beyond the pleasure of the person whom they move us to please; but

[1] BOOK II., part 2, sec. 2.

unless he regards them as desires for the pleasure which the subject of them experiences in the pleasure of another, there is no purpose in enlarging, as he does with much unction, on the special pleasantness of the pleasures which they produce. With such vagueness in his notions of what he meant by affections for ' self-good ' and for ' public good,' it is not strange that he should have failed to give any tenable account of the selfishness in which he conceived moral evil to consist. He could not apply such a term of reproach to the ' self-affections ' in general, without condemning as selfish the man who ' finds his own happiness in doing good,' and who is in truth indistinguishable from one to whom ' affection for public good ' has become, as we say, the law of his being. Nor could he identify selfishness, as he should have done, with all living for pleasure without a more complete rupture than he was capable of with the received doctrine of his time and without bringing affection for public good, in the form in which it was most generally conceived, and which was, at any rate, one of the forms under which he presented it to himself—as desire, namely, for sympathetic pleasure—into the same condemnation. His way out of the difficulty is, as we have seen, in violation of his own principle to find the characteristic of selfishness not in the motive of any affection but in its result; not in the fact that a man's desire has his own good for its object, which is true of one to whom his neighbour's good is as his own, nor in the fact that it has pleasure for its object, which Shaftesbury, as the child of his age, could scarcely help thinking was the case with every desire, but in the fact that it is stronger than is ' consistent with the interest of the species or public.'

24. Neither Butler nor Hutcheson[1] can claim to have carried the ethical controversy much beyond the point at which Shaftesbury left it. Each took for granted that the object of the ' self-affection ' was necessarily one's own happiness, and neither made any distinction between living for happiness and living for pleasure. They could not then identify selfishness with the living for pleasure without con-

[1] The works of Hutcheson, published before Hume's treatise was written, and which strongly affected it, were the ' Enquiry into the Original of our Ideas of Beauty and Virtue ' (1725), and the ' Essay on the Nature and Conduct of the Passions and Affections' (1728). In what follows I wrote with direct reference to his posthumous work, not published till after Hume's treatise, but which only reproduces more systematically his earlier views.

demning the self-affection, and with it the best man's
pursuit of his own highest good in the service of others,
altogether as evil. Nor in the absence of any better theory
of the object of the self-affection could the social affections,
which, according to Butler, are subject in the developed man
to the direction of self-love, escape the suggestion that they
are one mode of the general desire for pleasure. Butler and
Hutcheson, indeed, are quite clear that they are 'disinterested' in the sense of 'terminating upon their objects.'[1]
This means, what is sufficiently obvious when once pointed
out, (a) that a benevolent desire is not a desire for that
particular pleasure, or rather 'removal of uneasiness,' which
shall ensue when it is satisfied, and (b) that it cannot originally arise from the general desire for happiness, since this
creates no pleasures but merely directs us to the pursuit of
objects found pleasant independently of it, and thus, if it
directs us to benevolent acts, presupposes a pleasure previously found in them. This, however, as Butler points out,
is equally true of all particular desires whatever—of those
styled self-regarding, no less than of the social—and if it is
not incompatible with the former being desires for pleasure,
no more is it with the latter being so. Much confusion on
the matter, it may be truly said, arises from the loose way
in which the words 'affection' and 'passion' are used by
Butler and his contemporaries, not excluding Hume himself,
alike for appetite, desire, and emotion. In every case a
pleasure other than satisfaction of desire must have been
experienced before desire can be excited by the imagination
of it. A pleasure incidental to the satisfaction of *appetite*
must have been experienced before imagination of it could
excite the *desire* of the glutton. In like manner, social
affection, as *desire*, cannot be first excited by the pleasure
which shall arise when it is satisfied; it must previously
exist as the condition of that pleasure being experienced;
but it does not follow that it is other than a desire for
an imagined pleasure, for that sympathetic pleasure in the
pleasure of another in which the social affection as *emotion*
consists. Now though Butler and Hutcheson sufficiently
showed that it is no other pleasure than this which is the
original object of benevolent desires, they did not attempt
to show that it is not this; and failing such an attempt, the

[1] See in Preface to Butler's Sermons,
the part relating to Sermon XI., 'Besides, the only idea of an interested
pursuit' &c.; also the early part of
Sermon XI., 'Every man hath a general desire,' &c.

received doctrine that the object of all desire, social and self-regarding alike, is pleasure of one sort or another, would naturally be taken to stand. This admitted, there can be nothing in the fact that a certain pleasure depends on the pleasure of another, and that a certain other does not, to entitle an action moved by desire for the former sort of pleasure to be called unselfish in the way of praise, and one moved by desire for the latter sort selfish in the way of reproach. The motive—desire for his own pleasure—is the same to the doer in both cases. The distinction between the acts can only lie in that which Shaftesbury had said could not constitute moral good or ill—in the consequences by which society judges of them, but which do not form the motive of the agent. In other words, it will be a distinction fixed by that law of opinion or reputation, in which Locke had found the common measure of virtue and vice, though he had not entered on the question of the considerations by which that law is formed.

25. Such a conclusion would lie ready to hand for such a reader of Butler and Hutcheson as we may suppose Hume to have been, but it is needless to say that it is not that at which they themselves arrive. Butler, indeed, distinctly refuses to identify moral good and evil respectively with disinterested and interested action,[1] but neither does he admit that desire for pleasure or aversion from pain is the uniform motive of action in such a way as to compel the conclusion that moral good and ill represent a distinction, not of motives, but of consequences of action contemplated by the onlooker. An act is morally good, according to him, when it is approved by the ' reflex faculty of approbation,' bad when it is disapproved, but what it is that this ' faculty ' approves he never distinctly tells us. The good is what ' conscience ' approves, and conscience is what approves the good—that is the circle out of which he never escapes. If we insist on extracting from him any more satisfactory conclusion as to the object of moral approbation, it must be that it is the object which ' self-love ' pursues, i.e., the greatest happiness of the individual, a conclusion which in

---

[1] See preface to Sermons (about four pages from the end in most editions):— ' The goodness or badness of actions does not arise hence,' &c. The conclusion he there arrives at is that a good action is one which ' becomes such creatures as we are '; and this, read in the light of the second sermon, must be understood to mean an action ' suitable to our whole nature,' as containing a principle of ' reflex approbation.' In other words, the good action is so because approved by conscience.

some places he certainly adopts.[1] Hutcheson, on the other
hand, gives a plain definition of the object which this faculty
approves. It consists in 'affections tending to the happiness
of others and the moral perfection of the mind possessing
them.' If in this definition by 'tending to' may be understood ' of which the motive is '—an interpretation which
the general tenor of Hutcheson's view would justify—it
implies in effect that the morally good lies in desires of
which the object is not pleasure. That desire for moral
perfection, if there is such a thing, is not desire for pleasure
is obvious enough; nor could desire for the happiness of
others be taken to be so except through confusion between
determination by the conception of another's good, to which
his apparent pleasure is rightly or wrongly taken as a
guide, and by the imagination of a pleasure to be experienced
by oneself in sympathy with the pleasure of another. Nor
is it doubtful that Hutcheson himself, though he might
have hesitated to identify moral evil, as selfishness, with the
living for pleasure, yet understood by the morally good the
living for objects wholly different from pleasure. The
question is whether the recognition of such motives is
logically compatible with his doctrine that reason gives no
ends, but is only a ' subservient power ' of calculating means.
If feeling, undetermined by thought or reason, can alone
supply motives, and of feeling, thus undetermined, nothing
can be said but that it is pleasant or painful, what motive
can there be but imagination of one's own pleasure or pain
—*one's own*, for if imagination is merely the return of
feeling in fainter form, no one can imagine any feeling, any
more than he can originally feel it, except as his own ?

26. The work of reason in constituting the moral judgment
(' I ought '), as well as the moral motive (' I must, because I
ought '), could not find due recognition in an age which
took its notion of reason from Locke. The only theory then
known which found the source of moral distinctions in
reason was Clarke's, and Clarke's notion of reason was
essentially the same as that which appears in Locke's
account of demonstrative knowledge.[2] It was in truth

---

[1] See a passage towards the end of
Sermon III., 'Reasonable self-love and
conscience are the chief,' &c. &c.; also
a passage towards the end of Sermon
XI., 'Let it be allowed though virtue,'
&c. &c.

[2] See Clarke's Boyle Lectures, Vol.

ii., proposition 1. The germ of Clarke's
doctrine of morals is to be found in
Locke's occasional assimilation of
moral to mathematical truth and certainty. (Cf. Essay, Book iv, ch. 4, sec. 7,
and ch. 12, sec. 8.

derived from the procedure of mathematics, and only applicable to the comparison of quantities. Clarke talks loftily
about the Eternal Reason of things, but by this he means
nothing definite except the laws of proportion, and when he
finds the virtue of an act to consist in conformity to this
Eternal Reason, the inevitable rejoinder is the question—
Between what quantities is this virtue a proportion?[1] In
Shaftesbury first appears a doctrine of moral sense. Over
and above the social and self-regarding affections proper to
a 'sensible' creature, the characteristic of man is a 'rational
affection' for goodness as consisting in the proper adjustment of the two orders of 'sensible' affection. This rational
affection is not only a possible motive to action—it is the
only motive that can make that character good of which
human action is the expression ; for with Shaftesbury, though
a balance of the social and self-affections constitutes the
goodness of those affections, yet the man is only good as
actuated by affection for this goodness, and 'should the
sensible affections stand ever so much amiss, yet if they
prevail not because of those other rational affections spoken
of, the person is esteemed virtuous.'[2] Such a notion, it is
clear, if it had met with a psychology answering it, had only
to be worked out in order to become Kant's doctrine of the
rational will as determined by reverence for law; but
Shaftesbury had no such psychology, nor, with his aristo-
cratic indifference to completeness of system, does he seem
ever to have felt the want of it. He never asked himself
what precisely was the theory of reason implied in the
admission of an affection 'rational' in the sense, not that
reason calculates the means to its satisfaction, but that it is
determined by an object only possible for a rational as
distinct from a 'sensible' creature; and just because he did
not do so, he slipped into adaptations to the current view of
the good as pleasure and of desire as determined by the
pleasure incidental to its own satisfaction. Thus, to a
disciple, who wished to extract from Shaftesbury a more
definite system than Shaftesbury had himself formed, the
'rational affection' would become desire for a specific feeling
of pleasure supposed to arise on the view of good actions as
exhibiting a proper balance between social and self-regarding

[1] Cf. Hume, Vol. ii., p. 238.
[2] 'Inq. concern'ng Virtue,' Book i., pt. 2, sec. 4. Cf. Sec. 3 sub init.

affections. This pleasure is the 'moral sense,'[1] with which Shaftesbury's name has become specially associated, while the doctrine of rational affection, with which he certainly himself connected it, but which it essentially vitiates, has been forgotten.

27. That doctrine is of value as maintaining that those actions only are morally good of which the rational affection is the motive, in the sense that they spring from a character which this affection has fashioned. But if the rational affection is desire for the pleasure of moral sense, we find ourselves in the contradiction of supposing that the only motive which can produce good acts is one that cannot operate till after the good acts have been done. It is desire for a pleasure which yet can only have been experienced as a consequence of the previous existence of the desire. Shaftesbury himself, indeed, treats the moral sense of pleasure in the contemplation of good actions as a pleasure in the view of the right adjustment between the social and self-affections. If, however, on the strength of this, we suppose that certain actions are first done, not from the rational affection, but yet good, and that then remembrance of the pleasure found in the view of their goodness, exciting desire, becomes motive to another set of acts which are thus done from rational affection, we contradict his statement that only the rational affection forms the goodness of man, and are none the nearer to an account of what does form it. To say that it is the 'right adjustment' of the two orders of affection tells us nothing. Except as suggesting an analogy from the world of art, really inapplicable, but by which Shaftesbury was much influenced, this expression means no more than that goodness is a good state of the affections. From such a circle the outlet most consistent with the spirit of that philosophy, which had led Shaftesbury himself to bring down the rational affection to the level of a desire for pleasure, would lie in the notion that a state of the affections is good in proportion as it is productive of pleasure; which again would suggest the question whether the specific pleasure of moral sense itself, the supposed object of rational affection, is more than pleasure in that indefinite

---

[1] In using the term 'moral sense,' Shaftesbury himself, no doubt, meant to convey the notion that the moral faculty was one of 'intuition,' in Locke's sense of the word, as opposed to reason, the faculty of demonstration, rather than that it was a susceptibility of pleasure and pain.

anticipation of pleasure which the view of affections so ordered tends to raise in us.

28. Here, again, neither Butler nor Hutcheson, while they avoid the most obvious inconsistency of Shaftesbury's doctrine, do much for its positive development. With each the 'moral faculty,' though it is said to approve and disapprove, is still a 'sense' or 'sentiment,' a specific susceptibility of pleasure in the contemplation of goodness; and each again recognises a 'reflex affection' for—a desire to have—the goodness of which the view conveys this pleasure. But they neither have the merit of stating so explicitly as Shaftesbury does that this rational affection alone constitutes the goodness of man, as man; nor, on the other hand, do they lapse, as he does, into the representation of it as a desire for the pleasure which the view of goodness causes. Butler, indeed, having no account to give of the goodness which is approved or morally pleasing, but the fact that it is so pleasing, could logically have nothing to say against the view that this reflex affection is merely a desire for this particular sort of pleasure; but by representing it as equivalent in its highest form to the love of God, to the longing of the soul after Him as the perfectly good, he in effect gives it a wholly different character. Hutcheson, by his definition of the object of moral approbation,[1] which is also a definition of the object of the reflex affection, is fairly entitled to exclude, as he does, along with the notion that the goodness which we morally approve is the quality of exciting the pleasure of such approval, the notion that 'affection for goodness' means desire for this or any other pleasure. But, in spite of his express rejection of this view, the question will still return, how either a faculty of consciousness of which we only know that it is 'a kind of taste or relish,' or a desire from the determination of which reason is expressly excluded, can have any other object than pleasure or pain.

29. In contrast with these well-meant efforts to derive that distinction between the selfish and unselfish, between the pleasant and the morally good, which the Christian conscience requires, from principles that do not admit of it, Hume's system has the merit of relative consistency. He sees that the two sides of Locke's doctrine—one that thought originates nothing, but takes its objects as given in feeling, the other that the good which is object of desire is pleasant

---

[1] See above, sec. 25.

feeling—are inseparable. Hence he decisively rejects every notion of rational or unselfish affections, which would imply that they are other than desires for pleasure; of virtue, which would imply that it antecedently determines, rather than is constituted by, the specific pleasure of moral sense; and of this pleasure itself, which would imply that anything but the view of tendencies to produce pleasure can excite it. But here his consistency stops. The principle which forbade him to admit any object of desire but pleasure is practically forgotten in his account of the sources of pleasure, and its being so forgotten is the condition of the desire for pleasure being made plausibly to serve as a foundation for morals. It is the assumption of pleasures determined by objects only possible for reason, made in the treatise on the Passions, that prepares the way for the rejection of reason, as supplying either moral motive or moral standard, in the treatise on Morals.

30. 'The passions' is Hume's generic term for 'impressions of reflection'—appetites, desires, and emotions alike. He divides them into two main orders, 'direct and indirect,' both 'founded on pain and pleasure.' The *direct* passions are enumerated as 'desire and aversion, grief and joy, hope and fear, along with volition' or will. These 'arise from good and evil' (which are the same as pleasure and pain) 'most naturally and with least preparation.' 'Desire arises from good, aversion from evil, considered simply.' They become will or volition, 'when the good may be attained or evil avoided by any action of the mind or body'—will being simply 'the internal impression we feel and are conscious of, when we knowingly give rise to any new motion of our body or new perception of our mind.' 'When good is certain or probable it produces joy' (which is described also as a pleasure produced by pleasure or by the imagination of pleasure); 'when it is uncertain, it gives rise to hope.' To these the corresponding opposites are grief and fear. We must suppose them to be distinguished from desire and aversion as being what he elsewhere calls 'pure emotions'; such as do not, like desires, 'immediately excite us to action.' Given such an immediate impression of pleasure or pain as excites a 'distinct passion' of one or other of these kinds, and supposing it to 'arise from an object related to ourselves or others,' it excites mediately, through this relation, the new impressions of pride

or humility, love or hatred—pride when the object is related to oneself, love when it is related to another person. These are *indirect* passions. They do not tend to displace the immediate impression which is the condition of their excitement, but being themselves agreeable give it additional force. 'Thus a suit of fine clothes produces pleasure from their beauty; and this pleasure produces the direct passions, or the impressions of volition and desire. Again, when these clothes are considered as belonging to oneself, the double relation conveys to us the sentiment of pride, which is an indirect passion; and the pleasure which attends that passion returns back to the direct affections, and gives new force to our desire or volition, joy or hope.'[1]

31. Alongside of the unqualified statement that 'the passions, both direct and indirect, are founded on pain and pleasure,' and the consequent theory of them, we find the curiously cool admission that ' beside pain and pleasure, the direct passions frequently arise from a natural impulse or instinct, which is perfectly unaccountable. Of this kind is the desire of punishment to our enemies, and of happiness to our friends; hunger and lust, and a few other bodily appetites. These passions, properly speaking, produce good and evil, and proceed not from them like the other affections.'[2] In this casual way appears the recognition of that difference of the desire for imagined pleasure from appetite proper on the one side, and on the other from desire determined by reason, which it is the point of Hume's system to ignore. The question is, how many of the pleasures in which he finds the springs of human conduct are other than products of a desire which is not itself moved by pleasure, or emotions excited by objects which reason constitutes.

---

[1] Vol. II., pp. 214, 215. Cf. pp. 76, 90, 153 and 203.

[2] P. 215. The passage in the ' Dissertation on the Passions' (Vol. IV., 'Dissertation on the Passions,' sub init.), which corresponds to the one here quoted, throws light on the relation in which Hume's later redaction of his theory stands to the earlier, as occasionally disguising, but never removing, its inconsistencies. 'Some objects, by being naturally conformable or contrary to passion, excite an agreeable or painful sensation, and are thence called *good* or *evil*. The punishment of an adversary, by gratifying revenge, is good : the sickness of a companion, by affecting friendship, is evil.' Here he avoids the inconsistency of admitting in so many words a ' desire' which is not for a pleasure. But the inconsistency really remains. What is the passion, the 'conformability' to which of an object in the supposed cases constitutes pleasure ? Since it is neither an appetite (such as hunger), nor an emotion (such as pride), it remains that it is a desire, and a desire which, though the ' gratification' of it is a pleasure, cannot be a desire for that or any other pleasure.

32. In what sense, we have first to ask, do Hume's principles justify him in speaking of desire *for an object* at all. 'The appearance of an object to the senses' is the same thing as 'an impression becoming present to the mind,'[1] and if this is true of impressions of sense it cannot be less true of impressions of reflection. If sense 'offers not its object as anything distinct from itself,' neither can desire. Its object, according to Hume, is an idea of a past impression; but this, if we take him at his word, can merely mean that a feeling which, when at its liveliest, was pleasant, has passed into a fainter stage, which, in contrast with the livelier, is pain—the pain of want, which is also a wish for the renewal of the original pleasure. In fact, however, when Hume or anyone else (whether he admit the possibility of desiring an object not previously found pleasant, or no), speaks of desire for an object, he means something different from this. He means either desire for an object that causes pleasure, which is impossible except so far as the original pleasure has been—consciously to the subject feeling it— pleasure caused by an object, *i.e.*, a feeling determined by the conception of a thing under relations to self; or else desire for pleasure as an object, *i.e.*, not merely desire for the revival of some feeling which, having been pleasant as 'impression,' survives without being pleasant as 'idea,' but desire determined by the consciousness of self as a permanent subject that has been pleased, and is to be pleased again. It is here, then, as in the case of the attempted derivation of space, or of identity and substance, from impressions of sense. In order to give rise to such an impression of reflection as desire for an object is, either the original impression of sense, or the idea of this, must be other than Hume could allow it to be. Either the original impression must be other than a satisfaction of appetite, other than a sight, smell, sound, &c., or the idea must be other than a copy of the impression. One or other must be determined by conceptions not derived from feeling, the correlative conceptions of self and thing. Thus, in order to be able to interpret his primary class of impressions of reflection[2] as desires for objects, or for pleasures as good, Hume has already made the assumption that is needed for the transition to that

---

[1] See General Introduction, paragraph 208.   [2] See above, sec. 19.

secondary class of impressions through which he has to account for morality. He has assumed that thought determines feeling, and not merely reproduces it. Even if the materials out of which it constructs the determining object be merely remembered pleasures, the object is no more to be identified with these materials than the living body with its chemical constituents.

33. In the account of the 'indirect passions' the term *object* is no longer applied, as in the account of the direct ones, to the pleasure or pain which excites desire or aversion. It is expressly transferred to the self or other person, to whom the 'exciting causes' of pride and love must be severally related. 'Pride and humility, though directly contrary, have yet the same object,' viz., self; but since they are contrary, ''tis impossible this object can be their cause, or sufficient alone to excite them. . . . . We must therefore make a distinction betwixt that idea which excites them, and that to which they direct their view when excited. . . . . The first idea that is presented to the mind is that of the cause or productive principle. This excites the passion connected with it; and that passion, when excited, turns our view to another idea, which is that of self. . . . . The first idea represents the *cause*, the second the *object* of the passion.'[1] Again a further distinction must be made 'in the causes of the passion betwixt that *quality* which operates, and the *subject* on which it is placed. A man, for instance, is vain of a beautiful house which belongs to him, or which he has himself built or contrived. Here the object of the passion is himself, and the cause is the beautiful house; which cause again is subdivided into two parts, viz., the quality which operates upon the passion, and the subject in which the quality inheres. The quality is the beauty, and the subject is the house, considered as his property or contrivance.'[2] It is next found that the operative qualities which produce pride, however various, agree in this, that they produce pleasure—a 'separate pleasure,' independent of the resulting pride. In all cases, again, 'the subjects to which these qualities adhere are either parts of ourselves or something nearly related to us.' The conclusion is that 'the cause, which excites the passion, is related to the

object which nature has attributed to the passion; the sensation, which the cause separately produces, is related to the sensation of the passion: from this double relation of ideas and impressions the passion is derived.'[1] The ideas, it will be observed, are severally those of the exciting 'subject' (in the illustrative case quoted, the beautiful house) and of the 'object' self; the impressions are severally the pleasure immediately caused by the 'subject' (in the case given, the pleasure of feeling beauty) and the pleasure of pride. The relation between the ideas may be any of the 'natural ones' that regulate association.[2] In the supposed case it is that of cause and effect, since a man's property 'produces effects on him and he on it.' The relation between the impressions must be that of resemblance—this, as we are told by the way (somewhat strangely, if impressions are only stronger ideas), being the only possible relation between impressions—the resemblance of one pleasure to another.

34. Pride, then, is a special sort of pleasure excited by another special sort of pleasure, and the distinction of the two sorts of pleasure from each other depends on the character which each derives from an idea—one from the idea of self, the other from the idea of some 'quality in a subject,' which may be the beauty of a picture, or the achievement of an ancestor, or any other quality as unlike these as these are unlike each other, so long as the idea of it is capable of association with the idea of self. Apart from such determination by ideas, the pleasure of pride itself and the pleasure which excites it, on the separateness of which from each other Hume insists, could only be separate in time and degree of liveliness—a separation which might equally obtain between successive feelings of pride. Of neither could anything be said but that it was pleasant— more or less pleasant than the other, before or after it, as the case might be. Is the idea, then, that gives each impression its character, itself an impression grown fainter? It should be so, of course, if Hume's theory of consciousness is to hold good, either in its general form, or in its application to morals, according to which all actions, those moved by pride among the rest, have pleasure for their ultimate motive; and no doubt he would have said that it was so.

The idea of the beauty of a picture, for instance, is the original impression which it 'makes on the senses' as more faintly retained by the mind. But is the original impression *merely* an impression—an impression undetermined by conceptions, and of which, therefore, as it is to the subject of it, nothing can be said, but simply that it is pleasant? This, too, in the particular instance of beauty, Hume seems to hold;[1] but if it is so, the idea of beauty, as determined by reference to the impression, is determined by reference to the indeterminate, and we know no more of the separate pleasure that excites the pleasure of pride, when we are told that its source is an impression of beauty, than we did before. Apart from any other reference, we only know that pride is a pleasure excited by a pleasure which is itself excited by a pleasure grown fainter. Of effect, proximate cause, and ultimate cause, only one and the same thing can be said, viz., that each feels pleasant. Meanwhile in regard to that other relation from which the pleasure of pride, on its part, is supposed to take its character, the same question arises. This pleasure 'has self for its object.' Is self, then, an impression stronger or fainter? Can one feeling be said without nonsense to have another feeling for its object? If it can, what specification is gained for a pleasure or pain by reference to an object of which, as a mere feeling, nothing more can be said than that it is a pleasure or pain? If, on the other hand, the idea of self, relation to which makes the feeling of pride what it is, and through it determines action, is not a copy of any impression of sense or reflection—not a copy of any sight or sound, any passion or emotion[2]—how can it be true that the ultimate determination of action in all cases arises from pleasure or pain?

35. From the pressure of such questions as these Hume offers us two main subterfuges. One is furnished by his account of the self, as 'that succession of related ideas and impressions of which we have an intimate memory and consciousness'[3]—an account which, to an incurious reader, conveys the notion that 'self,' if not exactly an impression, is something in the nature of an impression, while yet it seems to give the required determination to the impression which has this for its 'object.' It is evident, however, that

[1] Vol. II., p. 96; IV., 'Dissertation on the Passions,' II. 7.

[2] Intr. to Vol. I., paragraph 208.

[3] Vol. II., p. 77, &c.

its plausibility depends entirely on the qualification of the
' succession, &c.,' as that of which we have an ' intimate consciousness.' The succession of impressions, simply as such,
and in the absence of relation to a single subject, is nothing
intelligible at all. Hume, indeed, elsewhere represents it as
constituting time, which, as we have previously shown,[1] by
itself it could not properly be said to do; but if it could,
the characterisation of pleasure as having time for its object
would not be much to the purpose. The successive impressions and ideas are further said to be ' related,' *i.e.*,
naturally related, according to Hume's sense of the term;
but this we have found means no more than that when two
feelings have been often felt to be either like each other or
' contiguous,' the recurrence of one is apt to be followed by
the recurrence in fainter form of the other. This characteristic of the succession brings it no nearer to the intelligible unity which it must have, in order to be an object of
which the idea makes the pleasure of pride what it is. The
notion of its having such unity is really conveyed by the
statement that we have an ' intimate consciousness ' of it.
It is through these words, so to speak, that we read into the
definition of self that conception of it which we carry with
us, but of which it states the reverse. Now, however
difficult it may be to say what this intimate consciousness is,
it is clear that it cannot be one of the feelings, stronger or
fainter—impressions or ideas—which the first part of the
definition tells us form a succession, for this would imply
that one of them was at the same time all the rest. Nor
yet can it be a compound of them all, for the fact that they
are a succession is incompatible with their forming a compound. Here, then, is a consciousness, which is not an
impression, and which we can only take to be derived from
impressions by supposing these to be what they first become
in relation to this consciousness. In saying that we have
such a consciousness of the succession of impressions, we
say in effect that we are other than the succession. How,
then, without contradiction, can our self be said to *be* the
succession of impressions, &c.—a succession which in the very
next word has to be qualified in a way that implies we are
other than it? This question, once put, will save us from

---

[1] Intr. to Vol. I., sec. 261.

surprise at finding that in one place, among frequent repetitions of the account of self already given, the 'succession &c.' is dropped, and for it substituted ' *the individual person* of whose actions and sentiments each of us is intimately conscious.' [1]

36. The other way of gaining an apparent determination for the impression, pride, without making it depend on relation to that which is not an impression at all, corresponds to that appeal to the 'anatomist' by the suggestion of which, it will be remembered, Hume avoids the troublesome question, how the simple impressions of sense, undetermined by relation, can have that definite character which they must have if they are to serve as the elements of knowledge. The question in that case being really one that concerns the simple impression, as it is for the consciousness of the subject of it, Hume's answer is in effect a reference to what it is for the physiologist. So in regard to pride; the question being what character it can have, for the conscious subject of it, to distinguish it from any other pleasant feeling, except such as is derived from a conception which is not an impression, Hume is ready on occasion to suggest that it has the distinctive character which for the physiologist it would derive from the nerves organic to it, if such nerves could be traced. ' We must suppose that nature has given to the organs of the human mind a certain disposition fitted to produce a peculiar impression or emotion, which we call PRIDE: to this emotion she has assigned a certain idea, viz., that of SELF, which it never fails to produce. This contrivance of nature is easily conceived. We have many instances of such a situation of affairs. The nerves of the nose and palate are so disposed, as in certain circumstances to convey such peculiar sensations to the mind; the sensations of lust and hunger always produce in us the idea of those peculiar objects, which are suitable to each appetite. These two circumstances are united in pride. The organs are so disposed as to produce the passion; and the passion, after its production, naturally produces a certain idea.' [2]

37. Here, it will be noticed, the doctrine, that the pleasant emotion of pride derives its specific character from relation to the idea of self, is dropped. The emotion we call pride is

[1] Vol. II., p. 84.   [2] Vol. II., p. 85.

supposed to be first produced, and then, in virtue of its specific character as pride, to *produce* the idea of self.[1] If the idea of self, then, does not give the pleasure its specific character, what does? 'That disposition fitted to produce it,' Hume answers, which belongs to the 'organs of the human mind.' Now either this is the old story of explaining the soporific qualities of opium by its *vis soporifica*, or it means that the distinction of the pleasure of pride from other pleasures, like the distinction of a smell from a taste, is due to a particular kind of nervous irritation that conditions it, and may presumably be ascertained by the physiologist. Whether such a physical condition of pride can be discovered or no, it is not to the purpose to dispute. The point to observe is that, if discovered, it would not afford an answer to the question to which an answer is being sought —to the question, namely, what the emotion of pride is to the conscious subject of it. If it were found to be conditioned by as specific a nervous irritation as the sensations of smell and taste to which Hume assimilates it, it would yet be no more the consciousness of such irritation than is the smell of a rose to the person smelling it. In the one case as in the other, the feeling, as it is to the subject of it, can only be determined by relation to other feelings or other modes of consciousness. It is by such a relation that, according to Hume's general account of it, pride is determined, but the relation is to the consciousness of an object which, not being any form of feeling, has no proper place in his psychology. Hence in the passage before us he tries to substitute for it a physical determination of the emotion, which for the subject of it is no determination at all; and, having gained an apparent specification for it in this way, to represent as its product that idea of a distinctive object which he had previously treated as necessary to constitute it. Pride produces the idea of self, just as 'the sensations of hunger and lust always produce in us the idea of those peculiar objects, which are suitable to each appetite.' Now it is a large assumption in regard to animals other than men, that, because hunger and lust move them to eat and generate, they so move them through the intervention of any ideas *of objects* whatever—an assumption which in the absence of

---

[1] Cf. Vol. IV., 'Dissertation on the Passions,' II. 2.

language on the part of the animals it is impossible to verify
—and one still more questionable, that the ideas of objects
which these appetites (if it be so) produce in the animals,
except as determined by self-consciousness, are ideas in the
same sense as the idea of self. But at any rate, if such
feelings produce ideas of peculiar objects, it must be in
virtue of the distinctive character which, as feelings, they
have for the subjects of them. The withdrawal, however,
of determination by the idea of self from the emotion of
pride, leaves it with no distinctive character whatever, and
therefore with nothing by which we may explain its production of that idea as analogous to the production by hunger,
if we admit such to take place, of the 'idea of the peculiar
object suited to it.'

38. If, in Hume's account of pride, for *pleasure*, wherever
it occurs, is substituted *pain*, it becomes his account of
humility. A criticism of one account is equally a criticism
of the other; and with him every passion that 'has self for
its object,' according as it is pleasant or painful, is included
under one or other of these designations. In like manner,
every passion that has 'some other thinking being' for its
object, according as it is pleasant or painful, is either love
or hatred. To these the key is to be found in the same
'double relation of impressions and ideas' by which pride
and humility are explained. If beautiful pictures, for
instance, belong not to oneself but to another person, they
tend to excite not pride but esteem, which is a form of love.
The idea of them is 'naturally related' to the idea of the
person to whom they belong, and they cause a separate
pleasure which naturally excites the resembling impression
of which this other person is the object. Write 'other
person,' in short, where before was written 'self,' and the
account of pride and humility becomes the account of love
and hatred. Of this pleasure determined by the idea of
another person, or of which such a person 'is the object,'
Hume gives no *rationale*, and, failing this, it must be taken
to imply the same power of determining feeling on the part
of a conception not derived from feeling, which we have
found to be implied in the pleasure of which self is the
object. All his pains and ingenuity in the second part of
the book 'on the Passions,' are spent on illustrating the
'double relation of impressions and ideas'—on characteris-

ing the separate pleasures which excite the pleasure of love,
and showing how the idea of the object of the exciting
pleasure is related to the idea of the beloved person. The
objection to this part of his theory, which most readily suggests itself to a reader, arises from the essential discrepancy
which in many cases seems to lie between the exciting and
the excited pleasure. The drinking of fine wine, and the
feeling of love, are doubtless 'resembling impressions,' so
far as each is pleasant, and from the idea of the wine the
transition is natural to that of the person who gives it; but
is there really anything, it will be asked, in my enjoyment
of a rich man's wine, that tends to make me love him, even
in the wide sense of 'love' which Hume admits? This
objection, it will be found, is so far anticipated by Hume,
that in most cases he treats the exciting pleasure as taking
its character from sympathy. Thus it is not chiefly the
pleasure of ear, sight, and palate, caused by the rich man's
music, and gardens, and wine, that excites our love for him,
but the pleasure we experience through sympathy with his
pleasure in them.[1] The explanation of love being thus
thrown back on sympathy (which had previously served to
explain that form of pride which is called 'love of fame'), we
have to ask whether sympathy is any less dependent than we
have found pride to be on an originative, as distinct from a
merely reproductive, reason.

39. 'When any affection is infused by sympathy, it is at
first known only by its effects, and by those external signs
in the countenance and conversation which convey an idea
of it.' By inference from effect to cause, 'we are convinced
of the reality of the passion,' conceiving it 'to belong to
another person, as we conceive any other matter of fact.'
This idea of another's affection 'is presently converted into
an impression, and acquires such a degree of force and vivacity as to become the very passion itself, and produce an
equal emotion as any original affection.' The conversion is
not difficult to account for when we reflect that 'all ideas
are borrowed from impressions, and that these two kinds of
perceptions differ only in the degrees of force and vivacity
with which they strike upon the soul. . . . As this difference
may be removed in some measure by a relation between the

impressions and ideas '—in the case before us, the relation
between the impression of one's own person and the idea
of another's, by which the vivacity of the former may be
conveyed to the latter—' 'tis no wonder an idea of a sentiment or passion may by this means be so enlivened as to
become the very sentiment or passion.'[1]

40. Upon this it must be remarked that the inference
from the external signs of an affection, according to Hume's
doctrine of inference, can only mean that certain impressions
of the other person's words and gestures call up the ideas
of their 'usual attendants'; which, again, must mean either
that they convey the belief in certain exciting circumstances
experienced by the other man, and the expectation of certain
acts to follow upon his words and gestures; or else that they
suggest to the spectator the memory of certain like manifestations on his own part and through these of the emotion
which in his own case was their antecedent. Either way,
the spectator's idea of the other person's affection is in no
sense a copy of it, or that affection in a fainter form. If it
is an idea of an impression *of reflection* at all, it is of such
an impression as experienced by the spectator himself, and
determined, as Hume admits, by his consciousness of himself;
nor could any conveyance of vivacity to the idea make it
other than that impression. How it should become to the
spectator consciously at once another's impression and his
own, remains unexplained. Hume only seems to explain it
by means of the equivocation lurking in the phrase, 'idea
of another's affection.' The reader, not reflecting that, according to the copying theory, so far as the idea is a copy
of anything *in the other*, it can only be a copy of certain
'external signs, &c.,' and so far as it is a copy *of an affection*,
only of an affection experienced by the man who has the idea,
thinks of it as being to the spectator the other's affection
minus a certain amount of vivacity—the restoration of which
will render it an impression at once his own and the other's.
It can in truth only be so in virtue (*a*) of an interpretation
of words and gestures, as related to a person, which no suggestion by impressions of their usual attendants can account
for, and in virtue (*b*) of there being such a conceived
identity, or unity in difference, between the spectator's own

person and the person of the other that the same impression, in being determined by his consciousness of himself, is determined also by his consciousness of the other as an ' alter ego.' Thus sympathy, according to Hume's account of it, so soon as that account is rationalized, is found to involve the determination of pleasure and pain, not merely by self-consciousness, but by a self-consciousness which is also self-identification with another. If self-consciousness cannot in any of its functions be reduced to an impression or succession of impressions, least of all can it in this. On the other hand, if it is only through its constitutive action, its reflection of itself upon successive impressions of sense, that these become the permanent objects which we know, we can understand how by a like action on certain impressions of reflection, certain emotions and desires, it constitutes those objects of interest which we love as ourselves.

41. Pride, love, and sympathy, then, are the motives which Hume must have granted him, if his moral theory is to march. Sympathy is not only necessary to his explanation of that most important form of pride which is the motive to a man in maintaining a character with his neighbours when ' nothing is to be gained by it '—nothing, that is, beyond the immediate pleasure it gives—and of all forms of ' love,' except those of which the exciting cause lies in the pleasures of beauty and sexual appetite : he finds in it also the ground of benevolence. Where he first treats of benevolence, indeed, this does not appear. Unlike pride and humility, we are told, which ' are pure emotions of the soul, unattended with any desire, and not immediately exciting us to action, love and hatred are not completed within themselves. . . Love is always followed by a desire of the happiness of the person beloved, and an aversion to his misery ; as hatred produces a desire of the misery, and an aversion to the happiness, of the person hated.' [1] This actual sequence of ' benevolence ' and ' anger ' severally upon love and hatred is due, it appears, to ' an original constitution of the mind ' which cannot be further accounted for. That benevolence is no essential part of love is clear from the fact that the latter passion ' may express itself in a hundred ways, and may subsist a considerable time, without our reflecting on the

happiness of its object.' Doubtless, when we do reflect on it, we desire the happiness; but, 'if nature had so pleased, love might have been unattended with any such desire.'[1] So far, the view given tallies with what we have already quoted from the summary account of the direct and indirect passions, where the 'desire of punishment to our enemies and happiness to our friends' is expressly left outside the general theory of the passions as a 'natural impulse wholly unaccountable,' a 'direct passion' which yet does not 'proceed from pleasure.' With his instinct for consistency, however, Hume could scarcely help seeking to assimilate this alien element to his definition of desire as universally for pleasure; and accordingly, while the above view of benevolence is never in so many words given up, an essentially different one appears a little further on, which by help of the doctrine of sympathy at once makes the connection of benevolence with love more accountable, and brings it under the general definition of desire. 'Benevolence,' we are there told, 'is an original pleasure arising from the pleasure of the person beloved, and a pain proceeding from his pain, from which correspondence of impressions there arises a subsequent desire of his pleasure and aversion to his pain.'[2]

42. Now, strictly construed, this passage seems to efface the one clear distinction of benevolence that had been previously insisted on—that it is a desire, namely, as opposed to a pure emotion. If benevolence *is* an 'original pleasure arising from the pleasure of the person beloved,' it is identical with love, so far as sympathy is an exciting cause of love, instead of being distinguished from it as desire from emotion. We must suppose, however, that the sentence was carelessly put together, and that Hume did not really mean to identify benevolence with the pleasure spoken of in the former part of it (for which his proper term is simply sympathy), but with the desire for that pleasure, spoken of in the latter part. In that case we find that benevolence forms no exception to the general definition of

[1] Vol. ii., p. 154.

[2] Vol. ii., p. 170. Compare Vol. iv., 'Inquiry concerning the Principles of Morals,' Appendix ii., *note* 3, where 'general benevolence,' also called 'humanity,' is identified with sympathy. 'Benevolence is naturally divided into two kinds, the *general* and the *particular*. The first is, where we have no friendship, or connection, or esteem for the person, but feel only a general sympathy with him, or a compassion for his pains, and a congratulation with his pleasures,' &c. &c.

desire. It is desire for one's own pleasure, but for a pleasure received through the communication by sympathy of the pleasure of another. In like manner, the sequence of benevolence upon love, instead of being an unaccountable 'disposition of nature,' would seem explicable, as merely the ordinary sequence upon a pleasant emotion of a desire for its renewal. Though it be not strictly the pleasant emotion of love, but that of sympathy, for which benevolence is the desire, yet if sympathy is necessary to the excitement of love, it will equally follow that benevolence attends on love. Pleasure sympathised with, we may suppose, first excites the secondary emotion of love, and afterwards, when reflected on, that desire for its continuance or renewal, which is benevolence. That love 'should express itself in a hundred ways, and subsist a considerable time' without any consciousness of benevolence, will merely be the natural relation of emotion to desire. When a pleasure is in full enjoyment, it cannot be so reflected on as to excite desire; and thus, if benevolence is desire for that pleasure in the pleasure of another, which is an exciting cause of love, the latter emotion must naturally subsist and express itself for some time before it reaches the stage in which reflection on its cause, and with it benevolent desire, ensues.

43. This *rationale*, however, of the relation between love and benevolence is not explicitly given by Hume himself. He nowhere expressly withdraws the exception, made in favour of benevolence, to the rule that all desire is for pleasure—an exception which, once admitted, undermines his whole system—or tells us in so many words that benevolence is desire for pleasure to oneself in the pleasure of another. In an important note to the Essays,[1] indeed, he distinctly puts benevolence on the same footing with such desires as avarice or ambition. 'A man is no more interested when he seeks his own glory, than when the happiness of his friend is the object of his wishes; nor is he any more disinterested when he sacrifices his own ease and quiet to public good, than when he labours for the gratification of avarice or ambition.' . . . 'Though the satisfaction of these latter passions gives us enjoyment, yet the prospect of this enjoyment is not the cause of the passion, but, on the

---

[1] 'Inquiry concerning Human Understanding,' note to sec. 1. In the editions after the second, this note was omitted.

contrary, the passion is antecedent to the enjoyment, and without the former the latter could not possibly exist.' In other words, if 'passion' means *desire*—and, as applied to *emotion*, the designation 'interested' or 'disinterested' has no meaning—every passion is equally disinterested in the sense of presupposing an 'enjoyment,' a pleasant emotion, antecedent to that which consists in its satisfaction; but at the same time equally interested in the sense of being a desire for such enjoyment. Whether from a wish to find acceptance, however, or because forms of man's good-will to man forced themselves on his notice which forbade the consistent development of his theory, Hume is always much more explicit about the disinterestedness of benevolence in the former sense than about its interestedness in the latter.[1] Accordingly he does not avail himself of such an explanation of its relation to love as that above indicated, which by avowedly reducing benevolence to a desire for pleasure, while it simplified his system, might have revolted the 'common sense' even of the eighteenth century. He prefers —as his manner is, when he comes upon a question which he cannot face—to fall back on a 'disposition of nature' as the ground of the 'conjunction' of benevolence with love. There is a form of benevolence, however, which would seem as little explicable by such natural conjunction as by reduction to a desire for sympathetic pleasure. How is it that active good-will is shown towards those whom, according to Hume's theory of love, it should be impossible to love—towards those with whom intercourse is impossible, or from whom, if intercourse is possible, we can derive no such pleasure as is supposed necessary to excite that pleasant emotion, but rather such pain, in sympathy with their pain, as according to the theory should excite hatred? To this question Hume in effect finds an answer in the simple device of using the same terms, 'pity' and 'compassion,' alike for the painful *emotion* produced by the spectacle of another's

[1] Attention should be called to a passage at the end of the account of 'self-love' in the Essays, where he seems to revert to the view of benevolence as a desire not *originally* produced by pleasure, but productive of it, and thus passing into a secondary stage in which it is combined with desire for pleasure. He suggests tentatively that 'from the original frame of our temper we may feel a desire for another's happiness or good, which, by means of that affection, becomes our own good, and is afterwards pursued from the combined motives of benevolence and self-enjoyment.' The passage might have been written by Butler. (Vol. IV., 'Inquiry concerning Principles of Morals,' Appendix II.)

pain and for 'desire for the happiness of another and aversion to his misery.' [1] According to the latter account of it, pity is already 'the same desire' as benevolence, though 'proceeding from a different principle,' and thus has a resemblance to the love with which benevolence is conjoined—a 'resemblance not of feeling or sentiment but of tendency or direction.' [2] Hence, whereas 'pity' in the former sense would make us hate those whose pain gives us pain, by understanding it in the latter sense we can explain how it leads us to love them, on the principle that one resembling passion excites another.

44. We are now in a position to review the possible motives of human action according to Hume. Reason, constituting no objects, affords no motives. 'It is only the slave of the passions, and can never pretend to any other office than to serve and obey them.' [3] To any logical thinker who accepted Locke's doctrine of reason, as having no other function but to 'lay in order intermediate ideas,' this followed of necessity. It is the clearness with which Hume points out that, as it cannot move, so neither can it restrain, action, that in this regard chiefly distinguishes him from Locke. The check to any passion, he points out, can only proceed from some counter-motive, and such a motive reason, 'having no original influence,' cannot give. Strictly speaking, then, a passion can only be called unreasonable, as accompanied by some false judgment, which on its part must consist in 'disagreement of ideas, considered as copies, with those objects which they represent;' and 'even then it is not the passion, properly speaking, which is unreasonable, but the judgment.' It is nothing against reason—not, as Locke had inadvertently said, a wrong judgment—'to prefer my own acknowledged lesser good to my greater.' The only unreasonableness would lie in supposing that 'my own acknowledged lesser good,' being preferred, could be attained by means that would not really lead to it. Hence 'we speak not strictly when we talk of the combat of reason and passion.' They can in truth never oppose each other. The supposition that they do so arises from a confusion between

---

[1] Book II., part 2, secs. 7 and 9. Within a few lines of each other will be found the statements (a) that 'pity is an uneasiness arising from the misery of others,' and (b) that 'pity is

desire for the happiness of another,' &c.

[2] 'Dissertation on the Passions' (in the Essays), sec. 3, sub-sec. 5.

[3] Vol. II., p. 195.

'calm passions' and reason—a confusion founded on the fact that the former 'produce little emotion in the mind, while the operation of reason produces none at all.' [1] Calm passions, undoubtedly, do often conflict with the violent ones and even prevail over them, and thus, as the violent passion causes most uneasiness, it is untrue to say with Locke [2] that it is the most pressing uneasiness which always determines action. The calmness of a passion is not to be confounded with weakness, nor its violence with strength. A desire may be calm either because its object is remote, or because it is customary. In the former case, it is true, the desire is likely to be relatively weak; but in the latter case, the calmer the desire, the greater is likely to be its strength, since the repetition of a desire has the twofold effect, on the one hand of diminishing the 'sensible emotion' that accompanies it, on the other hand of 'bestowing a facility in the performance of the action' corresponding to the desire, which in turn creates a new inclination or tendency that combines with the original desire. [3]

45. The distinction, then, between 'reasonable' and 'unreasonable' desires—and it is only *desires* that can be referred to when will, or the determination to action, is in question—in the only sense in which Hume can admit it, is a distinction not of objects but of our situation in regard to them. The object of desire in every case—whether near or remote, whether either by its novelty or by its contrariety to other passions it excites more or less 'sensible emotion'— is still 'good,' *i.e.* pleasure. The greater the pleasure in prospect, the stronger the desire. [4] The only proper question, then, according to Hume, as to the pleasure which in any particular case is an object of desire will be whether it

---

[1] Vol. ii., pp. 195, 196.
[2] Above, sec. 3.
[3] Vol. ii. pp. 198–200.

It will be found that here Hume might have stated his case much more succinctly by avoiding the equivocal use of 'passion' at once for 'desire' and 'emotion.' When a 'passion' is designated as 'calm' or 'violent,' 'passion' means emotion. When the terms 'strong' and 'weak' are applied to it, it means 'desire.' Since of the strength of any desire there is in truth no test but the resulting action, and habit facilitates action, if we will persist in asking the idle question about the relative strength of desires, we must suppose that the most habitual is the strongest.

[4] Cf. p. 198. 'The same good, when near, will cause a violent passion, which, when remote, produces only a calm one.' The expression, here, is obviously inaccurate. It cannot be the *same good* in Hume's sense, *i.e.* equally pleasant in prospect, when remote as when near.

is (*a*) an immediate impression of sense, or (*b*) a pleasure of pride, or (*c*) one of sympathy. Under the first head, apparently, he would include pleasures incidental to the satisfaction of appetite, and pleasures corresponding to the several senses—not only the smells and tastes we call 'sweet,' but the sights and sounds we call 'beautiful.'[1] Pleasures of this sort, we must suppose, are the *ultimate* 'exciting causes'[2] of all those secondary ones, which are distinguished from their 'exciting causes' as determined by the ideas either of self or of another thinking person—the pleasures, namely, of pride and sympathy. Sympathetic pleasure, again, will be of two kinds, according as the pleasure in the pleasure of another does or does not excite the further pleasure of love for the other person. If the object desired is none of these pleasures, nor the means to them, it only remains for the follower of Hume to suppose that it is 'pleasure in general'—the object of 'self love.'

46. Anyone reading the 'Treatise on Human Nature' alongside of Shaftesbury or Butler would be surprised to find that while sympathy and benevolence fill a very large place in it, self-love 'eo nomine' has a comparatively small one. At first, perhaps, he would please himself with thinking that he had come upon a more 'genial' system of morals. The true account of the matter, however, he will find to be that, whereas with Shaftesbury and his followers the notion of self-love was really determined by opposition to those desires for other objects than pleasure, in the existence of which they really believed, however much the current psychology may have embarrassed their belief, on the other hand with Hume's explicit reduction of all desire to desire for pleasure self-love loses the significance which this opposition gave it, and can have no meaning except as desire for 'pleasure in general' in distinction from this or that particular pleasure.

---

[1] No other account of pleasure in beauty can be extracted from Hume than this—that it is either a 'primary impression of sense,' so far co-ordinate with any pleasant taste or smell that but for an accident of language the term 'beautiful' might be equally applicable to these, or else a pleasure in that indefinite anticipation of pleasure which is called the contemplation of utility.

[2] *Ultimate* because according to Hume the *immediate* exciting cause of a pleasure of pride may be one of love, and *vice versa*. In that case, however, a more remote 'exciting cause' of the exciting pleasure must be found in some impressions of sense, if the doctrine that these are the sole 'original impressions' is to be maintained.

Passages from the Essays may be adduced, it is true, where self-love is spoken of under the same opposition under which Shaftesbury and Hutcheson conceived of it, but in these, it will be found, advantage is taken of the ambiguity between 'emotion' and 'desire,' covered by the term 'passion.' That there are sympathetic *emotions*—pleasures occasioned by the pleasure of others—is, no doubt, as cardinal a point in Hume's system as that all *desire* is for pleasure to self; but between such emotions and self-love there is no co-ordination. No emotion, as he points out, determines action directly, but only by exciting desire; which with him can only mean that the image of the pleasant emotion excites desire for its renewal. In other words, no emotion amounts to volition or will. Self-love, on the other hand, if it means anything, means desire and a possibly strongest desire, or will. It can thus be no more determined by opposition to generous or sympathetic *emotions* than can these by opposition to hunger and thirst. Hume, however, when he insists on the existence of generous 'passions' as showing that self-love is not our uniform motive, though he cannot consistently mean more than that desire for 'pleasure in general,' or desire for the satisfaction of desire, is not the uniform motive—which might equally be shown (as he admits) by pointing to such self-regarding 'passions' as love of fame, or such appetites as hunger—is yet apt, through the reader's interpretation of 'generous passions' as *desires* for something other than pleasure, to gain credit for recognising a possibility of living for others, in distinction from living for pleasure, which was in truth as completely excluded by his theory as by that of Hobbes. If he himself meant to convey any other distinction between self-love and the generous passions than one which would hold no less between it and every emotion whatever, it was through a fresh intrusion upon him of that notion of benevolence, as a 'desire not founded on pleasure,' which was in too direct contradiction to the first principles of his theory to be acquiesced in.[1]

---

[1] Cf. II. p. 197, where, speaking of 'calm desires,' he says they 'are of two kinds; either certain instincts originally implanted in our natures, such as benevolence and resentment, the love of life, and kindness to children; or the general appetite to good and aversion to evil, considered merely as such.' This seems to imply a twofold distinction of the 'general appetite to good' (a) from desires for particular pleasures, which are commonly not

47. Such desire, then, being excluded, what other motive than 'interest' remains, by contrast with which the latter may be defined? It has been explained above (§ 7) that since pleasure as such, or as a feeling, does not admit of generality, 'pleasure in general' is an impossible object. When the motive of an action is said to be 'pleasure in general,' what is really meant is that the action is determined by the conception of pleasure, or, more properly, of self as a subject to be pleased. Such determination, again, is distinguished by opposition to two other kinds—(a) to that sort of determination which is not by conception, but either by animal want, or by the animal *imagination* of pleasure, and (b) to determination by the conception of other objects than pleasure. By an author, however, who expressly excluded the latter sort of determination, and who did not recognise any distinction between the thinking and the animal subject, the motive in question could not thus be defined. Hence the difficulty of extracting from Hume himself any clear and consistent account of that which he variously describes as the 'general appetite for good, considered merely as such,' as 'interest,' and as 'self-love.' To say that he understood by it a desire for pleasure which is yet not a desire for any pleasure in particular, may seem a strange interpretation to put on one who regarded himself as a great liberator from abstractions, but there is no other which his statements, taken together, would justify. This desire for nothing, however, he converts into a desire for something by identify-

calm, and (b) from certain desires, which resemble the 'general appetite' in being calm but are not for pleasure at all. See above, sec. 31. In that section of the Essays where 'self-love' is expressly treated of, there is a still clearer appearance of the doctrine, that there are desires (in that instance called 'mental passions') which have not pleasure for their object any more than have such 'bodily wants' as hunger and thirst. From these self-love, as desire for pleasure, is distinguished, though, when the pleasure incidental to their satisfaction is discovered and reflected on, it is supposed to combine with them. (Vol. IV. Appendix on Self-love, near the end. See above, sec. 43 and note.) This amounts, in fact, to a complete withdrawal from Hume's original position and the adoption of one which

is most clearly stated in Hutcheson's posthumous treatise—the position, namely, that we begin with a multitude of 'particular' or 'violent' desires, severally 'terminating upon objects' which are not pleasures at all, and that, as reason developes, these gradually blend with, or are superseded by, the 'calm' desire for pleasure; so that moral growth means the access of conscious pleasure-seeking. This in effect seems to be Butler's view, and Hutcheson reckons it 'a lovely representation of human nature,' though he himself holds that benevolence may exist, not merely as one of the 'particular desires' controlled by self-love, but as itself a 'calm' and controlling principle, co-ordinate with self-love. (System of Moral Philosophy,' Vol. I. p. 51, &c.)

ing it on occasion, (1) with any desire for a pleasure of which the attainment is regarded as sufficiently remote to allow of calmness in the desire, and (2) with desire for the means of having all pleasures indifferently at command. It is in one or other of these senses—either as desire for some particular pleasure distinguished only by its calmness, or as desire for power—that he always understands 'interest' or 'self-love,' except where he gains a more precise meaning for it by the admission of desires, not for pleasure at all, to which it may be opposed. Now taken in the former sense, its difference from the desires for the several pleasures of 'sense,' 'pride,' and 'sympathy,' of which Hume's account has already been examined, cannot lie in the object, but—as he himself says of the distinction, which he regarded as an equivalent one, between 'reasonable and unreasonable' desires—in our situation with regard to it. If then the object of each of these desires, as we have shown to be implied in Hume's account of them, is one which only reason, as self-consciousness, can constitute, it cannot be less so when the desire is calm enough to be called self-love. Still more plainly is the desire in question determined by reason—by the conception of self as a permanent suscepti-bility of pleasure—if it is understood to be desire for power.

48. Having now before us a complete view of the possible motives to human action which Hume admits, we find that while he has carried to its furthest limit, and with the least verbal inconsistency possible, the effort to make thought deny its own originativeness in action, he has yet not suc-ceeded. He has made abstraction of everything in the objects of human interest but their relation to our nervous irritability—he has left nothing of the beautiful in nature or art but that which it has in common with a sweetmeat, nothing of that which is lovely and of good report to the saint or statesman but what they share with the dandy or diner-out—yet he cannot present even this poor residuum of an object, by which all action is to be explained, except under the character it derives from the thinking soul, which looks before and after, and determines everything by relation to itself. Thus if, as he says, the distinction between reasonable and unreasonable desires does not lie in the object, this will not be because reason has never anything to

do with the constitution of the object, but because it has always so much to do with it as renders selfishness—the self-conscious pursuit of pleasure—possible. Sensuality then will have been vindicated, the distinction between the 'higher' and 'lower' modes of life will have been erased, and after all the theoretic consistency—for the sake of which, and not, of course, to gratify any sinister interest, Hume made his philosophic venture—will not have been attained. Man will still not be ultimately passive, nor human action natural. Reason may be the 'slave of the passions,' but it will be a self-imposed subjection.

49. We have still, however, to explain how Hume himself completes the assimilation of the moral to the natural; how, on the supposition that the 'good' can only mean the 'pleasant,' he accounts for the apparent distinction between moral and other good, for the intrusion of the 'ought and ought not' of ethical propositions upon the 'is and is not' of truth concerning nature.[1] Here again he is faithful to his *rôle* as the expander and expurgator of Locke. With Locke, it will be remembered, the distinction of *moral* good lay in the channel through which the pleasure, that constitutes it, is derived. It was pleasure accruing through the intervention of law, as opposed to the operation of nature: and from the pleasure thus accruing the term 'morally good' was transferred to the act which, as 'conformable to some law,' occasions it.[2] This view Hume retains, merely remedying Locke's omissions and inconsistencies. Locke, as we saw, not only neglected to derive the existence of the laws, whose intervention he counted necessary to constitute the morally good, from the operation of that desire for pleasure which he pronounced the only motive of man; in speaking of moral goodness as consisting in conformity to law, he might, if taken at his word, be held to admit something quite different from pleasure alike as the standard and the motive of morality. Hume then had, in the first place, to account for the laws in question, and so account for them as to remove that absolute opposition between them and the operation of nature which Locke had taken for granted; secondly, to exhibit that conformity to law, in which the moral goodness of an act was held to consist, as

---

[1] Vol. ii. p. 245.　　　[2] Above, secs. 16–18.

itself a mode of pleasure—pleasure, namely, to the contemplator of the act; and thirdly, to show that not the moral goodness of the act, even thus understood, but pleasure to himself was the motive to the doer of it.[1]

50. It was a necessary incident of this process that Locke's notion of a Law of God, conformity to which rendered actions 'in their own nature right and wrong,' should disappear. The existence of such a law cannot be explained as a result of any desire for pleasure, nor conformity to it as a mode of pleasure. Locke, indeed, tries to bring the goodness, consisting in such conformity, under his general definition by treating it as equivalent to the production of pleasure in another world. This, however, is to seek refuge from the contradictory in the unmeaning. The question—Is it the pleasure it produces, or its conformity to law, that constitutes the goodness of an act?—remains unanswered, while the further one is suggested—What meaning has pleasure except as the pleasure we experience?[2] Between pleasure, then, and a 'conformity' irreducible to pleasure, as the moral standard, the reader of Locke had to chose. Clarke, supported by Locke's occasional assimilation of moral to mathematical truth, had elaborated the notion of conformity. To him an action was 'in its own nature right' when it conformed to the 'reason of things'—i.e. to certain 'eternal proportions,' by which God, 'qui omnia numero, ordine, mensurâ posuit,' obliges Himself to govern the world, and of which reason in us is 'the appearance.'[3] Thus reason, as an eternal 'agreement or disagreement of ideas,' was the standard to which action ought to conform, and, as our consciousness of such agreement, at once the judge of and motive to conformity. To this Hume's reply is in effect the challenge to instance any act, of which the morality consists either in any of those four relations, 'depending on the nature of the ideas related,' which he regarded as alone admitting of demonstration, or in any other of those relations (contiguity, identity, and cause and effect) which, as 'matters of fact,' can be 'discovered by the understanding.'[4] Such a challenge

---

[1] Of the three problems here specified, Hume's treatment of the *second* is discussed in the following secs. 50-54; of the *first* in secs. 55-58; of the *third* in secs. 60 to the end.

[2] Above, sec. 14.

[3] Boyle Lectures, Vol. II. prop. 1. secs. 1-4.

[4] BOOK III. part 1, sec. 1. (Cf. BOOK I. part 3, sec. 1, and Introduction to

admits of no reply, and no other function but the perception of such relations being allowed to reason or understanding in the school of Locke, it follows that it is not this faculty which either constitutes, or gives the consciousness of, the morally good. Reason excluded, feeling remains. No action, then, can be called 'right in its own nature,' if that is taken to imply (as 'conformity to divine law' must be), relation to something else than our feeling. It could only be so called with propriety in the sense of exciting some pleasure *immediately*, as distinct from an act which may be a condition of the attainment of pleasure, but does not directly convey it.

51. So far, however, there is nothing to distinguish the moral act either from any 'inanimate object,' which may equally excite immediate pleasure, or from actions which have no character, as virtuous or vicious, at all. Some further limitation, then, must be found for the immediate pleasure which constitutes the goodness called 'moral,' and of which praise is the expression. This Hume finds in the exciting object which must be (a) 'considered in general and without reference to our particular interest,' and (b) an object so 'related' (in the sense above [1] explained) to oneself or to another as that the pleasure which it excites shall cause the further pleasure either of pride or love.[2] The precise effect of such limitation he does not explain in detail. A man's pictures, gardens, and clothes, we have been told, tend to excite pride in himself and love in others. If then we can 'consider them in general and without reference to our particular interest,' and in such 'mere survey' find pleasure, this pleasure, according to Hume's showing, will constitute them morally good.[3] He usually takes for granted, however, a further limitation of the pleasure in

---

Vol. I. secs. 283 and ff.) It will be observed that throughout the polemic against Clarke and his congeners Hume writes as if there were a difference between objects of reason and feeling, which he could not consistently admit. He begins by putting the question thus (page 234), 'whether 'tis by means of our ideas or impressions we distinguish betwixt vice and virtue :' but if, as he tells us, 'the idea is merely the weaker impression, and the impression the stronger idea,' such a question has no meaning. In like manner he concludes by saying (page

245) that 'vice and virtue may be compared to sounds, colours, heat and cold, which are not qualities in objects, but perceptions in the mind.' But, since the whole drift of Book I. is to show that all 'objective relations' are such 'perceptions' or their succession, this still leaves us without any distinction between science and morality that shall be tenable according to his own doctrine.

[1] Sec. 33.

[2] Vol. II. pp. 247 and 248.

[3] Hume treats them as such in Book III. part 3, sec. 5.

question, as excited only by 'actions, sentiments, and characters,' and thus finds virtue to consist in the 'satisfaction produced to the spectator of an act or character by the mere view of it.'[1] Virtues and vices then mean, as Locke well said, the usual likes and dislikes of society. If we choose with him to call that virtue of an act, which really consists in the pleasure experienced by the spectator of it, 'conformity to the law of their opinion,' we may do so, provided we do not suppose that there is some other law, which this imperfectly reflects, and that the virtue is something other than the pleasure, but to be inferred from it. 'We do not infer a character to be virtuous, because it pleases; but in feeling that it pleases after such a particular manner, we in effect feel that it is virtuous.'[2]

52. Some further explanation, however, of the 'particular manner' of this pleasure was clearly needed in order at once to adjust it to the doctrine previously given of the passions (of which this, as a pleasant emotion, must be one), and to account for our speaking of the actions which excite it—at least of some of them—as actions which we *ought* to do. If we revert to the account of the passions, we can have no difficulty in fixing on that of which this peculiar pleasure, excited by the 'mere survey' of an action without reference to the spectator's 'particular interest,' must be a mode. It must be a kind of sympathy—pleasure felt by the spectator in the pleasure of another, as distinct from what might be felt in the prospect of pleasure to himself.[3] On the other hand, there seem to be certain discrepancies between pleasure and moral sentiment. We sympathise where we neither approve nor disapprove; and, conversely, we express approbation where it would seem there was no pleasure to sympathise with, *e.g.*, in regard to an act of simple justice, or where the person experiencing it was one with whom we could have no fellow-feeling—an enemy, a stranger, a character in history—or where the experience, being one not of pleasure but of pain (say, that of a martyr at the stake), should excite the reverse of approbation in the spectator, if approbation means pleasure sympathised with. Our sympathies, moreover, are highly variable, but our moral sentiments on the whole constant. How must 'sym-

---

[1] Vol. ii. p. 251. Cf. p. 225.   [2] Vol. ii. p. 247.   [3] Vol. ii. pp. 335-337.

pathy' be qualified, in order that, when we identify moral sentiment with it, these objections may be avoided ?

53. Hume's answer, in brief, is that the sympathy, which constitutes moral sentiment, is sympathy qualified by the consideration of 'general tendencies.' Thus we sympathise with the pleasure arising from any casual action, but the sympathy does not become moral approbation unless the act is regarded as a sign of some quality or character, generally and permanently agreeable or useful (*sc.* productive of pleasure directly or indirectly) to the agent or others. An act of justice may not be productive of any immediate pleasure with which we can sympathise ; nay, taken singly, it may cause pain both in itself and in its results, as when a judge 'takes from the poor to give to the rich, or bestows on the dissolute the labour of the industrious ;' but we sympathise with the general satisfaction resulting to society from 'the whole scheme of law and justice,' to which the act in question belongs, and approve it accordingly. The constancy which leads to a dungeon is a painful commodity to its possessor, but sympathy with his pain need not incapacitate a spectator for that other sympathy with the general pleasure caused by such a character to others, which constitutes it virtuous. Again, though remote situation or the state of one's temper may at any time modify or suppress sympathy with the pleasure caused by the good qualities of any particular person, we may still apply to him terms expressive of our liking. 'External beauty is determined merely by pleasure; and 'tis evident a beautiful countenance cannot give so much pleasure, when seen at a distance of twenty paces, as when it is brought nearer to us. We say not, however, that it appears to us less beautiful; because we know what effect it will have in such a position, and by that reflection we correct its momentary appearance.' As with the beautiful, so with the morally good. 'In order to correct the continual contradictions' in our judgment of it, that would arise from changes in personal temper or situation, 'we fix on some steady and general points of view, and always in our thoughts place ourselves in them, whatever may be our present situation.' Such a point of view is furnished by the consideration of 'the interest or pleasure of the person himself whose character is examined, and of the persons who have a connection with

him,' as distinct from the spectator's own. The imagination
in time learns to ' adhere to these general views, and distinguishes the feelings they produce from those which arise
from our particular and momentary situation.' Thus a certain
constancy is introduced into sentiments of blame and praise,
and the variations, to which they continue subject, do not
appear in language, which ' experience teaches us to
correct, even where our sentiments are more stubborn and
unalterable.' [1]

54. It thus appears that though the virtue of an act means
the pleasure which it causes to a spectator, and though this
again arises from sympathy with imagined pleasure of the
doer or others, yet the former may be a pleasure which no
particular spectator at any given time does actually feel—
he need only know that under other conditions on his part
he would feel it—and the latter pleasure may be one either
not felt at all by any existing person, or only felt as the
opposite of the uneasiness with which society witnesses a
departure from its general rules. Of the essential distinction between a feeling of pleasure or pain and a knowledge
of the conditions under which a pleasure or pain is generally
felt, Hume shows no suspicion ; nor, while he admits that
without substitution of the knowledge for the feeling there
could be no general standard of praise or blame, does he ask
himself what the quest for such a standard implies. As little
does he trouble himself to explain how there can be such
sympathy with an unfelt feeling—with a pleasure which no
one actually feels but which is possible for posterity—as will
explain our approval of the virtue which defies the world,
and which is only assumed, for the credit of a theory, to
bring pleasure to its possessor, because it certainly brings
pleasure to no one else. For the ' artificial ' virtue, however, of acts done in conformity with the ' general scheme of
justice,' or other social conventions, he accounts at length in
part II. of his Second Book—that entitled ' Of Justice and
Injustice.'

55. To a generation which has sufficiently freed itself
from all ' mystical ' views of law—which is aware that
' natural right,' if it means a right that existed in a ' state
of nature,' is a contradiction in terms ; that, since contracts

---

[1] Book III. vol. ii. part 3, sec. 1. Specially pp. 339, 342, 346, 349.

could not be made, or property exist apart from social convention, any question about a primitive obligation to respect
them is unmeaning—the negative side of this part of the
treatise can have little interest. That all rights and obligations are in some sense ' artificial,' we are as much agreed as
that without experience there can be no knowledge. The
question is, how the artifice, which constitutes them, is to be
understood, and what are its conditions. If we ask what
Hume understood by it, we can get no other answer than
that the artificial is the opposite of the natural. If we go
on to ask for the meaning of the natural, we only learn that
we must distinguish the senses in which it is opposed to the
miraculous and to the unusual from that in which it is
opposed to the artificial,[1] but not what the latter sense is.
The truth is that, if the first book of Hume's treatise has
fulfilled its purpose, the only conception of the natural,
which can give meaning to the doctrine that the obligation
to observe contracts and respect property is artificial, must
disappear. There are, we shall find, two different negations
which in different contexts this doctrine conveys. Sometimes it means that such an obligation did not exist for man
in a ' state of nature,' *i.e.*, as man was to begin with. But
in that sense the law of cause and effect, without which
there would be no nature at all, is, according to Hume, not
natural, for it—not merely our recognition of it, but the
law itself—is a habit of imagination, gradually formed.
Sometimes it conveys an opposition to Clarke's doctrine of
obligation as constituted by certain ' eternal relations and
proportions,' which also form the order of nature, and are
other than, though regulative of, the succession of our feelings. Nature, however, having been reduced by Hume to
the succession of our feelings, the ' artifice,' by which he
supposes obligations to be formed, cannot be determined by
opposition to it, unless the operation of motives, which explains the artifice, is something else than a succession of
feelings. But that it is nothing else is just what it is one
great object of the moral part of his treatise to show.

56. He is nowhere more happy than in exposing the
fallacies by which ' liberty of indifference '—the liberty supposed to consist in a possibility of unmotived action—was

---

[1] BOOK II. part 1, sec. 2.

defended.' Every act, he shows, is determined by a strongest
motive, and the relation between motive and act is no other
than that between any cause and effect in nature. In one
case, as in the other, ' necessity ' lies not in an ' esse ' but in
a ' percipi.' It is the ' determination of the thought of any
intelligent being, who considers ' an act or event, ' to infer its
existence from some preceding objects; '[2] and such determination is a habit formed by, and having a strength pro-
portionate to, the frequency with which certain phenomena
—actions or events—have followed certain others. The
weakness in this part of Hume's doctrine lies, not in the
assumption of an equal uniformity in the sequence of act
upon motive with that which obtains in nature, but in his
inability consistently to justify the assumption of an absolute
uniformity in either case. When there is an apparent
irregularity in the consequences of a given motive—when
according to one ' experiment ' action (a) follows upon it,
according to another action (b), and so on—although ' these
contrary experiments are entirely equal, we remove not the
notion of causes and necessity ; but, supposing that the
usual contrariety proceeds from the operation of contrary
and concealed causes, we conclude that the chance or indifference lies only in our judgment on account of our
imperfect knowledge, not in the things themselves, which are
in every case equally necessary, though to appearance not
equally constant or uniform.'[3] But we have already seen
that, if necessary connection were in truth only a habit
arising from the frequency with which certain phenomena
follow certain others, the cases of exception to a usual
sequence, or in which the balance of chances did not incline
one way more than another, could only so far weaken the
habit. The explanation of them by the ' operation of concealed causes' implies, as he here says, an opposition of real
necessity to apparent inconstancy, which, if necessity were
such a habit as he says it is, would be impossible.[4] This
difficulty, however, applying equally to moral and natural
sequences, can constitute no difference between them. It
cannot therefore be in the relation between motive and act
that the followers of Hume can find any ground for a dis-

---

[1] Book II. part 3, secs. 1 and 2.
[2] Vol. II. p. 189.
[3] Ibid., p. 185.

[4] See Introduction to Vol. I. secs.
323 and 336.

tinction between the process by which the conventions of
society are formed, and that succession of feelings which he
calls nature. May he then find it in the character of the
motive itself by which the 'invention' of justice is to be
accounted for ? Is this other than a feeling determined by a
previous, and determining a sequent, one ? Not, we must
answer, as Hume himself understood his own account of it,
which is as follows :—

57. He will examine, he says, 'two questions, viz., concerning the manner in which the rules of justice are
established by the artifice of men ; and concerning the
reasons which determine us to attribute to the observance or
neglect of these rules a moral beauty and deformity.'[1] Of
the motives which he recognises (§ 45) it is clear that only
two—'benevolence' and 'interest'—can be thought of in
this connection, and a little reflection suffices to show that
benevolence cannot account for the artifice in question.
Benevolence with Hume means either sympathy with pleasure—and this (though Hume could forget it on occasion [2])
must be a particular pleasure of some particular person—or
desire for the pleasure of such sympathy. Even if a benevolence may be admitted, which is not a desire for pleasure at
all but an impulse to please, still this can only be an impulse
to please some particular person, and the only effect of
thought upon it, which Hume recognises, is not to widen
its object but to render it 'interested.'[3] 'There is no such
passion in human minds as the love of mankind, merely as
such, independent of personal qualities, of services, or of
relation to ourself.'[4] The motive, then, to the institution
of rules of justice cannot be found in general benevolence.[5]
As little can it be found in private benevolence, for the
person to whom I am obliged to be just may be an object of
merited hatred. It is true that, 'though it be rare to meet
with one who loves any single person better than himself,
yet 'tis as rare to meet with one in whom all the kind affections, taken together, do not overbalance all the selfish' ; but
they are affections to his kinsfolk and acquaintance, and the
generosity which they prompt will constantly conflict with
justice.[6] 'Interest,' then, must be the motive we are in quest

[1] Book III. part 2, sec. 2.
[2] Cf. sec. 54.
[3] Cf. secs. 42, 43, and 46.
[4] Vol. II. p. 255.

[5] For the sense in which Hume did
admit a 'general benevolence,' see sec.
41, note.
[6] Vol. II. pp. 256 and 260.

of. Of the 'three species of goods which we are possessed of—the satisfaction of our minds, the advantages of our body, and the enjoyment of such possessions as we have acquired by our industry and good fortune '—the last only 'may be transferred without suffering any loss or alteration; while at the same time there is not sufficient quantity of them to supply every one's desires and necessities.' Hence a special instability in their possession. Reflection on the general loss caused by such instability leads to a 'tacit convention, entered into by all the members of a society, to abstain from each other's possessions;' and thereupon 'immediately arise the ideas of justice and injustice; as also those of property, right, and obligation.' It is not to be supposed, however, that the 'convention' is of the nature of a promise, for all promises presuppose it. 'It is only a general sense of common interest; which sense all the members of the society express to one another, and which induces them to regulate their conduct by certain rules;' and this 'general sense of common interest,' it need scarcely be said, is every man's sense of his own interest, as in fact coinciding with that of his neighbours. In short, ''tis only from the selfishness and confined generosity of man, along with the scanty provision nature has made for his wants, that justice derives its origin.'[1]

58. Thus the origin of rules of justice is explained, but the obligation to observe them so far appears only as 'interested,' not as 'moral.' In order that it may become 'moral,' a pleasure must be generally experienced in the spectacle of their observance, and a pain in that of their breach, apart from reference to any gain or loss likely to arise to the spectator himself from that observance or breach. In accounting for this experience Hume answers the second of the questions, proposed above. 'To the imposition and observance of these rules, both in general and in every particular instance, men are at first induced only by a regard to interest; and this motive, on the first formation of society, is sufficiently strong and forcible. But when society has become numerous, and has increased to a tribe or nation, this interest is more remote; nor do men so readily perceive that disorder and confusion follow upon each breach of these

---

[1] Vol. II. pp. 261, 263, 268.

rules, as in a more narrow and contracted society. But though, in our own actions, we may frequently lose sight of that interest which we have in maintaining order, and may follow a lesser and more present interest, we never fail to observe the prejudice we receive, either mediately or immediately, from the injustice of others. . . . . Nay, when the injustice is so distant from us, as no way to affect our interest, it still displeases us, because we consider it as prejudicial to human society, and pernicious to every one that approaches the person guilty of it. We partake of their uneasiness by *sympathy*; and as everything which gives uneasiness in human actions, upon the general survey, is called vice, and whatever produces satisfaction, in the same manner, denominated virtue, this is the reason why the sense of moral good and evil follows upon justice and injustice. And though this sense, in the present case, be derived only from contemplating the actions of others, yet we fail not to extend it even to our own actions. The *general rule* reaches beyond those instances from which it arose, while at the same time we naturally *sympathise* with others in the sentiments they entertain of us.'[1]

59. To this account of the process by which rules of justice have not only come into being, but come to bind our 'conscience' as they do, the modern critic will be prompt to object that it is still affected by the 'unhistorical' delusions of the systems against which it was directed. In expression, at any rate, it bears the marks of descent from Hobbes, and, if read without due allowance, might convey the notion that society first existed without any sort of justice, and that afterwards its members, finding universal war inconvenient, said to themselves, 'Go to; let us abstain from each other's goods.' It would be hard, however, to expect from Hume the full-blown terminology of development. He would probably have been the first to admit that rules of justice, as well as our feelings towards them, were not made but grew; and in his view of the 'passions,' whose operation this growth exhibits, he does not seriously differ from the ordinary exponents of the 'natural history' of ethics. These passions, we have seen, are 'Interest' and 'Sympathy,' which with Hume only differ from the pleasures

and desires we call 'animal' as any one of these differs from another—the pleasure of eating, for instance, from that of drinking, or desire for the former pleasure from desire for the latter. Nor do their effects in the regulation of society, and in the growth of 'artificial' virtues and vices, differ according to his account of them from sentiments which, because they 'occur to us whether we will or no,' he reckons purely natural, save in respect of the further extent to which the modifying influence of imagination—itself reacted on by language—must have been carried in order to their existence; and since this in his view is a merely 'natural' influence, there can only be a relative difference between the 'artificiality' of its more complex, and the 'naturalness' of its simpler, products. Locke's opposition, then, of 'moral' to other good, on the ground that other than natural instrumentality is implied in its attainment, will not hold even in regard to that good which, it is admitted, would not be what it is, *i.e.*, not a pleasure, but for the intervention of civil law.

60. The doctrine, which we have now traversed, of 'interested' and 'moral' obligation, implicitly answers the question as to the origin and significance of the ethical copula 'ought.' It originally expresses, we must suppose, obligation by positive law, or rather by that authoritative custom in which (as Hume would probably have been ready to admit) the 'general sense of common interest' first embodies itself. In this primitive meaning it already implies an opposition between the 'interest which each man has in maintaining order' and his 'lesser and more present interests.' Its meaning will be modified in proportion as the direct interest in maintaining order is reinforced or superseded by sympathy with the general uneasiness which any departure from the rules of justice causes. And as this uneasiness is not confined to cases where the law is directly or in the letter violated, the judgment, that an act *ought* to be done, not only need not imply a belief that the person, so judging, will himself gain anything by its being done or lose anything by its omission; it need not imply that any positive law requires it. Whether it is applicable to every act 'causing pleasure on the mere survey'—whether the range of 'imperfect obligation' is as wide as that of moral sentiment—Hume does not make clear. That every action

representing a quality 'fitted to give immediate pleasure to its possessor' should be virtuous—as according to Hume's account of the exciting cause of moral sentiment it must be—seems strange enough, but it would be stranger that we should judge of it as an act which *ought* to be done. It is less difficult, for instance, to suppose that it is virtuous to be witty, than that one ought to be so. Perhaps it would be open to a disciple of Hume to hold that as, according to his master's showing, an opposition between permanent and present interest is implied in the judgment of obligation as at first formed, so it is when the pleasure to be produced by an act, which gratifies moral sense, is remote rather than near, and a pleasure to others rather than to the doer, that the term 'ought' is appropriate to it.

61. But though Hume leaves some doubt on this point, he leaves none in regard to the sense in which alone any one can be said to do an action *because he ought*. This must mean that he does it to avoid either a legal penalty or that pain of shame which would arise upon the communication through sympathy of such uneasiness as a contrary act would excite in others upon the survey. So far from its being true that an act, in order to be thoroughly virtuous, must be done for virtue's sake, 'no action can be virtuous or morally good unless there is some motive to produce it, distinct from the sense of its morality.'[1] An act is virtuous on account of the pleasure which supervenes when it is contemplated as proceeding from a motive fitted to produce pleasure to the agent or to others. The presence of this motive, then, being the antecedent condition of the act's being regarded as virtuous, the motive cannot itself have been a regard to the virtue. It may be replied, indeed, that though this shows 'regard to virtue' or 'sense of morality' to be not the primary or only virtuous motive, it does not follow that it cannot be a motive at all. An action cannot be prompted for the first time by desire for a pleasure which can only be felt as a consequence of the action having been done, but it may be repeated, after experience of this pleasure, from desire for its renewal. In like manner, since with Hume the 'sense of morality' is not a desire at all but an emotion, and an emotion which cannot be felt till an

act of a certain kind has been done, it cannot be the original motive to such an action; but why may not desire for so pleasant an emotion, when once it has been experienced, lead to a repetition of the act? The answer to this question is that the pleasure of moral sentiment, as Hume thinks of it, is essentially a pleasure experienced by a spectator of an act who is other than the doer of it. If the doer and spectator were regarded as one person, there would be no meaning in the rule that the tendency to produce pleasure, which excites the sentiment of approbation, must be a tendency to produce it to the doer himself or others, as distinct from the spectator himself. Thus pleasure, in the specific form in which Hume would call it 'moral sentiment,' is not what any one could attain by his own action, and consequently cannot be a motive to action. Transferred by sympathy to the consciousness of the man whose act is approved, 'moral sentiment' becomes 'pride,' and desire for the pleasure of pride—otherwise called 'love of fame'—is one of the 'virtuous' motives on which Hume dwells most. When an action, however, is done for the sake of any such positive pleasure, he would not allow apparently that the agent does it 'from a sense of duty' or 'because he ought.' He would confine this description to cases where the object was rather the avoidance of humiliation. 'I ought' means 'it is expected of me.' 'When any virtuous motive or principle is common in human nature, a person who feels his heart devoid of that motive may hate himself' (strictly, according to Hume's usage of terms, 'despise himself') 'on that account, and may perform the action without the motive from a certain sense of duty, in order to acquire by practice that virtuous principle, or at least to disguise to himself as much as possible his want of it.'[1]

62. What difference, then, we have finally to ask, does Hume leave between one motive and another, which can give any significance to the assertion that an act, to be virtuous, must proceed from a virtuous motive? When a writer has so far distinguished between motive and action as to tell us that the moral value of an action depends on its motive—which is what Hume is on occasion ready to tell us—we naturally suppose that any predicate, which he pro-

[1] Vol. ii., p. 253.

ceeds to apply to the motive, is meant to represent what it is in relation to the subject of it. It cannot be so, however, when Hume calls a motive virtuous. This predicate, as he explains, refers not to an 'esse' but to a 'percipi;' which means that it does not represent what the motive is to the person whom it moves, but a pleasant feeling excited in the spectator of the act. To the excitement of this feeling it is necessary that the action should not merely from some temporary combination of circumstances produce pleasure for that time and turn, but that the desire, to which the spectator ascribes it, should be one according to his expectation 'fitted to produce pleasure to the agent or to others.' In this sense only can Hume consistently mean that virtue in the motive is the condition of virtue in the act, and in this sense the qualification has not much significance for the spectator of the act, and none at all in relation to the doer. It has not much for the spectator, because, according to it, no supposed desire will excite his displeasure and consequently be vicious unless in its general operation it produces a distinct overbalance of pain to the subject of it *and* to others;[1] and by this test it would be more difficult to show that an unseasonable passion for reforming mankind was *not* vicious than that moderate lechery was so. It has no significance at all for the person to whom vice or virtue is imputed, because a difference in the results, which others anticipate from any desire that moves him to action, makes no difference in that desire, as he feels and is moved by it. To him, according to Hume, it is simply desire for the pleasure of which the idea is for the time most lively, and, being most lively, cannot but excite the strongest desire. In this—in the character which they severally bear for the subjects of them—the virtuous motive and the vicious are alike. Hume, it is true, allows that the subject of a vicious desire may become conscious through sympathy of the uneasiness which the contemplation of it causes to others, but if this sympathy were strong enough to neutralize the

---

[1] I write 'AND to others,' not 'OR,' because according to Hume the production of pleasure to the agent alone is enough to render an action virtuous, if it proceeds from some permanent quality. Thus an action could not be unmistakably vicious unless it tended to produce pain *both* to the doer and to others. If, though tending to bring pain to others, it had a contrary tendency for the agent himself, there would be nothing to decide whether the viciousness of the former tendency was, or was not, balanced by the virtuousness of the latter.

imagination which excites the desire, the desire would not move him to act. That predominance of anticipated pain over pleasure in the effects of a motive, which renders it vicious to the spectator, cannot be transferred to the imagination of the subject of it without making it cease to be his motive because no longer his strongest desire. A vicious motive, in short, would be a contradiction in terms, if that productivity of pain, which belongs to the motive in the imagination of the spectator, belonged to it also in the imagination of the agent.

63. Thus the consequence, which we found to be involved in Locke's doctrine of motives, is virtually admitted by its most logical exponent. Locke's confusions began when he tried to reconcile his doctrine with the fact of self-condemnation, with the individual's consciousness of vice as a condition of himself; or, in his own words, to explain how the vicious man could be 'answerable to himself' for his vice. Consciousness of vice could only mean consciousness of pleasure wilfully foregone, and since pleasure could not be wilfully foregone, there could be no such consciousness. Hume, as we have seen, cuts the knot by disposing of the consciousness of vice, as a relation in which the individual stands to himself, altogether. A man's vice is someone else's displeasure with him, and, if we wish to be precise, we must not speak of self-condemnation or desire for excellence as influencing human conduct, but of aversion from the pain of humiliation and desire for the pleasure of pride—humiliation and pride of that sort of which each man's sympathy with the feeling of others about him is the condition.

64. That such a doctrine leaves large fields of human experience unexplained, few will now dispute. Wesley, Wordsworth, Fichte, Mazzini, and the German theologians, lie between us and the generation in which, to so healthy a nature as Hume's, and in so explicit a form, it could be possible. Enthusiasm—religious, political, and poetic—if it has not attained higher forms, has been forced to understand itself better since the time when Shaftesbury's thin and stilted rhapsody was its most intelligent expression. It is now generally agreed that the saint is not explained by being called a fanatic, that there is a patriotism which is not 'the last refuge of a scoundrel,' and that we know no more about the poet, when we have been told that he seeks

the beautiful, and that what is beautiful is pleasant, than we did before. This admitted, Hume's Hedonism needs only to be clearly stated to be found 'unsatisfactory.' If it ever tends to find acceptance with serious people, it is through confusion with that hybrid, though beneficent, utilitarianism which finds the moral good in the 'greatest happiness of the greatest number' without reflecting that desire for such an object, not being for a feeling of pleasure to be experienced by the subject of the desire, is with Hume impossible. Understood as he himself understood his doctrine, it is only 'respectability'—the temper of the man who 'naturally,' *i.e.*, without definite expectation of ulterior gain, seeks to stand well with his neighbours—that it will explain; and this it can only treat as a fixed quantity. Taking for granted the heroic virtue, for which it cannot account, it still must leave it a mystery how the heroic virtue of an earlier age can become the respectability of a later one. Recent literary fashion has led us perhaps unduly to depreciate respectability, but the avowed insufficiency of a moral theory to explain anything beyond it may fairly entitle us to enquire whether it can consistently explain even that. The reason, as we have sufficiently seen, why Hume's ethical speculation has such an issue is that he does not recognize the constitutive action of self-conscious thought. Misunderstanding our passivity in experience—unaware that it has no meaning except in relation to an object which thought itself projects, yet too clear-sighted to acquiesce in the vulgar notion of either laws of matter or laws of action, as simply thrust upon us from an unaccountable without—he seeks in the mere abstraction of passivity, of feeling which is a feeling of nothing, the explanation of the natural and moral world. Nature is a sequence of sensations, morality a succession of pleasures and pains. It is under the pressure of this abstraction that he so empties morality of its actual content as to leave only the residuum we have described. Yet to account even for this he has to admit such motives as 'pride,' 'love,' and 'interest; and each of these, as we have shown, implies that very constitutive action of reason, by ignoring which he compels himself to reduce all morality to that of the average man in his least exalted moments. The formative power of thought, as exhibited in such motives only differs in respect of the lower degree, to which it has fashioned its matter, from the same power as the source of the ' desire for excellence,' of the will autonomous in the service of mankind, of the forever (to us) unfilled ideal of a perfect society. It is because Hume de-rationalizes respectability, that he can find no *rationale*, and therefore no room, for the higher morality. This might warn us that an ' ideal ' theory of ethics tampers with its only sure foundation when it depreciates respectability; and if it were our business to extract a practical lesson from him, it would be that there is no other genuine ' enthusiasm of humanity ' than one which has travelled the common highway of reason—the life of the good neighbour and honest citizen—and can never forget that it is still only on a further stage of the same journey. Our business, however, has not been to moralise, but to show that the philosophy based on the abstraction of feeling, in regard to morals no less than to nature, was with Hume played out, and that the next step forward in speculation could only be an effort to re-think the process of nature and human action from its true beginning in thought. If this object has been in any way attained, so that the attention of Englishmen ' under five-and-twenty ' may be diverted from the anachronistic systems hitherto prevalent among us to the study of Kant and Hegel, an irksome labour will not have been in vain.